The Defiant One

ALSO BY AUBREY MALONE

Censoring Hollywood: Sex and Violence in Film and on the Cutting Room Floor (McFarland, 2011)

The Defiant One
A Biography of Tony Curtis

Aubrey Malone

McFarland & Company, Inc., Publishers
Jefferson, North Carolina, and London

LIBRARY OF CONGRESS CATALOGUING-IN-PUBLICATION DATA

Dillon-Malone, A. (Aubrey)
The defiant one : a biography of Tony Curtis / Aubrey Malone.
    pages cm
Includes bibliographical references and index.

ISBN 978-0-7864-7595-7
softcover : acid free paper ∞

1. Curtis, Tony, 1925–2010. 2. Motion picture actors
and actresses—United States—Biography. I. Title.
PN2287.C698D55 2013   791.4302'8092—dc23   [B]   2013033963

BRITISH LIBRARY CATALOGUING DATA ARE AVAILABLE

© 2013 Aubrey Malone. All rights reserved

*No part of this book may be reproduced or transmitted in any form
or by any means, electronic or mechanical, including photocopying
or recording, or by any information storage and retrieval system,
without permission in writing from the publisher.*

On the cover: This is one of the first publicity stills of
"Anthony" Curtis released by Universal-International shortly
after he signed with them in 1949 (author collection)

Manufactured in the United States of America

*McFarland & Company, Inc., Publishers
Box 611, Jefferson, North Carolina 28640
www.mcfarlandpub.com*

Acknowledgments

I would like to thank Ned Comstock of the University of South California for his immense help in tracking down material for me from his archives. Thanks also to Kristine Krueger of the Margaret Herrick Library for her conscientious labors on my behalf. Thank you to Ian O'Sullivan of the British Film Institute for his many profiles of Tony Curtis and features on him from the 1950s onwards, and to Rebecca Grant for giving me access to the library of the Irish Film Institute.

Special thanks to Mark Palmer for translating the books by Allegra Curtis and Christine Kaufmann for me, and to Hugh Comerford at Pearse Street Library for his help with the microfiche material.

Thank you to all the librarians from New York, London and Dublin for their help, to the film distribution companies who tracked down old Tony Curtis movies, to all the booksellers who found rare books for me, to Chris Smedley and Linda Tresham and anyone else who worked tirelessly behind the scenes, especially Melissa Gooley and, Derek Savage.

Table of Contents

Acknowledgments v
Preface 1
Introduction 3

1. The Outsider 5
2. Reform 12
3. Ollywood 17
4. Sultan of Shlock 30
5. Elite of the Milk Shake Set 37
6. High Wire Act 52
7. The Best of Everything 58
8. A-Lister 67
9. Boys Will Be Girls 78
10. Mixing with the Big Guns 88
11. New Beginnings 101
12. Lightweight 119
13. Into Strangler Hell 136
14. A Passionate Amoeba 144
15. Faded Grandeur 154
16. Author Author 161
17. The Road to Perdition 168
18. Fighting the Demons 177
19. Rendezvous in Dublin 189

20. Meltdown 204
21. Picasso of the Desert 213

Film and Television Listing 225
Chapter Notes 227
Bibliography 241
Index 247

Preface

I began this biography after interviewing Tony Curtis in March 1994. Shortly afterwards, sadly, he suffered a heart attack. Then his son Nicholas was found dead from a drug overdose. Finally, tragedies coming in threes, as they say, his marriage to Lisa Deutsch, his bride of just eighteen months, broke up. I put my book to one side but continued to chip away at it over the years. Now that Curtis is no longer with us, I felt the time was right to unearth my manuscript and use it to put his life and career into some kind of perspective.

Amazingly for such a major star, there's only one other biography of him extant, a fine book written by his friend Michael Munn called *Nobody's Perfect*. However, like all books — including Curtis' own two autobiographies — it has left some gaps. I've done my best to plug these with my own views of his life and career, as well as giving a more detailed treatment of his more important films than previous writers.

Introduction

When I received a phone call from the *Sunday Independent* in March 1994 to ask me if I would like to interview Tony Curtis, I greeted the offer with only mild enthusiasm. I had been interviewing stars off and on over the years, and almost invariably they fell below expectations. In some instances they were positively boorish. This had the adverse effect of making me turn off their movies after meeting them. I was reminded of the old Gustave Flaubert dictum: "Don't meet your idols. The gilt will rub off on your fingers."

Curtis had never been one of my favorite actors. I'd enjoyed him in the two films everyone talked about, *Some Like It Hot* and *Sweet Smell of Success*, but even in these I wasn't fully sure if it was Curtis himself I'd admired or the directors or the other stars. *The Boston Strangler*, his most critically acclaimed performance, I had found monotonous and morbid. Even *The Defiant Ones*, for which he garnered his one and only Oscar nomination, failed to impress me. (I felt it wore its earnestness too much on its sleeve.)

I changed my opinion of him after reading his autobiography. I had been blown away by it, imagining it to be one of the most engrossing confessional tomes from the inside track of Hollywood that had ever been written. If only Curtis could have acted as well as he wrote, I thought. He launched a full frontal assault on movies, on his background, his family, the people he worked with, his enemies and even his friends. It was a no-holds-barred trawl through Hollywood's mean streets and his own checkered past, beginning with an almost Dickensian upbringing as the dirt-poor son of dysfunctional Hungarian immigrants before he hit paydirt with Universal Studios in the late 1940s and managed to change Bernie Schwartz into Tony Curtis in a career that lasted over half a century.

He had also married four women by then and slept with hundreds more. He repeatedly insisted that he was finally reformed with his latest wife, Lisa Deutsch, but anyone who read the book would have had to greet that revelation with serious reservations. Would the man live up to the book? That was the main thought in my mind as he came over to shake my hand. As soon as I saw those merry eyes twinkling, though, I liked him already. He looked as if he was ready for some mischief.

He was every interviewer's dream, never dodging a question but turning enough of them on their heads to make you marvel at his wit. Talking to him, it was almost impossible to imagine him getting angry with anyone or chewing them out. He looked like a jovial old bear, and I imagined him to have been a jovial young bear as well. All you had to do was press a button and he was off into yet another anecdote. Or the same one you'd heard a hundred times before. But he always told them with a twist. It was like Take 2 (or 22), with added improvisations.

Lesley Salisbury once said that Curtis treated every question or comment of an interviewer as if it was the first time he heard it, that he laughed quietly at the least hint of a joke from an interviewer and loudly at his own *bon mots*. I certainly found that to be the case — on all counts. You didn't mind the loud laughter because you were part of it too. He made the interview fun. He wanted to be your buddy, pulling at your sleeve as he made a point, thinking on the spot and making things up as he went along. When he embellished his anecdotes he was giving a performance, perhaps the only kind of performance permitted to him after the film world had washed its hands of him. That made them even more precious, but also a little bit sad.

1

The Outsider

Tony Curtis once met a man who had the same birth name as himself, Bernie Schwartz, and also the same birthplace, New York. Their similarity seemed to be threatening to him. He turned to the man and said, "I don't come from Brooklyn. I was born in London and kidnapped by gypsies."[1] The truth was somewhat less exotic. In his autobiography he wrote about the jungle of East 78th Street and First Avenue where his pretty-boy looks made him a target for the local bullies.

He came into the world on June 3, 1925, the first son born to Emanuel ("Manny") and Helen Schwartz. Two more would follow. Emanuel and Helen were unhappy in their way. Emanuel had wanted to be an electrician but ended up becoming a tailor. Helen was physically abusive and also had schizophrenic tendencies. These were transmitted to her youngest son, Robert. (Robert would spend most of his life in an institution and die young.) The middle son was called Julius, or Julie. He was born four years after Bernie.

The Schwartzes were one of many immigrant Hungarian families in New York at the time. "For four blocks in every direction from where we lived," he remembered, "there were nothing but Hungarians, most of them as freshly over from Europe as we were, most of them hungry and poor."[2] As Curtis said once, "Hungary to me always meant hungry."

He began life in a part of New York called (with some reason) Hell's Kitchen, later moving to the Bronx. "We were always moving," he recalled, "because my father's shop didn't bring in enough money for us to pay the rent."[3] His father ran a cleaning and pressing business, but his customers often ran up debts and he was often too timid to ask them for the money. As a result he ran into money problems himself and found it difficult to pay his landlords what he owed them. It was cheaper to move than pay rent so they did that time and again. Or else they were thrown out. Curtis reckoned they moved house 27 times in ten years: "Sometimes we had no furniture and ate off my father's pressing table."[4]

Many of the buildings they moved into were little more than glorified tenements. Hoboes sometimes slept on the stairways, which reeked of stale booze. For Bernie the air on the street was cleaner.

"Manny" rarely complained. This was one of the reasons his business failed to thrive. As well as being slow to retrieve debts, he had a fatalistic attitude toward misfortune. In Curtis' words, "When some disaster would hit us, Pop would say God was punishing us for something bad we did. Something bad? Pop never did harm to anybody in his life."[5]

Emanuel smoked too much and in later life developed lung trouble. The family had to go on relief while he went up to a little room in the mountains to recuperate. Too many hours bent over the pressing machine made the problem worse. He was a hard worker, but his mind often drifted. He had been an actor in Budapest, but his limited English made it impossible to continue that in New York. As Curtis said, "He didn't speak the language and by the time he'd learned enough we were in the middle of the Depression."[6]

Curtis himself didn't speak English until he was seven. His education wasn't exactly auspicious. "I paid no attention in High School," he confessed. "Once I got every word wrong on a spelling test. The teacher gave me a minus zero because I even misspelled my name. I forgot to put the 't' in Schwartz!"[7]

His mother beat him repeatedly as Manny looked on helplessly. Bernie never really understood the motivation behind these beatings. "My mother was a child abuser," he concluded in later years. "She used to slap my face because she knew I was a goodlooking boy. But I wasn't going to let anyone mess up my face."[8] Even this early he seemed to sense that his handsomeness could be a ticket out of the ghetto.

Sometimes he imagined her violent behavior resulted from her being beaten by her own father, a man 45 years older than her mother and prone to rages. Along with her three sisters she'd been sent out to skivvy in strangers' homes from the age of six. Such an upbringing unhinged her, in Curtis' view. "What can you expect?" he suggested. "If you're raised by a schizophrenic you automatically absorb a schizophrenic's behavior pattern. You get beat up and you beat up. My mother used to slap me around because she got slapped around."[9]

To escape her he took to the streets, but here he endured different types of beatings. He was a tenderfoot and also Jewish, and not a native American — so there were three reasons for him to be targeted by the local bullies. "I never felt like I was an American," he said. "I never felt part of that environment."[10]

He was called "Jewish pig" in the streets. People shouted out, "You killed our Jesus!" at him. Or they'd say things like, "You know what a Jew is? A Jew is a nigger turned inside out."[11] There were job offers in shop windows looking for "Only non–Jews."

He offered this picture of the time: "Empty streets. Cloudless skies. There was a great deal of beauty in its spaciousness. The Bronx was uncrowded in those days, with pool halls, trolley cars, subways above the streets."[12]

His name embarrassed him because it was a giveaway as to his religion. He reminisced years later, "I'd get to a new school and when I'd have to stand up and give my name for the first time, I could feel resentment in the room."[13]

He described an encounter with one of the bullies: "He was staring me down and he was twice as tall and twice as heavy as I was. He was completely relaxed except for his tightened fists, which looked harder than the pavement." Bernie fled the scene, aware that he was being a coward, but in the following months he became determined to strengthen his muscles so that one day he could give the roughnecks a fight of it: "My arms developed and my shoulders broadened, meaning that when I went into a street scrap I could sometimes come out the winner."[14]

The increased bulk helped him confront a schoolmate who delighted in needling him. "I went apeshit one day. There was this guy called Webber. A German who kept calling me 'kike.' He used to ambush me every other day. But one day I jumped on his back and beat him senseless. I don't know what came over me. I was like a maniac. He never bothered me again."

Bernie's father looked elegant in photographs that have survived from these years, his brocaded hair combed backwards over his head. He was an aspiring dancer and one day he spotted an advertisement in the newspaper looking for dancers in Brooklyn. He put on his best suit and went to the address given. When he arrived he was told to take off his shoes and socks and to roll his trousers up to his knees. He was then shown a bunch of grapes and asked to dance on them until they turned into wine. It was all a humiliation, with no other dancing on offer at all. "I cried for him when I heard that story," Curtis said. "It killed off all his ambition."

It also seemed to kill off some of his humane qualities. Bernie noticed that he rarely showed affection to his wife. One day he saw him creeping up behind her smilingly when she was at the cooker and embracing her from behind. The fact that he would remember such a detail makes us aware of how rare it was. He never forgot it because it was so out of character.

When Bernie was seven, once again his parents were evicted from their home by bailiffs for non-payment of rent. They were thrown out onto the sidewalk with all their possessions, including some of Emanuel's customers' clothes. Eventually they found a condemned tenement house, and this became their new home.[15] It was boarded up with wooden planks that had expletives daubed on them. Manny removed them and moved in, using the front for his shop and the back for living quarters.

He was 36 now, but he still couldn't stop people from pushing his family around because he was so poor.[16] It was experiences like this that fortified Bernie with the notion that he would one day crawl out of this money trap and never go back. "I fought my way out of a garbage can," he would say years later.[17]

One night Manny was awakened after midnight by a burglar trying to steal his belongings. He picked up a wooden clobber he used for pressing and followed the intruder out of the building. Unfortunately, he couldn't catch him. Afterwards he stood under the bare electric bulb of the tenement in his nightshirt, groaning. "The damned fool," he kept saying to himself. "Couldn't he have sense enough to rob people who actually *have* something?"[18] The following year Bernie and Julie were placed in an orphanage for a month because Manny couldn't afford to feed them.

After the boys returned home, Manny built Bernie a shoeshine stand and gave him an old whisk broom. "Brush 'em off good," he advised, "and you'll get a tip." But times were hard, and he only got two or three shines a day. "If you don't get the nickels right at the moment you shine the shoes," Manny warned, "you're never going to see them."[19] For extra money Bernie began selling newspapers. "To work on a corner I would have to beat up the kid who was already there. For the most part the kids beat *me* up so I worked the middle of the road!" Sometimes he found the front page of a discarded paper and wrapped it around the previous day's edition to fool the customers and save a newspaper. If he didn't run away fast enough after they cottoned on to the trick he got a whack on the head.[20]

Bernie also delivered clothes for his father. "I'd have to hold [them] straight up high to keep them from dragging on the ground."[21] He also fished up lost change from sidewalk gratings using chewing gum that he placed on a stick.[22] He got another job working in a broom factory, cutting off the excessive straw from the ends as they came off the assembly line. His cutting wasn't particularly accurate, leaving him to conclude years later, "There are probably still housewives in New York sweeping their floors with odd-shaped brooms!"[23]

On other days he scrambled for dimes from the well-to-do outside hotels and restaurants: "One time the head waiter at Sardi's kicked me out for trying to get in to collect a tip." If he got lucky he'd bring it home to his mother and say, "Look, Mama, I got a buck."[24] One day a woman gave him $5 for no reason and he was overwhelmed. "It was a fortune then. I was too young to stop and wonder why a woman I'd never seen before should give me so much money."[25] Sometimes he went into stores not to shop but just to get out of the cold.

Another moneymaking ruse for the young Bernie was opening doors for people leaving their cars to go into hotels. (If they didn't tip him he let the air out of their tires.) He also robbed fruit from stands when he was especially hungry. He got caught at the latter activity once and found it exciting: "You felt so important with all those cops standing around with guns."[26] When nothing else was happening he threw discarded tomatoes at passers-by, especially visitors to the area.

One time after robbing a store a man claiming to be a plainclothes policeman hit him across the face with a gun and took all his money from him. Bernie later found out he was just a smalltime crook. The next time he saw the imposter he threw a brick at him. As the man fell, Bernie watched him fold like a dishrag. He thought he'd killed him but a few days later he spotted him with a bandage around his head, smoking a fat cigar.

Life on the streets was hectic for Bernie, and also tragic. One day a tenement collapsed and killed fifteen people. Bernie remembered staring at a woman cradling the body of her dead baby in the debris. Another day he saw a man chasing his wife down the street with a meat cleaver in his hand. Sometimes a man or woman jumped to their deaths from one of the high rooftops. Other times men and women made love on them, or his mother might cook a picnic supper there.

Bernie performed wild stunts, leaping onto moving trolley cars in response to senseless dares from his friends. Sometimes he went down to Third Avenue where the trolley cars ran on double tracks. It was exciting jumping from one to the other as they were going in opposite directions. Other times he and his friends took the rubber from the wheels of rollerskates and put a board on top of them at right angles so they could squat on them while skating through traffic.

He played a game called "Victim" which entailed dodging in and out of traffic and then pretending to be hit by passing cars and falling down in mock-pain. The idea was that the drivers in question would pay him for his "injuries." "Never once did any of them offer to take me to a hospital," Curtis reminisced wryly. "That was mean of them but it was good too because I'd have been arrested if any of them had."[27]

At home they ate simply. "Mama could always make a dinner out of *lotkes* and a bottle of cherry soda. She used to jazz it up some way. Christmas Eve we would beg. I would take off the warm jacket Dad had bought me and wring my hands and cry [at] how cold I was." One night a woman Bernie asked for money said no but as she did so a box fell from a bunch of packages she was carrying. Bernie saw his opportunity. "I almost slid under her car getting it. I ran home and gave it to my mother. She gave me such a rap. It was a black flimsy *negligee*. She knew I stole it."[28]

Curtis told me his parents showed a significant degree of "discontent and avarice" to him each day of their lives. "There wasn't enough—what's the word?—*living* for them. Every day was a struggle. Anybody who looked like they were doing a little bit better than my parents was envied. They didn't like it. They wanted a piece of any action that was going. But the discontent was in the outer family too. I remember once my mother borrowed $230 from her sister, my aunt, and my aunt got an attorney to sue her for the money when we weren't able to pay it back. He wrote to us for it. Of course $230 was a lot of money then and they made up afterwards, but I always thought that was peculiar. Even though I understood it, it still hurt to get those letters."

A dreamer by nature, Bernie walked through Central Park with his father imagining himself to be Emperor Franz Joseph of Austria parading through his grounds.[29] He also used to draw pictures to nurture such dreams. It was one of the few activities he had control over, an oasis of peace in a hostile world. "Looking back," he concluded years later, "I think the language barrier in my Hungarian-immigrant environment was what first motivated me to draw. I could express myself better with pictures than I could verbally."[30] He created images on the sidewalks with chalk and charcoal that formed the basis of his future style in acrylics.

Another hobby was going to the cinema. Movie houses were refuges too. For eleven cents he could sit for ten hours dreaming himself into the films he saw. Stars like Humphrey Bogart and James Cagney helped him deal with the Bronx jungle, whereas smoother actors like Cary Grant fed into his need for refinement.

He imitated all these stars when he left the cinema, often to the point of ridicule. "I once saw a movie where Errol Flynn bit into an onion. He chewed it and went on talking without crying or flinching." Bernie, as a result, ate "whole onions for a week steady. They ruined my nasal passages, my eyes and my ears. Not only that, nobody would sit near me on the subway."[31]

He would rhapsodize years later:

> I loved the movies. In those days we always went. It made no difference to me what the picture was, I just loved going. I liked going into a dark room and being amused and entertained. For a couple of hours it's not bad to just lose yourself in someone else's environment and be drawn along by it, to get all excited and then you go out and it's still snowing and your wife's left you and everything. That, I think, is what provoked me to be a movie star.[32]

Sitting in the cinema, he wrote once, he forgot everything around him. He had no sense of his body at all, just the moving images.[33]

He liked to tell interviewers he began preparing for his movie career "from about eight years old." This was partly what was behind his trolleycar escapades: "I figured one day they [the directors] were going to ask me to jump on something—and I wasn't talking about girls."[34] The acting bug extended into other situations as well. "I'd stiff up my leg and make myself a cripple. I'd buy a patch and put it over one eye and become a one-eyed person. I'd crinkle up my arm, my hand."[35]

Many of the films he saw at this time were action-oriented, "so I learned how to jump off one structure onto another, to climb up a wire fence, to play ball." The other part of his self-imposed regimen was more contemplative. "I just kept watching a lot of people. I knew instinctively that that was the secret of acting."

When Bernie was ten he jumped 25 feet from the top of a building on 76th Street onto another one on Second Avenue, but the leap didn't go to plan. He hit a chimney and was carried away on a stretcher. He suffered a concussion and four broken ribs and also had a temporary loss of hearing and double vision for many months afterwards.

By now he was tough enough for The Black Hand Gang to accept him as a member.

This was one of the most feared young gangs in the area. He wasn't sure where the name came from, but they meant business. It was largely comprised of Jews. Bernie and the other members developed an especial hatred of competing gangs who "ranted Nazi doctrine." When these hoods were marching on the streets, Bernie and his friends would climb up onto roofs and pour bottles of water down on them, "or more unpleasant liquids."[37]

Sometimes he dropped condoms full of urine on their heads from the tops of buildings. It was his way of gaining revenge for what Hitler was doing to his compatriots in Germany. Curtis documented this in a novel he once wrote as he chronicled scenes of himself and his friends hurling "missiles of love" down on the blonde, blue-eyed Nazis goosestepping up and down First Avenue with swastikas on their arms.

When Bernie was eleven, tragedy struck. What made it much worse was that he was complicit in it. It was an autumn day and he'd just watched the parade of the American Legion with his friends. Julie was nearby and came over to him to ask Bernie if he could play with him, but Bernie told him to get lost, to play with his own friends. Julie went away, but when he was crossing the street he got knocked down by a truck. In one recollection of the accident, Curtis said he actually heard the screech of the brakes. In another one he claimed to have been seized by a fit of laughing, as if he had some clairvoyant sense something terrible was happening and this was his nervous reaction to it.

In a 1954 account of the accident, Curtis is informed of it by a friend and identifies the body at the scene. "I wanted to run for my folks," he says. "I wanted to scream for my mother. [But] I knew I couldn't do it. I had to act grown up."[38] In his first autobiography he tells us he heard the news at home and had to go to the hospital to identify Julie.[39] Curtis often gave varying accounts of incidents throughout his life, perhaps even forgetting which was the true one.

It's almost certain he first saw Julie in the hospital, and also that he went there alone. Curtis suspected his parents didn't go with him because they couldn't face the possibility that it might be Julie. How much more harrowing must it have been for the young Bernie to make the chilling discovery on his own. "I don't know if they were trying to punish me for what happened," Curtis hypothesized. "Maybe it was their way of saying it was my fault. I often wondered about that because they never said anything about it."

Julie's head was swathed in bandages. Only his mouth was visible. Bernie recognized him from a tooth that had become chipped a few days before when some boys pushed him away from a water fountain. His legs were broken and so was his collarbone. He had compound fractures of the skull as well as internal injuries. But Bernie was told that he was still expected to live.

The next day he was sitting on the street waiting for news from the hospital when he saw his mother walking towards him. She was crying. "Julie died," she said flatly. Her father followed her into the house, not saying a word. Bernie looked after them, dumbstruck. Then he walked down to the East River. He sat on some pilings looking down into the dirty water where he used to push aside the floating garbage so he could swim.[40] He started to pray, begging God to let Julie live. "I won't tell anybody," he promised. "Just let me see him.[41]

The driver who knocked him down was drunk, so the family was entitled to compensation. Curtis said years later, "I'll never forget the lawyer for the trucking concern talking to my folks when they came to give us $2000 in settlement. 'Too bad the boy didn't live,' the guy said. 'That way you would have a steady income for life.'"⁴² This clashes with an account of the episode in Curtis' autobiography where he wrote, "My parents never got a dime from anybody after my brother's death."⁴³

Two months later, Manny's store was robbed again, the small consolation of the money received from the trucking firm wiped out by this latest calamity. Once more they were broke. Emanuel had a breakdown as a result. Bernie got more involved in the gang he belonged to, finding there the companionship he'd lost with the absence of Julie from his life.⁴⁴

Julie's death effectively ended Bernie's childhood. Afterwards his perspective on life changed dramatically. He became "very defensive, frightened, irritable."⁴⁵ He felt he was destined for a life of crime. He may well have been right, but then something happened to halt that. He was introduced to a man who, though he wasn't related to him, happened to share his surname.

2
Reform

Curtis always credited a community worker called Paul Schwartz with changing the course of his life. He met him when a truant officer dragged himself and a few of his friends to the Jones Memorial Settlement House for "treatment" for their dysfunctional behavior. Schwartz worked there and gave Bernie a hardline talk about where his life was going at that point — to hell in a handbasket. "He took the chips off my shoulder," was the way Curtis put it.[1]

Schwartz brought Bernie and his friends into his office and looked them up and down. He wasn't interested in telling them off or locking them away in a reformatory. He used psychology instead. "If you want to play cops and robbers," he suggested, "why don't you do it right?" Harnessing their testosterone for theatrical purposes, he designated his desk as a bank, his filing cabinet as a lookout post and his door as the getaway car. He said, "That's the setup. Now let's see one of you rob that bank and escape without being caught." They didn't like the idea at first but once they put flesh on the bones they ended up creating characters and writing a script for themselves. That script led to another and then another. The playlets became Bernie's training ground for a life in acting.

The first official play in which he appeared in the Settlement House was one about King Arthur. As a kind of prelude to his landmark role in *Some Like It Hot*, Bernie played a woman. The following year he wrote a letter to the gossip columnist Hedda Hopper asking her how he could become a movie actor. "Work hard," came the blunt answer, "and if you've got what it takes, it'll happen."[2] Bernie took solace from her encouragement.

Another welcome event at this time was the arrival of a new baby in the house. Bobby Schwartz was born in the fall of 1940, his birth seeming to presage an upturn in the family's fortunes. Bernie was now 15 and a freshman in Seward Park High School in Lower Manhattan, away from the tough gangs of the old neighborhood. After school he went to work for a watchmaker for $5 a week. He also worked out in the gym and sometimes helped polio victims do exercises. He even fell in love that year, with a girl called Gretchen, a "cute blonde with a hard little body and long legs."

Bernie was just six months away from graduating from High School when the Japanese bombed Pearl Harbor. America became part of the war effort, and so did he. He volunteered for the Navy, he said, "because the food was good." He also had a fascination with boats. As a child he'd built them out of broom handles, powered by tin propellers and elastic bands, which he then "launched" onto park ponds.[3] Two films he'd seen about the Navy fed into his fascination: *Destination Tokyo* with Cary Grant and *Crash Dive* with Tyrone

Power. Another advantage of the Navy was that one got to sleep with a roof over one's head rather than in a foxhole.

He served aboard the *USS Proteus*, a sub tender2 alongside which submarines would tie up while himself and the other crew members went aboard and scraped off the barnacles. After a short time in service he became a signalman.

Before he went into the Navy he'd been slow to take orders from anyone, but here it was different. This was his new family. He became "establishment," the first step towards the kind of conformity that would define his future. "One day an officer came onto the ship and asked which of us gobs would like to be officers. My hand shot up so fast I nearly pulled my arm out of the socket. The idea of wearing gold braid, of being constantly saluted, really reached me."[4] He was becoming a true son of Uncle Sam, more American than the Americans. Education became a goal for him for the first time in his life because he could see something at the end of it.

The only film available on the submarine was *Gunga Din*, starring Cary Grant. Bernie watched it over and over again and learned the dialogue by heart. Here his fascination with Grant continued. He even learned how to imitate his accent. He and his shipmates got to know the dialogue so well they eventually started turning down the sound and acting the film out on their own. They put on different voices, even going so far as to mimic the sounds of background animals.[5]

Bernie felt a strong kinship to his hero: "When Cary Grant was doing a scene in a movie, he was doing it for no one but me."[6] He also felt Grant was giving him subliminal advice in the scenes he watched. "Cary Grant would say to me, 'Bernie, watch the way I finesse this woman into giving me a kiss.' And I'd say, 'Ooh, that's good.'"[7]

One of his shipmates was Larry Storch, who became a lifelong friend and occasional costar. Bernie's buoyant personality made him irresistible company. Clive James captured it: "For men whose expectations of life varied between endless boredom and a kamikaze attack, he must have been good to have around, if harder to stave off than a suicide plane flown by someone with a different idea of glory."[8]

His father contracted lung cancer at this time and had to have a diseased lung removed. This reduced his quality of life significantly. From now on, in Curtis' estimation, he was only half a man. He was warned off cigarettes, which his surgeon referred to as "coffin nails." Bernie received compassionate leave to visit him in the hospital.

He wasn't too long back at the Navy base when a calamity befell him too. One day he was moving a torpedo when the winch chain broke and hit him in the back, throwing him forward into the water. When he was pulled back on board he was sent to the hospital. He was black and blue from his chest to his knees and all his fingers were broken. The pain was excruciating. A few days later he fell in love with his nurse, a woman called Louise. Louise gave him some books by Shakespeare and advised him to act out the parts with some of the other patients. He never saw her after he left the hospital but was grateful to her for her confidence in his vocal abilities.

When the war ended, the *Proteus* was ordered to round up surrendered Japanese submarines. On September 2, 1945, Bernie found himself in Tokyo Bay, watching General Douglas MacArthur effectively ending the war 300 yards away. He stood on the signal bridge watching the signing of the surrender document through a pair of binoculars. It was a seminal moment for him, he always maintained, one of the most moving of his life.

When he got out of the Navy the world of the Bronx seemed to have shrunk for him. Now that he had so much outside experience under his belt he was able to see it more clearly for what it was—or wasn't. No longer would he be intimidated by anyone, either by his mother or the local bullies. (He settled some old scores pretty quickly here.)

Life in the Schwartz household was the same, except more so. "You think things will have changed because time has elapsed," he reflected, "but the old home I left behind was as crazy as ever. My mother was still shouting her mouth off about nothing and my father still apologizing for being alive." The only real difference was Bobby. "He was acting funny and I didn't know why." It was the beginning of his schizophrenia starting to manifest itself, though it would be many years before this was diagnosed.

The day after Bernie got back he took a subway from his home to the street where Julie had been crushed to death. He knelt down and put his hand on the pavement where the accident occurred. It seemed extra warm, he thought, as though a part of his soul was still there.[9] He tried to put the accident out of his mind but he couldn't. In the following years it would continue to haunt him.

He made a halfhearted attempt to go back to school, but his heart wasn't in it. Like many ex-servicemen trying to adjust to civilian life, he felt restless. He rode the subway downtown and observed people going about their business, wondering what he'd do with the rest of his life. One thing was sure: he wouldn't be a henpecked husband like his father. Or a tailor like his father. You only got one shot at life and he was determined to make it count.

He hung around with some old friends. Drifting in and out of pool halls, they discussed their plans with him. One of them was considering holding up a supermarket. (He ended up in Sing Sing.) Another wanted to be a singer. Bernie thought about modeling for a brief time but decided it would be too mindless for him. Almost on a whim he decided to try acting for a living. The Paul Schwartz playlets, the Gunga Din adaptations, the Shakespearean readings in the hospital—all these played a part in his decision. His father understood it, having been an actor himself. But his grandfather was disapproving. "Why can't you be a professional man," he harangued—a doctor, maybe, or a dentist or an engineer. "Why must you want to be a bum?"[10]

The GI Bill of Rights enabled Bernie to enroll at the Dramatic Workshop in New York. As a war veteran, government funds subsidized his tuition and the cost of books. In February 1947 he joined Erwin Piscator's Acting School to learn the nuts and bolts of the trade. He did a mime rather than a line reading for his audition, already concerned that his Bronx accent might count against him. The work he chose to enact was *Dr. Jekyll and Mr. Hyde*. He didn't think he performed well but he was still accepted—perhaps out of pity, he imagined, for his persistence. "There was more perspiration in my performance than inspiration," he confessed, "but maybe my dedication shone through."

Walter Matthau was another student and he became friendly with Bernie. Matthau referred to the school as the "Neurotic Workshop of Sexual Research" on account of all the bedhopping that took place between classes. "A lot of sexual research went on there," Matthau remarked wryly, going on to conclude, "That's why people become actors. They want to get fucked from here to China."[11]

Bernie was starting to become interested in women by now. A childhood playmate had charged him ten cents for his first kiss.[12] Since then his relationship with the fair sex was complicated. "I was afraid of girls until I was fifteen," he admitted, "and from fifteen to nineteen I didn't like them as people. I'd force myself to make a date, then sweat it out right up to the time I'd get to the door. Then I'd take a fast powder, ending up at the beach alone. I was known as the most disappearing suitor on our block."[13] His good looks meant women showed an immediate interest in him but he had to fight off the attentions of other men interested in these women. The New York streets had girded his loins for these encounters.

He made his stage debut in a play called *Thunder Rock*, playing the idiot son of a lighthouse keeper. The man who would become famous for his hairstyle went bald for the role. "All in the line of duty," he smirked. (He wouldn't be as amenable in future years.) When his mother saw him she screamed and he fluffed his lines as a result.

Afterwards he joined a Jewish stock company on what was called the Borscht Circuit. With some other young actors he formed the Empire Players. They opened in Newark, New Jersey, making up the stage themselves to save money. They even slept at the theater. Their first play was *Dear Ruth*, but it turned out to be their last as well, as it didn't make enough money to make the production viable.[14] They played to tough crowds sometimes. As the saying went, "Jewish people aren't an audience, they're competition."[15] He then joined the Cherry Lane Players, appearing in a number of off–Broadway productions. "In those days," he pointed out, "off–Broadway meant over in Newark!"[16]

Most of the plays he did at this time were familiar period pieces: "I was in a succession of them for a solid year and a half without ever wearing a pair of pants."[17] His big break came when he was appearing in *Golden Boy* at the Cherry Lane Theater. Bob Goldstein, a talent scout for Universal Studios, came to see him. "The boy who played the lead got sick," Curtis recalled, "and I had the part for three nights. We filled the theater as far as possible with my relatives and friends because no one [else] wanted to see me."[18]

Accounts differ about what happened next, even accounts from Curtis himself. Sometimes when he told the story of how he was discovered he said it was by Goldstein himself, other times by somebody else.[19] What's certain is that he was now using an agent, Joyce Selznick. But even here he's inconsistent. In his first autobiography he wrote that Selznick "always said she was related to David O., but she wasn't."[20] In his second one he wrote, "She was the niece of David Selznick."[21] He got it right the second time.

"Do you want a screen career?" Goldstein asked him. Curtis replied, "Does a suffocating man want air?"[22] Goldstein offered him an interview, but where did this take place? Differing accounts of it jumble it up with a screen test at Universal Studios itself. Curtis told the *Herald-Examiner* in 1964 that he wanted to look taller than he was for the interview so he bought a deck of cards and cut it up, putting half of the deck in each shoe "with the two halves of the ace of spades face up for luck." After the interview Goldstein fed him the classic line, "Don't call us, we'll call you," which he took as a brush-off.[23]

One morning not long afterwards, however, he was playing stickball at home at 11 in the morning when his mother came running out of the house yelling, "Bernie! Bernie!" She told him he was wanted at an office downtown. He changed from his sneakers to his shoes but kept his sweatshirt on, that fact in itself testifying to his lack of belief that this could lead to any kind of big break. When he got to the office a woman handed him an envelope and said, "Here's your ticket. You're leaving at three o'clock Monday for Hollywood." It was that simple. Bernie borrowed money from an uncle over the weekend to buy a valise.

Then he jetted out.[24] "That one play brought me out to Hollywood," was the way he put it to Louella Parsons in the *L.A. Examiner*.[25] He gave a different version of the story in his book *American Prince*. Here Goldstein sends him to California for a screen test totally on the basis of his having been seen in *Golden Boy*. The *L.A. Examiner* recollection of the incident seems more likely, it being closer in time to it.[26]

Bernie met a man on the flight to Hollywood and told him about the screen test. He said he was looking forward to it more than he would have with a different studio like Warner Brothers. Warners, he chided, was being deserted by all the stars. "How do you know this?" the man asked him. "I'm a student of the movies," Bernie announced proudly. When they got off the plane, the man offered him a ride to his hotel. Bernie noticed that his chauffeur addressed him as "Mr. Warner." It was only then that the penny dropped; the man he'd been talking to all through the flight was Jack Warner.[27]

Afterwards he met Goldstein, who told him tartly, "Do you know how close you came to not getting the job? It was because of your walk in those boots. You walked funny."[28] Bernie then explained about the deck of cards. The ace of spades hadn't brought him much luck after all.

3
Ollywood

"When I first came to Hollywood," Curtis confessed, "I was really like a nature boy. You never saw such a left-footed, clumsy-looking bum." Amazingly, he'd never been in a private house up until this.[1]

He had been in Hollywood once before, as a Navy recruit: "I had nowhere to sleep when I arrived but I remember the sign that lit up the sky bearing the suburb's name. Part of it wasn't working and it just said Ollywood."[2]

His circumstances were somewhat different now, even though he still only had four dollars and twelve cents to his name.[3]

The first place he headed for was Shelley Winters' house. He presented himself at her door with a request that sounded more like a demand: "I'm Bernie Schwartz. My mother knows your Aunt Fanny in the Bronx and she said you should take care of me until I get settled." Winters remembered him as a "darkly handsome young sailor with a seabag at his side."[4] After she inviting him in (she didn't seem to have much choice in the matter), he deposited the seabag under her couch and proceeded to tell her he'd just been discharged from the Navy and was earning $75 a week at Universal as a trainee actor.[5]

"Bernie was nineteen," Winters wrote in her autobiography. "He was eager and sweet, completely without guile and totally starstruck."[6] The pair of them became friends, but Winters fretted that her brother might break in on them some day and suspect them of being lovers. That was far from the case. Winters became like an older sister to Curtis, fixing him up on dates as he waited for his career to take off.

She also put his name on the waiting list for Sycamore House, an accommodation shared by many young writers and actors at the time. When a vacancy came up, he was able to move out from her sofa and get himself into a proper bed.

Winters' memory of certain details about this time seem suspect. Curtis was only nineteen when he met her, but she said she set him up on dates with Janet Leigh, whom he didn't meet until the next year. She also said she was responsible for him changing his name from Schwartz to Curtis, and that she was on the set of *The Prince Who Was a Thief* when he delivered a line that doesn't come from that film at all: "Yonder lies da castle of my faddah."[7]

Universal was in a period of upheaval when Curtis arrived there. The postwar boom in sales was trailing off and audiences were becoming more discriminating.[8] Between 1948 and 1949 the studio was over $4 million in hock, so budgets were slashed even where major productions were concerned. "The studio was struggling and needed new talent," wrote

Phyllis Gates.[9] They were also cutting down on contract players. Between 1947 and 1956, as John Izod noted, the numbers had shrunk from 742 *in toto* to a mere 229.[10] Keeping people on contract when they weren't being used was an expensive business. Piper Laurie likened the "regular substantial paycheck" of a studio contract at this time to having a part in a television series today.[11]

Curtis first ran into Laurie at acting classes at Universal. In her autobiography she wrote about him flirting outrageously with her, "as if he would die if he didn't have me on the spot." She dated him briefly, regarding him as incredibly handsome and a great kisser, though she didn't like the shape of his mouth, which she thought resembled her "awful" brother-in-law's.[12]

When Curtis came to Universal the studio was riding high on the success of *Ma and Pa Kettle*, a film one writer described as "a cut-rate farce that recast the postwar baby/family/housing boom in comicsurrealist terms."[13] The war had decimated the studios' profit margins, which meant they had to be ultra-careful about which projects they took on. Andrew Dowdy claimed only one in ten movies made in the States in 1950 broke even, as opposed to eight out of ten before the war.[14] This meant they had to rely on overseas markets for their money, which explained the profusion of biblical epics and sex comedies made around this time.[15] The downside was that such features by definition acquired overtones of dutifulness. Because they were made with one eye on the box office it made cinemas more like retail outlets than dream palaces.[16]

Curtis first appeared on the Universal lot on June 3, 1948. His voice was a problem from the outset. Bob Goldstein likened it to that of "an immigrant taxi driver with a mouthful of hot bagel."[17] Another underwhelmed auditor said Curtis sounded like "an Armenian meter reader with a mouthful of razorblades."[18] Curtis tried to turn a deaf ear to such jibes, but they became so persistent it was hard to ignore them. "Some of the more snobbish critics at first criticized me because I didn't speak the King's English," he complained, "or even the President's English."[19]

Universal assigned him tongue exercises to eradicate the "dis" and "dat" from his delivery. He learned to say "Ninety nine nuns in an Indian nunnery." His pronunciation of words like "children" and "predicament" was also corrected.[20] The top brass at Universal were so perplexed by his accent they sent him to a speech instructor at MGM to help him with it.[21] The experience cut vast swathes through his self-confidence.

Curtis' early time in Hollywood, or Ollywood, were characterized by paranoia. "I was suspicious of everybody," he said. "I was certain that someone was trying to bust my contract or steal contracts from me. They were laying in wait for me outside like in the old Chicago gangster movies."[22] His first paycheck was for the hardly princely sum of $32.50. He cried when he saw it, thinking he could make more than that working for his father. He brought it back to the cashier, saying, "Man, this is a mistake." The cashier said, "It is. We forgot to deduct another $5."[23] The cost of his insurance, union membership, etc. had whittled his salary down to this meager amount.

He supplemented his income at this time by secretly escorting tourists around the studio backlot in a prewar Packard limousine, inventing wild stories about stars to impress them. When he was stopped by a policeman one day he pretended they were his relatives, even though three of them were Chinese.[24] He also sold "autographed" photographs of Deanna Durbin that he'd signed himself to make a few bucks on the side. Whatever he earned he spent as fast as he could. His self-esteem was so low he thought he'd be shipped home as soon as the studio found out he had no talent.[25]

After he paid all his expenses he found he only had $12 a week in his pocket. "It didn't leave much for taking out girls," he concluded, "so I got them to take *me* out. I'd look down the U-I [Universal-International] contract list, put a tick against the ones who had a car, and make my pitch. If she had an apartment that was even better because then I'd persuade her to cook dinner. If she shared the apartment with a girlfriend that was fine too because I could make two dates. On separate occasions, of course."[26]

The first big star he dated was Ann Blyth: "Somehow I got up the nerve to ask her to go out with me, expecting a polite turndown. She must have known I was a lonely guy. She said yes and I almost went through the floor."[27]

In those days sex wasn't as prevalent as it became later. Curtis found that if it was offered there were conditions attached to it. The girls he succeeded in getting into bed "almost made you sign a paper." It went like this in his mind: "I hereby declare that since I let you screw me, you must make sure that I'm introduced to Mr. Bob Goldstein, producer, Universal Pictures." The girls in question, according to Curtis, would "let you have three screws, but if you didn't produce you were out of there."[28]

He targeted starlets: "All those luscious tangerines would come out for a six month contract. The boyfriend would go back to Milwaukee but what he didn't know was that I was going to get them."[29] "There was a lot of pussy," he said, "I don't mean to be disrespectful but that was my main aim in life — the girls. I was a nice-looking guy. What was I gonna do, put it down? Say it's nothing? I had fun but I kept it polite."[30]

He met Marilyn Monroe at this time and they had a four-month fling. She was a redhead then but no less alluring on that account. The first time she sat in the back of his car, Curtis adjusted the mirror to get a better look at her legs.[31] Monroe wore see-through blouses even then, so heads turned each time she walked down a street. "We were both so empowered with wanting success," said Curtis, "we could never have shared it with each other. We could never have taken second billing to each other. We slowly stopped seeing each other." He then added, strangely, "We were never with each other long enough to start hating each other."[32] It was as if sex was a game they played, like jungle animals in a mating ritual.[33] "I don't think any guy could be a good lover to her," he said on another occasion. "Poor Marilyn, she never got much out of it."[34] It sounded like the ultimate irony for the world's most famous sex symbol.

Women were a ticket to the good life for Curtis but there were some lines they weren't allowed to cross. One night he was with a "glamour queen," who, as he put it, "had the world in the palm of her hand. She turned to me and, with her best Grade-B dramatic school diction, said, 'Let's go slumming downtown. It's fun to see how other people live.'" This hit a nerve with him. He was still too close to those mean streets to wish to revisit them. He replied, "Listen, honey, I used to live in a street that other people went slumming in. I don't go for slumming. It might make me homesick. I'll take you home instead."[35] The barbed wit was cruel but sharp; he would have no truck with this high-class dame who saw poverty as a spectacle sport, a temporary diversion from her well-heeled life.

Universal trained him in fencing, horse riding, speech and deportment. When it finally came time to display him before the public, it was in a bit part in a *noir* film called *Criss Cross*. He was to dance with Yvonne De Carlo, filling in time until Burt Lancaster came on the scene. Nobody expected him to be noticed. He would be "Anthony Curtis, dancer," so far down the credits as to be almost invisible.

He got the role as a result of meeting the film's director, Robert Siodmak, on the street one day. Like Curtis, Siodmak was Hungarian, "which helped a lot right away." He asked Curtis if he could dance. Curtis thought: I can barely walk. But he replied, "I can dance anything." Siodmak gave him the part without hesitation.

Curtis was supposed to dance a rhumba but it hardly looked like that. Luckily for him he was only photographed from the waist up (like Elvis Presley during some of his early TV shows), so it didn't really matter how he moved.[36]

Or did it? Everyone suddenly wanted to know who the handsome man doing the rhumba was. So much fan mail flooded into the studio that an extra secretary had to be employed to deal with it. Curtis hadn't been in more than a hundred feet of film and nobody knew what his voice sounded like but he was already a sensation. The minutes from a committee meeting Universal held in December 1949 testified to the fact that only two people were receiving more fan mail than "Anthony" Curtis: Ann Blyth and Yvonne de Carlo. Blyth got 1900 letters and De Carlo 1000. But Curtis had weighed in with 711, an incredible achievement for an unknown. There were also more money orders for photographs of him than for any of the established stars.[37]

This is one of the first publicity stills of "Anthony" Curtis released by Universal-International shortly after he signed with them in 1949. Already we can see the slick quiff hairstyle, the slightly Latin aura and the poster boy good looks that were exploited to such effect in his early movies, even those in which he only had walk-on parts.

"The world burst like a flower," Curtis gushed.[38] He couldn't understand the fuss about him but he decided to milk it. He was determined not to be a fly-by-night. In the next few years he appeared in whatever he was offered without a murmur. He took the soup Universal dished out, speaking the hammy lines, taking the humble dollars and serving his time. His logic was simple: "The movies weren't that good, but experience is experience."[39] "I was 24 years old," he said, "and suddenly I was King Kong." The films were cheap to make and were shot in little over a fortnight. "They went out and grossed $2.5 million, and that was on a 30 cent movie ticket. Universal were shooting dice that had no numbers on it so they could never lose. They were putting me in any kind of garbage they had."[40] But he still felt as if he could have "eaten the world."[41]

He worked hard and played hard. "At the end of the day we couldn't wait to get in our cars, go home, clean up.

Eight o'clock we'd eat at Dolores Drive-In, then hit the clubs: Morocco, Ciros, Mocambo, Lucy's and the Club Gala where Spago's restaurant is now. All-night madness. We didn't know there was a tomorrow."[42]

He kept his feet on the ground even as the fan mail poured in. One day he forgot to say hello to the studio gateman and asked his agent if that indicated he was becoming "high hat." "Don't worry, kid," his agent assured him, "when you *worry* about going high hat you never will."[43] It was a moot point.

He often wondered how he'd made such an impression on the public as a result of *Criss Cross*. Was it the way he moved? The way he dressed? Maybe De Carlo played a part too. He was always grateful to her for the way she looked at him in the scene. He thought it made people curious.

Curtis didn't only dance with Yvonne de Carlo, he went to bed with her. She was a trophy and he wanted to publicize the fact. One day when he was being driven in his limo he shouted out the window at Walter Matthau, whom he spotted standing at a corner, "I fucked Yvonne de Carlo!" He repeated this anecdote dozens of times throughout his life, apparently immune to Ms. De Carlo's possible sensitivity about it. Other people liked to tell it, too, like Frank Sinatra's wife Barbara.[44] In later years Curtis took to crowing, "Everybody in town has had Yvonne De Carlo!"[45]

Universal wanted to build on the publicity generated by *Criss Cross* but the studio heads weren't willing to risk Curtis in a main role. Neither did they want him to peak too soon. For the next few years he was a bit player in films that were largely mediocre. He allowed himself to be the blank canvas upon which the studio wrote its instructions. "I went gratefully to the U-I training school," he reminisced, "and tried to rehearse all my poor diction and my corny mannerisms out of myself."[46] He had few illusions about what he represented. "I was a sort of billboard and they just pasted the label onto me. I was a jerk. Little Bernie Schwartz who crawled out of an ash-can in the Bronx."[47]

In the half-dozen movies he made between 1949 and 1950, Curtis' dialogue was seldom more demanding than "They went that-a-way."[48] He knew these performances were guided more by testosterone than talent.[49] Abe Greenberg accused him of being associated with "more registered dogs than the American Kennel Club" in these years.[50] The scripts seemed to have been written by people with IQs somewhere below room temperature and he came in for a lot of ridicule from the press as a result. "I don't like being the brunt of jokes," he complained, "The gaps in my education bother me."[51] Having said that, he had a different kind of *nous*: "I maybe didn't know where Africa was, or how to spell 'cosmopolitan,' but I sure knew a phony when I saw one."[52]

Criss Cross was followed by another crime film, *City Across the River*. He was the fifth lead, his back to the camera most of the time, but he was philosophical about it: "A few people noticed me and wrote in to the studio." The critics were also "unbelievably kind."[53] (This wouldn't last long.)

Some of the shooting took place in downtown New York so he often spent nights at home. Most stars would have relished the chance to be back with their parents but not Curtis: "I didn't want to go home anymore; I was making my own life now."[54] All the "old shack" represented for him was the grey ordinariness of the everyday. It was like a step backwards.

The studio had lobbied for him to get the lead role in the movie, feeling his fan mail justified it, but Maxwell Shane, the director, disagreed. He doubted Curtis had enough experience under his belt to "carry" a film yet. This was a pity, as *City* could have become Curtis' *The Wild One* if he'd been given the reins.

He appealed mainly to the bobbysoxers at this time. David Shipman saw him as a "slick, greasy-haired yob who stood around outside poolrooms or chatted up the girls at the Saturday night hop."[55] He didn't exude the danger of a Marlon Brando or the torment of Montgomery Clift or James Dean, being more user-friendly than either. He didn't need to cry on one's shoulder, like Clift, or rub against it like Brando. All he wanted was some action and a fair shake. He wasn't lost but rather hungry for action.

Curtis didn't get on with Clift. Shortly after he arrived in Hollywood he was entertaining some people at a party when Clift got up from the table he was sitting at and called out, "Look at her [sic]. She thinks she's the king. Can you match her looks with mine?" He despised Clift from that moment on. Clift had hit him at a weak spot, his near-effeminate looks. The fact that Clift himself was gay was an extra irony. Shortly afterwards he received another insult from a colleague. Kirk Douglas came up to him at a party and hissed, "You think you're pretty good, don't you, you little prick?"[56] If it was a joke he wouldn't have minded but he got the impression Douglas meant it.

At this point he was in the middle of what Shipman referred to as "the Hollywood delinquent syndrome."[57] Hollywood delinquents weren't like real ones. They usually had sensitive streaks that were brought out either by sympathetic parents, kindly social workers or the love (and home cooking) of the local friendly sweetheart.

One of his costars in *City Across the River*, Barbara Whiting, became a close friend, though not a lover. She wasn't yet eighteen. "Tony spent a couple of years at our house," she told film archivist Doug McClelland — the "at" meaning "coming to" rather than "staying at." "I remember we once gave him a pair of alligator shoes." Curtis formed an attachment to Whiting's mother and visited her frequently over the years, no matter how inconvenient it was or what troubles he had. It was in gestures like this that his caring nature showed through. He continued to visit her until shortly before she died.[58]

His next movie was *The Lady Gambles*. Barbara Stanwyck played the eponymous character whose penchant for gambling all but wrecks her marriage. Curtis had a blink-and-you-miss-him cameo as a telegram deliverer, but he'd learned from *Criss Cross* that there was no such thing as a small part. It was what you did with it. He tried to convince himself this was the central scene of the movie. Michael Gordon, the director, told him to concentrate on the fact that he would be looking for a tip more than anything else. That advice gave him the motivation he needed to do the scene. Gordon's words impressed him so much they almost became a kind of mantra for him for everything he did afterwards in life, both in movies and outside them. He even called a chapter in one of his books "All You Want Is a Tip."

He kept one of the fan letters he received after *The Lady Gambles* was released. It said simply, "Who was the boy who delivered the telegram? Why doesn't he star in a picture?"[59] It was tantamount to an Oscar nomination to him at the time, this slender vote of confidence for the approval-hungry rookie.

He was a mute killer in *Johnny Stool Pigeon*, also released in 1949. It was a standard yarn about a convict being sprung from prison to smash a drug ring. Curtis, again billed as Anthony rather than Tony, died at the end, but he refused to let this detail squash his urge to have fun on the set. As the lid of his funeral casket closed, he tapped on it and cried out, "Please, the corpse is thirsty. A glass of water — how about it?"[60]

A 14-year-old filmgoer called Elvis Presley attended this movie with his mother at the Loew's State Theater on Main Street, Memphis, and was impressed. Mrs. Presley *et fils* had also liked Curtis in *City Across the River*. As his biographer noted, "It wasn't so much the movies Elvis and his mother liked as Tony's photogenic looks." Both of them noted that Curtis' black, curly hair helped to make him a more dynamic presence, "especially with his steely blue eyes — the same color as Elvis.'"[61]

Curtis was also bottom of the bill in *Francis* the following year. The first in a series of seven films about a talking mule, all but the last starred Donald O'Connor, who finally realized he'd had enough when the mule continued to get more fan mail than he did. Chill Wills did the voice, transforming the mule into a "four-legged Will Rogers."[62] Curtis then made *I Was a Shoplifter*, playing a man who bought stolen goods from the shoplifter in question. The detective on her tail was played by Rock Hudson, also starting out at Universal by now (his name came bottom of the bill). Curtis described it not so much as a B-movie as a Z one. Hudson and Curtis quickly became friends and occasionally went to clubs together. They weren't in competition for roles because Hudson looked older. (Curtis always sympathized with the fact that Universal held a stranglehold on Hudson, preventing him from getting quality parts.) He was aware of the fact that Hudson was gay even then. His agent, Henry Willson, was also gay, as were two more of Willson's clients, Tab Hunter and Sal Mineo.

Winchester 73 came next, with James Stewart and Shelley Winters in the leading roles. Though the film had a solid cast and a good director, the real star, in Winters' view, was "the goddam rifle."[63]

Stewart's agent at the time was Lew Wasserman. He would soon become Curtis'. Wasserman encouraged Stewart to ask for a percentage of the gross on the film. Stewart agreed and the resulting deal ended up making the actor rich.

Wasserman, in the words of Thomas Schatz, "reveled in his ability to dicker with studio bosses and jack up his clients' salaries."[64] (It was he who convinced Jack Warner to raise the salaries of Errol Flynn and Bette Davis after the war when their careers seemed to be going nowhere.) He got Stewart 50 percent of the gross for *Winchester 73* instead of a large salary.

Wasserman was born in Cleveland to Russian-Jewish immigrants and began his show-business career as a theater usher. Afterwards he became a booking agent for MCA, the Music Corporation of America, extending the organization's reach into non-musical forums. It was nicknamed "the Octopus" because of its reputation for crushing competition. Once a star belonged to it, they belonged exclusively to MCA-related productions.[65]

Wasserman said the Stewart deal came about not so much because of him insisting on it as the studio's lack of funds. Wasserman had demanded a salary of $200,000 per movie for Stewart, or half the movies' profits. Since Universal didn't have that kind of money available, it had to plump for the other option.[66]

Winchester 73 made Wasserman into the agent most budding stars, including Curtis, wanted to have. But there was a downside to this way of doing business, the freelance route being in many ways a double-edged sword for actors, many of whom would eventually come to believe they had merely traded in one set of feudal lords for another.[67] One of the reasons for this was that profits on movies were difficult to compute. Studio heads were past masters at cooking the books, or ramping up "endless and ingenious" arrays of expenses to deplete the status of their net gain on a given project. Gross profit, on the other hand, was "real money" one could touch immediately. It was a balancing act stars had faced from the inception of film. Stewart was an unusual catalyst for its present manifestation in the sense that he wasn't the biggest star in the Hollywood firmament. His career had also been stop-go since the war.[68]

Curtis appreciated the manner in which Wasserman refused to go in for palaver. Arthur Miller remembered him as "the only man I ever knew who offered to shake hands with the side of his hand against his flat stomach and his palm straight up."[69] He wanted to get away from the cigar-chomping, loud-clothed image agents often had, opting instead for a simple black suit with a white shirt and black tie.[70] He ushered in an age where agents surveyed a movie's earning potential and made decisions based on that prognosis. A byproduct of this was the rise of actors forming their own companies, like Burt Lancaster and Kirk Douglas, or Curtis himself when he set up Curtleigh with Janet Leigh.[71] This was one of the reasons Darryl F. Zanuck quit producing at Twentieth Century–Fox in 1956, complaining that actors had "taken over Hollywood completely with their agents....The producer hasn't got a chance to exercise any authority."[72]

Curtis now got a bit part in an Audie Murphy western, *Sierra*. At the premiere of the film in San Francisco in June 1950, screams went up from the audience when the name "Anthony Curtis" was announced. He had outshone Murphy and all the rest of the cast. He was so flummoxed he had to be pushed onto the stage to take his bow. "I couldn't understand it," he said afterwards of the attention he received. "I knew I wasn't getting it because of my acting because I hadn't done any. Then I realized people can like you just for your looks and personality. This was an odd experience for a guy who had never been accepted in his own neighborhood back in the Bronx and who had to fight for survival."[73]

He also had a pit part in another Audie Murphy western made that year, *Kansas Raiders*. This time he had to ride a horse. He told a lie to get the part, as he had with Robert Siodmak for *Criss Cross*. Asked if he could ride, he replied, "Very well." As Janet Leigh remarked, "Like all struggling performers, he would have said he could fly if it meant a job."[74] It was his first time on a horse, and he wasn't very good at it: "I kept looking for the gearshift."[75] "The only ones I'd seen before then were the horses in Central Park that people hired to drive them around in coaches."[76] (He also said he once dated a girl who *resembled* a horse, but that was a different story.)

Every trick in the book was used to keep him from falling off. At one stage the director even placed a black piece of velvet "about the size of a diaper" under him. He tied one end to a gun holster he was wearing and the other to the saddle. Curtis remarked, "I did everything but put silly glue on my ass so I wouldn't fly out of the saddle."[77] Some of the crew *wanted* him to fall off. After he climbed on, they loosened the saddle and stirrups so that when the horse bolted the saddle fell off, and him with it. As if this wasn't bad enough, "They picked up the tail of the horse and shoved a stick with kerosene soaked in it right up its ass and pulled it out. That fucking horse would go crazy with me on it. I had to fight for my life out there."[78]

He started dating Murphy's ex-wife, Wanda Hendrix, while the film was being made. Murphy was none too pleased about this. One day in a fit of pique he stuck a gun in Curtis' stomach and pulled the trigger. Curtis heard a "muffled explosion" as he did so and thought he'd been shot. He fell to the ground in a faint. After Curtis woke up, Murphy told him it was a prank, that the sound came from a cap gun he was hiding behind his back with his other hand. Curtis didn't really see the humor. Neither did he ever date Hendrix again.[79] "The fact that he'd killed half the German army during the war was a factor in my decision," said Curtis. (This was a slight exaggeration but Murphy was Hollywood's most decorated war hero.)

Asked what he liked most about Hollywood by an interviewer between takes on *Kansas Raiders*, Curtis replied, "The girls, the climate, the girls, the possibility of a career, the new car I just bought, and the girls." The car was a Buick, which he'd bought on the installment plan, "so I only own one hubcap. But it will be all mine if I live long enough, and I intend to live forever."[80] His happy-go-lucky attitude wasn't appreciated by the film's director, Ray Enright, especially when it shone through in some of the film's shots. "Don't act so happy," Enright castigated, "this is supposed to be a grim picture."[81]

Kansas Raiders was the first film he made as Tony Curtis. The transition from Bernie Schwartz had come about by circuitous means. (Schwartz was also too close to "schvartze," the Yiddish word for black.) At first he thought of changing it to Kertesz, the name of a Hungarian ancestor.[82] It was Bob Goldstein who came up with Curtis. He thought *James Curtis* worked, but Curtis liked the novel *Anthony Adverse* and suggested Anthony. He saw this rags-to-riches story as similar to his own.[83] "It conjures up images. I live like Anthony Adverse today, in a Mediterranean villa."[84] It was about being his own man, "a creation of myself."[85]

His hairstyle was also part of his new image. People talked about this as much as they talked about Curtis himself. At one point he even credited his hairstyle as being responsible for the birth of rock 'n' roll. "Without my hair," he declared extravagantly, "there would never have been rock music. Elvis Presley didn't invent rock'n'roll, my hair did."[86] After a while he came to believe the hair was such an important part of his success that if he lost it the fame would go too. He became paranoid, a movieland Samson living in terror of shorn locks.[87]

Curtis became Elvis Presley's favorite actor (before the King discovered Marlon Brando and James Dean), and a lot of that was down to the hair. Elvis put shoe polish on his own to make it to look like Curtis.' Presley never liked his natural blond hair—either for itself or its star possibilities. "There's no blondheaded icon except James Dean," was his thinking.[88] Elvis also adopted the Curtis quiff, sculpting his into "a perfect pompadour which curled into a greasy ducktail" at the nape of the neck.[89] After Presley started dying his hair he never reverted back to his blond roots except when he had to, in the army. This had the effect of making him look more like his mother than his father, a natural blond. In the words of his biographer Alanna Nash, the hair change "bolstered their bond, their oneness."[90]

Curtis told talkshow host Clive James he used a substance called Lanolin to accentuate his quiff and the greasy look. He had the same attitude towards his hair as he did towards his handsomeness in general—liking it for the way it moved his career forward but objecting when it became the thing people most associated him with. In time he would proclaim, "Marlon Brando will be known for his torn T-shirt and Levis, and Laurence Olivier for his speech, but I have my own mark in history—the Tony Curtis haircut. I'm famous all over the world for it." He went to London once and spotted his face in at least half a dozen barber shops.[91]

The haircut passed from merely being associated with him to being his essence. If someone walked into a barbershop and said, "I'll have a Tony Curtis," it was immediately known what he meant. It was a mixed blessing: "Every motherfucker grew his hair long, put a lot of pomade in it, curled it at the front, and there were 800 Tony Curtises roaming the city."[92]

By now he'd met Janet Leigh, the woman who was to form such an important part of his life both on and off the screen. The first time he saw her was in a publicity still standing beside Scott Brady. His heart went "Whump." On that occasion he didn't speak, playing a waiting game. Leigh thought him "too good-looking to have much of anything else to him."[93]

Their first "real" meeting was at a cocktail party for RKO Studios. Debbie Reynolds was in attendance and spoke of the resultant fireworks as being almost inevitable, like a Hollywood force of nature. Sometimes two people really clicked:

> Tony Curtis and Janet Leigh met one day when we were entertaining at Edwards Air Force Base. Janet was something to behold; beautiful as well as talented. Not jealous, not vindictive, not a bitch, not boring....Tony was a big, macho, Rambo-type guy: stunning, with gorgeous blue eyes and an ego on steroids. He took one look at her and the Fourth of July tripled.[94]

In later years Reynolds suggested their meeting was a set-up by the film industry's publicity department. "That's how [stars] would meet," she alleged. "They would [organize] premieres and each studio would have their new young stars meet the other new young stars and that's how we'd go out on dates. That's how Janet Leigh met Tony Curtis."[95]

Jamie Lee Curtis, Tony's daughter, agreed with this view. "Their publicists put them together," she maintained. "That's how they met. Nowadays a publicist would never put one star with another one. They may secretly be *schtupping*, but you don't see two stars going out on an arranged date [today]."[96]

Leigh thought Curtis had "a captivating boyish charm, yet there was an inner depth behind those penetrating eyes. Definitely someone worth investigating."[97] She had been married twice before, the first marriage lasting only the proverbial day. At 14 she ran off to Reno with a childhood sweetheart, having lied about her age. It was annulled when her parents heard about it. She hid it from people for years. When she eventually spoke about it, she described her husband as "dark and brooding." He sued her for the comment, alleging it suggested he was African, but the (ridiculous) suit was later dropped. Her second marriage was to a bandleader, Stan Reames, and that stumbled along for two years before collapsing.[98]

When Curtis met her she was going steady with a man called Arthur Loew. This was one of the reasons he didn't move in on her immediately. She was with Loew the day he met her, which made him all the more interested in her. Some nights he spied on her as she came home with other men. Before she got to the door he would have slipped notes under it with messages like "Don't kiss him, I'm watching," or "If he comes in, don't let him stay too long." Leigh groaned, "I had to read these notes in front of my dates."[99]

The first time Curtis kissed her, her heart rose. "My bells were definitely ringing," she exulted. "My built-in Geiger-counter was activated."[100] For the first few months of knowing her, Curtis only went on double dates with her, nervous about being alone with her in case things moved too fast between them — or didn't move at all. Eventually they went out alone, but Curtis couldn't afford to bring her to the "in" places like Ciro's or the Mocambo. He'd just made *Kansas Raiders* and had been temporarily laid off by the studio, as was the practice in those days to save money. He was more embarrassed about this state of affairs than she was. She didn't mind eating in, or going out to the local hamburger joint instead of having a six-course meal at an exclusive restaurant. Curtis was impressed by this. On the negative side, she found fault with his gauche ways at parties and tried to knock the rough edges off him. This led to many spats between them. He could "do" finesse, but not all the time. "Poise and sophistication aren't the most important things in life," he reasoned. "If I had to worry about them I'd go off the beam."[101]

Curtis and Leigh knew each other almost a year before they went steady. Considering the way the sparks flew between them when they met, this was unusual — especially for Hollywood. By now Curtis' parents and his brother Bobby had arrived in Hollywood. Not only did they expect him to put them up but to support them as well. Curtis found them an apartment. If things continued to go well for him he promised them a house of their own eventually. Their presence brought a huge thud of reality to his dream world. In a sense, the Bronx was back in his life.

Bobby was nine now and probably at the happiest period of his life. The schizophrenia that would blight his later years hadn't yet made too much of an impact, though there were suggestions of it. His mother was all sweetness and light to Tony, conveniently forgetting the way she brutalized him in childhood. She wanted him to put Bobby in the movies, being in denial about the cause of his sometimes weird behavior. Curtis tried to forget all these things and to look on the bright side. At least the bailiffs couldn't come in here and throw their furniture onto the street. It was a pretty apartment, if small, and sunshine came in through the windows. "We never had that before," he remarked piquantly.[102]

Sometimes he had more fun in the apartment than in his own posher home, enjoying his mother's potato pancakes and the casual banter of natural folk. The problems started when the "family" began to expand, with extended relatives being invited for visits. His expenses increased in direct proportion to what he was earning at Universal. As one of his friends put it, "Every time Tony gets his option picked up, another relative from the Bronx moves in with him."[103]

There were also some amusing moments. One day he brought his father out to the studio and they met the writer-producer Oscar Brodeny. Brodeny got Curtis' name-change back to front and said to his father, "Tell me, Mr. Schwartz, why didn't you like the name Curtis?"[104]

Curtis later got his father a job as his publicity agent. This was just an honorific term as he did little more than collect articles about the star. "Pop's a clipper," he informed Sidney Skolsky. "He clips my publicity."

Manny eventually designed film costumes. Here he relished his reflected glory when he saw the results on screen. He didn't necessarily look for his son at these movies but rather some other actor he'd outfitted. "That one on the left," he'd say, elbowing Curtis, "I made that."

While taking his first steps toward being a star, Curtis realized fame could be expensive. Apart from putting his relatives up and taking care of their expenses, the bigger his name became the less he was able to dine on hamburgers. Now he was a "big shot" and had to "splurge." He used to go to the beach and have a "million" laughs, but that wasn't possible anymore. Now it was the high life or nothing. He was enjoying success, but it was bankrupting him.[105]

He liked chronicling his list of expenses to interviewers: "I went in for a haircut and came out with a massage, a manicure and a shoeshine. They came at me from all angles." His tailor was giving him a hard time too. All of a sudden he "didn't have a thing" to sell that was under $130.[106]

Fame, they say, doesn't change the people who become famous, only those around them. It seemed so to Curtis. Bobby had also started to get strange with him, saying things like, "Good morning, Mr. Curtis."

Curtis was now rooming with no less a luminary than Marlon Brando. "We share an apartment," he told a journalist. "Marlon sleeps in the bed and I get the couch. But the night I got my promotion he let me have the bed — for eight whole hours."[107]

Brando and himself were both working on major movies. Curtis had just been cast in *The Prince Who Was a Thief*, the film that would make him famous, and Brando had just made *The Men* and was about to begin filming *A Streetcar Named Desire* with Elia Kazan. Curtis had seen the stage version of *Streetcar* (also with Brando) some years before. He got into it the way he'd secured entry to most shows in his youth — by sneaking in at the interval, without paying — so he only saw the second act. But it was still enough to make him thrill at Brando's brilliance. Curtis always admired Brando, but he took issue with the way he was always synonymized with the "Method" school of acting.

"He was great because he was Marlon, not because of the Method," he rightly concluded. "Why complicate the job of acting? Memorize your lines. Learn the part. Find out what the director wants. Then show up on time and act. The idea of trying to remember when your sister stole your peanut butter sandwich so you can give an angry performance is bullshit."[108]

"I knew Marlon didn't think much of my movies," said Curtis, "but he liked me and didn't give me a hard time over them." They went out together and enjoyed one another's company at parties, even if Brando tended to go out on a limb in groups. Curtis boasted that he once took a girl from Brando, a unique achievement.

Brando had a pet raccoon at this time that he called Russell. There are those who would say he treated the raccoon better than some of the women in his life at this time. He certainly seemed to have more fun with it. "For some reason," Curtis remembered, "Marlon always insisted Russell sleep in our oven. It's a good thing I didn't come home one night and heat up the oven for a midnight supper."[109] Shelley Winters told an even funnier story about Brando putting Russell into a bathtub and keeping it warm by aiming an electric heater at it in the winter months.[110]

Curtis had an interesting attitude toward Brando. "The rest of us were all boys in comparison to him," he believed. "His brain was so pristine and clear. It took me a lifetime to get to where he is. Marlon wasn't a kid when he was a kid. He wasn't like the rest of us who fucked our lives up."

"I didn't have the complexity of a Marlon Brando," Curtis once wrote, "because my life had been more primitive — trying to stay alive in those harsh New York streets, irritable, wary, every tooth in my mouth decayed."[111] Curtis liked Brando as a man but disparaged the acting school of Lee Strasberg that spawned him. "Everyone they turn out acts like Brando," he insisted. "And they can't act at all until they picture themselves in love with their sisters or their mothers as junkies."[112]

"The Lee Strasberg acting school should really have been called the Marlon Brando acting school," said Curtis. "Most of the things I saw happening in there were down to Marlon. He has a lot to answer for, but I don't say that in a way that might be critical of him. He can't be held responsible for the things that happened in his name." Curtis said he didn't engage in the fashionable practice of doing Brando impersonations ("My screen impersonations end with Cary Grant"), but he was amused by them. What was less easy to take were all the actors who thought that "because they walked and talked like Marlon, or scratched their face like him, they *were* him. That's what's sad, not that Stanislavski failed with most of Strasberg's students but that he never really tried. When you're as good as Marlon Brando, you kill off the opposition."

"There's no such thing as learning the craft of acting," Curtis declared. "Acting is of the moment. Acting is living. It's not more complicated than that....You must be careful not to fall into the trap of technique."[113]

Curtis despised the self-important airs of the Actor's Studio. Its reputation, he believed, came about from the "idiosyncrasies and genius" of one man: Marlon Brando. From him, not Strasberg or Stanislavski, came Dean, Clift, Newman, Cassavetes and so on.[114] This was a theory Brando himself hinted at when he said, "Acting is just an expression of one man's neurotic impulse."[115]

Brando didn't like Lee Strasberg any more than Curtis did. "Strasberg never taught me acting," he scowled, "Stella Adler did." Adler had taken Brando under her wing at Erwin Piscator's Dramatic Workshop. Like Piscator, she was Jewish and suffered for that. As Brando put it,

> If you looked Jewish you didn't get a part and couldn't make a living. You had to look like Kirk Douglas, Tony Curtis, Paul Muni or Paulette Goddard and change your name. They were Jewish but didn't 'look Jewish,' and employed the camouflage of non–Jewish names. Hence Julius Garfinkle became John Garfield, Emmanuel Goldenberg became Edward G. Robinson and Muni Weisenfreund became Paul Muni.[116]

And Bernie Schwartz became Tony Curtis. Inside himself, though, he would carry the ghost of his alter ego with him all his life. A name change was just the scratch of a pen on a piece of paper or a neon light on a marquee board. Identity went a bit deeper than that and would prove harder to shake off in the long run.

4

Sultan of Shlock

Curtis was now part of the "beefcake" set of stars, like Robert Mitchum, Jeff Chandler, John Derek, Scott Brady, etc. They'd become like male antidotes to their distaff "cheesecake" counterparts — Jane Russell, Maureen O'Hara, Esther Williams and so on. They were photographed bare-chested with their rippling biceps, which annoyed some of their female rivals.

"The idea of actors shedding their clothes for their art is just too ridiculous," Betty Grable complained. "Pin-up art is one field in which women were meant to be supreme. This invasion of the opposite sex's domain is as preposterous as if I were to set myself up as a prizefighter."[1] Jeanne Crain outlined another kind of difficulty experienced by beleaguered females: "It's somewhat disconcerting to play a love scene with an actor who's concentrating on flexing his chest muscles."[2]

Curtis was offered his first major role in *The Prince Who Was a Thief*, starring as a royal heir opposite Piper Laurie. It was one of the "Eastern" ventures with which he would become identified in the coming years. His eight screen appearances before this, as one writer put it, were "as fleeting as a snowflake at a barbecue." He totaled them as twelve minutes in all, an average of ninety seconds a film.[3]

The plot of *The Prince Who Was a Thief* had him as a prince called Julna who's about to be killed before his assigned assassin (Everett Sloane) takes pity on him and lets him live. Thereafter he fights his way back to his rightful throne and also manages to win the heart of his lady love, the commoner Tina (Laurie).

Curtis claimed Laurie was "less successful" than him at this point, but the fact remains that her career had taken off quicker than his.[4] She saw her role in the film as cartoon-like, "but at least it was a rather charming cartoon." She admired the choice of Rudolph Maté as director. He encouraged her to be experimental, and "laughed like a child" when she did something he liked.[5] The studio said the screenplay was based on a Theodore Dreiser tale but Laurie disputed this. Only the title was Dreiser's, she insisted: "It was essentially a Pygmalion story."[6] If this was so, Curtis was like a male Eliza Doolittle, with numerous fixers being commissioned to check "his hair, teeth, tan and fly-buttons."[7]

By now he was ranked second out of 150 stars vetted on the strength of their fan mail. Laurie was 12th on the female scale.[8] Curtis liked Laurie, but the studio wanted to trump up their emotional involvement offscreen and this created tension between them. Maybe if Janet Leigh wasn't in the frame something might have happened between Curtis and Laurie, but Curtis was contemplating marriage with Leigh by now.

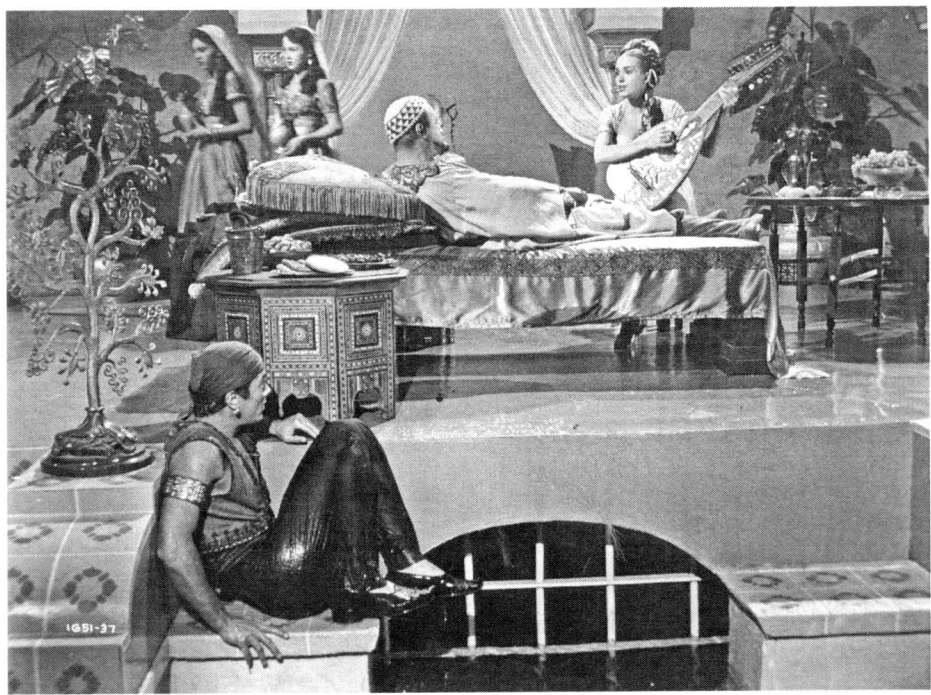

This scene is from the Rudolph Maté feature ***The Prince Who Was a Thief*** (1951), Curtis' first major role in what he would later term his "Arabian nights rubbish" phase. Nonetheless, he was glad of it at the time, not only for the money but also to boost his profile in the industry. The turban-sporting Curtis, as the dashing Prince Julna, crouches in hiding as his lady love Tina (Piper Laurie) diverts the attentions of the malevolent Prince Mustapha (Donald Randolph) by plucking her lute.

Leigh had also started to bond with Curtis' parents. This led to many trade paper features about "Janet's future in-laws."

One of these showed Curtis scouting around for a bigger house for "Mama and Papa." Janet adored his mother's cooking and was going to get fat on her stuffed cabbage. "Mama" was vetting a new jacket Curtis had bought. She'd gotten closer to her son since Julie died.[9] Everything was sanitized in yet another article streamlined to advance his career.

Curtis was warned he'd be letting his fans down if he married, so he came to a decision. "Okay, I'll make my bucks another way. I've a strong back and I can dig ditches. If all I'm offering my fans is my curly head and my flat belly, I want to find it out quick."[10]

After he became engaged to Leigh, people still tried to change his mind. "One big shot," he rasped, "sent word that if I go through with this he'll personally put me out of pictures. He thinks I want publicity. That bugs me." But the "big shot" was partly right. Curtis loved Leigh, but he also loved what she could do for his career. Neither did he have much respect for the institution he was about to enter: "All this talk about the sanctity of marriage is hooey. I resent it when it's called a holy experience."[11]

Universal threatened to drop his option if he married Leigh. The threat didn't work. "That hacked me and made me all the more determined to pursue her." Was it love? A career move? The two elements could have been present in his hunger for her. Even the objection of both sets of parents acted as a spur.[12] Leigh's father suspected he might have been after her money. Curtis' own parents would have preferred a "nice Jewish girl" for their son.

Promotion for *The Prince Who Was a Thief*, meanwhile, went on apace. A 26-city personal appearance tour was organized for Curtis and Laurie, and the film played to packed houses wherever they went. In Portland the audience was particularly noisy. When Curtis went to take his bow after it ended, a bunch of girls started screaming at him. He was so dumbfounded he froze on the edge of the stage. Lois Andrews, who had a small part in the movie, came to his rescue. "Get out there," she goaded. "This happens to a person only once in a lifetime." Outside the theater afterwards he was besieged by more fans. "One girl jerked my coat sleeve off. Another grabbed my necktie. My shirt was in tatters. A cop thought I'd been in a fight and wanted to run me in."[13] He was mobbed at many other locations too, causing his minders to finally dress him in "breakaway" suits. These came apart piecemeal in the hands of his admirers.

The world premiere was held in Detroit, Laurie's home town. This embarrassed her as she didn't feel she'd done anything particularly extraordinary in it. She took the train to Detroit with Curtis. They visited a hospital together. Then Laurie went back to her alma mater and Curtis checked out a local submarine. (His fans knew he'd been in the Navy.) Photographs were taken of these events and featured in *Motion Picture* magazine.[14] Everything was choreographed and tabulated to ramp up publicity for the movie.

They did a skit on stage together between showings of the film. Laurie was impressed when Curtis asked her parents to take a bow from the balcony. There was a party at her home that night and Curtis attended. Laurie showed him off. After he'd gone back to the hotel her young cousins "took turns using the bathroom that Tony Curtis had used."[15]

The pair of them toured other cities in the following days. Innumerable interviews and autograph parties were followed by red-eye flights or train journeys to the next destination. In the Bronx there was a marquee advertising "Bernie Schwartz and Rosetta Jacobs" (Laurie's real name) appearing in *The Goniff and the Maidle*, which was Yiddish for *The Thief and the Girl*.

Everything was done on the move. Laurie learned to apply false eyelashes "as a train rattled me up and down." She envied Curtis, who only had to change his clothes and shower to make himself presentable to fans. Her routine, in contrast, was "hats, jewelry, seams in my stockings, a few minutes on my face and a few more if my hair got wet."[16]

Curtis found it difficult to enjoy the tour. Leigh was on his mind most of the time. Would his marriage to her mean the end of all this? It was a decision he'd have to make sooner or later.

Then his father suffered a heart attack, which put matters into perspective. Everything was interrupted, giving him a reality check. His father survived, but from then on his health would be on Curtis' mind constantly.

His decision to marry Leigh met with strong opposition from the film industry. Leonard Goldstein thought the marriage could be a career-killer for the heart-throb and told him as much. Then Jerry Lewis, whom Goldstein had advised to do likewise, came out against it too. This proved too much for Leigh, and she fled Curtis in tears after an argument.

This seemed to wake him up to his priorities. "When you went out the door and I thought I could lose you," he reassured her, "the answer was clear. I told Leonard that if being single is my only chance for success then I'm in the wrong business."[17] Such a hiccup seemed to strengthen what they had, especially after Bernstein and Lewis both rang to apologize.

The prospective bride and groom grew closer, but Universal kept trying to change his mind. The "brass" wanted him to marry Laurie instead. It didn't matter that he didn't love her, nor she him. Only the film mattered. They offered him $30,000 to marry her, a huge sum of money at the time. A part of him was tempted to accept. It would have solved all his problems with his parents and Bobby. But he had no feelings for Laurie.

She behaved like a lady through everything. She was aware of the turmoil he was going through and sympathized with him. His attitude towards her was less philanthropic. He suspected her of trying to milk publicity for the movie for her own ends. For a time he even suspected she was behind the studio's plan to marry the pair of them off. He felt she was resentful of all the publicity he was getting.

Curtis now started badmouthing her to people and it got back to her. At first she didn't believe them but the more she heard the more suspicious she became. Curtis refused to admit to anything. One day after they came back from a trip he took her into a cubicle in the publicity department and started to cry. He said, "People who are envious of our good fortune might try to destroy our friendship."[18] She wasn't sure what he meant by this. He made her promise to tell him if she heard any unhealthy rumors about either of them from a third party. She agreed to this and they hugged one another.

It's probably true that he said the things Laurie heard he had. He was just about to break into the big time, and Laurie seemed to be blocking his light. He was also annoyed by her fussiness about makeup. This was in stark contrast to his own "Just do it" philosophy.

Curtis married Leigh on June 4th, 1951, the day after his 26th birthday. Jerry Lewis was the best man. Leigh was unaware of his overwrought state and looked a radiant bride. Neither of their parents attended the wedding.

"On the surface everything looked rosy," Curtis declared, "but there was a lot of tension. Janet's father thought she was marrying 'down.' I had the added problem of being Jewish — and pretty poor by movie star standards."

With their respective careers on full forward, the wedding was an anti-climax. It was wedged in between Leigh testing for a role in *Scaramouche* and Curtis on the road with Laurie. "We started married life without even an egg-beater," Leigh told Hedda Hopper.[19]

As the newlyweds honeymooned, Laurie found herself doing much of the promotion for the movie without Curtis. This didn't bother her, but as time went on she started hearing more stories about Curtis badmouthing her. One report had him saying she had actually tried to sabotage the wedding.

She tried to contact Curtis for him to confirm or deny the rumors but she couldn't get through to him. When he came back from his honeymoon she asked him about them, but he refused to talk to her: "He would walk away or leave if we were in the same room. His open hostility and coldness were bewildering. I was frankly afraid to confront him."[20]

By now their relationship was totally dysfunctional. Notwithstanding this, Universal rushed another "tits and sand" movie featuring the pair of them into production. *Son of Ali Baba* was a poor follow-up to *The Prince Who Was a Thief*. A sequel never equals, as they say, but it's also unwise to break a winning formula. *The Prince* had made so much money for the studio it was inevitable Universal would go back to the well for something similar.

Curtis and Laurie were wheeled out again to tramp across the sands and swoon into one another's arms, even though they were no longer on speaking terms.

Custis' fan Elvis Presley was working as a cinema usher in Memphis when *Son of Ali Baba* was released. Mary Lacker recalled, "Elvis thought [Curtis] had the ideal masculine look. He had that shiny black hair and blue eyes. Some people say Elvis copied his ducktail haircut [too]."[21]

Son of Ali Baba is the film in which Curtis spoke his most oft-quoted line: "Yonder in the valley of the sun is my father's castle." This is usually misquoted (in Bronxese dialect) as "Yondah lies the castle of my faddah." It's also usually attributed to *The Prince Who Was a Thief*. Curtis' friend Michael Munn made this mistake in his first biography of Curtis. (By the time he wrote his second one he corrected the error.)

Shelley Winters was another person who made this mistake, as mentioned already, her recollection of the line being complicated by the fact that she cites it as being delivered in front of Rudy Maté. But Maté wasn't the director of *Son of Ali Baba;* Kurt Neumann was. Winters claimed she told Maté to milk the situation for its comic potential.[22]

The Prince Who Was a Thief made so much money for U-I, they quickly rushed out the sequel pictured here, *The Son of Ali Baba* (1952). This also starred Curtis and Piper Laurie. Like most sequels, however, it didn't equal. Relations between Curtis and Laurie had deteriorated by now as well, not least due to Curtis' recent marriage to Janet Leigh. In yet another "Eastern" adventure where the plot and dialogue played second fiddle to Curtis' matinee idol appeal to the bobbysoxers of the time, this scene features him with Laurie, as well as costars Susan Cabot (holding the bow) and William Reynolds.

Curtis was always annoyed when Winters brought the subject up. He regarded her as a loudmouth, rationalizing his negative feelings about her with a remark that wasn't true: "She never really made it to the top tier of stardom, which really pissed her off."[23] It also annoyed him when she bragged about having "discovered" him. He was more inclined to confer that honor on a multitude of others before her—including a man with whom she had an extramarital affair, Burt Lancaster.[24]

His botching of the *Ali Baba* line came to haunt him. When Tab Hunter played a part in *La Freccia d'Oro* (*The Golden Arrow*), he was aghast to discover "page after page of truly horrendous dialogue." Hunter found a unique solution to deal with it: "All I could think of was Tony Curtis in *The Prince Who Was a Thief*."[25] Robert Wagner said of his hapless 1954 costumer *Prince Valiant* (costarring Janet Leigh), "I had no idea it would become for me what 'Yonda lies the castle of my faddah' was for Tony Curtis."[26]

Curtis expressed frustration about the issue to a British interviewer with this valid question: "How many movies have you seen in which the Nazis are all played by Englishmen?"[27] In later years John Wayne would be targeted for his Hollywood drawl as he played a Roman soldier at the foot of the cross where Christ was crucified in George Stevens' *The Greatest Story Ever Told*.[28] Max Von Sydow also left questions to be answered in that film, playing Christ with a Swedish inflection.

Some critics were more sympathetic than others. Clive James was one of these. "[Curtis] might not have been getting some of the consonants right," James speculated, "but he was always spot on with the emphasis and the impetus. Curtis weighed a line for rhythm and melody and said it as if it could be said in one way only, and no uddah."[29] Geoff Andrew had an unusual attitude toward Curtis' accent, pointing out that his vowel-mangling was probably the only way one could utter the dreadful lines he was being given in these kinds of films.[30]

Curtis came to despise films like *Son of Ali Baba* and all they represented. As for "that" line, "It would be a helluva thing if in the end, that's all I'm remembered for."[31] But he knew films like *Ali Baba* were buttering his bread. Asked in January 1951 if he would consider giving up costumers, he replied, "No ... because those Arabian fantasies have helped my career greatly."[32]

Piper Laurie said the film cost $200,000 to make.[33] Michael Munn put the cost at double that.[34] Barry Paris was more vague, computing it to be something under $1 million.[35] What was more important was what it earned, which was something in the region of $2 million. Neither Curtis nor Laurie was informed of this. All they knew was that they were given a huge raise in their salaries, so obviously somebody's till was ringing.[36]

Shooting simultaneously on the lot next to *Ali Baba* was a Frank Sinatra/Shelley Winters film, *Meet Danny Wilson*, in which Sinatra played a thinly-disguised version of himself. Curtis and his friend Jeff Chandler were asked to appear as themselves in a short scene where they pick a drunken Sinatra up off the floor of a nightclub.

Sinatra was temperamental on the set, as Winters outlined in her memoirs, because he was in the process of divorcing his wife Nancy to marry Ava Gardner at the time. He was kind to her in the musical scenes, but when he lost her to Alex Nicol at the end he changed the line "I'll have a cup of coffee and leave you two lovebirds alone" to "I'll go have a cup of Jack Daniels or I'm gonna pull that blond broad's hair out by its black roots."[37]

Curtis would make two more movies with Laurie before their screen pairing fizzled out and both of them went on to do other things. For years Laurie tried to break out of the genre stranglehold in which Hollywood held her but lacked the assertiveness to do anything about it.[38] Curtis' main problem continued to be his voice. To improve it he spent time with his next-door neighbor Dean Martin. Martin's daughter Deana was amused by his persistence as he borrowed her mother's tape recorder to work on it. She wrote in her memoirs: "Sitting in the den in his white turtleneck sweater he'd practice his elocution in an attempt to lose his Bronx accent while Mother listened and advised."[39]

Curtis always had a double-edged attitude toward this phase of his career, which put his name in lights but at some cost. "When I first got to Hollywood," he would tell a reporter years later, "I made $40 a week and they named a hairstyle after me and made me into a kind of male Yvonne de Carlo, fooling around in Arabian Nights rubbish."[40]

5

The Elite of the Milk Shake Set

Curtis' fanbase didn't trail off after his marriage to Leigh, as the studio bosses feared. Instead, it increased, as the minutes of a Universal Committee meeting on June 20 stated.[1] When the marriage didn't result in a mass exodus of the bobbysoxers from the cinemas, Curtis' detractors now got on to another tack, asking if it would last. There were stories in the press about marital squabbles, some of them quite graphic in their detailing of flared tempers and occasional flying cutlery. Curtis and Leigh admitted that they argued, but not always were plates smashed or frying pans hurled at one another.

The real (unreported) stresses sprung from other sources: money worries, the directions of their mutual careers, even having to appear at events they weren't madly excited about. They thought differently about life but spent an inordinate amount of time in each other's company. This fed certain tensions. If Leigh wanted to save what money they earned and Curtis wanted to spend it — or put it towards his parents' upkeep — Leigh grew distressed.

When reporters tired of writing about their rows they went to the other extreme and started placing them on twin pedestals. Upon such extremes did the publishing industry thrive. If one or the other blew their noses it made hot copy for publications that thrived on trivia. Their marriage, as Will Haygood put it, "rocketed both of them into the consciousness of the fan magazine crazies."[2]

Such "crazies" spouted predictable clichés about them. There was a 1951 piece in *Photoplay* which dealt with the hardly earth-shattering theme of their differing attitudes to timekeeping.[3] Every moment of their lives was tabulated in one form or another, including Leigh's fussiness. After they came back from their honeymoon, Curtis was sitting on a sofa reading a newspaper one night and asked Leigh for a glass of water. He took one sip of it, turned a page of his paper "and the fucking glass was gone." The table was also wiped dry. Had he knocked it over? "No, darling, I thought you were done."[4]

They were referred to as the elite of the milk shake set, two "Tennis, anyone?" types cooped up together for their mutual replenishment. What Douglas Fairbanks and Mary Pickford represented to a previous era, and what Brad Pitt and Angelina Jolie would be to a future one, they were to the fifties: Hollywood's Beautiful People.

Leigh had made a dozen films before she met Curtis and was shaping up nicely for an onslaught on the new decade. Once Curtis came into her life, however, she subjugated her career to his. Or, rather, audiences did. After they married, as one writer noted, "All her fans cared about was seeing another day in the superhappy life of Janet and Tony in the fan magazines."[5]

Curtis and his first wife Janet Leigh cosying up together shortly after their marriage in 1951. This was fairly typical of the kind of "Curtises at Home" photospreads in which the fanzines of the time specialized, "selling" their Golden Couple to a public more than anxious to hook their fantasies onto this dynamic duo on the cusp of superstardom.

"Janet and Tony" made a compliant couple — maybe too compliant. One columnist huffed, "They were fearfully ambitious kids, so determined to make it they were tiresome." Another one called them "over-eager, over-nice, over-everything."[6]

As testament to this, they won a joint award as Hollywood's Most Cooperative Stars. It was a dubious honor. The quality was seen by some as an ode to bovine servility. Far more exciting were the "problem" actors, the movie brats, the improvisers.

Curtis was sensitive but he didn't buckle under directorial fussiness. He said:

> A director is the toughest foreman or overseer. He has to get his product into the can as quickly as possible or he'll get fired. We actors are the raw material he has to deal with so he criticizes you, usually in front of a bunch of people, and you learn to take it even if you hate it. He criticizes your talk, your walk, your height, your coloring, your personality and your stupidity. It's

brutal and it's unjust, just as it is in other jobs. But if you can learn to take it you come out strong.[7]

Leigh seemed to mirror such blind obedience.

The first house they bought was a two-bedroomed one in Beverly Hills. Because both of them were under contract to their respective studios there was no problem getting a loan. "I'd never lived in a house before," Curtis confessed.[8] They entertained lavishly, and he enjoyed his newfound prosperity and "society" friends: "Debbie Reynolds' and Eddie Fisher's house had Christmas lights on the inside. It's the middle of July and you're sitting around looking at Christmas lights. Now that really was chic."[9]

He was aware his marriage to Leigh was, in part, a Hollywood construct. "We were like little children from two different families kind of playing house."[10] Such a remark was also attributed to Leigh.[11] At times they seemed like clones of one another.

The question most people asked was: How would Leigh's career continue now that she was married? Curtis seemed to disapprove of successful actresses, as we saw in his attitude toward Piper Laurie and Shelley Winters, if not Marilyn Monroe. "Name one big female star in this business," he challenged, "and I'll name you a miserable human being. The big-time actors seem to have a better shake. They have the ability to survive." Was he jealous of Leigh's career? "Marriage will not survive," he declared, "if both people are very successful."[12] In such a scenario it was obviously going to be the "successful" woman who fell on her sword and went home to cook dinner for "Toniola," as he called himself.

Leigh went along with his chauvinism. A stay-at-home girl when pushed to it, she said in 1952: "When I'm at the studio I'm Janet Leigh but anywhere else I prefer Mrs. Tony Curtis."[13] She played "the little lady," coming out with pronouncements like "I'm an old-fashioned wife who holds the currently unpopular opinion that a husband should be picked up after, catered to, babied, waited on and made comfortable." While Curtis painted and left the house in a mess after him, to her fell the duty of cleaning the mess up, leaving clean brushes and clothes for him for the next day, and seeing that "a piece of oilcloth is spread under the easel so gobs of paint won't dry on the rug."[14] She even let him supervise her hairdresser. When she liked an item of clothing she brought it home before buying it so he could approve it — or not.[15]

Leigh was like a trophy to him. That much is obvious from the way he spoke about her in conjunction with everything else in his life: "A $150 suit, custom-made shirts with my own monogram, those crazy cufflinks and Janet Leigh for a wife. Sometimes I ask myself: Is it for real?"[16] (He even put the cufflinks before her.)

He sought to improve himself under her tutelage. She referred him to classical music and middlebrow literature, a step up from his comic book fantasies. But in photographs taken at the time he always looked happiest playing with his train sets. He later admitted he didn't really enjoy them. He told a story about a time as a child when his parents managed to scrape enough dollars together one Christmas to buy one for him. When they plugged it in, the engine burned out in a cloud of smoke because they had the wrong current. His father tried to exchange it, but the store wouldn't take it back. His father promised him that one day he would have the biggest train on the street. Curtis was now trying to realize that dream. It wasn't the train he loved: He was trying to compensate for a childhood tragedy.[17]

The publicity machine made him into a "Bronx Hood Makes Good" figure with potted biographies that went from his poverty-stricken upbringing to features that portrayed him as a role model for the nation, advocating creative hobbies to the youth of America after his walk on the wild side with the Black Hand Gang.[18]

There were also potted biographies of him that told people everything they wanted to know about him, like this puff from *Screen Parade* in 1952: "He drinks no hard liquor, smokes less than a pack of cigarettes a day, works out daily, is an excellent boxer, wears no rings, lunches on steak and orange pop, spells badly, jitterbugs like a champion but stumbles on a tango, collects jazz records, will drive fifty miles to see an old Marx Brothers comedy, and numbers among his closest friends Jerry Lewis, Marlon Brando and anyone Janet thinks is nice."[19] There's a pretension towards completion in this grab-bag of tidbits, but one imagines it could have been put together by someone who never even met him.

Fame didn't change him, he insisted, even if he was temporarily awed by it. A friend rang him one night when he was in the bath, engrossed in looking at the "be-oo-tiful" tiles on the bathroom wall. He said he needed time to savor them, to taste their delights. It beat a coldwater apartment at the back of a tailor's shop hands down. But inside himself he was still "the same old schmoo."[20]

Fame for Curtis meant not only money and a luxurious lifestyle but also a change in his attitude toward people. Life in the fast lane made the world a more upbeat place. "I like people to smile at me," he acknowledged. "Maybe that goes back to when I was a boy. There was so much solemnness. People were so unhappy. Everybody was frowning. Anytime I could put a smile on somebody's face it made me feel good. It made me feel wanted."[21]

But he was still gullible. Studio pranksters sometimes dummied up letters for him to gauge his reaction. One such tulip went, "Dear Mr. Curtis, I want to adopt you. I'm a grandmother and I'm still alluring. So far I've adopted a ballplayer and a softshoe dancer but I like you a lot better. I promise not to hem you in. You can have two evenings off a week." He expressed bewilderment at the letter, saying, "Man, this is crazy."[22]

Money poured in, but most of it went to his parents, Leigh's higher salary covering their expenses until his equaled hers and he was able to pay her back. She was understanding about his predicament, but his commitment to his parents proved to be a constant strain. Such a strain continued to be hidden from the media, as magazines ran regular squibs about the Schwartzes and the Morrisons having a "practically perfect" relationship.[23] The only arguments that erupted between them were mock ones about who'd do the dishes, Mama Schwartz or General Leigh/Morrison.[24] But behind the scenes tensions were building. It wasn't much fun for Leigh watching Curtis' money going towards "Mama and Papa," or towards Bobby, who needed more and more care as his mental health declined. (He was still having his shoelaces tied by his mother at the age of thirteen.) One day he got a new bicycle, and Curtis offered him some chewing gum in exchange for it. Bobby happily agreed to the deal.[25]

Curtis was glad to be able to help his family. The problem was the constant dripfeed of need, 24/7. "Why couldn't we put up a sign at the end of a day's shooting saying 'Nobody bother me,'" he pleaded. "Why couldn't I just say, 'Hi, Mom. How much money do you need? $38 for a new suit? Then buy it, [but] leave me the fuck alone.'"[26] His mother never let him relax, which cut in on the concentration he needed for his performances.

His next movie was *Flesh and Fury*. He played a deaf boxer. As well as having hearing difficulties, he had to break away from a manipulative nightclub singer (Jan Sterling) who forced him into fights that damaged his ears more. As was par for the course in such ventures, the "bad" girl had to be complemented by a "good" one, so we also get Mona Freeman, Curtis' savior both in and out of the ring. It was the first of three films he made with Joseph Pevney, an underrated director he respected greatly. One day he suffered a black eye when he was rehearsing a boxing scene. As a result, he had his profile insured for $100,000 with Lloyds of London.[27] The insurance provided for any damage that might "mar, deface or otherwise make unsightly" his appearance.[28]

He took the part seriously. One day when a sparring partner got a little too physical for comfort he lost his temper and almost killed him in retaliation.[29] He was almost afraid of the innate violence inside himself that caused this reaction.[30] The best compliment he received for his performance was from a woman who spoke to him in sign language when he came out from a showing of the film. "It was a wonderful portrayal," she signaled, giving the perfect "review" to him with her hands.[31]

Shortly afterwards he made *No Room for the Groom*, a contemporary comedy in which he was again paired with Piper Laurie. (This time he didn't have to worry about getting into a doublet.) He played a soldier who elopes with his sweetheart but then comes down with smallpox and has to spend the honeymoon in the hospital. They keep the marriage a secret and he goes off to fight in Korea. When he comes home he finds Laurie's family have all moved into his home — hence the title of the movie.

It was a bore for the pair of them. Neither of them liked the director (Douglas Sirk) either. Laurie didn't even mention the film in her autobiography, the ultimate insult. Curtis had specifically asked for it as an antidote to his adventure films. He wanted to see if he was ready to be the next Cary Grant. The answer was a resounding no.

"Never mind the quality, feel the width," went the slogan. It certainly seemed to apply to Curtis. Inane films like this still sold tickets, and he was still receiving lots of fan mail (sometimes up to 1700 letters a week). These were "mostly from love-struck girls," some of them so intimate he was embarrassed to read them. He also received a few abusive ones each week from young men who blamed him for them losing their girlfriends.[32] The fan magazines continued to obsess over the details of his life with Leigh. In December 1952, *Screen Parade* ran a feature called "Tony and Janet Have Many Problems." In fact, there was just one: They were too busy to see much of one another. The style of writing was so melodramatic, one could have been forgiven for thinking the marriage was over.[33]

Paper didn't refuse ink. Many similar articles were fictionalized versions of flimsy truths, and Curtis and Leigh found themselves trying to live up to these fictions. If their movies were real life to cinemagoers, their real life became a movie. After coming home from the set each day they had to continue acting for journalists. They got so good at this that sometimes they didn't even know they were doing it. They were pictured at the beach, on vacation, in the kitchen and on the lawn, their life an open book for voyeurs to gaze at and adore. One photospread even showed them taking an afternoon nap, fully dressed (needless to say) on top of their bed, wrapped in each other's arms.[34]

A lot of the interviews Curtis did at this time had him using a *faux*-beatnik idiom that seemed inconsistent with his pretensions to suaveness. He would say things like "Hollywood is swell" or "I popped my cork at Janet" or "I don't dig hillbilly music." "America was crazy for celebrity couples," wrote Tab Hunter. "Maybe the movies were trying to restore an image of domestic bliss after the upheaval of World War II."[35] Elizabeth Taylor lived next door to them. In a few short years she too would suffer the same fate when she hooked up with Richard Burton, their burgeoning romance captured under the klieg lights of the paparazzi in every winsome (or, rather, wince-some) detail.

"Everybody is trying to run our lives for us," Curtis complained. "We try to ignore the wellwishers but they sure make us miserable."[36] This didn't seem to be the case when *Photoplay* magazine profiled them after their first year of marriage. The uxorious Leigh was presented almost as Curtis' secretary ("She has me organized so I don't make three appointments for the same time"), his cook ("If she has an early call at the studio she leaves the table set, the coffee perking. All I have to do is plug in the toaster"), and a glowing admirer of his painting ("Janet wants to frame and hang everything I do"). No wonder he imagined marriage to be "wonderful."[37]

In 1953 the idea of putting them together in a film — it had to happen sooner or later — came to fruition with *Houdini*. Curtis played the famed escapologist, and Leigh was his wife Bess. He had mixed feelings about the project. "It was another double act," he said, "like myself and Piper all over again, except this time I was sleeping with my leading lady." Leigh believed being married to him helped both of them give better performances: "Because we were in love we could be uninhibited with each other." *Houdini* was the first of five films they made together. "I like working with Janet," Curtis said jocosely, "she's the only leading lady who also cleans my dressing room every morning."[38]

He had a lot in common with Houdini. First of all they were both Jews who'd changed their names. (Houdini's was Ehrich Weiss.) Secondly, they were both fascinated by magic from youth. Curtis practiced card tricks with Jerry Lewis to get himself in the mood for the role. "Look," he gushed to Lewis one day, "I've got a trick that'll cut your hair." Lewis replied, undaunted, "Swell, kid, but first lemme show you the one where you pick a card and without you telling me what it is, I find it in East Pasadena." Curtis wasn't amused by this putdown: "Jerry, I'm doing the tricks. I'm Houdini in the picture. You're still doing those comedies with a guy called Dean Martin."[39]

As well as practicing card tricks in preparation for the role, Curtis also had a magician, George London, coaching him in more sophisticated routines. London was amazed at his prowess. "Tony is doing tricks after eleven days that most new magicians would have to work on for thirty weeks," he announced.[40] He was able to drive to the studio with one hand on the wheel while the other sliced the deck and flicked cards in between his fingers.

Leigh found it harrowing to watch him trying to escape from a straitjacket in one scene from the movie. "I was ready for one myself when I watched Tony suspended by his ankles, hanging upside down in midair while bound in one." Another scene had him tied on a moving platform that edged towards a whirring buzzsaw. "I was afraid I'd only have half a husband," she gasped.

Curtis himself had different kinds of tensions. He didn't mind the action sequences, but he was shy when he came to do his first romantic scene with her. He'd made love to dozens of actresses on screen, but it was different with Leigh. "I can't kiss my wife in front of all these people," he protested, gazing at the crew. It was Leigh who took the initiative, plonking a kiss straight on his mouth with the words, "That should break the ice, honey."[41]

The film had pluses and minuses. Curtis' fascination with his stunts shone through the role, but he needed to bulk up more for it. In Hollywood's refracted vision, the escapologist was transformed from an audacious apostle of grueling physical activity into a leading

5. *Elite of the Milk Shake Set* 43

Curtis dons a straitjacket to test his powers of escapology in George Marshall's *Houdini* (1953). When he hung upside down in it and was suspended by his ankles, Leigh became so agitated she said she was almost ready to be placed in a straitjacket herself. As filming went on she relaxed more. In fact, in the romantic scenes it was Curtis who was more bashful than she was.

Curtis prepares to have himself handcuffed in a drum in another one of the stunts pioneered by the famous escapologist, overseen by two assistants. *Houdini* (1953) was the first of five films in which Curtis appeared with Janet Leigh. Here she played his wife Bess, but their relationship wasn't examined in very much depth, Marshall preferring to place the emphasis on the action sequences.

man with silver screen appeal.[42] Being Hollywood, the romance with Leigh also took center stage when it should have been sidelined.

The most important scene of the movie, as Gordon Gow pointed out, was the one where he immersed himself in the Detroit River while incarcerated in a padlocked box. He managed to get out of the box but had trouble trying to break through the frozen surface of the water: "Airless time went by as he moved beneath the heavy layer of ice. A cut to the anxious crowd above: some desperate, unsuccessful work with grappling hooks. Houdini's wife then fainted and was taken away. Night came. And then, in a memorable frame, the dark hole in the ice was guarded by a solitary figure, Houdini's German assistant and latterday mentor, Torin Thatcher."[43]

Gow speculated that the actual events could hardly have been as prolonged or dramatic as the fictional one, "but that single image of the waiting man, exerting some wishful power of his own, went beyond hokum: it held a dark strength."[44] In another scene Curtis was suspended upside down in a tank of water and handcuffed. He negotiated the handcuffs easily enough when the scene was being shot, though one wonders why he was cuffed at all. (Could they not have used some trick photography?) So easily, in fact, that he decided to pretend he was choking to give the scene some added drama. The crew panicked as they watched this. They ended up breaking the tank with axes, with water flooding all over the set as Curtis fell onto the floor. "It turned out my acting was a little too good," he remarked.[45] But was it really that funny? Was there not a possibility he was choking for real in this scene but was too proud to admit it? Surely he would have told the director beforehand if he had any intentions of pulling a stunt like this.

Curtis dies in the film after trying to escape from the tank of water. Again this was Hollywood fiction. Houdini's actual death was caused by a man named J. Gordon Whitehead, who asked him if it was true that he could resist "the hardest blows struck to the abdomen." When Houdini said it was, Whitehead administered four or five "forcible, deliberate, well-directed blows" to him.[46] The following day another man punched him viciously in the stomach as he sat reading a newspaper in a hotel lobby, the cumulative effect of the blows resulting in his premature demise.[47]

Houdini was a fascinating man, and we have Curtis to thank for the regeneration of interest in his life.[48] As Lance Staedler remarked, "If you think of Houdini you think of Tony Curtis breathing under the ice, you don't think of Houdini."[49] What a pity, then, that more effort wasn't expended in making Curtis look like him. Apart from Curtis' slighter build, his face was also different, Houdini having a round face that looked like a cross between Frederic March and Victor Buono. A greater pity was that an attempt wasn't made to divine the inner essence of the man, or the complexities of his relationship with Bess. (They were often waspish with one another.) It was a formulaic movie so the emphasis had to be on love's young dream cut short by fate. The magic was wrapped inside the love story rather than vice versa. Houdini, as a result, came across as a kind of Superman wannabe rather than a serious thinker about spirituality, the afterlife and the occult.

The critics were lukewarm about the film. *The New York Times* dismissed it as "standard screen fiction."[50] *The Chicago Daily Tribune* was even more scathing, accusing it of presenting "tricks a-plenty, but in other respects being rather soggy."[51] The novelist E.L. Doctorow presented us with a more tortured Houdini in his novel *Ragtime*, published in 1975. Here he's plagued by inner tensions, as his early fame is superseded by other vaudeville performers who make him think up more and more dangerous escapes to keep pace with them.[52] The Curtis depiction is more straightforward, refusing to delve into any complications in Houdini's psyche, the emphasis being placed squarely on the stunts and the love story. The movie was a hit, though, and fortified the position of both stars. Curtis had enjoyed working with Leigh despite his initial reservations, and hoped it would become a habit.

He didn't like being away from her for long stretches, as happened when he made his next movie, *Beachhead*, a forgettable venture that stuck in his mind mainly for that reason: It was made on the island of Kauai. "Will you take me there some day, honey?" Leigh asked her husband as the pair of them did a joint interview to promote it in conjunction with *Prince Valiant*, which Leigh had just completed on another set. "Sure," he replied, "when I get time off—about twenty years from now."[53] It wasn't altogether a joke: the pressures were beginning to catch up to both of them. The dual career seemed to suit Leigh more than Curtis, his irritation at the draining work schedule only slightly apparent through the weak jibe.

One of the reasons for such a schedule was the continuing influence of Lew Wasserman on Curtis' career. Being a workaholic, Wasserman rarely let up in his negotiations on his clients' behalf. "With Lew," Curtis said once, "the deal was the sex and the movie the cigarette."

Wasserman rose at dawn and worked into the small hours. "When I'm in Hollywood," he said, "I'm in early because I have to talk to New York and they're three hours ahead. And when I'm in New York I'm in the office until 9 P.M. because it's still 6 o'clock on the Coast."[54] In later years, when he spent more time at home, he took to watching three TV sets simultaneously to keep abreast of any news that might be relevant to him.[55] Connie Bruck defined him as the "gold standard" of agents. "If Hollywood was Mount Olympus," Jack Valenti speculated, "Lew Wasserman is Zeus." Steven Spielberg identified him so much with movies he even thought his glasses looked like two film screens.[56]

Wasserman also liked to indulge his clients. Curtis' star being on the rise, he presented him with a Rolls-Royce. When Curtis said he'd like to have his initials inscribed on the door, Wasserman arranged to have it custom-made and shipped over from England.[57] "I only started doing really well when I found Lew," Curtis acknowledged. "I was like a good soldier. Lew would say, 'Go here. Do this. Then go there. Do that.' And I would say, 'Yes sir!' I always kept my trunk packed, like a guy who was ready to ship out."[58]

Though Wasserman had a genial manner, his velvet glove hid an iron fist. He rarely came out second best in a deal. The former movie theater usher would go on to run MCA and Universal. "As long as I've known Lew," Curtis opined in a left-handed compliment, "everyone's been frightened of him."[59] Leigh concurred with that, even though she never found herself in that position.

Leigh miscarried her first child in 1953 (not 1954 as is often reported). She asked her doctor if this meant she might never give birth. He reassured her by informing her that one in every four pregnancies resulted in a miscarriage. It was Nature's way of "taking care of what is not meant to be." Curtis took the sad news well. "We'll have a dozen," he consoled, "six sets of twins."[60] "Tony did everything he could to reassure me," Leigh praised. He emphasized the fact that they were still young and had "ample time" to raise a family. "All this while trying to disguise his own disappointment."[61]

More films followed in quick succession. *The All-American* had him as a football player but was nothing to write home about. The humor, as one writer remarked, was limited to jokes about his hair.[62] He then made *Forbidden*, another Rudolph Maté film about a hood recruiting him to find his girlfriend (Joanne Dru) who also shares a past with Curtis. After that came *Johnny Dark*. This was his last appearance with Piper Laurie. He played an auto designer. Thoug no masterpiece, it wasn't a bad film with which to end their pairing, even if the best performance was given by the car.

Curtis told a curious anecdote about an incident that happened after the movie came out. He'd been trying to date a girl when the movie was being shot, but she kept putting him off and he felt too awkward to take things further. (Bear in mind he'd now been married to Leigh for over three years.) After the movie was released, a fan came up to him and said, "Gee, you were great with that girl in the picture. A real powerhouse. Strong stuff, the way you told her off and she jumped. That's the way to handle 'em." Curtis realized the disjunction between his onscreen firmness and his off-screen timidity. After the conversation he rang the girl who was putting him off and more or less demanded she go out with him. "I learned from this stranger what he learned from me.... From then on we had all the dates I wanted."[63] Leigh's reaction to all of this wasn't documented.

The Black Shield of Falworth (1954) was another costumer, again directed by Maté and again costarring Leigh. It didn't tax anyone's energies unduly. Curtis came in for the usual abuse from the critics, one reviewer sneering that he was as *papier maché* as the medieval England settings.[64]

According to author Wendy Leigh, Curtis had an affair with Grace Kelly when she was making *The Country Girl* the same year. Leigh alleged they met at a party given by Charles Lederer in Beverly Hills and that Curtis was entranced by Kelly, having found her to have dropped her Ice Queen persona. He'd wanted things to go further with her, but she was looking for "bigger grapes" than him. Curtis was quoted as saying Kelly was "hot," and "a horny Philadelphia girl" in Leigh's version of events.[65] If this happened it's unusual that Curtis, a garrulous Lothario, wouldn't have gone into such details in any of his books. Were princesses off limits? Hardly for this man. He admitted to having necked with her at some parties in L.A. before she got married, but that was the extent of it. Bing Crosby and William Holden had flings with her during *The Country Girl* too.[66]

Curtis made his only musical that year. Some would say this was just as well. *So This Is Paris* was an unexceptional Richard Quine offering, Curtis playing a sailor on shore leave putting on a fundraising show for orphans. He asked Gene Kelly what he thought of his dancing and got the duff reply, "Keep fencing."[67]

Afterwards he went on a promotional tour to New York. One day he passed the street where he grew up. A "stab of recognition" hit him as he watched the boys in the street playing stickball. He became self-conscious of his sharp attire, almost as self-conscious as he had been wearing tattered clothing as a child. Then he spotted two teenagers standing in front of a theater without any money to go in. The sight catapulted him back to the times when he was in that position himself, when he foraged through his mother's purse for a nickel or a quarter and then found it wasn't worth it, his enjoyment of the film in question being tarnished by feelings of guilt and shame. He paid for the teenagers' tickets, mindful of how much it would have meant to him if someone had done that for him at their age.[68]

His next film was *Six Bridges to Cross*. He played a robber and drew some positive notices, but the fact that his character was Italian led to some hate mail from Italians who felt Hollywood had stacked the dice unfairly against their nation.

Sal Mineo, who would die tragically some years later after being stabbed in an alleyway, played the young Curtis in the movie. Curtis' mother, blithely unaware of how the casting system in Hollywood worked, thought Bobby should have got the role and tried to pressure Curtis into arranging this. He made an overture on Bobby's behalf and some pictures were even taken of him with the part in mind, but his mental instability made him too big a risk so it didn't go any further.

The film gave Curtis some much-needed "street cred." By now he was slotted comfortably into Hollywood's penchant for what were termed "juvenile delinquency" films. Many of these exploited a contrast between "wild" and "mild" youth.[69] Curtis obviously wasn't in the Brando league as a rebel hero, but *Six Bridges to Cross* established him as a victim rather than an aggressor, a strain that would be preserved in many other films of this time. By the end of the fifties, as Andrew Dowdy remarked, the industry had flattered youth so much that in an adult world of vicious behavior, maybe only they could be truly trusted or admired.[70]

Life magazine now ran a feature called "The Stronger Sex" which listed Curtis, Rock Hudson and Robert Wagner as the "Big Three for Bobbysoxers." The idea was that they would do for a younger generation what the likes of Gable, Tracy and Stewart did for a more mature one some time before. In a picture spread, a photographer got them to pose on a ladder "struggling for a higher rung against each other."[71] This was the kind of thing for which Universal was notorious in trying to market its merchandise.

The heat was being turned up on Hudson regarding his closet homosexuality at this time. Henry Willson, his manager, got wind of the fact that Robert Harrison's sleazy scandal magazine, *Confidential*, was planning to run a story "outing" him. He couldn't let this happen, as it would have killed Hudson's career even before it got off the ground, so he organized a trade-off to publish one on Rory Calhoun instead.[72] George Nader, a minor closet gay, was also part of the trade-off.[73] "Harrison tried to destroy Rock's career," Curtis fumed. "When that didn't pan out, they went for the expendable guy. But it backfired. A lot of people on the inside of the business were glad about that. Harrison was a rat."

The Calhoun story focused on his criminal past, including a conviction for armed robbery. It was entitled "But for the Grace of God Still a Convict."[74] Instead of turning the public against him it made him into a kind of hero from the standpoint of the Reformed Robber.[75] In the autobiography of *Confidential* informant Fred Otash there's a record of a conversation between Hudson and his wife in which Hudson admits he's gay.[76] That wife was Phyllis Gates, Willson's secretary, who Hudson married in November 1955 as a cosmetic exercise to quash the rumors. Hudson didn't even wear a wedding ring for the ceremony, giving the lame excuse that he'd have to keep removing it for movie roles.[77]

Hudson had a good time with women, Curtis stated, "but he liked the other team better."[78] After Gates married him she wanted to call her mother to tell her the news, but Willson said, "Oh no, you've got to call Hedda [Hopper] and Louella [Parsons] first. They'll still have time to make the home editions."[79] She could hardly have asked for a clearer indication of the reason for the marriage. They divorced in 1958, and she never saw Hudson again. He died of AIDS in 1985, the disease finally blowing his cover. Curtis never fell out with Hudson and was always sympathetic to his plight. "I was tagged with being gay myself when I went to Hollywood first," he said. "I knew how it felt."

People assumed good looks suggested one was gay, in Curtis' view, or even a transvestite. When he was growing up there was a rumor he was working in a New York club as "a ravishing dark-haired beauty," a woman by night and a mild-mannered Jewish boy by day.[80] He hated homophobia. "'I don't ask people what they do in bed," he said, "and I don't expect them to ask me. I don't mind what you do as long as you don't frighten the horses."

He made three movies in 1955, a western called *The Rawhide Years*, a boxing film (*The Square Jungle*) and *The Purple Mask*. He and Leigh moved into a new house during the filming of the latter, and the move was played up by Universal to help sell the movie. It did that, and also netted the couple some unasked-for gifts from the public. A farmer from Dodge City sent them a frozen side of beef with this message: "Kinda thought you might be out of ready money with all the expenses of a new house. This will keep you eating."[81]

Set in France during the Napoleonic era, *The Purple Mask* had Curtis as a nobleman rescuing revolutionaries from the guillotine. Angela Lansbury played a seamstress. She appeared friendly to Curtis on the set but was afterwards quoted as saying, "Things got so bad for me in the fifties, I had to make a movie with Tony Curtis."[82] The remark made him furious. He thought it came from a book she wrote herself, but it was actually from a biography of her written by Margaret Wander Bonanno in 1987 where she's quoted indirectly — though 21 years earlier Rex Reed had quoted her in a similar vein in *The New York Times*.[83] Curtis' confidence was in tatters by now, having had so many flops in a row. "I had little to contribute but my good looks," he admitted. Further, "Nobody cared whether I could act or not. I'd get on the set to do a scene and I'd have trouble with the dialogue. If I took more than four takes, the director would stop and say, 'Don't worry about it, kid, we'll change it.'"[84]

His success bewildered him. "I'm perfectly truthful when I say I don't know what made me click," he stated, "any more than I know why the public got all excited about the hula hoop."[85] Maybe his secret was his versatility. As one writer observed, "He moved from enjoyable hokum via adventure spectacle to classic light comedy, with more than the odd flabby costume drama failure in between."[86]

One part of him was saying, "Grab what you can and run with it," while another part was going, "You're a schnook and you're distasteful and you're dishonest and you're just nothing." He was like a *tabula rasa* upon which the director *de jour* made his imprints: "Everything I did fitted my personality. If I played a prizefighter or a knight in armor, it was basically the same story."[87]

But the pressure was beginning to tell: "I was working so hard I thought I'd burn out." Casting director Bob Raines advised him to see an analyst, Marco Frym. Curtis poured his heart out to him about his troubled upbringing and the problems fame brought. The studio paid for his sessions. This was important, as he was still having a hard time supporting his family now. It was the trendy thing for stars to have their own private analyst at this time, but Curtis' reasons were more genuine. There were few people with whom he could share the tangled skein of his mind at this time. All Frym had to do was listen and he felt better.

The therapy gave him confidence in himself. "I was tongue-tied," he informed a reporter. "I was pretty shy. Can you imagine that? Now I go on talking for a week. Not that I was a crazy, mixed-up kid who chased girls in the park or picked his toe in public. I just needed help."[88]

A problem that refused to go away was his pronounced distrust of others. It was something that plagued him all his life to some extent. When Leigh was making *My Sister Eileen* in 1955, Curtis suspected she was having an affair with Bob Fosse, the choreographer of the movie. He had intercepted from Fosse a note which contained the words, "I can't wait to see you. When you're coming, let me know."[89] This sounded like something more than a professional interest in Leigh, but it could also have been just that, combined with a deep affection. Curtis chose to think of it as evidence of an affair between them, though he never found any other indication that they were carrying on. More significantly, he used the letter as a rationalization for having affairs himself (even though, on his own admission, he'd had many of these already).

He never pretended the marriage was sunshine and roses. "Sure we quarrel," he admitted. "I can come home as dragged as the next guy and take out my fatigue on Janet, or vice versa." But the quarrels are only part of the necessary way of getting to know one another. "My folks had Janie's and my kind of marriage too, full of laughter, color, enthusiasm and a few rousing rows." It was give and take, like all marriages. He had to learn punctuality and neatness, and she had to learn not to be "on the dot and on the dime" all the time.[90]

Curtis socialized with Jerry Lewis frequently at this time, often calling round to his ranch house in Pacific Palisades. One evening he told him he was frustrated by the substandard roles foisted on him by Universal. "Truth is," he confided to Lewis, "I'm sick of wearing tight uniforms and having to look so damned honorable all the time. But those guys don't listen. They can't see me playing something nutty for a change."[91]

He may have been indirectly asking Lewis to put him into one of the goofy capers he was making with Dean Martin at the time. Lewis couldn't arrange this, but he did the next best thing. "Tell you what," he offered, "I'll write a funny part for you and we'll make a movie right here." Curtis agreed and they made a string of wacky home movies together.[92] The first one they shot was about two men trying to smuggle a hernia across a border.[93] Another one had Errol Flynn as the star. It ran over schedule because Flynn grabbed the heroine's buttocks "and then tried to make a three-point landing on her bones." They had premieres on Lewis' front lawn, "a battery of revolving klieg lights" stabbing the night sky while at the curb scores of limousines were lined up bumper to bumper, with a red carpet placed beside them, leading to the playhouse.[94]

In the spring of 1956 Leigh announced she was pregnant "with the same degree of expectation that might well have been accorded the re-birth of the savior."[95] Afterwards they sold their Beverly Hills home and moved to San Ysidro Drive. "We were moving up the ladder of real estate," Curtis crowed. "That's what you did. You got in the movies and bought real estate."[96]

Leigh was ecstatic. She told Hedda Hopper, "This is going to be our home for a long time — we'll probably see our kids married in it." Hopper thought that was premature. How right she was.[97]

The house had a pool, a bath house and a badminton court. "When we have some loot," Leigh predicted, "we'll make it into a tennis court." She told Hopper she had "Dad's okay" on the house. Hopper remarked, "I remember he handles your finances. You wouldn't even buy a sweater without asking his permission."[98] Leigh laughed, but maybe she shouldn't have. Her father's excessive involvement in her affairs would ultimately prove detrimental to her — and him.

The child was born in mid–1956 and christened Kelly. Curtis had dramatic notions about the birth: "Ever since I learned Janet was pregnant I waited for the day that I could speed toward the hospital, flag down a policeman on the way, shout, 'Follow me, my wife's having a baby,' and weave through streams of traffic with the sirens screaming behind me." What happened, in effect, was that Leigh got her labor pains on a quiet Sunday morning.

"Everybody else in Los Angeles was sleeping. There was no traffic to weave through. There was no policeman. I didn't even get a chance to run the red lights. Every time I came to a signal, it turned green."[99]

They lived the gala life with their new addition. It seemed to round off their identity as Hollywood's Golden Couple. No expense was spared as they wined and dined the great and good of Hollywood's glitterati in the following years. Billy Wilder's daughter Vicki remembered being at a party Curtis threw for Leigh one night: "I remember they had a pool with an electronically operated cover which rolled itself up when you pressed a button, the only one of its kind I ever saw. During the party a plane circled overhead with a streamer saying, 'Happy Birthday Janet.'"[100]

The luxurious indulgences continued but so did the poor movies. One day when Curtis was feeling particularly bad about his career, Lew Wasserman had an idea. He took him to the offices of *The New York Times* and rummaged through old reviews of the early films of Cary Grant, Clark Gable and James Cagney, most of which were diabolical. "I couldn't believe it," Curtis groaned, "they'd all been slaughtered."[101]

Wasserman told him it was going to take him ten "hard, heavy years" to become a star. Curtis felt this was probably true. He believed everything Wasserman told him. In fact, he carried cards around with him that said, "I can't make a deal" and gave them to people, listing Wasserman's name and phone number at the bottom.[102] He felt Wasserman had an instinct for knowing what people liked: "He wouldn't make a boring picture, like what I call *Breakfast at Nuremberg*."[103]

Curtis had been a studio product for some years now. Things reached a nadir the time he was given away as a prize in a "Win Tony Curtis for a Weekend" competition. He was quite taken with the woman who won it after he visited her in her home in Washington, but the feeling wasn't mutual. "She'd been hoping for second prize," Curtis gasped, "a new stove."[104] Feeling sorry for her, he bought her one anyway.

He tried not to take negative comments about him too seriously, abiding by the dictum of Anton Chekhov: "If I'd listened to the critics I'd have died drunk in the gutter."[105] By now he'd made nearly twenty films. He'd been in a variety of genres — westerns, period films, crime capers — but none of them really stood out. His old housemate Marlon Brando had won an Oscar for playing the punchdrunk dockhand in Elia Kazan's *On the Waterfront* in 1954. The following year Ernest Borgnine, Curtis' costar in *The Square Jungle*, had surprised everyone by walking off with a statuette for *Marty*, a movie that looked like it would play a week at some drive-in and then disappear. It didn't, but Curtis was still laboring in the vineyard of sword-and-sandal films that were little more than chewing gum for the eyes. Was this going to be his destiny, to go for the short end dives (as Brando's *On the Waterfront* character might say) and then get a one-way ticket to Palookaville?

He hoped not. He'd started to exercise in a gym with Burt Lancaster and they got on well together. During one of their workouts, Lancaster mentioned a new movie he was about to make in Paris called *Trapeze*, and Curtis pricked up his ears.

6

High Wire Act

When Curtis expressed an interest in being in *Trapeze*, Lew Wasserman pointed out an obvious stumbling block to him. It was a United Artists film, but Curtis was "hog-tied" to Universal. Would the studio loan him out? Ed Muhl, the Universal boss at the time, said no at first, but Burt Lancaster won him round.

Trapeze was based on Max Catto's 1950 novel *The Killing Frost*, the tale of a man called Tino Orsini who was executed for the murder of a beautiful woman before it was discovered that it was actually his mentor in a circus act who did it. Lancaster's company (Hecht-Hill-Lancaster) was producing it.

It was to be filmed almost entirely in Paris. This gave Curtis some pause as he didn't like to be away from Leigh for too long. To accommodate him she took on the movie *Safari*. It was to be made in London and Africa, "to ensure our presence in the same vicinity, except for my few weeks in Africa. At the conclusion of *Safari* I would remain in Paris with Tony. Everything was wonderful."[1]

Trapeze was being directed by Sir Carol Reed. Curtis was playing Orsini, a trapeze artist who vies with his colleague Mike Ribble (Lancaster) for the attentions of the delectable Lola (Gina Lollobrigida). Orsini wants Ribble to train him to perform a potentially fatal triple somersault, an exploit that forms the fulcrum of the action.

In the novel the characters played by Curtis and Lancaster were gay. Ribble murders Lola because he's jealous of her love for Orsini.

There were rumors Lancaster himself was gay because of his close relationship with James Hill, his partner in Hecht-Hill-Lancaster, but Curtis scotched these. Burt only liked girls, he made it clear, and girls with "big knockers" at that.[2]

Lancaster wanted Curtis for the role for a number of reasons. Firstly because he liked him and secondly because he felt he was athletic enough for it. "Burt was the main reason I got the part," Curtis always insisted.[3]

It was Reed's first major Hollywood project. He was so eager to work with Lancaster he said yes without even reading the script. Lollobrigida was offered $160,000 for the role, at the time the highest fee ever paid to a European star.

Leigh was doing preproduction for *Safari* in Elstree Studios in London by now. Her shooting schedule was five weeks while Curtis' was six. She flew to Paris every weekend to spend it with him. On his time off they arranged to meet for walks by the Seine and romantic meals in the penthouse suite of the Georges V hotel as they looked down on the panoramic splendor of Paris. Back at work she gasped every time he fell from the trapeze onto the safety net that had been placed beneath him to protect the "yugos" (apprentice flyers). There was a French holiday before Janet took off for Kenya, so Tony took the opportunity to fly to London with her for the day, as the train would have taken too long. For Leigh, this was indisputable proof of how much those few shared hours meant to him because he hated flying.[4]

Before filming on *Trapeze* began, the entire crew paraded up and down the Champs-Elysses and Parisians turned out in droves to welcome them. Afterwards they based themselves at the famous Cirque d'Hiver, the vast arena where most of the action sequences were shot. Leigh sat beside Curtis and observed that the animals seemed fiercer in this circus than in American ones. When the film began shooting, a new lion tamer was being trained, the former one having been mauled to death by one of his charges.[5]

Lancaster had worked in a circus as a youth. Curtis' great grandfather was a Budapest strongman with an astounding height of seven feet, eight inches. When he died, a special coffin had to be made for him.[6] Curtis hadn't liked circuses as a child himself: "Anytime I sneaked into something it was a movie."[7] But now it was different. He was doing the stunts, understanding the passion.

The first time he looked up at the platform he almost succumbed to vertigo. He had to do a backbend to see it. For Lancaster it was a platform but as far as Curtis was concerned it was "one level short of heaven."[8]

Lollobrigida's past contained no circuses — nor any American movies either. Clive James didn't think much of her in the part. "Since Lancaster was a genuine athlete," he speculated, "and Curtis knew how to look like one, the film is ridiculous only when Lollobrigida pretends to fly."[9] He had a point, but her body was so lubricious most hotblooded males in the audience weren't too bothered by this. Neither were people too bothered about the love triangle between Lollobrigida, Curtis and Lancaster. There were enough vertiginous thrills to divert one's mind from its predictability.

Lancaster had a troubled relationship with Lollobrigida both on and off screen. His dislike of her was evident the day he asked, "How's your cunt?" taunting her about the fact that she had little to offer except her sex appeal. Luckily for Lancaster's sake she didn't know what the "C" word meant. Curtis thought fast and muttered, "He means how is your *country?*"[10]

Curtis was flattered that Universal were loaning him out for the film. "When I saw those representatives of a billion-dollar agency walk into my dressing-room and tell me the Lancaster schedule had been juggled around just to fit my time, I flipped."[11] It was the first time he'd ever been made to feel really important. "Up until that point I hadn't been much more than a part of Universal's furniture. With *Trapeze* I moved into a new room in a new house." He meant figuratively, but it was a geographical change too.

Lancaster and Curtis had a lot in common: a domineering mother, a tough upbringing on the streets of New York ... and a love of movies. They were also both very concerned with physical fitness. They bonded immediately on the set, sometimes at the expense of Lollobrigida, who failed to adapt to Hollywood as readily as Reed might have hoped.

When Lancaster wasn't trying his best to annoy "Lollo," he spent his time playing practical jokes on Curtis. One day he sent him on a wild goose chase for a "left-handed" can of film. Another time, after Curtis had had a tryst with a lady of the night, he soaked a towel he was using in a steam room with eucalyptus oil. When Curtis went to dry his pelvic area, the pain in his penis convinced him she'd given him gonorrhea. Lancaster howled with laughter as he watched Curtis writhe in agony.

Curtis used to visit Lancaster in his hotel some nights, climbing up to his room from outside, his early years of clambering across fire escapes in the Bronx standing him in good stead. "You're doing overtime," Lancaster laughed one night as he watched him scurrying up the trestle. "Yeah," Curtis replied, "only this time there's no safety net if I slip." "Don't worry," Lancaster assured him, "I'll give you so much to drink you won't feel a thing even if you do."

As well as drink, there were women. One night Curtis met Marlene Dietrich at a function in Paris and she started flirting with him. When he intimated that his marriage to Leigh prevented him from going further with her, she said, "Don't let a little thing like that stop you."[12] This exchange is from Curtis' first autobiography. In his second one it's in London where he meets Dietrich, not Paris, but the same flirting takes place.[13] Which account should we believe? In the first one, Leigh is hundreds of miles away. In the second she's only a few feet away. How could his memory let him down like this? In both recollections of the event he remembers Dietrich leaning on a fireplace with a drink in her hand. She was 55 at the time, over twenty years older than Curtis. He usually liked it the other way round. (This was more likely the reason for his reticence than marital fidelity.) Dietrich would have been shocked to learn that he would have balked at dating a woman of his *own* age, never mind a 55 year old.

He had his hair in a tight cut for the film. One writer thought he looked like "a high school undergraduate dressed for the annual costume party."[14] Curtis claimed Lollobrigida was responsible for this.[15] Carol Reed's nephew Oliver begged to differ, saying it was his uncle who was behind it. In Oliver Reed's autobiography, his uncle said to his assistant as the film began, "Tell Tony Curtis to get his hair cut." The assistant refused, fearing Curtis would be aghast. "The hairstyle is part of his image," he maintained, "he'd have a fit." Reed responded gamely, "Why is that? He's supposed to be a circus flier, isn't he?" Reed then approached Curtis in his dressing-room, saying simply to him, "By the way, Tony, we start shooting on Monday. Could you get your hair cut before then?" Curtis apparently replied, "Fine," making Reed wonder why his assistant had been so nervous. It was only later, when he looked at a dossier of Curtis' stills, that he realized what the assistant meant.[16]

Oliver Reed told another story in his book about how his uncle dealt with Lancaster's perfectionism. At one point he wanted to print the first take of a scene Lancaster did with Lollobrigida, but Lancaster insisted on doing it again and again, sixteen times in all. Finally Lancaster was satisfied. Reed went over to him and said, "How right you were. That last take was ideal." Then he printed the first one.[17]

The film was arduous for Curtis but also fulfilling. "Some of the stunts were so dangerous," he quipped, "even the doubles had doubles."[18] The powerful Cinemascope bulbs also meant many of the cameramen had to endure temperatures of over 100 degrees. They wore special reflector hoods to stop the lights from blinding the trapeze artists when they flew through the air.

The emotional convolutions of the plot seemed to play second fiddle to the highwire thrills and spills. Today these are what the film is primarily remembered for. That said, the love triangle was credibly played, the offscreen antagonism between Lancaster and Lollobrigida conveniently bleeding into their dramatic tensions in the film.[19] Curtis found Lol-

The smiles displayed here on the faces of Curtis and his *Trapeze* (1956) costars Burt Lancaster and Gina Lollobrigida conceal the fact that there was much friction between Lancaster and Lollobrigida on the set. (This ironically helped their performances, as they were at loggerheads in the plot as well.) For Curtis it was a landmark movie, his first "outside" picture made in his Universal years and the one he always credited with giving him confidence to go toe-to-toe with an acknowledged talent like Lancaster, though critics of the movie debunked its storyline as being subservient to the high jinks on display.

lobrigida easier to deal with, though he thought she lied about her age and that bugged him.[20]

He believed the film gave him a greater challenge than anything he'd done up to this. "Before it had been like the blind leading the blind. In most of my U-I [Universal-International] films I'd been teamed with players who were like me: fairly new and inexperienced. But here I was matched against top performers with a top director. It kept me light on my toes." Lancaster was the main driving force for him. "What an actor. In my scenes with him it was like being in a furnace."[21]

What about the fact that he was being farmed out by Universal? "It had to happen. It was only a matter of time. I had to break away from the other beefcakes." He was referring to Jeff Chandler and Rock Hudson, who were also branching out. "[Universal] gave birth to three babies," he deduced, "and we turned into monsters." He didn't want his fans to think him disloyal. There was nothing personal in it; it was simply a career change.[22]

He always credited *Trapeze* with initiating his changeover from the "Son of Islam" roles to more substantial parts. When he started in the movies, he told Abe Greenberg, "Studios used a shotgun technique with new players. They'd collect 500 kids and sign them all, hoping one would become a Gable or a Grant." It was only force of will that enabled him to get through those years. "When I struck out on my own, playing with Lancaster in *Trapeze*, I made the turn upwards. Up till then I played one Caliph's son after another."[23]

Even though *Trapeze* pushed him in a new direction, he was aware Lew Wasserman was right to steer him away from leading man roles just yet. He was happy to "ride shotgun" with Lancaster. He seemed to prefer appearing opposite men than women. "There are no leading ladies left in Hollywood," he pronounced, one of those classic Curtis howlers that always left interviewers scratching their heads. They must have wondered if he was serious or just having a gigantic laugh at their expense.[24]

Trapeze made over $4 million during its opening week. No film had ever done that kind of business before. It would go on to earn over $10 million eventually. Notwithstanding that, many of the critics were sniffy about its soap-operatic overtones. Bosley Crowther dismissed it as "a hackneyed story that's almost as old and sawdust-littered as the one about the brokenhearted clown."[25]

Curtis became seriously interested in art around now. People like John Levee and Jules Stein's brother David, who was living in Paris at the time, were the catalysts for this. Levee gave him an interest in artists like Picasso and Chagall. Curtis bought over $3000 worth of lithographs and etchings "when prices were on another scale." Later on, Billy Wilder and his wife Audrey deepened this passion for him. "Art influences the way I live," Curtis said. "It's a never-ending growth process. As far as I'm concerned, collecting helps a man or woman to establish an identity. I know myself better because of the things I've surrounded myself with."[26]

He also formed his own production company with Leigh at this time. He was high on Curtleigh, as the company was called, but Leigh felt it fomented tensions between them. As time went on, she felt these tensions spilling over into her relationship with her father, who was also involved in the company, as well as looking after her business affairs generally. (In her autobiography she pondered the possibility that Curtleigh spelt "the beginning of the end" of her marriage.)[27]

Curtis' next film was *Mr. Cory*. It was directed by Blake Edwards, somebody he would work with many times. They also became friends. He played a poor boy making good. Martha Hyer was the society lady keen on him. He drew good notices for the role, as he did for another film he made at this time, *The Midnight Story*. The latter was one of his rare ventures into *noir* territory. He played a motorcycle policeman looking for a priest's killer. It was his last collaboration with Joseph Pevney, a director who never really achieved his full potential, arguably because he was traumatized by the death of his wife from cancer at age 48 in 1969. "He hurt his career," Curtis believed, "by not demanding the quality of production he really needed."[28] The film also marked the end of Curtis' original contract with Universal. Wasserman arranged that from now on Curtis only made one film a year with the studio, leaving him open to more lucrative offers from elsewhere without having to be loaned out like before.

Curtis' career was growing more and more seaworthy, but his marriage continued to spring leaks. He didn't seem to know what he wanted from Leigh anymore. He flirted with women in her absence, and slept with some of them, but he still felt lonely for her when she was away. So much so that after *Safari* he had a clause inserted in her contract stating that the only films she could make on location from now on were ones in which he also appeared.

This despite the fact that he had all but had an affair with his *Beachhead* costar, Mary Murphy. "I didn't want to jeopardize my already fragile marriage," he explained. "It was a case of my eyes saying yes but the rest of me saying no. This was difficult for me, because saying yes was a helluva lot more fun."[29]

7

The Best of Everything

Curtis gave what many people regard as the best performance of his career in *Sweet Smell of Success* in 1957. In it he played the sleazy press agent Sidney Falco, who fed hawk-like newspaper columnist J.J. Hunsecker (Burt Lancaster) snippets to make and break reputations. A film awash with the tawdry sewers of New York, it proved to the public that, given the right script and direction, Curtis could go toe-to-toe with the best of them.

It began as a short story written by the press agent Ernest Lehman for *Colliers* magazine in 1948. Lehman called it "Hunsecker Fights the World." It was widely believed that he wrote it as a kind of *apologia* for the dirt-digging exploits he engaged in when he worked for leading New York press agent Irving Hoffman. Another view was that it was a thinly-disguised hatchet job on the redoubtable Walter Winchell, a syndicated columnist who held court at Manhattan's famous Stork Club in the 1930s. People feared Winchell's power, with good reason. His pen ripped acid. He had an elephantine memory for slights and waited in the long grass to take revenge on his enemies. "I'm not a fighter, I'm a waiter," he said. "I wait until I can catch an ingrate with his fly open and then I take a picture of it."[1]

The main plot of the film concerned Hunsecker's efforts to break up the romance of his sister Susan (Susan Harrison) with guitar player Steve Dallas (Marty Milner). In real life Winchell had a daughter who was dating a man he disapproved of and wanted out of her life. Perhaps this is one of the reasons the script lay gathering dust on Hollywood's shelves for so many years. Producers felt it was too hot to handle.

Lehman knew he was treading on a lot of toes with his corrosive tale. After it morphed from a story into a novella it was published in *Cosmopolitan* under the title *Tell Me About It Tomorrow* in 1950. Lehman waited for the backlash from Winchell or anyone else who might have deemed themselves to be maligned by the piece. Hoffman didn't speak to Lehman for over a year after he read it. Winchell seemed to take it even worse. Lehman had tried to make Hunsecker different from Winchell by putting golf trophies in his study (Winchell didn't play golf) and changing the number of his table at the Stork Club from 50 to 21, but everything about the character screamed Winchell. The trivial differences only served to emphasize that fact more trenchantly.[2]

Lehman sold the story to Hecht-Hill-Lancaster, insisting that he produce and direct the film version as well. This was a bold move considering his lack of experience in the movies, but they wanted it so much they agreed. Harold Hecht predicted the film would be a flop.

Lehman bowed out of the directing job without a fight when it got too much for him. "I was too close to the material," he admitted. "I'd lived it; it was part of my life."[3] Curtis argued precisely the opposite case when he sought the part of Falco: he too had lived that life, therefore he was ideal for it. Universal didn't want him to take the role, imagining it would alienate his fans. He feared this too, but it was a risk he was willing to take. "It was like the difference between hitting a golf ball down the middle of the fairway or going for the pin," he imagined, "and I wanted to go for the pin." He grabbed the part with both hands. "All they had to tell me was New York," he said. "I was raised in that city."[4]

Hecht recommended that Alexander Mackendrick direct the movie in the absence of Lehman. Up until then, Mackendrick, who hailed from Scotland, had been working with more lighthearted material at Ealing Studios. On the surface he was a fish out of water but there was also a perception that the "twisted satire" of his 1955 feature *The Ladykillers* might serve him well for what would eventually be termed "one of the darkest films ever to emerge from Hollywood."[5]

Mackendrick's main problem was the fact that Lehman's screenplay was too "talky." Lehman agreed to flesh it out but it still felt wrong to Mackendrick. He came up with the idea of shooting more outdoor scenes, New York's bustling streets relieving the claustrophobia of Lehman's original treatment. New York became almost as important a character in the final film as Falco or Hunsecker, James Wong Howe's camera inching its way into every seedy pore as the pair of them cooked up a backstory to snuff out the threat of Dallas to Hunsecker.

Philip Kemp felt Mackendrick was an ideal choice for director precisely because of his outsider status: "The American in Scotland, the Scot in England, the Briton in America." Such a *crise d'identité* stood him in good stead to approach the recalcitrant material Lehman thrust in front of him.[6] Lehman (who was still a nominal producer of the movie) wondered how Mackendrick could have known anything about the world of Broadway and New York night life. In Curtis' view, "The challenge gave him an extra surge of energy." The fact that he didn't live in Hollywood offered him a better chance to view its venality more objectively. (Mackendrick liked to tell people his mistrust of Hollywood was so strong it was "prenatal.")[7]

Curtis marveled at his punctiliousness on the set. "Even if everything went perfectly he would still want to reshoot. In the middle of a scene he'd yell, 'Shut up!' Everyone tiptoed round him. Burt would get mad because they couldn't afford all the reshooting."[8] (Lancaster's attitude toward retakes had changed drastically since *Trapeze* because he was footing the bill now.)

Mackendrick was aware of Lancaster's reputation for eating directors alive. He became edgy around him as a result. As the tensions increased, Lehman developed colon problems. He decided he needed to be off the movie altogether. His doctor advised him to take a holiday in Tahiti so Lehman ceded the producer's job to James Hill.

With Lehman gone, the question now was: Who was going to write the screenplay? Paddy Chayefsky was the first suggestion, but Mackendrick favored Clifford Odets, and Hill concurred. "Clifford was a God," he enthused. "The most talented writer of his day." Chayefsky was young, "full of piss and vinegar," but Odets was "a craftsman, he was first class."[9] Mackendrick had grown up watching his plays. Though he was now almost a forgotten man, he thought it would be an honor to work with him.

Odets had "named names" during the HUAC investigations. He felt as badly about this as Lehman had about working for Irving Hoffman. Like Lehman, he saw *Sweet Smell* as a chance to expiate his past by dint of a script which denounced whistleblowers like

Winchell. Both men felt they'd stabbed people in the back. They were looking for vicarious exoneration, a kind of forgiveness from the public by confessing their sins through the medium of film.

Odets thought he'd have the screenplay completed in three weeks but it took him as many months, working around the clock. The pressure became so intense that Mackendrick was pulling pages from Odets' typewriter as the actors waited for their cues.

Curtis remembered seeing Odets cooped up in his hotel room one night as he rummaged through vast amounts of pages in his pajamas. Only grudgingly was he allowed to go down to Times Square in a prop truck to get out of the room. Curtis heard him tapping away at his typewriter in the truck after 3 A.M. and went in to see him. He asked bemusedly, "What the hell are you doing here at this time of night?" Odets replied, "I've got to finish this sequence." Curtis joined him in the truck. A few moments later Odets flashed him a look as if he'd just happened on a "eureka" experience. "Come here, kid," he exhorted, "I want to show you something." Curtis went over and saw in front of him one of the most famous lines from the film: "The cat's in the bag and the bag's in the river." Odets was thrilled to show it to him and Curtis was equally thrilled to see it. It took his breath away. "Right from his brain to my brain," he glowed.[10]

Odets, like Mackendrick, found Lancaster heavy duty. He described the actor as being a unique blend of "enigmatic, creepy, cocksure, exuberant, paternal, vulgar, cruel and mischievous"—a behavioral mosaic of which his celluloid alter ego would no doubt have been proud.[11] Curtis, in contrast, was an androgynous figure for Odets. He called him "Boychick." For the character of Falco he transmuted such androgyny into a kind of babyfaced menace that Curtis enjoyed playing with.

"Don't be still with Sidney," Odets advised. "Don't ever let him sit down comfortably." For Curtis this was easy because he was naturally nimble anyway: "I was able to grace the part with little physical innuendoes. I wanted to make him an excellent athlete, growing up in the streets of New York, playing stickball. He punched, he boxed, he did everything, always on his feet, always moving."[12]

Curtis also empathized with Falco's upwardly mobile aspirations. Sam Kashner pointed out that Falco's ambitions in life (delivered in an early speech to his secretary) were probably Curtis' as well. "Hunsecker is a golden ladder to the places I want to get," he tells her, "way up high, Sal, where it's always balmy and no one snaps his fingers and says, 'Hey, shrimp, rack the balls.' From now on, Sally, the best of everything is good enough for me."[13] Geoffrey McNab believed these aspirations weren't totally mercenary: "He's hopelessly compromised but still has a vulnerability about him, and even a sense of idealism."[14]

The rest of the characters in the film were peripheral figures to Falco and Hunsecker. Barbara Nichols played Falco's friend Rita. Emile Meyer was Harry Kello, the policeman.

"I love this dirty town," Hunsecker snarls in the first scene. He chops up the words, as his biographer Kate Buford put it, "into bloody bits of raw meat." Falco is behind him, as ever. "You stand still and I'll circle around you," Curtis suggested to Lancaster, adhering to Odets' advice. Lancaster was happy to comply.[15]

Lancaster regarded Mackendrick as overly precious in his direction. He fought with him almost every day. Was this an extension of Hunsecker's megalomania? Curtis thought so.[16]

7. The Best of Everything   61

Sweet Smell of Success (1957): Playing the parasitic press agent Sidney Falco with zeal, Curtis gazes hungrily at his nemesis J.J. Hunsecker (Burt Lancaster), the ruthless columnist who both makes and breaks him in Alexander Mackendrick's coruscating revelation of the murky depths to which syndicated journalists descend. It became one of Curtis' most highly-rated roles, but the film itself failed at the box office and hastened the end of Lancaster's production company, Hecht-Hill-Lancaster.

Curtis and Lancaster are polar opposites in the film. If Curtis is a sinewy snake, Lancaster is the dull crab who counterpoints the latter's constant movement with an equally potent stasis. Lancaster had to work hard to keep still in the role, his natural instinct for brisk movement reduced to grim stares. His eyes always carry the threat of danger, like an iguana that could flip his tongue out in an instant and snatch its prey. He adopted an unusual combination of menace and staidness. The manner in which he drank his tea looked almost effeminate at times, holding the cup handle effetely with his thumb and forefinger. This made his pronouncements even more threatening. He looked like a human version of a frog as he sat monolithically behind his desk, consigning minions to their fates.

He also wore glasses, ostensibly to befit his profession as a man who spent his life reading and writing, but more significantly to remove him from the world around him. Sam Kashner thought the glasses gave him a violent presence, "the skeletal look of a walking corpse."[17] After a while Howe started putting Vaseline on them to make them opaque, thereby fortifying his baleful edge.[18]

Hunsecker puts Falco down at every turn, sometimes even refusing to speak to him in the first person when others are present. In an early scene when Falco presents himself to him at the 21 Club, Hunsecker sighs to the company, "Mr. Falco, whom I did not invite to sit at this table tonight, is a hungry press agent." What's interesting about Curtis here is the manner in which he shows no reaction at all to the slight. It's almost as if he expects it. He's insensitive to Hunsecker's grossness because it doesn't register with him as long as he gets his precious column inches from him. To this extent, Hunsecker's sardonicism is wasted.

"You're a cookie full of arsenic," Hunsecker tells Falco. Elsewhere the language is formal: "We shall see what we shall see, Sidney." "Come here, J.J., I want to chastise you."

One of the film's key phrases entered film lore. That was Hunsecker's "Match me, Sidney," delivered to Falco every time he wants a light. In one writer's view, this contains a *double entendre*, because that's exactly what the ambitious Falco wanted to do — i.e. "match" (meaning "equal") Hunsecker.[19]

The language throughout is stylized, even Kello's. "Rectify me a certain thing," he says, a far cry from the routine "Book him, Dano" verbiage more expectable from movie cops of the time. Even Hunsecker's secretary is infected with it, as one writer noted. Instead of telling Hunsecker he's only interested in money, she says, "You're so immersed in the theology of making a fast buck." It's times like this that one is most aware of Odets' theatrical past.

Mackendrick felt the script was too literary by far. Odets defended himself by saying, "Play the scenes not for the words but for the situations. Play them 'on the run' and they'll work just fine." Curtis and Lancaster did that. Their chemistry was embellished by Howe's atmospheric camerawork. He shot the movie largely from a worm's eye view so they looked as if they were, in the words of screenwriter Stephen Schiff, "knifing up through the air, poised for the kill."[20] Sets were built two feet off the ground so Howe could "light the smoke."[21]

The characters eventually merge into this smoky twilight, the astringent jazz score acting both as background music and a kind of shrieking commentary on Falco and Hunsecker. One writer saw Curtis as the "whining clarinet" to Lancaster's "bass bassoon."[22]

For Philip Kemp the film's visual richness was one of its stand-out qualities: "The gleam of rain-washed streets, by this stage a cliché of the *noir* style, is here revitalized by being extended to the interiors so that everything, both indoors and out, seems to glisten with a flashy lubricant sheen."[23] Howe was behind this, having placed mushroom photoflood globes in the bars, afterwards washing the walls with oil.[24] Clive James paid him a huge compliment when he attested to the fact that his visual style had a fluency unseen since the heyday of Max Ophuls, a director who started the trend of filming scenes in one take.[25] This increased the sense of claustrophobia.

Many of the outdoor shots had a documentary feel to them. We see real people going about their business in the background as Mackendrick's characters goad one another or send their sentiments into the cold night air. (Shooting occasionally had to stop when fans of Curtis broke through police barriers to touch their idol.)

If the film was *noir*, it was only mutedly so. For starters, nobody was killed in it, a *noirish* staple.[26] But its endemic pulse — the jazzy soundtrack, the cacophonous streets, the quickfire dialogue, the general mood of stylized menace — all placed it firmly within this genre. Another *noir* element was the manner in which Falco tried to finagle Rita into sleeping with a client of his. In the view of David Shipman, cinema hadn't seen this kind of thing since the pre–Code days.[27] The scene caused problems for the censors and was passed only on condition that Nichols play Rita as a crushed woman.[28]

What makes Falco especially intriguing isn't so much his moral duplicity or his ruthlessness to get ahead, but rather the crude honesty he displays so unselfconsciously to his secretary. "I'm nice to people where it pays me to be nice," he confesses. His self-belief is boundless, even in the face of Hunsecker's frequent threats to put him out of business.

For Curtis the part was a Kierkegaardian leap into faith. If audiences didn't like him he knew his career could be over. It would be difficult to climb up on a masthead in doublets after the film, or even a trapeze in white tights. Mackendrick alluded to this at the preview when he remarked, "What you had was an audience that liked Tony Curtis and thought he was a nice, open-faced kid on the make. When it slowly dawned on them that he was the shit of all time, the result was physical. You could see them curling up, crossing their arms and legs, recoiling from the screen in disgust." James Hill witnessed a similar culture shock in Lancaster's fans, who "kept waiting to see Burt jump out of a tree."[29] But there were no trees in this jungle.

The film was a double-edged sword for Curtis. If he was convincing as "the shit of all time," he risked losing the bobbysoxers. If he wasn't, the film could self-destruct. The latter possibility was always on the cards. Many people wondered how "the boy with the ice cream face" could move from this to Hunsecker's "cookie full of arsenic."

One of the factors that made *Sweet Smell* so fulfilling for him was the open-ended shooting schedule. Universal was like a sausage factory in the sense that "you had an 18-day schedule and that was it. You got to the end of the 18th day and they would just stop shooting. So each picture didn't have that delicate care."[30] At H-H-L, on the other hand, Mackendrick could shoot and re-shoot 'till the cows came home. And on some days they almost did.

Susan Harrison was excellent as Susie, the girl who crawls out from under her brother's shadow at the end of the movie, having been scarred by his near-incestuous manipulation of her. She had been emotionally damaged in real life too. Before she made the film, Harrison had a fall from a building, which she admitted might have been a "veiled suicide attempt." (She was suffering from depression at the time.) From this point of view the tension she bestows on the part — Falco stops her from throwing herself off a building here too — carries an added edge. Curtis thought her lack of acting experience made himself and Lancaster drive her "down into nowhere." As a result, she seemed lost in the film.[31] But it was this lost quality that gave her performance its resonance.

Harrison was only eighteen when the film was made. "I didn't know what I was doing when I was in front of the camera," she admitted, "but it looked good."[32] Like everyone else she seemed to be operating on her instincts. These were spot-on because her hesitancy was just what the part called for. In the film, as in life, she wasn't quite sure which way to turn, surrounded as she was by the dull-but-sweet lover, the controlling brother, the obsequious lackey.

Of course the central irony of Falco is that he's been pulling tricks for Hunsecker for years and getting away with it, and is then deemed guilty for something he didn't do at all (i.e. seduce Susie). Maybe there was a sense of poetic justice in this tense dynamic.

The relationship between Susan and Dallas is boring by contrast. Not only do they look bland: we don't see them in day-to-day situations, so we never get a chance to know them — if there's anything to know. Milner seems less like a musician than an accountant. He displays little passion either for jazz or Susie. To that extent our sympathy for his plight is undermined. The storyline tells us they care for one another but it isn't evident in their interaction. Their only relevance to the film is what happens to them. If they weren't being threatened by one circumstance or another we'd probably yawn watching them.

In the novella Susan frames Falco to punish her brother. In the movie her revenge is more convoluted. She causes Hunsecker to suspect a lie, and Falco has to try and talk his way out of a sticky situation. But Hunsecker isn't buying it. Falco's goose is effectively cooked.

The film's ending posed a problem for all concerned. Would the final scene be between Hunsecker and Susan or Hunsecker and Falco? Lancaster favored the latter, perhaps misogynistically. "You can't bring in a two-bit actress to play the last scene," he barked at Mackendrick, making an unnecessary reference to his disrespect for Harrison's acting ability.[33] The remark underlined how obsessed he was with Falco, as if he was actually turning into Hunsecker in real life as well. (In Lehman's original story, Hunsecker kills Falco after suspecting him of raping Susie. In the film he merely turns him over to the police.)

Hunsecker's final tragedy — the ability to control a city but not his sister — arrives with the suddenness of his own bullet-like liquidations. Susie can't be embarrassed in print, or hauled off by Kello to the local precinct for interrogation. She has no secrets to hide so his poison ink is irrelevant. Her final words, outlining her wish to be with anyone but him, aren't literary or ornate, but they cut deeper than any of his own barbed witticisms. After ninety minutes of suggestiveness, this simple declaration jolts us into an awareness of a life outside syndicated columns.

The film failed miserably at the box office, being too far ahead of its time in its evocation of sleaziness. In many ways Odets' screenplay was *too* good because nobody is as articulate as these characters in real life. We needed some light relief to leaven it. As it was, some classic lines ended up falling flat. Audiences would have much preferred to hear the Curtis and Lancaster of *Trapeze* dripping hamfisted clichés about lost loves. They would also have preferred to gaze at Gina Lollobrigida's gravity-defying curves rather than Susan Harrison's angst-ridden visage.

The critics tried in vain to relate this Tony Curtis to the one they knew and loved from previous movies. Was there something in Falco's childhood that could explain his "unscrupulous drive"?[34] *The Evening Standard* commended the film for having the "cold-blooded excitement" of a stroll through a reptile house.[35] But *The Observer* pounced on one of its main weaknesses, labeling it "slightly arty-crafty."[36]

The film also went way over budget, which Lancaster blamed both on Odets' huge salary demands (he earned $300,000 in all) and Lehman's absenting himself from the set in mid-shoot for that trip to Tahiti. "I ought to punch you in the jaw," Lancaster said to Lehman when he saw him at the post-premiere party, to which Lehman replied, "Go ahead, I need the money."[37]

Odets, in the end, could have been accused of over-finessing things. The words were always in the right place, but stagecraft was his *métier*. They would have worked better in the theater than the cinema. In real life people didn't speak in such post–Victorian soundbites. Even though Lancaster and Curtis breathed an inspired kind of life into the honey-tongued syllables, they came across to audiences as just that: words, words and more words. Harold Hecht wallowed in its commercial failure, taking some solace in the fact that he'd been right after all to be leery of it, a discomfiting example of *schadenfreude* from a man who'd just been hit in the pocket to the tune of $600,000.[38]

Some critics gave it grudging approval, its ambiguous appeal best summed up in William Zinseer's comment that "*Sweet Smell of Success* is such a sordid movie that you might want to go outside occasionally for a breath of fresh air. But it is so good that you will end up ... keeping your seat."[39] (Sadly, not many people did.)

The New York Times praised it for its "high-toned street vernacular that no real New Yorker has ever spoken, but that every real New Yorker wishes he could." The enthusiasm was shared by *The New York Observer*, which advised, "The main incentive to see this movie is its pungent and idiomatic dialogue, such as you never hear on the screen anymore in this age of special-effects illiteracy." The sad thing was that such illiteracy was in the ascendancy now. It would continue its leap over wordy screenplays even moreso in the decades to come.

Mackendrick referred to it as his "worst film."[40] One suspects an element of tongue-in-cheek here. He knew he brought home the bacon even if the public didn't agree. He'd never forget the summer of 1957 when he received a baptism by fire in the way American filmmakers operated, and gossip columnists too. Two years later Lancaster had him fired from *The Devil's Disciple*. Curtis believed it was his meticulousness that was behind his dismissal.[41] For Lancaster it was revenge of a sort for what he regarded as the monumental failure of *Sweet Smell*.

For Curtis, though, The Sweet Smell of Success proved to be just that. The role came to define him. Years later he would declare, "In all the films I've done, I've never lost Sidney."[42] His character became a byword for sleazy sycophancy, so much so that, as one writer noted, "Even today people talk about going into Sidney Falco mode."[43] Tony Parsons gave him this accolade: "In probably his greatest role, he said something about the fallibility of human nature, the empty core of the American Dream."[44] For another critic, Curtis' greasy hair seemed to "lubricate Falco's unscrupulousness, making him quite simply the most terrifying evocation of the American success ethic." It was a performance, he reckoned, "to make even Nixonians squirm"— high praise indeed.[45] Peter Bradshaw credited him with having a kind of "sixth sense" for how and where to play to the camera in the film.[46] This was definitely true, even if part of this was due to Odets' urgings. Roderick Mann saw him as the "white rabbit" of movies, always on the move.[47]

Clive James was also unequivocal in his praise of Curtis: "His Sidney Falco is one of the definitive performances of the American cinema, the galvanic answer to the perennial question of what makes Sammy run. There's something marvelous about the way he varies the pace of his dialogue between the cockiness he parades among his fellow grifters and the servility he lavishes on Lancaster's magisterially ruthless Hunsecker."[48]

As well as claiming he "was" Falco, Curtis went on to exclaim cynically, "We're all Sidney. We'll all do anything for success if it doesn't look like we're going to get out of the quagmire we're in."[49] David Thomson praised him for giving a fine portrayal of unprincipled ambition "and the collapsible personality that goes with it."[50] Philip Kemp talked about the manner in which even his character's name carried predatory undertones, Falco resembling "falcon."[51] Curtis was humbled by all the hosannas and bowed to everyone who helped him reach this pinnacle of his career — Lancaster, Mackendrick, Odets. He even acknowledged a debt to Sammy Davis Jr.'s press agent Jess Rand, from whom he got the idea of constantly chewing his nails to convey Falco's restlessness.[52]

Because the film flopped, it spelt the end of the careers of many people associated with it. Harrison disappeared off the Hollywood radar almost totally, making only one other film, the tacky *Key Witness* in 1965. Hecht-Hill-Lancaster folded its tent in 1960, imagining itself to be too experimental for its own good as a company. Odets' career also went downhill after the film. He was reduced to writing scripts for the likes of Elvis Presley (*Wild in the Country*, 1961), afterwards busying himself with mediocre television work, most notably for Richard Boone in *Have Gun, Will Travel*. His primary love continued to be the theater. Hollywood had been a comedown for him. A friend revealed, "He was miserable out there. All of his dreams were of escaping from it, of writing plays and coming back to the theater. He never made peace with his defeat."[53] He died in 1964, his passing captured in the Winchell-like pun of *Time* magazine's obituary heading; "Odets, where is thy sting?"[54]

The film, in the words of one writer, "drowned in a river of red ink and popular repugnance." Before he died, Mackendrick lamented, "*Sweet Smell of Success* destroyed us all." In time, though, it became the property of buffs and cultists. It's now regarded as a *success d'estime*, something Mackendrick himself acknowledged when he said, "The moments of your greatest fear are also the moments you look back on as your greatest thrill. The danger is an aphrodisiac."[55]

Philip Kemp has argued that it's one of the most restless movies ever made. "Rarely does the camera stay still for more than a few seconds," he observed. "Even in a scene of relative emotional tranquility such as Susan's acceptance of Steve's [marriage] proposal, it prowls and sidles around the lovers, nervously framing and reframing as though checking out every angle from which danger might emerge."[56] Another viewer even saw a subtext of McCarthyism in its ambience of snoopers and informers.[57]

Though it will always have appeal, the world it captured so tellingly has all but passed. Personnel guru Mark Borkowski summed it up:

> There's still a perception of PR that relies on the image put forward by *Sweet Smell of Success*, the drop-a-story-in-and-see-things-happen approach, but the successful public relations merchants today are as much media strategists as press agents, weaving interlocking campaigns that bring a modernity of thought to the old publicity process. It's telling that *Sweet Smell of Success* came out in the late 1950s, casting its beady, dystopian eye on an era that was passing.[58]

Or, as J.J. Hunsecker might say, "You're dead, son, get yourself buried."

8

A-Lister

Janet Leigh announced that she was pregnant for the second time in the summer of 1958. Shortly afterwards, "The Tony Curtises," as they were called, bought a plush new house in Beverly Hills. It was situated just above Pickfair, the residence of Douglas Fairbanks and Mary Pickford. Curtis could now look down at his former idol from his bedroom window.[1]

It had 18 rooms. "I counted them to make sure," he informed Hedda Hopper. "We had one and a half rooms in the house in New York City where I was born. I never realized I'd end up a country gentleman. People would have given you odds I wouldn't even wind up a gentleman." Hopper liked his attitude, commenting, "This boy from a poor Manhattan family keeps the picture of his early youth before him deliberately, I think, so he won't fall into the luxury trap which Hollywood lays for its favorites."[2] His saving grace was that he didn't take anything for granted; he knew it could fade.

The house also had a swimming pool. Leigh objected to the idea at first. "A pool?" she exclaimed incredulously, "When we don't even have any living-room furniture?" Curtis pacified her with, "It'll give you a rest. We'll live outdoors around the pool. No cooking, cold food and paper plates. And I'll keep an eye on the kids."[3] His psychology worked and she gave in — as she usually did in matters like this.

Things weren't going quite as well with his "other" family. By now Bobby had started to deteriorate psychologically and was put in therapy. Curtis also kept seeing his own therapist at this time. Bobby's sessions were considerably more expensive than his.

After *Sweet Smell* was released, he was contracted to appear in another H-H-L production, *Cat Ballou*. It would have been his fourth appearance in a Lancaster movie but Harold Hecht ended up producing it in 1965 without either of them. Lee Marvin won an Oscar for playing the lead role.

Curtis made *The Vikings* instead, costarring Kirk Douglas, Leigh and Ernest Borgnine. He played a former slave, Eric, vying with the one-eyed warrior Einar (Douglas) for the hand of an English princess, Morgana (Leigh). It was directed by Richard Fleischer.

Douglas made the film with his own company, Bryna, named after his mother. "Now that I'm producing my own pictures," he joked, "I can rarely afford to hire myself. Apart from that, I can't stand myself as an actor. I'm too temperamental." He saw the film as a Norse opera, "a sort of Scandinavian Western. I always think of that time as being similar to our Wild West period."[4] He justified his choice of having American stars play Norse characters by arguing that they had a rougher quality.[5] This may have been true of Borgnine and himself, but Curtis was cast for his pulling power at the box office.

The film was shot mostly on location in Norway. Douglas employed experts from the Netherlands to advise him on period details, like the architecture of the time and the dimensions of the boats used. He organized flights for Curtis, Leigh and Borgnine to various places the film was going to be shot to give them a feel for it before the cameras rolled. The fact that Curtis was an avowed white-knuckler when it came to flying meant he was none too pleased about this. "No-fly" clauses were generally written into his contracts.[6]

He'd flown with Leigh a few times in their early days because it was unmacho not to, some sedatives calming his nerves. But one night they hit a fog so thick he couldn't even see the window-sill of the plane. Then one of the motors caught fire and he had a panic attack. Somehow the plane managed to land. As they got to ground there were fire engines and ambulances everywhere. Curtis walked to his hotel and collapsed, vowing, "I'm never taking my feet off the ground again."[7]

Leigh was glad to be working with him a second time. "The worst threat to Hollywood marriages," she ventured, "or any marriage, is prolonged separation."[8] Curtis had to wear a beard to look suitably hirsute for the role. At first he donned a false one but then he grew his own, saving the studio both time and money on makeup by doing so. Leigh thought it gave him maturity. He was relieved to be free of the fake beard, which was held on with spirit gum. It had stiffened his face so much he could hardly eat.[9]

Douglas originally intended to spend just a month in Norway. That stretched to two when the weather proved inclement. Set-ups for the scenes were also more complex than he'd anticipated. The budget, as a result, was increased by $1 million. This caused him some sleepless nights because a lot of his own money had been invested in the production. "In sixty days we only got eleven days of sunshine," he lamented, "and two of them were on Sundays when we couldn't shoot."[10] He eventually decided to film through the rain rather than around it. "Does it always rain here in Norway?" he asked an extra one day and got the tart reply, "I don't know. I'm only eighteen."[11]

Richard Fleischer, the film's director, was the recipient of a similar Norse witticism. The weather for the first day of preproduction was sunny, and everyone worked with their shirts off. Towards evening one of the Vikings came up to him and asked, "Well, how did you like our summer?" Fleischer said his cynicism was unfounded because summer actually lasted for "a good two weeks."[12]

Notwithstanding the difficult conditions, work went on apace. Dozens of bearded men who were members of rowing clubs in Norway and Denmark were hired and trained to maneuver boats in unison. One of the problems with the boats was that the oarholes were too close together when the American crew took over, Scandinavian men being shorter in stature. The rowers kept banging against one another because their arms were too long, so every second hole had to be plugged up. The rudders were also too shallow, so an extension had to be added to the bottom of them to allow the boats to be turned properly over short distances. Another problem with filming so far north was the continuous light. This made it difficult to sleep at night, so curtains had to be placed over the windows.[13]

There were other problems too. "There wasn't a shot in the film that was easy," said Curtis. "I had an accident and nearly lost an eye. Janet was ill and almost had jaundice. Then Kirk was ill. Ernest Borgnine was having domestic troubles."[14] Fleischer also found Douglas a nightmare to work with. He threw temper tantrums, accused him of not being properly familiar with the story of the movie, and in general tried to wrongfoot him for little or no reason. Curtis knew Douglas hated to be upstaged and would do anything to prevent that happening. If the camera was over Douglas' shoulder on Curtis in a scene, "By the time the shot was over it was over my shoulder. That was the deal. You took it because Douglas was a killer.... He would take no prisoners."[15]

Fleischer was surprised by Curtis during a scene which called on him to strike Borgnine before capturing him after Borgnine fell from a ship. Curtis refused to hit him because, as he told Fleischer, "It would be bad for my image. My fans wouldn't like it if I hit an old man."[16] It was ironic that Bernie Schwartz had gained dignity in the tough New York streets by proving himself man enough to punch local hoods. In his new identity he was maintaining that dignity by *pulling* those same punches.

Everyone was exhausted when filming finally drew to a close. Douglas threw a party for the local extras who'd been in the rowing scenes and everyone got drunk. Curtis and Douglas hammed it up with a juggling exhibition. Janet Leigh even did a mock striptease. The following morning the Norwegians demanded a salary increase. Douglas was disgusted at their lack of appreciation for his generosity to them thus far. He knew they'd never earned as much money in their lives. Infuriated, he closed down the production on the spot and decided to complete the filming in Munich. The Norwegians now backtracked and said they'd work for the original rates. But Douglas, a tough taskmaster, was unbending. The entire crew upped stakes the following day.

Douglas wrote about these events in his autobiography but failed to mention one very salient point: he'd planned to leave the country anyway, even before the money was asked for by the extras. The weather had made everything too costly for him so he'd decided to do post-production on the sound stages of Munich instead of Norway. When the Norwegians became demanding, according to Fleischer, it actually suited him because he was now able to sack them all and still preserve the air of "the injured man."[17] He won in every way, holding the high moral ground and also the purse strings. Curtis scoffed, "Kirk left Norway with the thirty pieces of silver and the crown of thorns as well."

The Vikings was a solid production but hardly art. It had Fleischer's familiar flourishes but also his escapist gloss. One critic remarked that Curtis looked more like he'd just stepped out of a salon than a Northumbrian boat.[18] "You're never quite convinced that these guys are the mead-guzzling, maiden-ravishing ninth century stalwarts of macho legend," he went on, "though Douglas' fullblooded tearaway gives it a good go."[19] But Curtis wasn't complaining. He'd done the movie for 5 percent of the gross rather than a flat fee, a wise decision as things turned out. It made over $15 million, and this netted him a tidy sum. "He started getting money before I did," Douglas complained.[20] Neither was Curtis shy about cashing his checks. "This idea of 'Let's do it all for nothing' is ridiculous," he proclaimed. "An actor deserves whatever he can get. These are the rules of the game." The context of these remarks was the brouhaha surrounding the fact that Elizabeth Taylor had recently received a whopping $1 million for *Cleopatra*— an unprecedented sum in film history. Not only did Curtis feel she was good for the money, he went so far as to say she could have been cheated if her value to the film were to be computed.[21] (One imagines he meant "underpaid" rather than cheated.) He expected to earn $1 million from *The Vikings* eventually. Rod Steiger saw the situation in plain terms: "It's basically a fight between the older generation and the younger one."[22] In other words, moguls versus actors.

Curtis' belief had always been that actors sold movies. It was essential for a star to have his name above the title. If studios didn't do this it was "like Chrysler spending millions on a new convertible, then taking its name off it." Did producers honestly believe the title sold the picture? "If they do, they're out of their heads. No title matches Cary Grant's name." He believed studios tried to "minimize the actor's position so he'll make less trouble in the future."[23] They didn't want stars becoming like two-headed hydras. "Create a star," Jack Warner liked to say, "and you create a monster."

Picturegoer magazine caught up with Curtis as the film was awaiting release and found him to be in top form. "Without a doubt, Tony Curtis is the happiest star I've ever met," his interviewer beamed. Curtis had just said, "Where else would I get the chance to be a Viking, a boxer, a dancer, a trapeze artist, a conjurer? Why, I even wear a beard and get away with it." His enthusiasm, the magazine felt, was a welcome antidote to the "average tortured self-doubting Hollywood actor."[24] (Were there really that many of these about then?)

Curtis was also excited about the possibilities offered by Curtleigh: "Too many actors complain that when they're under contract they don't like the films they're given. They can't wait to be free. So what happens? When they're free they make exactly the same kind of movies they've been making under contract. A lot of actors use the studios as a scapegoat."[25]

His next movie, *Kings Go Forth*, linked him with two people who would become long-term acquaintances: Frank Sinatra and Natalie Wood. The movie's plot was controversial, having a racism theme, but, unfortunately, this was buried under the romantic triangle.

Sinatra and Curtis played two radically diverse army men in France during World War II. Sinatra is battle-hardened, and Curtis is like light relief when he joins Sinatra's troop as a privileged radio operator. Sinatra softens when he falls for Wood, but when he hears her father was a "negro" (sic) it discommodes him. Curtis is more interested in her as a conquest than anything else. Curtis drops her when he learns of her heritage, despite appearing unconcerned about this at first. Will Sinatra, who isn't racist, go back to her? Or is she too heartbroken over Curtis? Matters are resolved a mite too tidily when Curtis is killed by departing German soldiers at the end, thereby paving the way for Sinatra to rekindle his relationship with her. The three of them give adequate performances, but as one critic pointed out, there's nothing about Wood that suggests she's African-American.[26] Curtis' performance wasn't rated by the critics. *Films and Filming* was unduly harsh with this barb: "Tony Curtis' part is at least consistent and provides him with the kind of role in which he is always good — that of a stinker."

Wood's main fear on the set was that Sinatra would make a play for her — he had this reputation. He tried to early on, but she staved him off. Amazingly, he took it in good spirits. The two of them became friends then, and eventually lovers.

She had a less felicitous time with Curtis, according to her biographer Gavin Lambert, finding him "aggressively self-important."[27] If this was so, the feeling wasn't mutual. In his autobiography Curtis wrote of Wood being "engaging and sweet, with an impudent personality." He was sexually attracted to her but didn't do anything about it because of "R.J. Wagner and Janet Leigh."[28] Years later, when Curtis moved to London, Wagner and Wood rented his house. This casts doubts on Lambert's claim of Wood's relationship with Curtis being negative.[29]

After *Kings Go Forth* was released, Curtis was deemed to be an honorary member of Sinatra's famous Rat Pack. He enjoyed the company of Sinatra and his entourage, but only up to a point.[30] He didn't think Sinatra's gambler lifestyle was for him. "How long could I go on playing cards and find that one week I was out $1800? What in my background made me Nick the Greek all of a sudden?"³¹ It was also a strain trying to be "funnier than Dean Martin" at parties.³²

"Sinatra is a helluva human being," Curtis said after finishing the movie. "This is the most mixed-up, sad man with great inner beauty, the most thrilling, exciting man I ever met."³³ He liked Sinatra's "didn't give a fuck" attitude to life: "There was no club that was too big or too small for him."³⁴ If he wanted to go somewhere, he went. He did it His Way. Shirley MacLaine told Curtis she gave Sinatra a gift once and he gave her a bigger one back. Curtis noticed that quality in him too but didn't find it a problem. He didn't have difficulty accepting his position on the ladder:

> I played the small boy with him, the kid brother. He'd ring and say, "Bernie, we're going out tonight," and I almost always said yes. He set the time and the pace. When he laughed you laughed. His jokes had to be the best. When the night was over for him it was over for you. Not everyone would have been happy with that arrangement but it worked for me.

Kings Go Forth was the only film Curtis made with Sinatra, and that's the way he wanted it. "Lew [Wasserman] told me that was enough. If I did any more I ran the risk of

Frank Sinatra huddles in a trench with Curtis in their 1958 war movie *Kings Go Forth*, directed by Delmer Daves and featuring an anti-racist subplot involving Natalie Wood. It was Curtis' only film with Sinatra, though the pair of them became lifelong friends after it wrapped. Curtis' agent, Lew Wasserman, dissuaded him from becoming too involved with Sinatra, though he did become an honorary (albeit part-time) member of Ol' Blue Eyes' infamous "Rat Pack."

being embraced within the fold of the 'padrone.' Lew said that could have strangled me more than any studio straitjacket."

Curtis was lucky to be allowed to flit in and out of the Rat Pack because Sinatra, being Sinatra, usually demanded nothing less than 100 percent commitment from his acolytes. As the self-appointed Chairman of the Board, he was like a monarch presiding over those who came and went in his gilded domain, cosseting his friends and punching out his enemies (or having them dealt with by his many bodyguards). Curtis was liked for his engaging personality and the manner in which he indulged Sinatra's vagaries.

Curtis regarded Sinatra as a father figure, one of the many he had in life. He didn't see the nasty side of him much because he wasn't around him enough, but he knew it was there. He gave Sinatra a wide berth if danger threatened. "I never crossed Frank," he said. "The word on the street was that if you did you might end up with a horse's head in your bed. Or sleeping with the fishes."

He didn't mind being a gofer for Sinatra. He would occasionally be called upon to sweet-talk women into joining the Rat Pack for drinks, breaking the ice with showgirls at the Sands Hotel before they were invited back to Sinatra's room. Everyone else got the leftovers.

In August 1958 Curtis and Leigh were involved in a potentially life-threatening car crash after a night out with Sinatra. They'd been at a party at Peter Lawford's house. On the way home their car was rammed. Leigh became hysterical. Sinatra, traveling in a car behind them, rang for an ambulance on his car radio. Leigh was pregnant with Jamie Lee at the time and was terrified she'd lose the baby. She started screaming. She was rushed to the hospital where she received the good news that the smash-up hadn't endangered her pregnancy.

The incident had its funny side. After Sinatra called the hospital and everyone stood around on tenterhooks wondering what damage had been done, a fan of Curtis happened upon the scene and said, "Gee, Mr. Curtis, I seen you in *The Vikings*. You was great! Ya mind tellin' me, how'd they cut your hand off?"[35] (He was referring to one of the film's more disturbing scenes.)

Jamie Lee was born on November 22, a date that would go down as one of the blackest in U.S. history five years later when John F. Kennedy was assassinated in Dallas. She was a healthy baby despite a tear in the wall of her intestine causing a hernia, which had to be operated on.[36] With two daughters in the house now, Curtis was prevailed upon to spend more time at home. The comedian Richard Lewis made fun of him trying to juggle the roles of father and actor as he mimicked a fictional speech he might have given to Leigh: "I'm sorry, honey, I can't play Barbies with you right now. I'm duelling with Kirk Douglas." Jamie Lee disapproved of Lewis' routine. "It wasn't that bad," she insisted. "Actors aren't too different from doctors or any other people who had to be out a lot."[37]

Curtis didn't live like a monk as a result of his new situation. He still partied, but less frequently, cutting down on his nights out with Sinatra and his cronies. He saw a lot of Sammy Davis Jr. around this time. Like Curtis, Davis dropped in and out of the Rat Pack. On one occasion he spoke out against Sinatra during his nightclub routine and was frozen out of Sinatra's life for years afterwards. That was one thing you didn't do with Las Vegas' Don Corleone.

Davis was interested in appearing in a Stanley Kramer film that was about to be made.

It dealt with two bigoted convicts, one black and one white, on the run from prison. They're handcuffed together and forced to unite in many ways to make good their escape. Elvis Presley, who was a friend of Davis', had brought the idea to his attention. Kramer had been considering Presley for the main role. When he saw him socializing with Davis he thought he had his costar too.

"He's been thinking of me for the white guy," an excited Presley told Davis, "but he didn't have any ideas about the colored guy till he saw you with me a few nights ago. He saw us shaking hands and liked our chemistry." Davis was over the moon about the idea. For Presley it would have been a rare challenging role. "I'm up to here in these beach-and-bikini pictures," he's quoted as saying in Davis' autobiography.[38] (This has to be an apocryphal quote, as Presley didn't get into such movies until the sixties, after he came out of the army.)

Presley sent Davis the script, and the next day they acted it out together. Presley was jubilant. "I'm going to be an actor!" he bellowed at Davis, "Do you think the kids'll be interested in me without the guitar and the tight pants and the pompadour?"[39]

Curtis met Davis a few days after this conversation. He invited him to a party at his house, and Davis said he'd be delighted to come. It was at this party that Davis met Kim Novak. Curtis said they spent the evening "deep in thought."[40] Davis talked about being held back in his career by his skin color, while Novak complained about being manacled by Harry Cohn.[41] The following day the story of their meeting was all over the papers. Racists were livid, but the pair of them enjoyed the danger of the relationship. Davis said he had to do everything but wear "a cloak and mustache" when meeting Novak on their clandestine dates.[42]

He was made to feel even more like a criminal when the subject of *The Defiant Ones* came up. Presley had run the idea of Davis being in the movie with him by his manager and received an emphatic "No" in response because "all those people who buy my albums, among them are lots who won't want to see me chained to a colored guy and end up liking him."[43]

Davis' relationship with Novak ended when he heard Harry Cohn was connected to the Mafia and had put out a contract on him. If he didn't stop seeing her, he learned, both of his legs would be broken.[44] Davis is also alleged to have received a visit from two of Cohn's thugs, who said to him, "You have one eye now, want to try for none? That's the way the future looks if you don't marry a colored girl."[45]

With Presley and Davis out of the running for the film, Kramer had to look elsewhere for his two leading stars. Billy Wilder told a joke about the casting: "First they went to Marlon Brando and asked him to be in the movie. Marlon said, 'Yes I'll be in it but I want to play the black man.' Then they went to Robert Mitchum. Mitchum said, 'Hell, I'm not going to be in any picture with no nigger.' So then they went to Kirk Douglas and asked him and Douglas said, 'Yes I'll be in it. But I want to play both parts!'"[46]

Kramer's concerns about Curtis being in the movie were understandable. He wrote in his autobiography: "He was an actor you cast beside Janet Leigh, not Vivien Leigh." He thought of him only because there was a lack of other suitable actors available at the time: "By this point I had gotten around to considering several actors who made Tony Curtis look like Laurence Olivier."[47]

Curtis was delighted to get the call. "I spend all of my days trying to think of ways to escape the prettyboy rut I'm in," he told Kramer. "I don't ever want to think about another Junior Prom or rich father-in-law. I've been begging producers to let me prove I can act, but you're the first one even to consider it."[48]

Sidney Poitier wasn't everyone's choice for the other role either. Some people felt he didn't represent black culture so much as a white man's perception of it. He was, in a sense, a white black man. If one took away the color of his skin — which was, admittedly, a very big if— one could have been looking at another Curtis.

Kramer had reservations about Poitier from another perspective too. He had heard some reports that Poitier didn't want to play a bigot. It had taken him a lot of time to establish himself as a respectable black actor, and he thought the role might alienate many of his fans. But Kramer talked him round. As Curtis said, "He told Sidney, 'Black men have as much a right to negative character traits as the rest of us, maybe more so.' It was inversely racist to glorify them."

Curtis insisted Poitier be given equal billing with him. This was in itself a validation of the ethos of the film: "I thought it was unfair for him to be a featured player when it was a picture of a black and white. I was offended by that."[49]

The obvious risk the film ran was of being too blatant in its polemical edge, the literal and metaphorical black-white bonding screaming "Tolerance" a little too stridently.[50] Kramer was a good enough director not to make it too much like a Sunday School lesson, but in another director's hands it could have teetered over into bathos.

Poitier saw the characters as being more convoluted than that. "Each misunderstood the other," he wrote in his autobiography, "but they also misunderstood their own individual limitations, so they scapegoated each other." Much of their disaffectedness came from their impoverished circumstances: "They were poor, and that pissed them off. Each used the other to justify his anger."[51]

For Poitier the film was about bonding: "That's why, at the end, they wound up on that railroad trestle, one guy holding the other guy, struggling to survive. Hanging on but singing a song, a song of hope."[52] Many blacks objected to such camaraderie. They wanted "payback" for all the years of white oppression. Their anger reached a boiling point as a result of the last scene where Poitier sacrifices his freedom to jump off the train to be with Curtis, who's too weak to catch it. Their attitude was "Screw that guy." Poitier was sympathetic to that position but took a softer line with the view that "all of us were molded out of the same clay."[53]

Curtis changed his nose to make himself look less handsome. When shooting started, he was humble enough to take acting tips from Poitier. He was impressed by the staccato manner in which he delivered his lines and took to aping him. Poitier was momentarily discommoded by this, but as time went on Curtis developed his own style of delivery and the ebony/ivory chemistry took off in earnest.

Poitier never expressed any misgivings in print about Curtis' lack of suitability for the role. "He was a big part of Hollywood's last twenty five years," he knew, "but this town ain't too cool with you when you're in the afterglow of your stardom."[54] One day Poitier walked into Kramer's office and said, "I think Curtis is doing a hell of a job." That was the moment all Kramer's fears dissipated. He knew his brave casting choice had been vindicated.[55]

Poitier liked Kramer. He saw him as someone who looked the world in the eye and said, "You're not quite structured the way I like, and here comes a little energy to move you around a little."[56]

The *Defiant Ones* outgrew its thin storyline in the latter scenes when Curtis and Poitier softened towards one another. This was mainly down to Kramer's nuanced direction. Gordon Gow called it right when he said, "If sentiment often bordered on sentimentality, he knew just how far to let it ride, [knew] when to rein it in."[57] Mark Honigsbaum felt the would-be "messageathon" played better as a high-concept thriller than a statement about race relations, partly because both stars were too pretty to play underclass convicts. Having said that, he appreciated the understated finale in which Poitier sacrifices his freedom for his new white friend.[58]

The radical black writer James Baldwin disagreed. He held a cynical view of the two leads' eventual decision to "buddy-buddy back together to the same old Jim Crow chain gang."[59] When Baldwin saw the film in a well-heeled district, his black friends applauded the brotherhood theme, but then he watched it again in Harlem the audience there hooted at Poitier for forgiving his white brother. Why, Baldwin asked, was it necessary for Kramer to demonstrate the fact that the Negro had "forgiven and forgotten all. Maybe he has. That's not the problem. You haven't. *That's* the problem."[60]

But the film was a giant leap forward in many ways. We may carp at its coy ending, but it's important to see it in the context of the time in which it was made. (Some Deep South theater chains wouldn't even screen it.)[61]

When Oscar nominations were announced that year, both Curtis and Poitier were cited in the Best Actor category, something that rubbed Curtis the wrong way.[62] He felt they'd cancel each other out. "It was a token nomination," he sneered, "a Jew and a black guy."[63] The only reason the nominations were proffered, he held, was because the Academy would have been ashamed not to do so.[64] Poitier's nomination signaled the first time in the Academy's thirty-year history that a non-white had been in the running for a Best Actor award.[65]

Curtis attended the Oscar ceremonies with Leigh. "I told her to expect nothing,' he said. "The Academy patted myself and Sidney on the head by stepping up to the racist plate, but it wasn't going to go any further. The only way either of us could have won is if they found a way to cut the statue in half."

His prediction came to pass. David Niven won Best Actor for *Separate Tables*, and Vincente Minnelli beat Kramer to the Best Director award by winning for *Gigi*. This prompted one writer to remark that directors who won for "big, logistically challenging films" was a reflection of Hollywood's view of the director as a "damage containment expert" rather than an artist.[66]

Curtis' performance validated him in the eyes of the critics, however, and in his own eyes too. "I used to feel a sort of shame at accepting my paychecks," he said, speaking of his early days. "It seemed almost like stealing. I was in a long line of mediocre pictures [and because] the pictures got panned, I got panned too. But then a few years ago, somehow I changed. I got the urge to improve." But had he improved as much as some reviewers suggested? He didn't think so. "I am," he offered soberly, "neither as bad as critics once claimed I was nor as good as they now say I am."[67]

He imagined the nomination would open the door for more serious roles in the future, but this wasn't the way things panned out. The phone didn't ring with offers, and neither

This iconic image from Stanley Kramer's influential prison drama *The Defiant Ones* (1958) aptly conveys the "ebony-ivory" theme of the film. Curtis finds himself handcuffed to the equally bigoted Sidney Poitier after the pair of them go on the run together and form an unlikely camaraderie, united by the common purpose of trying to evade recapture. Both were nominated for Oscars for their performances, but Curtis believed this hurt both of their chances, a theory which may well have been true, as neither won.

did quality scripts find their way to his mailbox. Curtis railed, "It damn near broke my heart when I got no recognition for *The Defiant Ones* and *Sweet Smell of Success*. I thought I wasn't bad in them but nothing happened. Nothing. If I'd come from the same distinguished theatrical background as Brando I'd have awards for both films, I'm sure."[68]

It was now back to the drawing board, another piece of fluff with Leigh called *The Perfect Furlough*. It featured Curtis as a sex-starved army man winning a vacation to Paris where he has to pretend to have sexual thrills that he can relate to his army buddies back in the Arctic, where they're stationed, to relieve their frustrations. (Surely such disclosures would make them worse?) Leigh is his psychologist-cum-chaperone and Linda Cristal a film star he has to pretend to romance. Will he fall for her for real or end up with Leigh? One didn't have to be a genius to guess which eventuality would transpire. Matters speed up when Cristal becomes pregnant. There's also a phantom pregnancy from Leigh to woo Curtis. It's all harmless nonsense. Keenan Wynn and Elaine Stritch brought up the rear in supporting roles.

Curtis and Leigh enjoyed a giddy time on the set of the movie, largely due to the lackadaisical atmosphere created by its director Blake Edwards, a good friend to them both. A talented writer as well as a director, Edwards was plagued by clumsiness. He reacted to mishaps he caused with much good cheer. Clumsiness was also something to which Leigh was prone: "Blake and I must have been related way back when we were swinging in the trees because we were both charter members of the Klutz Club."[69]

The film was hammered by the toffee-nosed press. Curtis complained:

> Every time I make a picture I always end up as the butt of critics' jokes. Whenever I appear in a bad production they call it "another lousy Tony Curtis picture," but if it turns out well they say, "This time Curtis has somehow been able to get himself a good director." That gets me. I tried to fight back once by writing a letter to a critic on a Dallas newspaper who not only doesn't know how to review movies but misquoted me in an interview. I wrote him that he wouldn't know a good actor if one sat on his face, but it didn't do any good. He's still writing the same garbage.[70]

Universal was in deep debt by now. During the previous year it had spent almost $40 million on 32 films that sat on a shelf awaiting release. The movies that did go into release, meanwhile, were losing money hand over fist. The studio was recording an annual loss of $2 million. Leigh received positive notices for Orson Welles' cult film *Touch of Evil*, but it didn't turn a profit until years afterwards. Would the studio go under and force the couple out of their luxurious lifestyle?

Just as the storm clouds began to gather, Lew Wasserman rode over the hill like the Seventh Cavalry. He had a film for Curtis that was going to be made not by Universal but rather the Mirisch company. It concerned two men on the run from the Mob who have to dress up as women in an all-girl band to stay alive.

9

Boys Will Be Girls

"Some intrepid souls are drawn to high-risk adventures like cobra-kissing," Don Widener wrote, "or sailing out where there be dragons." Billy Wilder's zeal for masochism expressed itself in *Some Like It Hot*.[1]

Loosely based on a minor German film called *Fanfaren der Liebe*, it had Curtis and Jack Lemmon as two out-of-work musicians who witness the Valentine's Day Massacre and then have to make themselves scarce after they're spotted by hoods with orders to wipe them out. Where else would they go but to the all-girl band Sweet Sue and Her Society Syncopators, presided over by a whiskey-sipping bubblehead played by, who else, Marilyn Monroe.

Wilder originally considered either Danny Kaye or Bob Hope for the role Curtis ended up playing. Frank Sinatra was even in the running for a time. It's unlikely Sinatra would have subjected himself to Wilder's rigorous directorial technique, the actor's least favorite phrase being "Take Two."[2] Wilder had wanted Edward G. Robinson and George Raft to play the two hoods. Raft came on board but Robinson refused to star with him, so the lesser known Nehemiah Persoff stepped in. Raft was difficult on set. He refused to do a scene where he was asked to kick a toothpick from the mouth of fellow hood George E. Stone. Raft was afraid he'd kick Stone in the head by accident, which annoyed Wilder so much he said he'd give him a demonstration himself. Wilder did, and Stone ended up in the hospital.[3]

The writer Angie Errigo picked up on Wilder's "neat *noir* touch of shooting Raft's key entrances from the dandy footwear upward."[4]

The most controversial casting choice of all was Marilyn Monroe as Sugar Kane. She was slow to take the role because of its "dumb blond" overtones.[5] For years she'd been anxiously looking for a script that might counter her "dim bulb" image.[6] "I've been dumb," she said, referring to Sugar Kane's failure to see through the genderbending disguises of Curtis and Lemmon, "but not *that* dumb."[7] It was her husband, Arthur Miller, who persuaded her to take the part.

Harold Mirisch, who was producing the film, threw a party for Monroe and Miller when they got to Hollywood. They arrived at 11.20 P.M. The party was breaking up by then but became "unbroken" when she came in.[8] "There was no doubt in anyone's mind who was the star of the movie," Curtis huffed. Her dominance was reflected by her salary. She received $300,000 and 10 percent of the gross. Curtis and Lemmon were only offered $100,000 each and 5 percent of the gross. Laurence Maslon noted that in this particular game of poker a Queen beat a Jack, "and a Tony too."[9]

Like Monroe, Lemmon had reservations about being in the movie. "People thought

Billy was crazy to attempt such a film," he said. "Friends told me I could be ruined because the audience would think I was faggy or had a yen to be a transvestite."[10]

Monroe was having marital difficulties with Miller at this time. She was also depressed over aging and losing that marvelous physique. She still looked sexy but she was starting to put on weight.[11] The film was to be shot in black and white and she wasn't over the moon about this. Wilder decided on this because of the gaudy makeup he had to apply to Curtis and Lemmon to make them look like women, which came out green.[12] The film's gangster element was also best served by monochrome.

Monroe had worked with Wilder once before, on *The Seven Year Itch*. She threw tantrums on that movie and had also been unpunctual frequently, so Wilder was expecting some problems with her. In the four years between *Itch* and *Some Like It Hot* her world had changed: "She had become one of the most celebrated personalities in the world. She had divorced Joe DiMaggio. She had married Arthur Miller. She had become a disciple of Lee Strasberg. She was seriously studying acting."[13]

Wilder started shooting on August 4, 1958, with a projected filming schedule of 45 days. He was concerned about the excessive influence being wielded over her by her acting coach, Paula Strasberg. Curtis didn't think much of Strasberg. Monroe was paying her $1500 a week, he thought, to tell her to relax.[14]

She insisted on accompanying Monroe to the set each day. Curtis thought her expression gave off an "I'm a King Shit here" vibe which Wilder picked up. One day he had had enough of this. After a take Wilder looked around at Strasberg and inquired, "How was that for you, Paula?"[15]

Curtis admired Wilder. He took the part of Josephine "five seconds" after Wilder offered it to him. But Wilder's dictatorial approach to directing "scared the shit" out of him. He also felt the least important of the three main players: "I always knew Marilyn was going to be Billy's first priority but what I didn't bank on was that Jack would be his second." Wilder and Lemmon would go on to make many movies together after this one, but it would be Curtis' only collaboration with Wilder. He summed up their relationship in a telling comment: "I didn't avoid Billy but I kept my distance."[16]

Getting into costume involved much time and energy for Curtis and Lemmon. "We had to hold our arms palms down so our muscles didn't show," Curtis remembered, "which was a bigger problem for me than Jack. I'd played a boxer."[17] They also had their legs and chests shaved and their eyebrows plucked. Another problem was getting out of costume to relieve themselves for bathroom breaks. (They'd both been fitted with metal jock straps to conceal their private parts.) Curtis rigged up an ingenious "relief tube" that ran down his leg. He didn't tell Lemmon, who marveled at his perceived restraint in that department. "How do you hold it?" Lemmon would inquire repeatedly. Curtis thought the tube worked so well he even considered patenting it.[18]

The first time Curtis and Lemmon tried out their new apparel they went into a Ladies room to see if they could pass themselves off as women. Lemmon couldn't wait to try out his disguise but Curtis was terrified. He had to be coaxed out by Wilder. When he faced the women he was amazed to discover none of them showed any interest in himself or Lemmon. "They just thought we were extras or bit players doing a period piece. But they thought we were women."[19] Lemmon was satisfied at this, as well he might have been, but Curtis looked deeper. He imagined they were ignored because they were ugly. He insisted on going back to makeup for more mascara and higher heels. Also, "I had my boobs enhanced, as they say, and Jack had his rump reupholstered." The result this time was disastrous. No sooner had they reentered the Ladies than one of the girls in there said, "Hi, Tony."[20]

Back in the original get-up, Curtis thought he looked like Eve Arden. Lemmon tried to relax him but it was no easy task. "My nickname was Vanity Curtis on that set," he said. "I couldn't stop looking in mirrors. Jack told me to pull myself together, that I wasn't going for Miss World. That needed to be said. At first I didn't just want to be a woman; I wanted to be a *pretty* woman." It was important for Curtis to make that shift in attitude, but in a strange way, as Angie Errigo pointed out, his self-consciousness actually helped his performance, giving him a kind of "aloof control."[21]

Lemmon decided to take his part, Daphne, to the cleaners from the off, exaggerating his walk and flashing a banana-shaped grin.

Curtis was more reserved. He tried to model Josephine on women he knew — his mother, Grace Kelly, anyone he could think of. Janet Leigh was also on his mind. Sometimes Leigh got mad at him, he said, and looked at him with a "sophisticated, hoity-toity" expression that seemed to say, "What is it?"[22]

Leigh was amused that her husband was finally realizing that being a woman wasn't all peaches and cream. "Those high heels were uncomfortable and it was difficult to keep on balance. The wigs were hot and itchy, and they had a heck of a time with the makeup and the five o'clock shadow."[23]

Lemmon and himself suffered "the tortures of the damned" with muscle cramps. Such tortures were only mitigated when Wilder called "Cut" and they were able to douse their feet in ice-cold buckets of water. Afterwards they poured lotion on them to make them ready for the next take. Curtis found it helpful to let go of his muscles to get into the part. Otherwise they became too defined. He wanted to look "slinky, supple."[24]

Wilder recruited the famous Texan transvestite Barbette as a consultant to Curtis and Lemmon. Barbette, who had been born Vander Clyde, was now in retirement. He'd had a glittering circus career before it ended prematurely due to poor health. Curtis took his advice as regards to how to walk like a woman and so on, but Lemmon was more intractable. After three days Barbette blew up at Wilder. "Curtis can be magnificent [but] Lemmon is hopeless," he snapped.[25] Curtis explained what happened:

> Jack told Barbette he didn't want anything to do with him. He said he didn't want to walk like a woman. He wanted to walk like a man trying to walk like a woman. He was so right. We should have been hamming it up as much as we could. And of course Jack did that. The reason I didn't was because I wanted to give him something to bounce off. I played the straight man — or should I say straight woman — to him. We were going screwball.

Curtis was to be admired for telling the story against himself. There's a difference between imitation and impersonation. He always maintained he wanted Josephine to be stylish. Daphne was different. "For a two dollar bill she'd go with anyone."[26] Because Curtis wasn't camping the part up as much as Lemmon he was more amenable to Barbette's advice. He felt his self-consciousness about being in drag could be lessened by coming across as a genuine woman rather than a hysterical man going bananas.

"I was too inhibited to go all out like Jack did," Curtis confessed, "but it worked out all right because it gave us some yin and yang. Jack was afraid if he listened to Barbette there'd be nothing of himself in the part. He'd become Daphne and lose Jack. He preferred to keep half of each. It was a wise move and Billy approved of it, so he let Barbette go."

Monroe had different kinds of problems with her character. Despite Miller's reassurances, she was still put out by the fact that Sugar Kane couldn't see through the "comically bad" disguises of Curtis and Lemmon. This "overpowered" her.[27]

Monroe used an imaginative technique to suspend her disbelief over the fact that Curtis and Lemmon were really men in drag. Paula Strasberg came up with it. Strasberg advised her to use "substitution," i.e. to envisage them as women she knew — or one particular woman. Monroe chose her former roommate Shelley Winters. She told Winters, "I pretended Tony Curtis was you and Jack Lemmon was you too. I pretended I was talking to you and put your face over their made-up, silly faces. I think it worked great."[28]

Monroe also had a problem with the first scene of the film, where she felt upstaged by Curtis and Lemmon. She walked off the set after it was shot, muttering, "I'm not going back into that fucking film until Wilder reshoots my opening scene. When Marilyn Monroe comes into a room, nobody's going to be looking at Tony Curtis playing Joan Crawford. They're going to be looking at Marilyn Monroe."[29] She was speaking about her scene at the train station where she's compared to "jello on springs." She thought her entrance was boring, and Wilder agreed. To give it some fizz he came up with the idea of having the steam from the train hit her on the backside and hoosh her along. This worked a treat and settled her down.

Soon afterwards she showed her diva qualities in a different way — by taking a fancy to one of the dresses Orry-Kelly had designed for Lemmon and grabbing it for herself. Afterwards the wardrobe department had to make another one up for Lemmon.[30] This was the beginning of her becoming "difficult."

Monroe had to go to the hospital shortly after filming began. When she came back to work she was frequently late on set, causing Wilder to rasp, "Do you think maybe there's a little watchmaker in Zurich [who] makes a living producing special watches only for Marilyn?"[31] Her lateness, for him, was reflective of a general waywardness in her headspace. He remembered being in her car once and surveying the chaotic mess of the back seat. "There's blouses lying there, and slacks, girdles, skirts, shoes, old plane tickets, old lovers for all I know...."[32]

One day the excuse she gave for being late to the set was having gotten lost on her way to the studio. At this time she'd been working there seven years. For anyone else this would have been regarded as a bad joke, but with Monroe — a riddle wrapped inside a mystery wrapped inside an enigma — Wilder took it seriously. He became so frustrated by her he took to drinking martinis at lunch.[33] Most of the damage, he thought, was caused by Strasberg. He compared the situation to a man writing a song like "How Much Is That Doggie in the Window" and then being asked to write symphonies for Toscanini. "She is being taught acting by the kind of people who don't believe in underarm deodorants," he bristled. "They believe in sitting on the floor even if there are six comfortable chairs. They'll make her into another Julie Harris."[34]

Wilder believed stars who had to do scenes repeatedly lost their spontaneity. Monroe put it down to shyness on her part.[35] "Billy thought this was baloney," Curtis maintained. "He saw it as just attention-grabbing and so did I. You couldn't call yourself shy when you were responsible for holding up a whole operation."

Monroe's inability to master short takes became legendary. One scene which required her to just say, "It's me, Sugar," went on forever. Another in which she had also had only a few words necessitated forty takes. She was losing the plot — in every sense of the term.

"Her unhappiness was so tangible," said Lemmon, "it was catching."[36] It got so bad that over time he used to wake up in the middle of the night in a sweat, "and I've dreamt that we're now on Take 55 and Marilyn has gotten her lines right and I blew it."[37]

"Marilyn had a kind of inbuilt alarm system," according to Lemmon. "It would go off in the middle of a scene if that scene wasn't right for her. She'd stand there with her eyes closed, biting her lip and kind of wringing her hands until she had it worked out."[38]

Even though she was ditzy, he thought she had an innate sense of survival: "She simply isn't like other people. If we were all in the same building and it began to fall down, we'd all run. But Marilyn would probably run in a totally different direction. The point is, she wouldn't get hit by any falling bricks because she's not only different, she's smart."[39]

Lemmon was able to be more understanding of her than Curtis because he didn't share too many scenes with her. He realized it was different for Curtis. "Tony had one in the third act that ran twelve minutes with Marilyn. When you consider she had a habit of showing up late, had a tendency to act *at* instead of *with* you, and you were never sure of getting through a scene before she stopped it, it's understandable she drove Tony a little cuckoo."[40]

The scene where Lemmon tells Curtis about his "engagement" to Joe E. Brown was Lemmon's favorite in the movie. When that scene was written, Lemmon couldn't think of anything to do while delivering his lines, but "Billy suggested that, since I'd just been dancing the fandango with Joe, it would be natural for me to come home playing the maracas. The idea pumped energy into my action and gave the entire scene flavor."[41]

"I'm convinced Joe kept Jack sane on the movie," Curtis believed. "He took his mind off Marilyn. Unfortunately, there was no Joe E. Brown for me. I only had Marilyn. Can I honestly say I would have preferred to be dancing with Joe with a rose in my teeth than making out with the so-called sexiest woman in the world? Sadly, yes. No matter how much of a freak that makes me sound."

One day Curtis bet Lemmon that Monroe would "get" a take at the fortieth attempt. She didn't get it until Take 47, so Lemmon won.[42] Sometimes she stopped takes that Wilder felt were going well if she didn't agree. Curtis remembered a day Wilder made a tactful suggestion to her about a line reading. She snarled back at him, "Don't talk to me now. I'm thinking about how I'm going to play the scene."[43]

As her problems grew, so did the gap between herself and the rest of the cast. Matthew Smith wrote, "If Marilyn had problems to share, her costars would not have been the people to share them with."[44] He was right. Curtis and Lemmon were too angry at her to sympathize with her.

Curtis developed insomnia from the stress. One day he went to Wilder and droned, "I'm having trouble sleeping because of all the shit with Marilyn." Wilder gave him some suppositories to help him. "Slip one in your tuchis," he advised, "and you'll sleep all night." Curtis did as he was told. The next morning Wilder asked him if it worked. A relieved Curtis replied, "My ass fell asleep instantly!"[45] No matter how much Marilyn was draining him, she couldn't take away his sense of humor.

Another day Wilder told Monroe his back was bothering him, but she didn't believe him, going back to Strasberg with the story that he was "inventing" things like this to drum up sympathy for himself. "Only Marilyn was supposed to feel pain," Maurice Zolotov concluded.[46]

Donald Wolfe believed her tantrums were deliberately orchestrated by her to take power away from Wilder, who'd been annoying her with his rapidfire direction.[47] James Bacon also held this view. He believed Monroe had been using tactics similar to this as far back as 1952 when she made *Clash by Night* with Fritz Lang. She drove her costars crazy with her tardiness on that film too, and apparently told Bacon she muffed lines deliberately to get things her way: "When I liked it, I said the line perfectly."[48] Izzy Diamond believed her histrionics were simply caused by her wishing to throw her weight around. "Having reached the top," he argued, "she was paying the world back for all the rotten things she'd had to go through."[49]

Wolfe, like Bacon and Diamond, felt there was "a Method to her madness."[50] Perhaps, but there may also have been madness in her Method. "I'm not a quick study," she said. "I envy these people who can go from a bright quip and gay laugh into a scene."[51]

Curtis said Monroe had sex with him in the Coronado Hotel during the shooting of the film. Why? He wasn't quite sure. Maybe she was lonely, Strasberg and Miller both being away at the time. "I stroked her hair," he recounted, "and my hands moved all over her. Touching her, any part of her, never felt obscene or vulgar. I couldn't be vulgar with her." But he didn't know if it brought her closer to him or not: "She was an actress."[52] When she became pregnant soon afterwards he firmly believed it was with his child.

By now Arthur Miller had started to realize she was on a collision course with disaster. He suspended his writing, giving her the kind of emotional support he hoped would convince her she was no longer alone in the world — the heart of the problem.[53] He also became more visible on the set.

Curtis thought Miller strange in the sense of being in on himself. "He looked like Abraham Lincoln," he remarked. "But then all of Marilyn's husbands did."[54] DiMaggio and Miller certainly had the wrinkled Lincoln visage, but hardly Jim Dougherty. Nonetheless, Curtis was right to point out that she tended to go for craggy men. Even one of her last lovers, Yves Montand, had a wrinkled appearance.[55]

Towards the end of his book on *Some Like It Hot*, Curtis documented a scene between himself, Monroe and Miller where everything comes out into the open about his sexual relationship with Monroe and the possibility that he might have impregnated her. This is taking things a notch higher than his 2008 autobiography, and many notches higher than his 1994 one.[56] It's a fascinating interchange, but one wonders how much of it actually happened this way. As we know from his novels, Curtis had a very active imagination.

Matters reached a nadir with Monroe the day it took her over fifty takes to say "Where's the bourbon?" the way Wilder wanted her to, either because she "moved off cue, froze on her line or spoke it wrong — even after Wilder pasted slips of paper with the dialogue in all the bureau drawers she opened."[57]

Wilder explained the circumstances of the disastrous bourbon scene in some detail to fellow director Cameron Crowe: "There was the whole afternoon trying to get it because she cried after every take and then she had to be made up again. And then also we lost the morning because she didn't show up, and we lost the afternoon because she didn't remember the line."[58] The irony is that in the finished film the line is played on her back. Crowe asked Wilder why he spent a day and a half on a close-up he ended up not even using. Wilder replied, "Maybe I was just stupid!"⁵⁹ (And they called Marilyn Monroe dumb?)

One day in a fit of anger, Curtis yelled at Wilder, "Billy, how many fuckin' takes are we gonna do?" Wilder replied, "When Marilyn gets it right, that's the take I'm going to use."⁶⁰ Because the perfect Marilyn take was always the one Wilder printed, Curtis and Lemmon had to take care not to have their finger in their ear, as Wilder warned, at the time. On one occasion Lemmon *tripped* during a take, but it was still printed because Wilder liked Marilyn in it.⁶¹

Monroe continued to weep after the botched takes. This meant even more time delays having her makeup reapplied.⁶² She also continued to flub her dialogue, her delays causing the movie's budget to skyrocket.⁶³ Wilder realized her unpredictability was the price he paid for her appeal. As he wisecracked more than once, "I have an Aunt Minnie whom I love and she's always on time. But who would buy tickets to see her?"⁶⁴ Monroe became a necessary evil to him, one of the inmates running the movie asylum.

The hapless director groaned, "We were in mid-flight and I knew there was a nut on the plane."⁶⁵ The stuntman Ted Jordan, in his book about her, said she contemplated throwing herself into the Hudson river many times at this point of her life.⁶⁶ But then Jordan makes many even more extravagant claims about her in a book that reads more like a penny dreadful novel than a memoir proper. But Jordan was right about her being an accident waiting to happen. During the last month of filming she was so "out of it" she read many of her lines from an off-camera blackboard. Her eyes can be seen moving in the scene where she talks to Curtis on the phone.⁶⁷

This was one of the most challenging parts of the film for Curtis, as he was now called upon to essay his "third" role in the movie — that of Junior, the Shell Oil millionaire that Monroe falls for.

When Wilder informed him he'd have to put on a different accent for Junior he wasn't too pleased. The accent he was using for Joe was fine, but it couldn't work for Junior because Sugar Kane would recognize it instantly. Now that he had to put on another voice, there was really only one option for him: Cary Grant. He'd been impersonating Grant on and off since the days watching *Gunga Din* in the Navy. In fact, the first time he asked Janet Leigh out on a date he did so using Grant's voice. (She didn't fall for it.)⁶⁸

Curtis didn't want to do a straight take-off on Grant: "I played it saucy. I kicked up my voice a little bit higher, which told you right away that this guy wasn't English. He's a New Yorker trying to sound English."⁶⁹

James Naremore compared the accent to that of a "middle class Englishman trying hard to sound cultivated."⁷⁰ Wilder described it as "a lowbrow's idea of a highbrow."⁷¹ Whatever way one looked at it, it was a curious phenomenon in the context of the movie considering Grant hadn't even been born at the time in which it's set.⁷²

When Curtis impersonated Grant for the first time, he wrote in *Me, Marilyn and the Movie*, Wilder didn't like it.⁷³ He gave a different version of events to Charlotte Chandler when she asked him about Wilder's first reaction to the Grant accent. In this version, Wilder was enthralled by his new voice and actually kissed him in appreciation.⁷⁴

Elsewhere when Curtis was asked what Cary Grant said when he first heard it, Curtis put on Grant's voice and answered, "Cary said 'Neubawdy taulks loike that!'" The truth of the matter is that Grant adored Curtis' impersonation of him. According to Wilder, he roared with laughter when he talked about it with him.⁷⁵

In later years people sometimes accused Curtis of speaking like Grant even in ordinary life. Curtis disputed that, claiming he "nasalized" his voice for the movie.[76] He felt the accent would work for people who didn't even know who Grant was. Time has proved him right. It's even become a benchmark for *other* accents.[77] Curtis was glad he did it but he wasn't cocky enough to imagine he could ever emulate his hero's sophistication: "Nobody plays Cary Grant like Cary Grant."[78]

The second thing most people remember about Junior is the fact that he had a strange experience with Marilyn Monroe on a sofa towards the end of the film. Because he's impotent. It was Wilder's idea to make Sugar Kane seduce Junior rather than vice versa. It gave the scene an added kick and gave Curtis the chance to make his character something other than the kind of stud one might have expected. In the original script, Junior tried to get Sugar Kane in a compromising position on the sofa. Wilder realized this would probably be the only ordinary scene in an extraordinary movie, and that wouldn't do. He told the director Cameron Crowe:

> The idea was that Curtis invites Monroe back to the boat of Mr. Shell and it's all set up, they're alone. Now there's going to be sex, right? I woke up in the middle of the night thinking: This is no good, this is expected. What we'll do is that he plays it impotent. And she suggests the sex. And she fucks him. Seduced and screwed by Marilyn Monroe, what could be better?[79]

The revamped script allowed Wilder to claim Curtis' family spent a fortune trying to cure him without success. Whereupon Monroe asks, "May I try?" Wilder told Crowe the idea of Curtis' leg going up in the air as she kisses him gave viewers an inkling of his real feelings without having to worry about censorship problems. The "cure" for his impotence was transmitted metaphorically. And comically.

Wilder boasted, "I always played an honest game with the censors. Sex is in my pictures, but it is dramatic or it is funny. The scene between Monroe and Curtis on the boat is just one laugh after another. That the censors forgave me."[80] Being seduced by Marilyn Monroe was a ubiquitous male fantasy; Curtis got to realize it and make half the male world feel madly jealous by extension — including Wilder himself. In fact, when Crowe asked Wilder what character he would most like to have been in all his movies he replied with refreshing frankness, "I would like to have been Tony Curtis in *Some Like It Hot*."[81]

Monroe increased censorship problems for Wilder in the scene by removing the pieces of cloth in her dress that covered her nipples. When Curtis expressed fears about this she dismissed them, evincing a need to be "more organic." She also drank champagne to prepare herself for the scene. "She wanted me to have some too," Curtis said, "but I held off. I felt if it took her as many takes to seduce me as it did to say, 'It's me, Sugar,' I'd have been unconscious on the floor before Billy yelled, 'Print.'"

Having her towering over him and misting up his spectacles made the scene into a whole new ballgame for him. "When you're making *Some Like It Hot*," he surmised, "and Marilyn Monroe sticks her tongue in your mouth all the way down to your navel, that's not moviemaking, my friend, that's life."[82] At one stage he even got an erection. "She was grinding away and really tight against me." She acknowledged his excitement with a kind of "I gotcha," according to Curtis, "and she liked that. There was nothing salacious about it. She knew she could still do it to me."[83] It was like the days—or nights—of 1949 all over again.

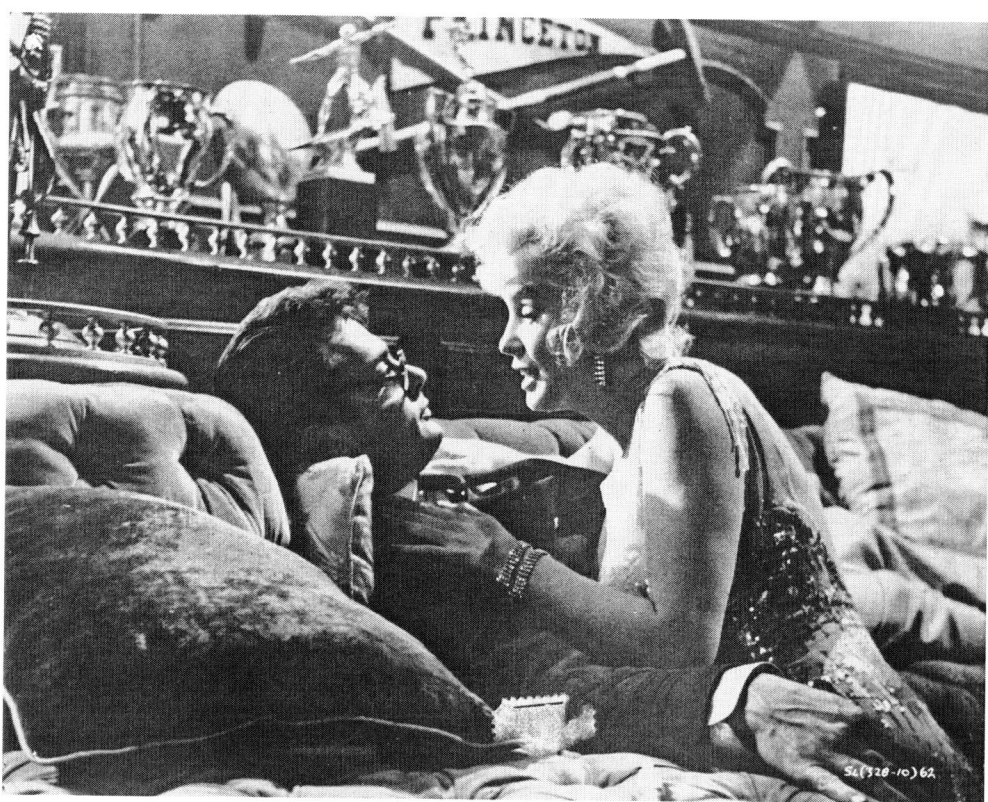

Here we have the famous love scene that occurs towards the end of Billy Wilder's genderbending comedy *Some Like It Hot* (1959), where Marilyn Monroe, as the pneumatic song-and-dance girl Sugar Kane, attempts to "cure" Junior (Curtis), the Shell Oil heir, of his fabricated impotence. Curtis was driven mad by Monroe's unpredictable behavior on the set, so much so that on one occasion he said kissing her was "like kissing Hitler." The remark haunted him for the rest of his life and was inevitably trotted out by interviewers whenever they quizzed him about his mercurial relationship with the troubled sex symbol.

One critic described this scene as the high water mark of Monroe's "onscreen carnality."[84] Considering Curtis' "growing" ardor, it's amazing that what the Curtis/Monroe relationship is primarily remembered for today isn't this scene but rather Curtis' infamous comment afterwards that "Kissing Marilyn was like kissing Hitler."

At various times over the years he gave different versions of why he said it. It wasn't because he didn't enjoy the physical act of kissing her. It was because, "Here was this woman, beautifully endowed, treating all men like shit. Why did I have to take that?"[85]

Elsewhere he claimed it was meant to be ironic: "Come on. Kissing the most desirable woman in the world and then being asked repeatedly what it was like is a no-brainer. It began to annoy me. What was I supposed to say, that it was like skiing down a snow-covered mountain and being launched into the air by a ski-jump and then floating to earth on gossamer wings?"[86]

Whatever his reasons, Monroe didn't like it. She's alleged to have retorted, "He only said that because I wore prettier dresses than he did."[87] (Yes, thanks to her filching Lemmon's Orry-Kelly frock.)

Another account of her reaction went into more bitter detail: "You've read that there was some actor that said kissing me was like kissing Hitler. Well I think that's his problem. If I have to do intimate love scenes with somebody who has these kind of feelings towards me, my fantasy can come into play. In other words, out with him and in with my fantasy. He was never there."[88]

This is interesting, but Curtis actually made the comment *after* their love scene, not during it, so she wouldn't have needed to bring her fantasies into play. And what did she mean by him not being there? Was it not herself that wasn't there if her mind was on her fantasy?

It's likely that her "He was never there" jibe was a retrospective putdown to pay him back for the Hitler analogy. It flies in the face of Curtis' memory of her looking down bemusedly at his aroused member and admonishing, "There you are, you naughty boy!"[89]

Filming concluded on November 6, 1958, 29 days over schedule. On the last day of shooting Curtis arranged for a stripper to jump out of a life-sized cake pop that was used to gun down one of the gangsters. Wilder, unfortunately, wasn't amused when she approached him to plant a kiss on his lips. Too much had gone on. It was probably the only time in his life that the great director was impervious to a practical joke. "Marilyn had exhausted him so much he just wanted to get out of Dodge," was the way Curtis put it.

The following day there was a promotional photo shoot but Monroe failed to turn up, a double having to stand in for her. (Her face was superimposed on the shots later). It was probably as a result of this final slight that Wilder refused to invite her to the wrap party. Donald Wolfe thought that was shabby of him considering she'd been the glue that held his film together "and kept it from falling into the kinetic mayhem of his subsequent farce, *One, Two, Three*."[90] This was unfair. *One, Two, Three* wasn't one of Wilder's triumphs, but he made many brilliant films without Monroe. Though she enhanced this one delectably, it would still have been a riot even if she hadn't been in it.

James Bacon also felt Wilder should have forgiven Monroe. She may have added $1 million to the film's budget, he allowed, but she probably added five times that amount to its profit margin as well.[91] These are all tenable arguments, but they were being put forth by people who weren't in the eye of the storm in the fall of 1958. It's easier to forgive from the purview of history, especially since Monroe's death a few years later acquired the proportions of a Greek tragedy in some people's eyes.

When the film was previewed for critics it didn't garner much of a reaction. A distraught Wilder burst into tears as a result. The agent Irving Lazar, who was with him at the time, related the story to Michael Caine. Caine remarked that he ought to have known that a "paper house" (i.e. a non-paying audience) never laughed.[92] As a film critic of some years standing, the present writer can testify to the veracity of this dictum.

When Curtis was asked if it was the most difficult film he ever made, he hedged. "They're all difficult in different ways. Whatever I suffered on that set was made up to me a hundredfold by the fond memories people have of it. Hardly a day goes by but someone mentions it to me. The fact that I made two and a half million dollars out of it also helps."

10
Mixing with the Big Guns

Two events took place within a week of one another in 1958 that changed Curtis' life significantly: his father died and his daughter Jamie Lee was born. "A door to the past was closing," he said, "and one to the future opening a little wider."

He had a great devotion to his father even if he couldn't always express it. He was also angry at him for not making more of his life even though the odds were stacked against him. He revered his humility, his quietness. His father was both a gentleman and a "gentle" man, Curtis said. In fact, he inscribed his gravestone with these two words: "Gentle man."[1]

If they disagreed on something, more often than not it was a friendly spat. "Nothing was too trivial for us to argue about," he pointed out:

> We once had a quarrel that got so bad we didn't talk to each other for nearly a week. We made up one night drinking wine and wound up quarreling about who started the fight. I said it was my fault. He said it was his. The more wine we drank, the louder we got. Finally I said, "Okay, it was your fault." Dad took a long swallow of his wine, looked me straight in the eye and said, "Are you trying to start another fight, Bernie?" That broke me up. We started crying and laughing.[2]

Jamie Lee, like so many of Curtis' daughters, came into the world at a time when his nerves were shot to pieces. His biographer Michael Munn contended that his grieving over his father at this time may have been one of the reasons his relationship with Jamie was more problematic than that with any of his other children.[3] This is possible, but grief after a birth would be more likely to affect a mother-child bond than a father-child one, considering the umbilical connection. One would have thought the two-year-old Kelly would have suffered more than Jamie from his inattention at this time.

A third event took place that year which had different kinds of reverberations for him: MCA bought out Universal Studios. What this meant in effect was that Lew Wasserman couldn't be his agent anymore, having too much on his plate as a studio executive. Wasserman assured him he'd continue to have his best interests at heart and loan him out whenever he wanted, but it was still a seismic change for Curtis. "I lost two fathers that year," was his reaction to the news.

Wilder sneak-previewed *Some Like It Hot* at the Bay Theater in Pacific Palisades in December. It was featured on a double bill with Joe Mankiewicz' *Suddenly Last Summer*, an abominable mess of a film that tried to juxtapose themes like homosexuality, cannibalism and mental illness with a distressing lack of cohesion.[4] A disgusted audience wasn't in form for a screwball comedy afterwards, so *Some Like It Hot* fell flat. One commentator remarked,

"Perhaps they thought Curtis would chop up Monroe for dinner."[5] David O. Selznick was in the audience and predicted Wilder's film would be a disaster at the box office. When it was shown to a younger audience in New York, however, they greeted almost every line with uproarious laughter.[6]

When Marilyn Monroe saw the finished cut she wasn't impressed, complaining to her husband that Wilder made her resemble "a fat pig."[7] Geoff Andrew thought he betrayed her in a different manner: "The way the film leers at her body is depressing, not because the body isn't worth looking at but because the viewpoint is shifty."[8]

The film became hugely popular. It was "modern in its sexual approach [and] nostalgic in its tribute to screwball comedies."[9] *Time* magazine thought it parodied gangster films while also recalling the "pie-throwing farce" of cinema's infant days.[10] Curtis was also praised, though more guardedly. Robyn Karney thought he exuded "sisterly warmth" in the role.[11] He wasn't nominated for an Oscar, though Lemmon was. "I took it personally, man," he admitted to a reporter years later. "At a time when I needed the accolades of my peers, they turned their back on me."[12]

The fact that Lemmon had drawn the lion's share of Wilder's attention on the set seemed to drive the point home. One of the reasons he thought Wilder played "favorites" with Lemmon was to protect himself from Monroe. This is a theory which should perhaps be explored in more detail.[13] Some critics believed Curtis was better than Lemmon in the movie. Kate Muir thought his fine features totally suited lipstick, "and his staggering high-heeled swagger proved he was a great *physical* comedian."[14] Clive James felt Lemmon indulged himself too much with a "stuttering false-start technique" only unfunny actors thought funny. Curtis, in contrast, spoke with the kind of "clean bite" that would have made Cary Grant proud.[15] For Curtis the irony was that someone who became famous for his "pumped up testosterone image" was having his finest moments dressed in drag.[16]

"Something in the chaotic thwartedness of his character's admiration for Monroe," Peter Bradshaw contended, "brought out the comic charm of his personality, which remained ineffably boyish."[17] Wilder was also nominated for an Oscar, as was Orry-Kelly for Costume Design, but the film was "trampled on" by *Ben-Hur*, and only Orry-Kelly came away with a statuette.[18]

Innocuous as the humor appeared to be, America's rabid Legion of Decency found some of the *doubles entendres* to be "outright smut," while the central theme of transvestism, "with its clear implications of homosexuality and lesbianism," constituted a serious breach of the Production Code.[19] "Even in a time of sexual revolution," wrote Vito Russo, "when traditional roles are being examined and challenged every day, there's something about a man who acts like a woman that people find fundamentally distasteful." Such a sense was heightened here "because Jack Lemmon seemed to be enjoying his role too much."[20] Rebecca Bell-Metereau described Curtis as a "feminine" matinee idol in the tradition of Rudolph Valentino."[21] Speaking of androgyny in general, Curtis espoused the view that "we're all half man and half woman; we come from the two cells."[22]

Monroe miscarried her child on December 17, the very day the film previewed. Her depression increased over the Christmas period, the freneticism of the film's shoot having been replaced with too much time to brood over her tragedy. It was the last time she became pregnant. She felt her inability to have a baby would drive Miller away from her.[23]

Monroe had mixed feelings about the film's success. "That's it," she railed, "I'm a dumb blond forever now. I'm stuck. I've ruined everything for myself."[24] She tried to forget what she perceived as Wilder's cruelty to her, but it was all brought back to her when he gave an interview to Joe Hyams in which he rehashed all of the acrimony that had spilled over between them. Monroe threw a fit when she read the interview. Nina Pepitone, her maid, remembered her leaping out of her bed and running into Miller's study screaming, "It's your damn fault. You better do something about it, you bleeding-heart bastard!"[25] Miller fired off a telegram to Wilder berating him for his cruelty to a woman who was unable to work a full day on account of her pregnancy and who'd suffered a miscarriage so soon after the film ended.[26]

Wilder wrote back defending himself, and thus a "telegram duel" developed, ending with Wilder's, "Dear Arthur, in order to hasten the burial of the hatchet I hereby acknowledge that good wife Marilyn is a unique personality and I am the beast of Belsen, but in the immortal words of Joe E. Brown, quote, 'Nobody is perfect,' end quote."[27]

Monroe overdosed shortly afterwards. Pepitone found her unconscious on her bedroom floor, her face caked with vomit. She was rushed to the hospital and had her stomach pumped. When she regained consciousness she was asked how she was. She replied weakly, "Alive ... bad luck."[28] One of her main problems on the film, Miller contended, was that Wilder hadn't allowed her even "the slightest deviation" from the script because it had been so tightly composed.[29]

Miller thought Monroe's difficulties on her next and final film, *The Misfits*, resulted from the same cause — i.e. trying too hard to improvise.[30] Her misbehavior on that set had repercussions for another film. She was due to play opposite Cary Grant in *Let's Make Love* the following year, but after Curtis told Grant some horrifying tales about her behavior on the *Some Like It Hot* set he backed off.[31] Curtis resolved never to work with her again either. Pressed on the issue by Wilder, he replied, "Definitely not in the United States, but in Paris it might not be so bad. While we were waiting we could all take painting lessons on the side."[32]

Curtis became elated after the success of *Some Like It Hot*. He could virtually set his own contractual terms now. Even his fiercest critics were starting to think they'd been unduly harsh on the Noo Yawk *naif*. *Operation Petticoat*, his next movie, was a special one because his costar was none other than Cary Grant. It was a harmless comedy about an attempt to rescue a submarine from the scrapheap, aided and abetted by a group of nurses. The film is notable for featuring probably the only pink submarine in cinema history as its centerpiece. Blake Edwards again directed.

Today's audiences don't realize how big a star Grant was in his day, or Curtis' fascination with him, but as Ronnie Wood said once, "At the time Tony Curtis met Grant, he was so popular groupies used to yell, 'Cary Grant, it's Jesus Christ!'"[33] Janet Leigh said Curtis was "a gibbering mass of mush" at the prospect of finally costarring with his idol.[34] He was so in awe of working with him he thought it might affect his performance, but as the days went on he went from being a fan to a *bona fide* costar. Their relationship strengthened, so much so that Curtis ended up allowing Grant to stay in one of his houses to escape the media glare when he wanted to spend some time with his daughter Jennifer.[35] In his dressing room Curtis had a Jules Feiffer cartoon that said, "I woke up this morning and thought I was Cary Grant." He also went to L.A. Dodgers games with Grant, and dined with him at the Aware Inn.[36]

Grant wouldn't be everyone's idea of an acting coach, but he became Curtis' Svengali.

"Just relate to the person you're working with," he advised the young *ingénue* if he found himself cast opposite someone he didn't admire. "Even if they can't play the part properly and you don't believe a word of the dialogue, you must use that. Use everything you hear and be ready to adjust like a good acrobat."[37] Watching Grant, Curtis once said, taught him everything from "how to behave with a woman to how to dress for dinner."[38] "[He] told me once that the way you judge a bottle of white wine is that when it's chilled, it tastes like a glass of cool water. It's so artful it's artless. Nice, isn't it? Well, I feel acting is like that."[39]

This made a profound impact on Curtis, who said afterwards, "I never forgot it. I work in an artless world. Everything must look like an improvisation. How many movies have you seen where you know what's going to happen?" He liked people to be "unprepared for what they're gonna see."[40] In a like vein, he warned, "What you have to avoid is acting. The words do the acting. When I say, 'I love you,' I've transmitted some information. That's not acting to me, that's just a matter of reading a line well." Acting, in contrast, was "things left unsaid."[41]

Curtis once said he could learn more from watching Grant drinking a cup of coffee

Blake Edwards' offbeat service comedy *Operation Petticoat* (1960), dealing with a series of frantic attempts to make a battered pink submarine seaworthy again, was one of Curtis' most commercially successful films and was doubly sweet for him because it afforded him the opportunity to appear opposite his idol Cary Grant, seen here in discussion with him. Dina Merrill is the female interest. The fellow at right is unidentified.

"than by spending six months with a Method actor."[42] Marc Eliot thought Grant was also thrilled to be working with Curtis, probably seeing "something of his younger self in the handsome, dark-haired romantic leading man." He also believed working with Curtis would make him more accessible to younger audiences.[43] Whatever Grant's motivation for taking the part, the pair of them fed off each other comfortably, embellishing whatever humor was in the original script.[44]

Curtis' character in the film was like a jokey version of Sidney Falco.[45] Curtis also imitated Frank Sinatra in a scene. "I loved his skulls," he confided, meaning Sinatra's dumb expression used to indicate confusion. "He gets a quizzical look in his eyes as if to say, 'I didn't quite understand what you said.' So I do that at one point."[46]

Curtis enjoyed the film for its merging of romantic frolics with the idea of Grant trying to run a tight ship while at war with the Japanese.[47] He also valued the experience because his friendship with Grant helped him forget about various problems he was having with Leigh at the time. Leigh seemed blithely unaware of these problems. She regarded the time they spent together on Curtis' free days as equivalent to a "second honeymoon."[48]

Grant was a canny businessman and managed to pocket three-quarters of the profits from the film, as well as gaining sole ownership of it after eight years.[49] When the TV series *McHale's Navy* used footage from it some years later, the ever-vigilant star made Universal pay him a percentage every time the footage was shown.[50] The profit participation deal Lew Wasserman negotiated for his production company (Granarte) on the movie made him the highest paid actor in Hollywood history at that point.[51] Charles Higham contended that it netted him a cool $3 million.[52]

By now Curtis was almost as refined as his sometime hero. "Elegance," he reflected, "is going through all the inelegance of life and finding out why it is. Giving up the easy way and making it the hard way is elegant."[53] After *Operation Petticoat* wrapped he was profiled in a newspaper article called "The Wonderful World of Tony Curtis." The article began, "As a boy in New York he sometimes used to steal the toys his parents were too poor to buy, but last year he made more than $1 million before taxes."[54]

Everything looked rosy in the garden. In eleven years he'd made no less than 34 films. His fan mail averaged 15,000 letters a month, his yearly bill for autographed pictures of himself running to nearly $35,000. A few months ago he'd been voted the most popular actor of 1958. He was earning upwards of $700,000 per movie. He'd also bought some property in California and a share in a basketball team called the Phoenix Suns.

Inside his head, though, the old tensions kept bedevilling him. Between 1955 and 1959 he was reputed to have spent over $30,000 on analysis, visiting his Beverly Hills psychiatrist up to four times a week. Some people thought this was a pose but Curtis needed it. A part of him felt unworthy of his success. (It's interesting to note that Lloyds, his insurance firm, refused to give him accident cover on the set of *The Vikings* because of his much-publicized therapy sessions — some very strange logic.)

Much of the reason for his attending therapy was to try to deal with the guilt he felt over Julie's death. One day his psychiatrist asked him if Julie ever had any other accidents. Curtis suddenly remembered he had. Just a few months before he was killed he'd been knocked down crossing the street. He had to stay in bed for a few days afterwards, as he'd gotten a bump on his head. The recollection of this incident lessened his feelings of culpability.[55]

Therapy gave him an avid listener in a world where few cared:

10. Mixing with the Big Guns

I thought it was wonderful to have somebody to tell those dark and dreadful things I had never told anybody, someone to finally listen to all my problems. To get somebody to be concerned about me for 55 minutes was terrific. How often do you get that in a normal conversation? I would have spilled my guts to anybody with a receptive ear.[56]

This makes for sad reading. The man who was getting all that fan mail, whose pin-up was on teenage girls' bedroom walls throughout the U.S., couldn't find anyone to listen to him without paying them by the hour.

One imagines his conversations with Marco Frym were deeper than all his film scripts put together. The dross continued with *Who Was That Lady?*, yet another frothy comedy with Leigh. The two of them were having more serious marital tensions now, but they seemed to be able to put such tensions on the back burner when they were making movies. Or at least camouflage them. It was their last cinematic pairing and perhaps this was for the best. The fizz seemed to be gone.

Dean Martin was also in the cast. The storyline involved him trumping up a fake FBI identity for Curtis to justify Curtis kissing a woman who wasn't his wife. Such a storyline was so ridiculous that one critic suggested the film should have been called *Who's Kidding Who?* instead of *Who Was That Lady?* The fact that the three of them succeeded in making it half-way credible was a tribute to their comedic powers.

Leigh spent a lot of time with Martin on the set. "She was in denial about the problems we were having," Curtis accused. That was possibly true, or maybe she just needed a break from them. Of Martin, she exulted, "I felt Dean had great depths that hadn't been plumbed. He's a naturally funny and very sweet man with tremendous potential."[57] Martin's lazy style of acting gave him an enviable naturalness. Many viewers thought he was drunk in some scenes.[58]

The film ran out of steam long before the end, as Curtis tried to keep a straight face. "The only way we could get through it was by playing it straight," he stated. This was a ploy he often used in lifeless farces: refusing to mug. "Doing a comedy or doing a drama is the same thing," he said once. "The emphasis may be on another syllable but that is all it is."[59] Actors were as close to laughter as they were to tears, he believed. The trick was to negotiate that nuance depending on which genre one was working in.

The critics were mixed about the movie, *Variety* giving Martin a lefthanded compliment when it said of him, "He strengthens the false impression that he isn't acting at all."[60] He was paid $200,000 for the role. With an expected filming schedule of eight weeks, as one writer surmised, it worked out at roughly the equivalent of what he was earning singing in nightclubs at the time, which was $25,000 a week.[61]

Curtis' next film was *The Rat Race.* This had him playing a saxophonist opposite Debbie Reynolds, with whom he falls in love when they share an apartment. It was directed by Robert Mulligan and scripted by Garson Kanin from his play. Curtis showed how serious he was about the role by learning the saxophone, and playing records between takes that he felt suited his character.[62] Elvis Presley had originally been considered for it but the script described him as a "naive, innocent boy," and studio executives felt he didn't look like that.[63] This seems weird in view of the fact that Curtis was ten years older than Presley.

Michael Munn stated in his biography of Curtis that Sinatra gave him an expensive flute as a gift to help him with his saxophone-playing in the film.[64] Curtis himself wrote that the flute was given to him by Sinatra when he was learning to play it for *Sweet Smell of Success*.[65] This doesn't seem to make sense either. Why would he have wanted it for that movie?

Curtis afterwards embarked on *Spartacus*, another epic in which he only had a minor role. He was again working with Kirk Douglas. It concerned a Roman slave who spearheads an uprising among slave-gladiators against the might of a man called Crassus. The novel was written by the Marxist, Howard Fast. Douglas asked Fast to write a screenplay and brought it to United Artists. When the studio refused it, Douglas could see why. It was like a watered-down version of the novel without the drama.

Douglas now went to the blacklisted writer Dalton Trumbo for help. Trumbo wrote a treatment for him under the pseudonym Sam Johnson, one of many he used so he could put bread on the table without coming to the attention of the HUAC watchdogs.

Trumbo was one of the infamous "Hollywood Ten" screenwriters. He had been indicted in 1947 for refusing to answer questions about his leftwing sympathies. He was cited for contempt of court and served ten months in jail. Upon his release he was blacklisted but carved out an underground career using a number of aliases. He wrote in *The Nation* in 1957, "The studios, while operating a blacklist, were in the market purchasing plays and other material without crediting the authors."[66] Douglas decided to let him use his own name, afterwards priding himself upon having "broken" the blacklist. He was being unduly self-congratulatory here. That distinction belonged to Jules Dassim, who was openly credited for directing *Rififi* in 1954.[67]

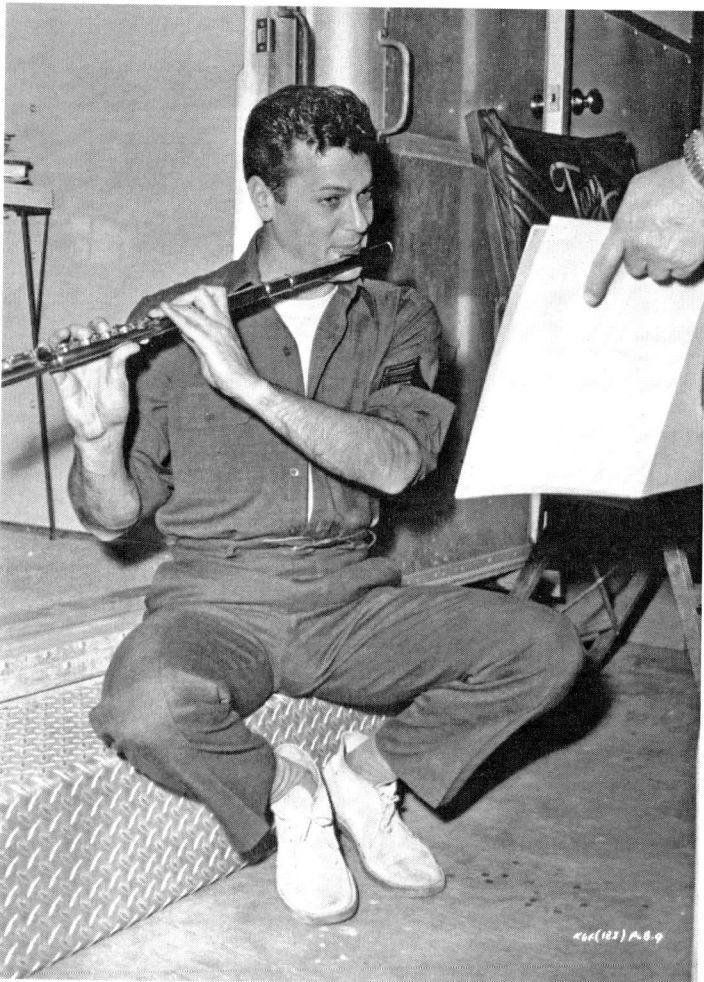

Curtis learned to play the clarinet for *The Rat Race*, Robert Mulligan's 1960 comedy-drama in which he played an aspiring musician sharing an apartment with Debbie Reynolds before they fall in love. Though the film only took 46 days to shoot, Curtis also mastered the saxophone and flute for the role.

The casting of the film was Douglas' next challenge. He pulled off a major coup by recruiting three major league stars: Laurence Olivier, Charles Laughton and Peter Ustinov.

United Artists were contemplating a competitive film about Spartacus called *The Gladiators*, set to star Yul Brynner and to be directed by Martin Ritt. This galvanized Douglas into action. He mobilized all his resources and snuffed out the threat of the other movie, which was abandoned before his own film began.

Brynner's son Rock felt Douglas "beat Yul to the jump" partly because his father didn't make himself available for meetings and conferences in Hollywood due to his other commitments. After *The Gladiators* was shelved, Brynner was furious.[68]

Curtis asked Douglas if he could be in the film. Douglas had some reservations about him but he asked Trumbo to draft up a part he could play. That became the character of Antoninus, the poetic slave.

Douglas liked what Curtis had done in *The Vikings*. Having him in *Spartacus* gave the movie box office security.[69] "There were too many old fogeys in it," Curtis pointed out. "Kirk knew what he was doing by putting me into the mix."

Douglas prepared himself conscientiously for the film but Curtis ribbed him over his hairstyle, which to him looked far too modern. He imagined him going into a Beverly Hills barber and saying, "Give me a crewcut — I'm doing a scene in a Roman arena!" The pair of them also joked about the fact that the script called for Douglas to kill Curtis at the end of the movie. For him this was poetic justice, as Curtis had killed Douglas in *The Vikings*.[70]

Douglas had difficulty finding a suitable director for the film. Anthony Mann was the first choice but Douglas dismissed him after a week, claiming he wasn't up to the challenge. This was unlikely. It's more probable Douglas gave him his walking papers because Mann criticized Douglas' depiction of Spartacus in the film's early scenes, finding him "mongoloid" and "neanderthal."[71] Douglas claimed it was the studio's decision, not his.

In Mann's place, Douglas decided upon the novice director Stanley Kubrick. Kubrick didn't have as much control as he wanted on the film. "When Kirk offered me the job," he commented ruefully, "I thought I might be able to make something of it if the script could be changed, but my experience proved that if it's not explicitly stipulated in the contract that your decisions will be respected there's a very good chance they won't be."[72] But Douglas bit off more than he could chew with Kubrick. In the words of his biographer, John Baxter, he took charge of "any part of the movie that wasn't nailed down."[73] This contradicts Kubrick's version of events.

Kubrick was disparaging both of Fast's novel and Trumbo's screenplay. Both of them had, in his view, everything but a good story.[74] He was aware Spartacus was a minor historical character, the revolt he led not causing quite as many ripples as Fast would have had his readers believe. Fast's novel had also been excessively agitprop. Trumbo thought this diminished its dramatic impulse. He referred to Fast as a "cocktail party communist." He toned down this element of Fast's novel to make it more palatable for mainstream Hollywood.[75] Trumbo's rewrites stretched to a whopping 1400 pages before Kubrick ordered them to be whittled down.

Spartacus was unusual in the sense that it was probably the first Hollywood sword-and-sandal epic that didn't have religious overtones, its main character predating Christ by two generations. Hollywood rarely presents their heroes to us as they were and this was no exception. "They took the sparse historical records of the time," M.J. Trow wrote, "and wove their own wonderful tapestries."[76]

On the first day of shooting, Douglas made a mistake by saying to Olivier, "In film you don't have to do a lot," as if the stage thespian was unaware of the difference between the two mediums. After that the egos started to collide in earnest.[77] Olivier's emotions were confused on the production. He had become alienated from his wife Vivien Leigh and was about to take up with Joan Plowright. His life, he said later about this time, was comprised of "horror of what I'm going through and guilt for what I plan to go through."[78]

Shortly into the shoot Curtis injured himself playing tennis at Douglas' house. He limped off the court muttering to Douglas, "I'm not like you, some goddam Cossack who can ride a horse for ninety hours straight."[79] He was a victim of excessive enthusiasm, being new to the game and trying too hard to impress. It was only the following day when he realized how much he'd injured himself. The pain increased, and he was rushed to Cedars-Sinai hospital where he was diagnosed with a severed Achilles tendon. The doctors had to go all the way up his leg to pull the tendon down and secure it. Leigh said he was "fit to be tied." In actual fact, he was — literally. His foot was placed in a cast for six weeks, which only increased his frustration. "It was harder to keep him under control than Kelly," Leigh sighed.[80] Kubrick, luckily, was able to shoot around him for the duration.

When he'd recovered he anxiously reported back to the set. Here he was duly presented with a scene Dalton Trumbo had written for him. He had to play opposite Olivier in a bathtub. It was the scene for which the film would be mostly remembered. The gay Crassus tries to seduce him by asking him if he prefers snails or oysters, offering the information that he himself is partial to both (as well as the belief that appetites have nothing to do with morals).

The censors immediately decoded Olivier's language, fully aware he was transmitting his bisexuality to Curtis. They suggested the scene might be allowed to stay in if "snails and oysters" was changed to "artichokes and truffles," a ludicrous idea that, thankfully for the film, didn't materialize. But the scene still ended up on the cutting-room floor.

The Production Code Administration jumped all over it, as did the Legion of Decency. "It was killed because of the Legion," wrote Murray Schumach.[81] Geoffrey Shurlock, the chief censor of the time, was unbending in his attitude.

Shurlock strenuously objected to the manner in which Antoninus speedily departs the bathtub after the exchange of dialogue with Crassus, insisting that the reason for his "frantic escape" would have to be "something other than the fact that he's repelled by Crassus' suggestive approach to him."[82]

Curtis was well aware the scene was rife with sexual symbolism, and also that there was no way the censors of the time would allow it to pass. He liked the subtlety of the scene, and also Olivier's restraint. It was like, "Take me out to dinner first. Don't throw me in the tub and drop the soap!"[83] Did it bother him being in a tub with a man like Olivier who was possibly gay? "Not much. It was better than being in one with Fatty Arbuckle!"[84]

Olivier's portrayal of Crassus, wrote one critic, is "everything we expect of a Roman general. With his impossible white armor, riding his impossibly white horse, he is devious, haughty, decadent, perverted and, above all, disgustingly rich."[85] Olivier was an actor who orated more than spoke but here it seemed somehow appropriate.

Peter Ustinov played a slave trader, Batiatus, who tries to wrest control of the government from him. Their confrontational relationship onscreen was mirrored by a real-life rivalry, each trying to upstage the other. Charles Laughton, as the sly senator Gracchus, also fell into this. Simon Callow claimed Douglas sent each member of the cast a version

10. Mixing with the Big Guns

"Shall we dance?" Kirk Douglas clowns with Curtis between scenes of Stanley Kubrick's gladiatorial epic *Spartacus* (1960). Curtis was cast as the poetic slave Antoninus, a relatively minor role which nonetheless had vast repercussions because of a scene he shot in a bathtub with Laurence Olivier. It was excised from the movie by the censors because of gay overtones and not reinstated until 1990.

of the script "in which he or she appeared to have the largest, most interesting part."[86] This is a story corroborated by Ustinov.[87]

Laughton and Olivier had an unusual relationship on the set. Callow painted a vivid picture of their similarities and contrasts: "Laughton envied Olivier's capacity to *do*; Olivier was jealous of Laughton's ability to *be*."[88] Said Curtis, "At times they looked like two old queens, quibbling about the slice of the cake they were about to get."

Laughton was the more temperamental of the two. He accused Douglas of hijacking his role to favor Olivier's. As he continued to sulk over Olivier's grandiose grandstanding, Ustinov bemusedly remarked that the film was "as full of intrigue as a Balkan government in the good old days."[89] Laughton had little cause to carp, though. He earned a whopping $41,000 for a mere thirteen days work.

To Ustinov fell the task of placating Laughton if Olivier tried to step on his lines. Ustinov and Laughton spent a lot of time rewriting their dialogue together, with Kubrick's blessing. Time dragged on and costs mounted. Douglas was constantly late on the set and kept Curtis and the rest of the cast needlessly waiting around.[90]

Callow saw Olivier's performance in the film as similar to a knife, an "entirely linear" experience.[91] From this viewpoint, the suggestiveness of the bathtub scene lent it a much needed layer of color. It also had a historical bearing on the time. "Much sought after were the 'soft' boys sold as cooks, cupbearers and bath attendants," M.J. Trow wrote. Good looks were also highly prized. "Powerful Romans wanted beautiful people around them, and that included their slaves."[92]

When Curtis was asked if he thought Olivier was more partial to snails or oysters himself in real life, he replied, "As far as I was concerned he just liked oysters."[93] He didn't go into the rumors circulating about Olivier having had a homosexual relationship with Danny Kaye in 1950 but he knew they were there.[94] "We didn't talk about anything like that on the set," he said. "We just knew we had a good scene — probably my best. And then the bastards went and cut it out."

The excision of the scene, followed by the slipping away of Antoninus to join Spartacus, doesn't make sense in the context of the film. Vito Russo wrote, "What is lost is all indication of Antoninus' fear of being homosexually involved with Crassus."[95] His departure became meaningless. An opportunity for real drama was lost. What a shame, as the film needed a degree of intimacy. It was over-served with crowd scenes at the expense of this.

Curtis enjoyed working with Olivier. Olivier imparted some advice to him on the craft of acting in exchange for an unusual favor, he told me:

> One day Larry said to me, "How do you get arms like that, Tony?" I said, "Follow me, sir." I led him out of the room. I got him to do push-ups with me every morning after that and he built his muscles up. Not a huge amount but a little bit. I got two ten pound weights and between shots he and I would be working all the time. Then one day I said to him, "All right, Larry, I'm helping you with your arms. I hope you like it." He said, "It's wonderful." I said, "Now I want you to do something for me." He said, "Name it." I told him I wanted him to give me some tips about acting. Then he said an unusual thing to me. He said, "Clothes make the man, Tony. When you look in the mirror, dress as the person you want to be. Keep trying different jackets on until finally you get a look you like and that's the person you'll be." I loved that. He was absolutely right.

The previous year Curtis had had problems with the dresses he was offered for *Some Like It Hot*, dismissing them with the putdown, "They didn't fit right. They puckered up.

I knew this. My father was a tailor."[96] Curtis probably exaggerated Olivier's point about dress. He hadn't meant it to apply to all roles. When Olivier was making *Dracula* with Frank Langella he told his costar Robert Wagner there was "a bit too much [going on] with the cloak." Wagner took this mean that the older actor was fearful of relying too much on props instead of communicating a given character's emotions to an audience.[97]

Spartacus was a tough experience for Curtis but a rewarding one. He liked working with veterans. Their wisdom, he believed, rubbed off on him. He also liked Kubrick's open-ended approach. The opposite of a Billy Wilder, he often transmitted his wishes through expressions rather than words. He refused, as Curtis stated, to "articulate in the grand manner." He was punctilious in his preparation but still allowed for improvisation: "He had us coming in before we were supposed to. An actor would say a line and before he could finish it another actor would say his one. It had a roll and a spill to it."[98]

> One day Curtis told Kubrick his accent had been made fun of through much of his career. Kubrick advised him not to worry. So had his, he mentioned. "It's okay for you," Curtis replied, "You're not in front of the camera." Kubrick laughed at that.

Douglas had a fractious relationship with Kubrick but he still admired his approach. Douglas liked the way Kubrick adapted Trumbo's script in the scene where Spartacus meets Varinia (Jean Simmons). He cut the dialogue out totally, which made the expression of Spartacus' desire for her all the more manifest. Simmons praised Kubrick for being able to direct "on the wing." She told Michael Munn, "It was very difficult for Stanley because he came on at the last minute so he had no preparation with the script."[99] Curtis enjoyed working in what he called this "heel-against-the-head" manner. Because there was nothing set in stone it gave him more freedom than he'd have had otherwise. "Stanley was good enough to step up to the plate in his own style," he praised.

One of the great ironies of Curtis' career is that, while he was most famous for being a ladies man, three of his most acclaimed performances were in films where he was paired with men. He had good chemistry with Burt Lancaster in *Sweet Smell of Success*, with Sidney Poitier in *The Defiant Ones*, and then with Jack Lemmon in *Some Like It Hot*, his third major buddy-buddy movie, as it were. (His scenes with Marilyn Monroe were, of course, hilarious in the latter movie, but it was his double act with Lemmon that's primarily remembered.)

Curtis said about *Spartacus* that it was essentially "the love story of three men": Douglas, Olivier and himself. He always felt that should have been the basis of the movie, not the relationship between Douglas and Jean Simmons: "That's done in all the movies. Sure the guy fucks a girl and makes a baby. Sure our freedom is being trounced on by everybody, black, white, all nationalities or religion. Yet we delicately avoid the physical love between men. We never really discuss those scenes, and if we do they're always salacious and lewd and never really capture the real sense of what we are as people."[100] Kubrick would have been open to Curtis' interpretation of events but not Douglas. He was more interested in a traditional approach. It was like a recap of the situation in *Ben-Hur* where screenwriter Gore Vidal wanted William Wyler to emphasize what he perceived as a gay relationship between Charlton Heston and Stephen Boyd. In the end this became marginalized, much like the Olivier/Curtis scene in *Spartacus*.[101] Said Curtis, "The studio couldn't handle the fact that these three men were in love with each other so they loaded the picture with Spartacus and his wife."[102]

Either due to Kubrick's eccentricity or his inexperience — or both — Douglas was nervous about how the film would fare at the box office. He knew he was facing opposition from diverse camps. Everyone from Hedda Hopper to those who saw him as championing a Communist weighed in with their ten cents worth of huffing and puffing. For Douglas, *Spartacus* was simply a symbol of the evils of slavery, but Joseph McCarthy and his ilk had left a long shadow on the postwar *zeitgeist*. "Don't go and see it," the matronly Hopper barked. "The story was sold to Universal from a book written by a commie. The screen script was also written by a Commie."[103] Notwithstanding such paranoia, the film became a huge hit.

Curtis was only supposed to be in it for twelve days but his participation went on considerably longer than that — and not only because of his tennis injury. The film itself took over a year to complete, Kubrick agonizing over every nuance. One day after five months, Curtis was sitting on a hill with Simmons waiting to do a scene. He came out with the immortal line, "Who do you have to fuck to get off this picture?"[104] (Laurence Olivier, perhaps?)

The repeated delays in shooting disturbed some of the stars more than others. One of Peter Ustinov's daughters was born while it was being made. As she grew up, she often heard Ustinov complaining about Kubrick's fussiness — so much so that one day when a classmate asked her what her father did for a living, she replied without a moment's hesitation, "*Spartacus!*"[105]

11

New Beginnings

Curtis' career had progressed in leaps and bounds since he met Janet Leigh, but Leigh's hadn't, at least until 1960 when she landed a role in Alfred Hitchcock's *Psycho*. When she met the famous director for the first time he told her she'd be expected to be like one of the famous "cattle" he had once compared to actors.[1] Her reaction to this was unusual: "I realized he was in actuality complimenting our profession.... He was proposing a challenge, throwing down the gauntlet to our ingenuity."[2]

Leigh was always upset that people wanted to talk about the famous shower scene in *Psycho* rather than anything else about it, or indeed anything else in her career. She spent much of her time talking about how he avoided censorship difficulties in the scene.[3] People also seemed to have a fascination with asking her if she took showers after it was over. (The answer was no.)[4] She sidestepped the issue of whether Hitchcock used a nude model for it, though she did point out that audiences didn't actually see Anthony Perkins' knife touch her flesh.[5]

The shower scene became as identified with Hitchcock as it did with Leigh. One man wrote to him to say that after seeing the film his daughter was avoiding the shower room so much she was now beginning to smell. The man asked Hitchcock what he should do. The Master of the Macabre replied, "Send her to the dry cleaners!"[6] From another point of view, as Michael Musto observed, *Psycho* was the prototype for the "drag queen as evil murderer" motif which became more prevalent in future movies, far from the innocuousness of films like *Some Like It Hot*.[7]

Curtis admired Leigh's performance but his claim that she "walks away with the movie" was excessive. He believed she was "the only one that brought a kind of brittle vulnerability" to the film. "Everybody else was bigger than life. But there she is, trying to hide the money, fucking a guy in a motel room — so gritty, and at a time when nobody wanted to deal with that or show that; least of all Universal, least of all Alfred Hitchcock."[8] This is an extraordinary claim. He made Leigh, rather than Hitchcock, out to be the person behind the raunchiness.

Leigh never worked with Hitchcock again. For audiences, he told her, she would always be Marion Crane. It's incredible to think the film had such an impact on her career, considering she was only three weeks on set.[9]

It was also a film that was analyzed out of all proportion regarding Hitchcock's motivation for making it.[10] Some critics also used it to poke fun at Curtis. Writing about Crane in the opening scene where she cavorts in a hotel room with John Gavin, David Thomson sniped: "Marion says she has never been married but she has a ripe carnal body and a face that seems to know about sex — even if it was sex with Tony Curtis."[11]

Curtis got to know Hitchcock socially during the shoot and found him amusing. One day Hitchcock told him he had an idea for a movie that involved a parachutist jumping out of a plane. When he reaches the ground he takes off the jumpsuit he's wearing and underneath it is a tuxedo. He walks towards a restaurant in the tuxedo, puts on white gloves, goes in and then emerges as the *maitre d'*. Curtis listened, entranced, to this scenario and asked him what happened next. Hitchcock replied, "I haven't got the rest of it yet!"[12]

Leigh was thrilled to be nominated for an Oscar for her performance. She attended the Oscar ceremonies with a mixture of expectation and dread. When Shirley Jones was announced as the winner (for *Elmer Gantry*), she felt strangely relieved.[13] Both she and Curtis were now bridesmaids at the Oscar wedding. They would stay like this for the rest of their careers.

The double disappointment seemed to amplify tensions between the pair of them in the ensuing months.[14] When Curtis said he was thinking of buying a Rolls-Royce convertible, tensions only increased. Leigh disapproved of them splashing out on such a luxury even though they were both earning good money. Why rock the financial boat, she argued. Curtis demurred; he wanted to enjoy the fruits of his success here and now. Leigh, as always, caved in, stretching their credit limit to the hilt when he got the car.

Curtis said Leigh started to drink a lot after the attention *Psycho* brought her. This placed an added strain on a relationship that was already in deep trouble. They bickered constantly, and Curtis stayed out of the house as much as he could, running to his friend Hugh Hefner — and Hefner's stable of nubile lasses — for solace. "Marriage is hard in Hollywood," Leigh reflected, "but then it's hard everywhere."[15] This knowledge made her want to try harder than her husband. She was in it for the long haul, despite the brickbats.

Curtis' next film was *The Great Imposter*. In it he got a chance to play the multiple roles of teacher, Trappist monk, prison warden, surgeon, dentist and so on. He was cast as the con man Ferdinand Waldo Demara, capturing his versatility admirably in the good-natured romp. The film was based on the Robert Crichton book of the same name. It playfully reenacted the life and wild times of "one of the last sad playboys of the western world."[16]

In Lawrence, the town where he was born, Crichton wrote that there was "no America to melt into. The result was a series of enclaves — islands of each nationality clinging together like barnacles on pier piles — clustering with each other in rows of crowded, rotting buildings."[17] Demara escaped this sense of anonymity by stamping his personality on everything he touched. "I always had the feeling that he was laughing at us," one of his contemporaries related. "Not hard, you know, or nasty, but laughing like he was enjoying a great big secret all his own."[18] Maybe his disguises were a kind of revenge against the staid blandness of Lawrence.

He was a complex character, but, as was the case with Harry Houdini, a Hollywood film about his life could only be allowed to scratch the surface. It would capture him through his stunts rather than the mindset that inspired them. The whys and wherefores of his quixotic behavior were never sufficiently explained. The main brief of Robert Mulligan, the film's director, was to keep things light.[19]

Curtis fortified his relationship with the Rat Pack after the film went into release. His involvement with Sinatra increased when Sinatra lobbied to get John F. Kennedy elected

Enjoying life between scenes of *The Great Imposter* (1961) with costar Sue Ann Langdon. Curtis always regarded this role as symptomatic of his general life as an actor, considering the fact that the character he played, Ferdinand W. Demara, was, like most actors, a chameleon by nature.

to the presidency in 1960. Sinatra's biographer Anthony Summers wrote about him being at Curtis' house in Beverly Hills organizing fundraisers, charging people $50 a head to hear him sing from the top of Curtis' diving board.[20] After Kennedy won the Democratic nomination, Curtis and Leigh threw a party to congratulate him, but he didn't show up for it. This is something Curtis neglects to mention in either of his autobiographies, but Gore Vidal was present at the *soirée*. His account of the dismal scene went as follows:

It was a dreadful evening. Curtis gave an all-star party for the victor and Jack didn't come. There were a lot of tables, about two or three hundred movie stars, and I was waiting there at the main round table where Janet Leigh presided with Frank Sinatra and some bimbo. They waited for Jack and they waited for Jack. Eunice [Kennedy] went to the phone. Came back to report, "He's gone to the movies." Which meant that Jack was off fucking. I looked at Sinatra and it was [like looking at] Attila the Hun. If he could have killed Jack and half the earth he would have.[21]

Kennedy's opponent was Richard Nixon. It was a race that could have gone either way. On the night that Kennedy squeaked past Nixon, Curtis and Leigh held a party at their home to watch the returns. Sinatra turned up as well. The signs looked good as the night wore on, and Sinatra grew increasingly excited. But Nixon refused to throw in the towel, which drove Sinatra up the wall. Leigh remembered him getting drunk and yelling at the television screen, "Concede, you son-of-a-bitch, concede!"[22] He even had a colleague ring the hotel at which Nixon was staying to "encourage" him to do so. But Nixon didn't. It wasn't until the next morning that America knew who its new president was. "Skinny" D'Amato, one of Sinatra's shady night club connections, believed Sinatra won Kennedy the election.[23]

On the night of his inauguration, Curtis met Kennedy. The incumbent president told him he'd enjoyed *The Great Imposter* so much he almost fell on the floor laughing at the scene where Curtis, taking on the role of a dentist, yanked one of Edmond O'Brien's teeth out. It wasn't every day that an actor received a commendation from the President of the United States and he savored the moment.

Curtis knew JFK only slightly. He became better friends with his father Joe. He was having a drink with Joe one night after a game of golf when the phone rang. It was Kennedy calling his father to try out his inaugural speech on him, the one that contained the famous line "Ask not what your country can do for you, but what you can do for your country." Apart from JFK's father, Curtis was the first person in the world to hear that line. Joe pointed the phone towards him as his son was speaking. This was a big moment for Curtis, being privy to history in the making.

In his first autobiography Curtis said he didn't realize the importance of the line at the time.[24] When he wrote his second one, however, it gave him "goosebumps."[25] This is typical of the way Curtis retold anecdotes with different emphases over the years. In the second version he also tells the president-elect that the line impressed him, but in the first he doesn't. It's amazing that somebody would forget speaking to the most important man on the planet on such a night. One imagines that the mischievous Curtis tacked on this last bit in his capacity as creative reinventor of events.

It's surprising that he got along as well with Joe Kennedy as he did. George Jacobs, Frank Sinatra's valet, portrayed Joe Kennedy as rabidly anti–Semitic in a book he wrote on Sinatra. "Kennedy was, if anything, crueler about Jews than he was about blacks," Jacobs wrote. "To him they were 'Sheenic rag traders.'" He referred to the august Louis B. Mayer as a "kike junkman," according to Jacobs, and also told anti–Jewish jokes like, "What's the difference between a Jew and a pizza? Answer? The pizza doesn't cry on its way to the oven."[26]

Election fever over, Curtis wanted Blake Edwards to put him in his new movie, *Breakfast at Tiffany's*, but George Peppard got the part instead. Curtis saw this as disloyalty on Edwards' part. Why hadn't he pushed for him after all they'd been through together? They'd become good friends offscreen as well. "One drunken night," Curtis wrote in his autobiography, "we went so far as to see whose dick was too big to fit through the hole of a 45 rpm record."[27] Unfortunately, such exalted behavior didn't necessarily guarantee one film roles.

Instead he made *The Outsider*, playing Ira Hayes, the American Indian who raised the flag on Iwo Jima at the end of World War II. It was one of his most underrated performances. In some ways it's an autobiographical one. He played a man who suffered for his fame and descended into a vortex of substance abuse afterwards. The difference between them was that Curtis craved fame whereas Hayes instead sought out anonymity.

After raising the flag on Iwo Jima it was all downhill traffic for Hayes. He failed to accommodate himself to civilian life, mainly because the memories of war (and the death of his friend Jim Sorenson) were too heartbreaking. To those who hadn't been in the trenches the war was a noble affair, but for Hayes all it represented was death and dismemberment. His descent into alcoholism reflected that.

One critic thought Curtis' "dedicated and energetic" performance was unable to disguise the fact that he was miscast. He also felt the friendship with Sorenson, played by James Franciscus, was underdeveloped, possibly from fear of a perceived homosexual undercurrent.[28] After Franciscus dies, Curtis listens to a song which contains the words, "Where can you be without me, I thought you cared about me," which suggest something beyond mere grief. Afterwards he wanders into the desert and dies.

A scene from *The Outsider* (1961), one of Curtis' most underrated movies, with Norma Yost. Curtis played Ira Hayes, the Indian who raised the American flag on Iwo Jima. He never felt he received the proper recognition for his performance here, partly because many of his scenes ended up on the cutting room floor.

Sorenson's death was a contributing factor to Hayes' subsequent alcoholism. Curtis' depiction of this was reputed to contain his finest acting, but it was edited out before the film reached the public. If it had been kept in he might well have earned the Oscar nomination he quietly expected for his performance.

Marital discord with Leigh intensified for him after the Oscar hoopla. Kelly saw him crying one day, and he became embarrassed as a result. "I heard tell it wasn't the sort of thing you did in front of your kids. Yet that was the only true emotion I showed to my daughter." It was a release for him, the emotional irrigation of tear ducts — but also an admission of how bad things were.

In May 1961 his friend Jeff Chandler died from complications after back surgery. Curtis took the news badly. Chandler had been with him from the beginning and was a great support valve in times of trouble, like when his father died. Chandler also had great admiration for Curtis' ebullient personality. "He gets a tremendous thump out of everything," he said once. "Such enthusiasm I've never seen."[29]

Three months later Leigh's father committed suicide, which threw everyone's life into turmoil. He had separated from her mother, Helen, beforehand. Helen rang Curtis to ask him to look in on him in his office one day, as she wasn't able to contact him and had become concerned. (Leigh was in Monaco at a Red Cross ball at the time.) When Curtis got to his office he found him dead beside a typewriter. In the typewriter was a note he'd written to Helen. It said, "I hope you're satisfied, you bitch." Curtis took the note out of the typewriter and put it in his pocket, not showing it to the police. As a result they initially believed his death to be the result of natural causes. Fred Morrison never looked like the kind of man to kill himself. Neither Leigh nor Curtis knew he'd been depressed.

To Curtis fell the hard task of telling Leigh what had happened over the phone. Her reaction was unusual. "The waves of the ocean relentlessly washed over me," she wrote in her autobiography, "and I let myself be swept away." This was poetic, but she didn't quiz her husband about exactly what happened. Her thoughts resemble the kind of reflective attitude one might have weeks or even months later, not moments after hearing the news. Her purple prose continued: "How could I find him to tell him I loved him? How could he see the children grow if I couldn't find him to stop him? How could he go away from me?"[30]

Curtis said there were no pills beside his body. Leigh claimed there were. He also said Helen Morrison never saw Fred's note to her. This may have been true, but he also left an "extended and tortured" letter addressed to her blaming her for his torment. This she did see.[31] It traumatized her and cast a huge pall over her remaining years.

Why did Fred kill himself? It was probably a combination of marital strife and stress about money. Having appointed himself as Curtis' financial advisor he overstepped the mark, interfering too much in his affairs. He was also short of cash himself. With Helen he had approached Curtis and Leigh in this regard more than once, and this led to tensions between them. "These are my folks," Leigh pleaded with her extravagant husband not long after a lavish party thrown to celebrate her and Tony's tenth anniversary. "If it was your family you damn well would help."

This hit a nerve with Curtis. He was always telling Leigh they should spend their money rather than hoard it. She was the one who had advocated pragmatism anytime he splashed out on a new car or similar indulgence. "Oh, so now it's okay to spend money," he roared at her. "Not if I want something, but if your dad does, that's all right." This set-to was acted out in front of Leigh's father. He was humiliated. "Jesus," he sighed, "do you think I *like* coming here asking for a loan?"[32]

Leigh's mother moved in with Curtis and herself after Fred died. This made things even worse between them. She needed to be consoled. In her grief she wasn't aware she was intensifying their own growing rift. Leigh and her mother bonded, driving Curtis further into a shell. The marriage built on glitz couldn't hold itself together. Real Life had started to intrude.

Curtis' next movie was the historical epic *Taras Bulba*. It was shot in Argentina. He decided to bring Leigh with him to take her mind off her father's death. This proved to be a bad idea as they really needed to be apart at this time.

She wanted to fly to the location but he didn't. Kelly, Jamie Lee and the pair of them took a train to Miami to begin the first leg of their journey, but in a hotel room in Miami a row broke out between them. It was so fractious that Curtis saw it as the point at which their marriage became irreparably damaged.

Other events conspired to increase the tension between them. One Sunday he was playing with Jamie in an amusement park and he dropped her. She fell awkwardly on her shoulder and broke her clavicle. Then Leigh came down with food poisoning. Curtis himself got a throat infection. Everything seemed to be going wrong so Leigh decided to go home with the children.

Set in 16th-century Ukraine, *Taras Bulba* was produced by Yul Brynner. Brynner also played the role of the eponymous tyrant. Curtis was cast as his son. The film was directed by J. Lee Thompson.

"There was never a film he cared about more," Brynner's son Rock insisted, "not even *The Brothers Karamazov*." But as the shooting progressed he became totally disenchanted with the venture.[33]

The reason for this was "some stupid dialogue and the worst painted backdrops of medieval Poland you've ever seen." The film was also butchered in the editing room to make it short enough to show on a double bill.[34]

There was a clash of egos between Curtis and Brynner from the outset. Curtis had top billing. This angered Brynner no end, as he was playing the more significant role.[35] His anger dissipated somewhat when he was offered an extra $100,000 in his salary. Playing second banana to the upstart from the Bronx didn't seem so bad now.

The female interest was supplied by the 17-year-old German actress Christine Kaufmann. She caught Curtis' eye immediately. Before long they were "an item." Her youth allowed him to be the father figure, a unique experience for him. For once he was the leader rather than the led. She hung on his every word, allowing him to teach her the ways of the world. Bored with boys her own age, she blossomed in this May–December relationship. Curtis became infatuated with Kaufmann's "rosy face, her green eyes, her narrow waist."[36]

He tried to keep his mind off his infatuation with her as the film was being made. It was characterized more by bold flourishes than anything else, but he admired the subdued manner in which Thompson directed the final scene where Brynner shoots him, a little hole in his breast plate marking the spot. Curtis' performance was adequate, but his voice continued to be a sore point with critics. *Time* magazine suggested that his accent would pass as Russian "only when the Gowanus flows into the Don."[37]

The film drew harsh words from the press. Bosley Crowther wrote in the *New York Times*: "It is one of those pictures in which masses of horses and men are the main attractions, and most of the action scenes have been slashed.[38] Brynner agreed. He hated the movie, telling his son, "From here on in I'm just there for the money like everyone else. I can't go on being the only one who cares. I'll just pick up my check and go my way. A great performance in a lousy picture isn't going to get seen by anybody."[39]

The film did well at the box office but much of the money went astray. "I was ripped off on *Taras Bulba*," Curtis told me. "Nobody cared. They didn't give a fuck. That sort of thing happens a lot in this business. After I came off that movie I told the studio, 'I'm not coming back until you guys give me the money you stole from me.' They bumrapped me by telling them I held up the production and that pissed me off too. Everybody uses everybody else for an excuse in this business."

He returned from Argentina by land, taking a train to Buenos Aires and then a boat to New York and another train to Hollywood. Leigh had flown home earlier, as mentioned, because of illness. Their separate itineraries caused tongues to wag about possible problems in the marriage. Curtis dismissed such notions out of hand.

"Janet flies, I don't. It's as simple as that. Except that it isn't that simple. Whenever we go on a trip separately, whoosh, the rumors start. We had a fight. We're separated. We're getting a divorce." He was entitled to say this, as he had a legitimate phobia, but in this case, ironically, the rumors were true. Curtis was never going to admit this. "As a matter of record," he gleamed, putting on his PR hat, "we're better off than we've ever been."[40]

He sounded more convincing when he discussed his flying phobia. It started during his early years at Universal when he made all those personal appearances with Piper Laurie for his first big movie. "They'd have me visiting twenty cities in twenty days, flying in any kind of plane in any kind of weather. I figure I used up all my luck in those days."[41] Famous now and able to afford more leisurely forms of transport, he wasn't going to press that luck.

Curtis' devotion to the teenage German beauty Christine Kaufmann, the woman who broke up his marriage with Janet Leigh, can clearly be seen in this scene from J. Lee Thompson's 1962 historical epic ***Taras Bulba***, which also starred Yul Brynner. Curtis fell in love with Kaufmann on the set, and after the movie was completed he divorced Janet Leigh and married Kaufmann.

Instead he took planes and boats: "A couple of well-placed bucks here and there and I'm locked in a room with all the privacy I want."[42]

He was sleeping with Kaufmann now, their onscreen romance having spilled over into real life. Leigh suspected something but hadn't caught them in the act. "The sneaking around," Curtis wrote in his autobiography, "made our trysts even more romantic."[43] (Only Tony Curtis could use the word "romantic" to describe himself cheating on his wife.)

Back in the States for postproduction, he left Leigh at dawn some days and continued his trysts with Kaufmann at her apartment in Hollywood before the pair of them drove separately to the studio. This he also found "romantic." By now he was resigned to the fact that his days with Leigh were numbered. One of his main concerns was how the public would react to this. If the Golden Couple was sundered, as the gossip press had been whispering about for a decade now, would he be regarded as the culprit? One of his friends even said, "Where am I going to go for dinner if you two divorce?"[44]

Leigh denied there was anything between Curtis and Kaufmann. It wasn't the first time he'd been associated with a leading lady. Rumors about the marriage being in trouble started "while we were cutting the wedding cake. Regularly since then we've been either splitting up or having a baby. One columnist announced my pregnancy every few months for five years. When I finally did get pregnant he wrote, 'Remember, I had it first.'"[45]

In March 1962 Curtis finally plucked up the courage to say to his wife of ten years, "I think we should get a divorce. I don't want to be married anymore." She wasn't surprised but she was still stunned. She expressed it well in her autobiography:

> Even though you know something is coming, and perhaps even understand and agree to a certain extent, when it becomes an actuality it's still a shock. You struggle to cling to the existing state of affairs, yet knowing that state is bankrupt. You go through the motions of denial, of pseudoassurance. It will pass, it will be resolved. But of course it doesn't pass....[46]

So the great love affair was finished, *kaput*, over. After ten and a half years this Cinderella and her Prince Charming didn't live happily ever after.

She wasn't looking for any easy explanations. "If only we could wrap it all up in a neat package and place the blame on one doorstep. Our life had too many doors for that simplicity."[47]

She put her finger on the nub of the issue when she said she married Bernie Schwartz but was divorced by Tony Curtis. He didn't want to be reminded of his past. The new lady in his life knew little or nothing of Schwartz, so she relaxed him. She was part of his reinvention. "Perhaps Christine Kaufmann provided the timely bridge to that other world; she was European, she spoke various languages, and she knew only the new Tony Curtis."[48]

Her thoughts turned to the children. How would she tell them? She didn't want to "scare or scar" them. She preferred to simply say "Mommy goofed." In time they'd make up their own minds about what went wrong. For now she tried to kill any stories that might upset them in the press. "Suppositions ran rampant. Hell, it was a jungle. Only I didn't have Tarzan anymore."[49]

Her reaction to the split seems mature here, but Curtis claimed she tried to take an overdose one night around this time. At her dressing-table he watched her pop 14 sleeping pills into her mouth without stopping: "I hit her really hard on the back so they all flew out of her. It was at that moment I knew the marriage was over."[50]

Just as the image of marital bliss had fed the fan magazines for years, details of their split now provided different kinds of headlines. Curtis was philosophical about this: "If you blew your nose it was news. That's always been the way with my life. I saw the tide turning. That didn't mean I liked it. But I wasn't going to throw my toys out of the pram."

Journalists lined up to give their ten cents worth of "insight" into what went wrong. Was it too much too soon? Money problems? Different careers? The seven (or eleven) year itch? "I shouldn't have gotten married," Curtis admitted, "but there was a lot of things I shouldn't have done. Janet had an *entrée* to everybody in the movies so to me it was very valuable." At the end of the day, "I had a good life with her, and two kids."[51] When he added it all up, that was the only legacy. Eleven years of hype but no nostalgia, both of them now moving on to the next phase. This always seemed to be the case in an industry where most marriages broke down sooner or later — mostly sooner.

Maybe the problem was that they spent too much time with one another. "When we split up it was like Jack leaving Jill. We used to go to work together, come home together, go to a producer's house for dinner together, then go to bed and have five hours sleep."[52] Another problem was the high expectations their fans had of their liaison. Since it was largely acted out in the public gaze, they became, by extension, public property. Allowing themselves to be filmed in so many "The Curtises at Home" spreads gave them a responsibility to live up to the Pleasantville overtones of such stories. The public felt they owned them.

"Hollywood has a history of heartache headlines," Douglas Thompson wrote. "There were marriages that were thought unbreakable and, because of happy-ever-after fan magazine coverage, when they disintegrated, shocked even more. Janet Leigh and Tony Curtis, Debbie Reynolds and Eddie Fisher, Robert Wagner and Natalie Wood."[53] It was like: "How dare you. We made you. You can't do this to us." Such marriages were part of the stock iconography of pop culture; they gave ordinary people a sense of their own permanence writ large. When the plaster temple toppled, everyone seemed the poorer for it.

The question also had to be asked: Were these so-called "unbreakable" marriages all they were cracked up to be? In Fisher's autobiography he wrote about mixing with other glamour couples like Curtis and Leigh in the golden years when they were on the A-list party scene. He ends one paragraph like this: "It was rarely quite as wonderful as it seemed to be when I read about it later."[54]

Curtis liked Fisher but he wasn't sure he could rely on Reynolds. She'd made fun of his accent after *The Son of Ali Baba*, and he also suspected her of being anti–Jewish, though this was unlikely considering she'd married Fisher. He felt she was only friendly to him because she liked Leigh.

When Reynolds and Fisher broke up, most of the public anger was foisted on Fisher. Curtis expected the same fate. For him this was tunnel vision: it took two to tango — or to stop tangoing.

After the Fisher/Reynolds split, Elizabeth Taylor was blamed for "stealing" Fisher from his wife. Curtis felt this was a misreading of the situation. He thought Reynolds and Fisher were finished long before Taylor came along, and Kaufmann could say the same thing about Curtis and Leigh. But the public didn't think like that. There had to be a good cop/bad cop scenario to feed the fanzines their tittle-tattle.

Curtis had been surprised Taylor married Fisher in the first place. He felt she was in a different league. He suspected she went for him because she was in shock from the recent death of Mike Todd in a plane crash. It was as if she was too emotionally fragile to think straight. Fisher was her crutch, but it wasn't really love. (This view would seem to be corroborated by their acrimonious split soon afterwards.)

An added problem for Curtis with the divorce from Leigh was the fact that he was walking out on his two daughters as well. As he packed his bags to leave his home for the last time, Leigh stood in the doorway with Kelly and Jamie in her arms. "She looked pleadingly at me," he said, "which made me feel like a heel. But there was no going back now. I couldn't excuse it. I just knew I had to do it."

Asked what was going through his mind as he prepared to spend the night in a hotel, he replied:

> A crazy thought. When we were making *The Vikings* there was a call one night from London to say Kelly was sick. It was from the nurse that was minding her. Janet and myself panicked. It turned out to be nothing in the end but that night I drove five miles on unpaved roads to get to a phone. And now I was walking away from that little girl. I could never get my head around that.

Neither could the public. They couldn't square the doting father image with a man who was now dating a woman who wasn't even allowed to travel abroad without her mother in tow.[55]

To mitigate the damage to his reputation (and maybe his self-esteem) he was generous to Leigh in their divorce settlement. As well as custody of the children, he gave her half of everything he had, and a Cadillac, to help her begin her new life. She was now dating the stockbroker Robert Brandt, a man he both liked and admired.

Curtis told Louella Parsons he had no immediate plans to marry Kaufmann. She was a lovely girl but he wasn't going to rush into anything. Leigh was also a "wonderful human being." He was thrilled to hear she was about to marry Brandt. They were both being very civilized about the break-up and she was letting him see the children "any time under any condition." He also wished to clear up the rumor that Kaufmann had caused the marital rift: "Janet and I were just not compatible."[56] Parsons might have asked him why it took him eleven years to cotton onto this.

"When you're 18," he assured Kaufmann, "I'll marry you." (He would do exactly that. The fact that she waited for him, in the view of Curtis' later daughter Allegra, must have meant she wanted him as much as he wanted her.)[57]

Despite her maturity, Kaufmann's age gave many people pause. In Germany, where the law was stricter, she was still technically a child. Such a law permitted her parents to confiscate half of her income until she was eighteen. This was a more pragmatic reason for Curtis to delay marrying her. There was also more of a social stigma in Germany than the U.S. regarding a divorced man living with a woman.[58]

Apart from their age there was a culture gap, a religious gap, a family gap and a nationality gap. The only difference in their favor, as Norma Gideon pointed out, was that Curtis was a man and Kaufmann a woman. Curtis added, "You can get pretty good mileage out of that."[59]

Was he flirting with disaster heading into a marriage with a woman he hardly knew, a woman who was so young she hardly knew herself? Deborah Kerr said once, "When a man leaves his wife for a younger woman I always wish him luck—because he's going to need it." To the outside world, Curtis seemed to be throwing away what it took ten years to build up because of an adolescent infatuation.

Kaufmann had been born in Austria in 1945, a time when many of Curtis' fellow Jews were rotting in concentration camps and mass graves. She grew up in Germany, becoming a child actress. Her mother was a trained doctor but she couldn't find work so she took a job as a makeup artist in a film studio to tide her over. Her father was a major in the German Air Force.

She wasn't unduly concerned about the twenty-year age gap between herself and Curtis. It was "neither visible nor important." She didn't care if they got married or not, or if she ever worked again. "Neither marriage nor career interest me," she pronounced, "only life." Because of her own parents' unhappy marriage, the institution had less appeal for her. It was "nebulous."[60]

She saw Curtis and herself as two outsiders against the world. She loved the "creative madness" of his paintings. In many ways it was he who was the child in the relationship: "I was more mature than he was." She was advised not to marry him because she was too cultivated for him. Curtis, in contrast, was perceived as a philistine. "He hadn't read Nietzsche and couldn't speak five languages." Her reaction to this was: Who cares?[61]

There was an irony to Curtis falling in love with Kaufmann, considering she came from the country that had given his ancestors such grief. He would say to his children sometimes in the following years, "In Germany they hate Jews and you're half Jew." Or even, "You've got a Nazi mother!"[62]

Kaufmann's mother, who was anti–Semitic, didn't approve of the liaison. Curtis gave her $10,000 to stay out of his life, and she agreed. He found her father more cordial by far.

In September 1962 Leigh went to Mexico for a divorce decree. She married Brandt the following day. Curtis married Kaufmann in February 1963 in the Riviera hotel in Las Vegas. Kirk Douglas was best man. Afterwards they moved into their luxury house in Coldwater Canyon. (The address would have an ironic relevance when things went sour with them.)

After they got married they surveyed the headlines of the newspaper: "Tony Curtis Marries Teenager." Curtis felt more like the teenager.

Some of his subsequent remarks on her were hilarious: "She's European and she likes being bossed so I boss her. I am a benevolent despot. All men should be locked up until they're 35, and then only allowed to marry 20-year-old girls."[63]

The same columnists who had rhapsodized about everything he'd done with Leigh turned against him with a vengeance after he deserted her. Leading the charge were Rona Barrett and Radie Harris, two ladies Curtis described charmingly as "cancers on the rectum of the [film] industry." When Barrett hinted that she could ruin him he had his press agent threaten legal action against her, so she backed off.[64] But his honeymoon with the media was over. Almost before the ink was dry on his marriage certificate, hacks were sharpening their pens for news of divorce proceedings between himself and his new bride. "How can they last?" went the headlines. "He likes Frank Sinatra and she goes for Bob Dylan."

Curtis was relieved more than angered when Leigh married Brandt. It took the heat off him as the "bad guy" who walked out on the marriage. "She's happier and the kids are [too]," he volunteered. "She's married to a great guy and I don't resent the fact that my kids look up to him and treat me as a happy-go-lucky uncle. If I'd stayed on as I was they'd have maybe made an idol out of me and then found the feet of clay."[65]

Notwithstanding the heartache, it had been best for them to split. They were pulling each other down every which way. The speed with which both of them remarried seemed to underline his point.

Leigh was more cut up about it, being an old-fashioned romantic. "I sometimes think life is like one of my old flicks," she surmised, "because I'm determined there will be that happy ending."[66] To her credit, she found that with Brandt. She was so optimistic that Jamie Lee referred to her as Pollyanna.

Jamie grew up with very negative feelings about Curtis' desertion of the family home. "Bob [Brandt] is my father," she insisted. "He raised me. Tony is my biological father but I never lived with him when I was growing up and I don't remember him very much when I was young. He was like a ghost."[67] Even so, she wasn't able to shake off his influence when she went to boarding school. Here she wasn't Jamie Lee Curtis so much as Jamie "Janet Leigh and Tony Curtis's daughter" Curtis. "I had the longest middle name in the world," she pronounced. "That was the way I was introduced. It went with me everywhere."[68]

Curtis became bitter about Leigh in future years, both in interviews and his writings. "I couldn't be with Janet anymore," he ranted in one unexplained outpouring. "She was disappearing into her own madness." Such obliqueness was countered by the admission, "I married Janet for my career. I realized the two of us could get more attention together. It wasn't enough for a man to be cute. He had to be connected to the right woman."[69] And yet in his autobiography he berated Ray Milland for being "one of the people who subscribed to the theory that I had married Janet Leigh as a career move."[70]

The fan magazines called his marriage to Leigh a storybook romance. Curtis hardly agreed: "I thought: Who are they talking about? Are they kidding me? It was just driving around, going to premieres and parties, dressed up to kill."[71] That was hardly a considered evaluation of over ten years and two children.

Curtis said Leigh did her utmost to turn him into her idea of a gentleman because she found him "crude and clumsy."[72] Elsewhere he admitted having married her for what he termed "fucking privileges."[73] He was working so hard he didn't have time for a relationship so he decided to get married instead. With this kind of mindset it's a miracle they lasted so long together, or that he didn't find a Christine Kaufmann sooner.

Curtis said once, "I didn't marry Christine for her youth, but rather my own one. Janet put an old head on my young shoulders. It wasn't her fault but she made me even more self-conscious than I was before I met her, which is saying something." He always felt she was watching him, "especially when we were out. Did you use the right fork? Who were you talking to? That kind of thing. She probably meant it for my good but for me it was like a continuation of the induction process at Universal — after hours. I never got that with Christine. How could I? She was hardly out of the cradle [when I met her]."

He looked ecstatic in photographs taken with Kaufmann around this time. But even this early in the marriage he made some comments which hinted at problems down the road. Like: "Ten years ago if I'd met her as she is now she wouldn't have given me a second glance." What was he suggesting here — that she only married him for his fame? What was more worrying about the comment was the fact that he seemed to be saying it in a complimentary way about her, as if he defined his own worth by these standards as well. Whatever way one interpreted it, it didn't sound like a great recipe for their future together. It was as if his success was an aphrodisiac. Regarding her acting plans, he said, "I'm not sure. She's been in films since she was five but she doesn't like it. That doesn't mean to say she's going to be a housewife because she doesn't like housework either."[74] Reading between the lines, it sounded like Kaufmann was going to be high maintenance.

Curtis started to focus on different things after hooking up with her. If he married Leigh for self-advancement, that urge was gone now. His present priority was what Fellini called "La Dolce Vita," the sweet life. It had been a struggle to crawl out of the Bronx, and equally to make it in Hollywood. He married Leigh almost immediately after that transition had been realized. He grew up so fast he'd never really had a childhood, and then married without having had time to absorb the great freedom of life as an actor. That freedom was open to him now that he'd grown out of the decade-long life with Leigh.

It had a lot of good things in it, but he was out of that world now. He needed to be more in control, not the small boy sitting at the big girl's table. Kaufmann allowed him to mentor her, a father figure as well as a sex partner. Now firmly established on the Hollywood totem pole, she could take him to the next level. As was the case with Leigh, he asked her to wind down her acting when she was with him. But their relationship, he thought, would be more real than the largely manufactured one with Leigh. (The fact that they'd formed a company together seemed apt testimony to its functional nature.)

"Four years ago," Curtis reflected, "I bought a Rolls-Royce. It cost $24,000 and was the most beautiful thing in the world. For me it was proof I'd arrived, the last word on status symbols. But it's not that anymore: Now it's just a magnificent automobile."[75] He was suddenly starting to talk like a mature man.

Kaufmann retired from acting soon after they got married, announcing boldly to the press, "You cannot be a woman and an actress." This no doubt sounded problematic to the thousands of female thespians around the globe.

Pretty soon she seemed to be speaking in Curtis' voice: "A successful glamour girl becomes a restless, driving individual. She loses her femininity, and eventually her husband."[76] (A further comment, "I don't think I'll be missed," was more to the point.)[77]

Curtis' first post-marital movie was one that never got made at all. He was contracted to appear in a film called *Lady L*. Lew Wasserman had secured a deal in which he'd earn $500,000 and a percentage of the gross. It was to be directed by George Cukor. Cukor wanted Sophia Loren for the lead. The studio favored the younger Gina Lollobrigida. Cukor was unhappy with this. Neither did he like the script that he was presented with. A stand-off developed.

It looked like the film was going to be shut down, which meant Curtis would have lost a lot of money. This was where Wasserman's guile came into play. Not for nothing had Arthur Miller labeled him a "sly eagle."[78] He told Curtis to report for work each day even if nothing was happening. He did this. Cukor, meanwhile, became more frustrated as the days, and then weeks, dragged on.

Lollobrigida knew Cukor didn't want her. She became uncomfortable in his presence. Cukor, for his part, found Lollobrigida both "unpleasant and untalented." Cukor eventually begged off the job, complaining of an ulcer. The production was shut down. It was the first time in his career he'd ever missed work due to sickness.[79]

In his first autobiography, Curtis tells us he was paid "$50,000 a week for ten weeks" on the set of *Lady L*, despite it not being made.[80] In his second one he wrote that he was merely *offered* the money if the film got made, implying that he forfeited it because the project fell through: "And boy, did I need that money. I had painted myself into a corner and I needed to find a way out."[81] This passage comes at the end of him telling us he had huge financial problems after his divorce from Leigh, and being cheated out of a percentage of the profits of *Taras Bulba* by Harold Hecht. It's as if he'd forgotten what he'd told us in his previous book.

Lady L was eventually made with Paul Newman, but it was a fiasco. Newman was cast as a French bomb-thrower. He asked to be allowed to grow a mustache for the part. "I couldn't find even one photograph of an anarchist without a mustache," he grumbled.[82] The search was symptomatic of his general discomfiture in the role. "The film made me aware that I'm stuck in an American skin," he admitted. "I doubt I'll ever play a foreigner again."[83]

Newman's biographer Daniel O'Brien colluded with this view. He thought Curtis would have been better in the role because of his gift for comedy.[84] Curtis contented himself with having made big bucks for sitting on his rear end. Later in the year he filed a Superior Court suit against the studio to prevent them from reclaiming the money paid to him, a move suggested to him by Wasserman.[85]

It kept the wolf from the door, but he would have preferred a good part. His perceived lack of talent still ate at him. He felt like a fraud, a studio product who made it to the top on very flimsy credentials.[86] All he had going for him was a lack of pretentiousness. When people came up to him for acting tips, he replied, "Make faces at your aunts and uncles, hang out with actors to learn what it's like, have little secrets inside of you. And don't go to too many schools. All I learned in actor's school was that there were a lot of actors unemployed."[87]

He now considered making a movie about the life and times of *Playboy* publisher and friend Hugh Hefner. He spent some time in Chicago where Hefner's office was located, discussing the project with him. Curtis thought the movie would work best as a comedy in the style of *The Apartment*, featuring a man who was trying to juggle different girlfriends and prevent them from finding out about one another. Hefner had more grandiose ideas in mind.

Far from producing a sitcom in "French farce" mode, Hefner wanted to use the movie to intellectualize sex, an ambition Curtis transmuted into the phrase "Dostoevsky in the nude." Hefner wanted the film to be six hours long. This was obviously never going to work with a major studio. When Curtis received voluminous drafts of the script from Hefner he began to go cold on the idea. "I don't even have to read them," he exclaimed frustratedly. "I just have to *weigh* them to know we're never ever going to make this movie."[88]

Hefner was disappointed by his reaction. He saw himself as the Moses of Permissiveness, leading America out of the Dark Ages of fifties chastity into the enlightenment of dropping out, tuning in and getting high — an ambition that seems positively quaint today.[89] Curtis agreed broadly with Hefner's viewpoint but was practical enough to know that even if the American public was willing to embrace his saucy credos they wouldn't have wanted them rammed down their throats over six hours of permissiveness.

Hefner's treatment was rejected. It was replaced with a more accessible studio one, which Hefner in turn rejected. After much to-ing and fro-ing the project was abandoned, mercifully. But Hefner continued to publish his magazine to enthusiastic denizens of the New Morality (or, as the "bluenoses" would have it, *lack* of morality) for the next half century. Curtis also kept up his friendship with him. He appeared at his mansion from time to time and was hardly impervious to the charms of the scantily-clad ladies who appeared in its corridors, or their willingness to get up close and personal with him.

This was a transitional period in Curtis' life, and not only because of his new wife. After abandoning the Hefner project he started to paint more. The activity seemed to enable him to tap into the bohemianism he now craved.

He exhibited one of his paintings in Barnsdall Park in Los Angeles in May 1961, but its abstract nature didn't impress everyone. Dick Williams, the entertainment editor of the *Los Angeles Mirror*, huffed, "I was gratified to discover I'm not the only 'square' when it comes to abstract paintings. The Holly woods are full of them. Nobody could figure what Tony was up to." Producer William Perlberg, Hollywood's leading Picasso collector, suggested it should have been called "Sunrise at Campobello," but Williams preferred the more mundane "Spilled Eggs in a Greenwich Village Alley." This kind of philistinism didn't impress Curtis. He snapped back, "If anybody else asks what it is, I'm going to cut off my ear like Van Gogh."[90]

He wondered where his movie career would go from here. He needed money to support Kaufmann and also something to stimulate himself. He knew he'd lost many of his fans after the break-up with Leigh. Wasserman had also cooled towards him after the divorce.

When Wasserman bought Universal in 1962 it was near bankruptcy following the huge popularity of television and the consequent diminishing returns in theaters across the country. The film business was changing. Could Curtis count on its security anymore? He didn't know. Would he ever find an agent as good as Wasserman? He doubted it.

Other things were changing too. At the beginning of 1962 the relationship between Frank Sinatra and John F. Kennedy broke down. In January, Peter Lawford rang Sinatra to tell him JFK was coming to California on a political trip and wanted to know if he could stay at Sinatra's Palm Springs house for a few days. Sinatra was over the moon at the prospect but then Kennedy changed his mind, Sinatra's alleged connections with the Mafia proving too much of a hot potato for the new president. Sinatra was livid at the snub.

In August of that year, Marilyn Monroe was found dead in her bedroom from a suspected overdose. A flood of rumors circulated about her being murdered by the Mafia, the Kennedys or the CIA. There was even a theory she was murdered by the administration of a Nembutal suppository.[91] Conspiracy theorists had a field day rewriting her life story. Then the resurrection came, and her canonization. As Billy Wilder put it, Monroe became Hollywood's Joan of Arc, "our Ultimate Sacrificial Lamb."[92]

Curtis speculated:

> When you look at the condition of the room she died in, it's not hard to see the state she was in herself at that time. Here we had the sexiest girl in the world going home to this dumpy room. There are those who would say that the place you go back to is the person you are. I don't hold totally with that but it was a sign. And yet people still tell us she was murdered.

The last time he saw her was at Peter Lawford's beach house not long before she died. The old Marilyn was gone; she'd lost her ju-ju. Their conversation was flat. She asked him about an old car he had, a green convertible. He told her ominously that it was "in Buick heaven."[93] They didn't have too much to say to one another. He felt worried about her, but he didn't think there was anything he could do for her. She looked like "death warmed over."[94]

Curtis believed Monroe wouldn't have been as plagued by her demons if she wasn't so endearing. "Somebody would have put her away somewhere, or she'd have settled down someplace where these terrible tensions and power struggles would have just bypassed it."[95] Being the most popular actress of her time, he thought, "bent" her. He felt she died because she was "fulfilling her personal life in the press."[96] He would have known all about that as a result of his very public marriage to Janet Leigh.

Curtis told Charlotte Chandler he thought Monroe's main problem was the fact that she'd been robbed of her childhood by her unhinged mother, leading to all those years in foster homes. "Marilyn didn't know how to play," he said during the shoot of *Some Like It Hot*. "She always seemed tense and intense, afraid of a shadow, especially her own. Sometimes she would talk this baby talk, but a girl who looked like that had to know a lot." This is a *non-sequitur*, but one grasps his meaning. He concluded that she had a kind of "voluptuous naiveté."[97]

It might sound strange to say it, but he was probably more upset by the death of another star that year, Ernie Kovacs. Kovacs had died in January after losing control of his car while under the influence of drink. He'd been a great friend to Curtis and also shared Hungarian roots with him. They used to play poker and gin rummy together in his Beverly Hills home. Kovacs nearly always lost but never minded. A larger-than-life personality, he basically drank himself to death. Curtis missed him terribly. Leigh also took the loss hard, referring to him as a genius in her autobiography.[98] She also mentioned him in her novel *House of Destiny*, seeming to ally his death with that of another famous Ernest — Ernest Hemingway, who also self-destructed after a lifetime of excessive drinking.[99]

Another tragedy Leigh documented in her novel was the assassination of John F. Kennedy, transferring the shock of the event onto her characters.[100] Surprisingly, she didn't go into this in her autobiography, nor did Curtis in either of his. Considering both of them campaigned for him, this was strange. The fact that he was assassinated on Jamie Lee's fifth birthday may have had something to do with their silence on the matter. (Christine Kaufmann was also told she was pregnant with her daughter Alexandra on the day of the assassination.)[101]

Sinatra was shooting a scene in *Robin and the Seven Hoods* when he received the news. He had a mixed reaction to it, his natural feelings of grief undermined by a carry-over of the old anger he felt at Kennedy for having snubbed him after being elected. He'd been shooting a scene in a Los Angeles' cemetery earlier in the day and had ominously spotted a headstone marked "John F. Kennedy."[102] When he heard what happened, he left L.A. for Palm Springs and drowned his sorrows in Jack Daniels. He wasn't invited to the funeral. His wife Barbara said he locked himself in his room to try and deal with the tragedy, much as he'd done the previous year when Monroe died.[103]

Janet Leigh had just made her last great movie at this time, but, as was the case with *Psycho*, it had negative repercussions for her. She didn't appear in *The Manchurian Candidate* until half-way through (the corollary of her *Psycho* experience) and wasn't central to the action, but it was still a quality performance from her. The film featured Laurence Harvey as a brainwashed war veteran and Frank Sinatra as the man who tries to stop him shooting the president of the U.S. It was because of this that Sinatra ordered it pulled from circulation after Kennedy was assassinated.[104] Leigh regarded it as her most challenging role. As director John Frankenheimer said to her, she had only twenty seconds to grab the audience's attention, the characters of Harvey and Sinatra already having been established when she finally appeared.[105]

Curtis watched Leigh's career rise and fall as he tried to morph into his own new identity. The new decade had begun strangely for him: the divorce from Leigh, the death of Monroe and the assassination of JFK all affected him in significant ways. Suddenly nothing seemed the same anymore. Where would his relationship with Kaufmann go from here? Or his career? He was heading into *terra incognita*.

12

Lightweight

For much of the sixties Curtis seemed content to immerse himself in mindless fluff, appearing in a string of sex comedies where he played what Alexander Walker referred to as "the playboy hero." Walker summed up this character succinctly: "From the composite picture provided by Rock Hudson, Frank Sinatra, Cary Grant and Tony Curtis at one time or another, he is handsome, oversexed, promiscuous and sophisticated, able to telephone two girls simultaneously and woo each with the same amorous monologue, and adept not only at taking a girl for a ride but also encouraging her to pay for the gas and leaving her feeling it was a privilege." According to Walker, the playboy hero only has one fear: "A castrating apprehension of marriage, the tender trap."[1]

Curtis didn't take to the sex comedies with any great relish in the beginning, preferring movies that ended with only the suggestion of the boudoir, with "glistening eyes and a long yearning kiss."[2] But as the decade went on he was made aware of the fact that this was the way the industry was going, that such fare was all that was available to him.

He joined a select band of handsome stars who acted as safe but desirable bets for the professional virgins of the burgeoning film industry. The smart money was behind "the bubbling teenage Cinderella, a new genre of heroine who bounced from the high school prom into the conjugal bed as fast as she could wrap her bridal veil around Tony Curtis, Tab Hunter, Rock Hudson, Robert Wagner or, later, Troy Donahue."[3]

Before the decade took him over with such fluff he had a few varied roles which stretched him in different ways. In *Forty Pounds of Trouble*, a remake of *Little Miss Marker*, he made the most of his role as a softhearted casino manager bonding with a young girl left with him as a bookie's marker. He would also like to have bonded with his pretty leading lady, Suzanne Pleshette, if Kaufmann hadn't entered his life. Shortly after filming ended he received a phone call from the director Richard Quine asking him if he could do a few days on a comedy called *Paris When It Sizzles*. He was to cover for William Holden, who was drying out from a bender and couldn't do his scenes with costar Audrey Hepburn.

Hepburn had made *Sabrina* with Holden years before. They were thought to have had an affair on the set. Holden was married to Brenda Marshall at the time but said of Hepburn, "I was determined to wipe Audrey out of my mind by screwing a woman in every country I visited."[4]

Holden had been apprehensive about making the film from the moment he touched down at Orly Airport in Paris: "I realized that I had to face Audrey and that I had to deal with my drinking. And I didn't think I could handle either situation."[5] He was right on both counts. He drank almost nonstop, sometimes resulting in Quine having to shut down the production. Holden sniffed around her like a puppy dog, craving even the tiniest trickle of affection. If she gave it, it led to the expectation of more. If that wasn't forthcoming he grew morose and sank into a haze of booze and self-pity.

The plot had him as a screenwriter acting out movie fantasies in an attempt to finish a script. Hepburn played his secretary. Curtis had a few scenes written in for him to be shot as Holden dried out. He played one of those hippy-dippy sixties characters prevalent in movies at the time, all bluff and jargon. He seemed to enjoy the experience, but the film itself was a disaster. Quine himself must have realized this as it wasn't released until two years after filming wrapped. *Paris When It Flops* might have been a more appropriate title.

Michael Freedland commended Curtis for his neat satire of a "self-important, vainglorious and frivolous young actor," and for giving the film some of its funniest moments.[6] Curtis' beatnik crowing of lines like "Tut a lur, baby" (a loose Bronx rendition of the French for "See you later") went down a treat with reviewers, as did his wheat-colored Levis.[7]

Kaufmann was making a movie in Munich at this time, and Curtis went over to see her after finishing *Paris When It Sizzles*, driving to Germany in a car he'd bought in London. In between scenes they sat in the car together and chatted and then he went back to his hotel. One morning the doorman of the hotel took him aside and told him the exhaust pipe of the car had rags stuffed into it. The rags had been tightened with masking tape. Curtis was aghast. He suspected some neo–Nazis were trying to murder him. The weather was so cold he often fell asleep with the heater on while waiting for Kaufmann. If his suspicions were right, the vigilant doorman could have saved his life.[8]

His next movie was *Captain Newman M.D.* It was loosely based on the life of the psychiatrist Ralph Greenson. Gregory Peck essayed the title role. Curtis played Jackson Laibowitz, a wacky orderly working for Newman. Angie Dickinson was Newman's nurse. Other roles were played by Eddie Albert and a then-unknown Robert Duvall. The singer Bobby Darin also appeared in a minor part.

Steve Blauner, Darin's agent, originally wanted Darin to play the Curtis role, but he accepted the fact that Curtis was hired instead. "I couldn't quibble with that," he sighed resignedly. "Tony Curtis is ten times what Bobby Darin is worth."[9] Such humility was followed up by a request that Darin take a smaller role, that of the shellshocked Jim Tompkins. The studio didn't think they could afford him, but Blauner offered him for a modest $25,000 and the offer was accepted.

It proved to be a judicious decision. Darin didn't have much screen time, but Tompkins was an interesting character, a guitar-strumming Southerner who covers up his remorse over not rescuing a friend who was decapitated by the Nazis during the war by drinking too much and sublimating it in music. Newman finally succeeds in getting him to confront his guilt by injecting him with the truth serum sodium pentathol. Curtis thought Darin overacted horrendously, but Darin still earned an Oscar nomination for his performance. It was a decision that bewildered Curtis. The critics were mixed about his portrayal. Bosley Crowther commended him in the *New York Times*, but the *New York Herald Tribune* found his behavior under the sodium pentathol embarrassing.[10]

Curtis talked to Joseph Finnigan of the *Milwaukee Journal* about the way he was feeling about life in general after the film went into general release. From the way he spoke it was clear he was still finding it difficult to slough off his past. "Everybody has that little kid inside them," he attested, "and mine is a kid who walked the streets of New York. I'm paying off that kid. He's going to Europe first class [to] look at a Picasso. That kid is always with me. He reminds me when I'm wrong and pats me on the back when I do something good. For years people told me I didn't know anything, didn't have anything and wouldn't get anywhere. Well, here I am."[11]

He seemed to need to prop himself up like this all the time, and to tell people fame hadn't changed him: "My relationship with people would be the same if I were a butcher." One couldn't help feeling this was true, especially when he followed it up with the self-deprecatory, "I'm more surprised than my enemies that I made it." Now that he had, he was able to say, "This is a nice gravy train trip, I'll ride it till they kick me off."[12]

His next few films were lackluster. He had a brief cameo in John Huston's whodunit *The List of Adrian Messenger*, one of the great director's rare misfires. The gimmick was that Curtis and a bevy of other stars would appear in disguise — including drag — and stir the brew. But having Curtis, Frank Sinatra, Burt Lancaster, Kirk Douglas, Robert Mitchum, George C. Scott and Dana Wynter on the same set doesn't automatically ensure chemistry. The removal of the disguises is about as good as it gets, suspense being sorely lacking.[13] Douglas is the killer, if anyone cares. Most viewers contented themselves with engaging in a "Guess who that is?" exercise in the absence of anything more stimulating to think about.

Curtis now made a film with Kaufmann, carrying on the husband/wife scenario that worked so well with Leigh, at least in their early films. This was less felicitous, a spoof called *Wild and Wonderful*, which was neither. It was set in France but filmed on a backlot which looked like ... a backlot. The plot concerned a French poodle, which ended up giving the film's best performance. (This was only right, as the poodle was a star in France.) Curtis was as breezily confident as ever but Kaufmann looked miscast, her delicate features aligning themselves more with emotional roles. The film had three screenwriters, in itself a worrying sign.

Goodbye Charlie, which followed it, seemed to have more potential. It told the story of a gangster who dies and comes back to life as a woman. She passes herself off as the gangster's widow and proceeds to bribe the women he slept with. Curtis played a friend of the gangster who's simultaneously horrified by the reincarnated hood (played by Debbie Reynolds) and attracted to her. It was based on a George Axelrod play that had run on Broadway to lukewarm reviews. It was directed by Vincente Minnelli and featured supporting roles by Pat Boone and Walter Matthau. Marilyn Monroe had been considered for the lead role when the project was first set in motion in 1961. She pulled out when George Cukor, who was set to direct it, began to have problems on the set of *Lady L*, as mentioned.[14]

One critic regarded *Goodbye Charlie* as the apotheosis of a predominant trend in sex comedies of the sixties whereby "the man gets weaker and more febrile or impotent while the woman gets more masculine and dominant."[15] This was true, but Reynolds didn't have the dynamism to properly enliven the role. In her autobiography she wrote about having difficulty with a kitchen scene with Curtis which involved her holding coffee, orange juice, eggs and toast and only having two hands. She asked her friend Agnes Moorehead how she should solve the problem. Moorehead came up with the suggestion that she play the scene with the toast in her mouth. The fact that putting toast in her mouth while delivering a speech to Curtis remained her abiding memory of the film perhaps tells us all we need to know about her attitude toward it.[16]

Kaufmann also appeared with Curtis in Michael Anderson's *Wild and Wonderful* (1964), a frothy comedy about a French poodle. It was set in Paris but made in Hollywood. It ushered in a decade of like-minded fare which bolstered Curtis' bank balance if not his credibility with top-flight directors.

Reynolds only took the part because she wanted to work with Minnelli. He didn't think she'd be up to the challenge of playing it, envisaging her as "too crass and uneducated to tackle the complexity of a man reincarnated as a woman." Reynolds had the opposite problem, seeing her character as a "one joke" contrivance.[17]

The production values were shoddy, most of the film being shot in the studio. This, as Emanuel Levy observed, "underscored the tale's claustrophobic staginess." Curtis did his best with lines like, "It's as if I've been a gourmet all my life and suddenly I'm a lamb chop," but the fact that Axelrod hammered home the same point about a chauvinist's reform time and again — Charlie now finally realizing what it means to be a woman — meant that Reynolds' reference to the material's thinness militated against him taking it on to another level. One writer intoned wearily, "As his new self, Charlie is even duller than the male he was."[18]

Curtis liked working with Minnelli. He admired his perfectionism almost as much as he had that of Kubrick and Wilder. Minnelli also liked Curtis, appreciating the way he was underplaying the role. Reynolds, on the other hand, annoyed Minnelli with her histrionics. An atmosphere developed between the pair of them. One day she came on the set and chirped, "Good morning, everybody!" She then asked Minnelli, "How was that for you, Vincente?"[19] It was like a re-run of the line Wilder fed to Paula Strasberg on the set of *Some Like It Hot*. The film was a critical disaster. It also did poor business at the box office. For Curtis it was yet another case of a quality director failing to deliver for him.

He had greater hopes for *Sex and the Single Girl*. This had him as the editor of a sex magazine trying to seduce a psychiatrist (Natalie Wood). It was supposedly based on the Helen Gurley Brown book of the same name, but the connection was merely cosmetic. Henry Fonda and Lauren Bacall costarred as a bickering couple.

Brown's book had been published to some notoriety in 1962. It dealt generally with the idea of women using sex as a weapon to get what they wanted from men. She seemed to be carrying on where Alfred Kinsey had left off in the previous decade. Elaine Tyler Mae remarked that Kinsey had become aligned in the public imagination with "other postwar" threats like homosexuality and Communism among the "family value" contingent who preached monogamy and women's subordination.[20] Brown didn't have to undergo taunts like this, but she still felt Kinsey's work needed to be elaborated upon. Maureen Dowd once called Brown "the perfect twin" to Hugh Hefner, and the analogy held up.[21]

Her book was written in a fast-paced style which engaged the reader immediately. She documented the importance to women of men, money, work and sex — though not necessarily in that order. She refused to see men as the enemy, preferring a policy of peaceful coexistence. If men made the rules, she argued, women could at least manipulate them.[22] She accepted the concept that, for many husbands, monogamy was monotony. "Man is not monogamous," she wrote, "no matter how much religion and social rites tell him he is. You don't like your adorable Persian kitty dragging a maimed half-alive pigeon into your living-room, but that's the nature of Persian kitties."[23]

She didn't disapprove of divorce but believed in saving marriages even when errant husbands were involved, a distinctly unfeminist notion. "A wife," she wrote blithely, "if she is loving and smart, will get her husband back every time. He doesn't really want her not to. He's only playing."[24]

Apart from Kinsey there were two female authors in the fifties who'd rocked the U.S. with steamy tomes. Rona Jaffe's *The Best of Everything* and Grace Metalious' *Peyton Place* predated Brown. One of the central tenets of Metalious' book was that "Women wanted sex and enjoyed it, that sex was not something [they] simply acquiesced to."[25] This was in stark contrast to the mindset of *Life* magazine in 1957, which not only denied the single woman sex but also a career.[26] Sex was natural and therefore good, Brown argued, but there was much more to it than sexual intercourse: "It begins with the delicious feeling of attraction between two people. It may never go further, but sex it is."[27]

She had much to say about matters outside the *boudoir* as well. She urged women to work hard, whether they were secretaries, flight attendants, *Playboy* bunnies or corporate executives.[28] Her secret was that she appealed to all age groups, a characteristic captured by a *New Yorker* cartoon which pictured a teenager trying to buy her book from a middleaged clerk but being refused because she was too young. "Don't worry," the teenager assured the harassed clerk, "it's not for me, it's for my mother."[29] The book was banned in both Ireland and Spain but went on to enjoy robust sales in 35 countries, despite people like Norman Vincent Peale dismissing it as "one long glorification of indiscriminate sex."[30]

Warner Brothers bought the film rights for $200,000 but once they'd paid the money they didn't know where to go next. One studio executive complained that the book had no plot. He was right, but Brown never laid claim to one, the book being non-fiction. "I told you that $100,000 ago," producer Saul David replied.[31] The next step was to find a screenwriter who could conceive one. Joseph Heller, hot off of *Catch-22*, was brought on board.

He decided to adapt Joseph Hoffman's *How to Make Love and Like It* instead of the Brown book. This was good thinking, but it meant Warners had basically paid $200,000 for a *title*. This worked out at $40,000 per word, an expensive purchase by any standards. One wondered if Hoffman's title wasn't just as eye-catching. (It would also have been significantly cheaper.)

Heller started work with a colleague called David R. Schwartz (no relation to Curtis). He was offered a staggering $5000 a week to rework the script after another screenwriter who'd first been offered the job failed to do much with it. He was advised to "spice things up" with a car chase.[32]

He duly obliged, but he was confused. It would have been more usual to be given a film about cars and then asked to "spice things up" with some sex. Still, at $5000 a week, he didn't want to ask too many questions, as the studio was growing increasingly nervous about their high-priced (and, to some, directionless) commodity. The eventual car chase, in one writer's view, was extraneous to the story "but all the more welcome for that."[33]

When the film finally reached cinemas the credits left many audience members confused. They went: "Based on the book *Sex and the Single Girl* by Helen Gurley Brown. Screenplay by David R. Schwartz and Joseph Heller. Story by Joseph Hoffman." Brown wisely laughed her way to the bank, remaining far away from the studio. "You should leave movies in the hands of people who know what they're doing," she advised.[34] But did they? "They paid a king's ransom for a white elephant," Curtis concluded.

Wood told Heller she hated the movie, only taking it because she was contractually obligated to do so. Heller thought she had a natural gift for comedy but subjugated it to become a quote-unquote "serious actress." Curtis told Heller he took the part because he needed the money for his divorce. "That's what I like best about the movie industry," Heller carped, "the art and idealism."[35] One imagines he could have written a good book on this theme (*Catch-23*?).

In order to seduce Wood, Curtis feigns sexual inadequacy, a reprise of the acute shyness his character evinced in *Some Like It Hot*.[36] The difference here is that it's the woman who has to be stimulated. This isn't too difficult. As Alexander Walker pointed out, the simple act of itemizing the erogenous areas of his body acts as an aphrodisiac for her.[37]

The film worked well as a satire on psychology in the early scenes but afterwards degenerated into farce as the question of Wood staying a virgin took center stage.[38] Today it looks tame, many of the innuendoes having been toned down to avoid censorship problems.[39]

Wood's biographer, Gavin Lambert, alleged that Wood didn't like Curtis here any more than she did on their previous movie together, *Kings Go Forth*. He contended that she found him "aggressively self-important."[40] There's no evidence to support this view. In his autobiography Curtis tells us he enjoyed a very friendly relationship with Wood on the set of both movies, though he did once remark obliquely of her, "She would have been much happier as a nun or a hooker."[41]

The reviews were harsh but fair. *The New York Times* slammed it for reinforcing stereotypes about strong women who secretly wanted a man, and unfaithful women who wanted strong women to prevent them from straying. The finest scene, the newspaper rightly pointed out, had the two main leads "yammering about love and Freud at a zoo, tiredly watched by monkeys and baboons."[42] This was funnier than the so-called racy scenes, which seem "pathetically coy" to a post–*Sex and the City* audience.[43]

Curtis made "secret little pilgrimages" back to the Bronx at this time. As he revealed to Earl Wilson, "I stop the car a block away [from where I'm going] and walk a mile for my memories. I always pick out some spot to revisit. The other day I found my initials in cement on Prospect Avenue. In 1937 they were re-doing a school there. Some of us snuck in under the fence and scratched our initials. I found mine there. B.S. for Bernard Schwartz."[44] Sometimes he ran into old friends from his childhood. "What are the dames like in Hollywood?" they asked him. "No different from the Bronx," he replied.

On one trip he dined at Sardi's. He once sold newspapers outside the door. Now he wore a tuxedo and got the best table in the joint. Who would have believed it, a guy from "the curb" making the big time?

Sometimes he ran into Elvis Presley on the Paramount lot. He remembered Elvis as being shy with him. He thought the singer might have looked up to him the way he himself had once looked up to Cary Grant. There was always somebody who went before you that formed you in some way — or in many ways.

He shared a lot in common with Presley apart from the hairstyle. They were both born on the wrong side of the tracks and both became sex symbols. This made Hollywood not take them as seriously as they might have wished, leading them to settle once too often for the almighty dollar when a superior script might have paid more long-term dividends. They both also harbored ambitions to emulate Marlon Brando's brooding genius before becoming manacled in more wholesome fare.

One day Curtis was going for a walk around the lot when the door of a camper opened and Presley appeared. He reached down to Curtis, took his arm and said, "Mr. Curtis, won't you please come in for a minute? I've been a fan of yours since I was a kid. I want you to meet my buddies." Curtis went into the camper and was introduced to Elvis' entourage, the self-styled Memphis Mafia. Elvis said, "What a joy, what an experience, Mr. Curtis, to finally meet you." Curtis replied, "Excuse me, please, don't call me Mr. Curtis, call me Tony." Presley agreed and called him Tony. Then Curtis said, "And what shall I call you?" Presley thought for a second and then said, "Call me Mr. Presley!"[45] Curtis enjoyed Presley's sense of humor (not often commented on by writers). After this exchange he began to see him more like a brother than an icon. (Who would have thought he'd outlive Presley, who was born ten years after him, by over thirty years?)

When Curtis accused Presley of "stealing" his hairstyle, Presley in turn accused Curtis of taking *his* part in *The Defiant Ones*. He told Curtis he liked him in that movie. Curtis said he liked Presley in *King Creole*. "Maybe we needed to pat ourselves on the back," he said. "Nobody else was doing it. When I got to Hollywood first, people said, 'They've finally found an actor worse than Elvis Presley.' Why did people come out with stuff like that? Who was it helping?"

Curtis and Presley didn't quite become friends. "He always had an army of people around him. I don't know why. He didn't need it. Maybe he was trying to make up for something that was missing in his childhood. I tried that for a while but it didn't get me anywhere. You lose yourself."

Asked if he would like to have made a movie with Presley, Curtis replied, "Definitely. The critics mightn't have liked it but we'd have drawn some crowds." How did he feel about the way Presley died? "It could have been me. It *should* have been me. Elvis got caught up in the same stuff as I did. We didn't talk about it but I read he started popping pills in the army to keep himself awake on the red eye shift. I took uppers too. They were a gateway to what happened later. Elvis thought that if something came from over the counter it couldn't kill you, but they all kill you." Curtis' general feelings about Presley were similar to those about his own career. Hollywood had guillotined him by downplaying his talents. Basically he believed Presley failed because he made acting look too easy.[46]

In the spring of 1964 Curtis gave a dinner party for cinema's elite. A top national magazine photographer called to ask if he could bring his camera and join the group. Curtis said no, despite the photographer's assurance that the pictures would be featured in a multi-million-dollar-selling publication. "Ten years ago," he teased, "you'd have been happy to let me cover you on the way to the john." Curtis replied, "Ten years ago I really thought people were interested in my going to the john."[47]

He'd changed in the interim. He was less media-hungry now. Years in the artistic abyss had made him more sardonic, less zesty. He could afford to pick and choose his handlers now. Challenging opportunities were bypassing him, and he was becoming more philosophical about that fact, relaxing into a groove. "It took a while," he said, "but it finally dawned on me that there was no correlation between job and party offers. I stopped going to parties when I couldn't decide whether it was duller and more stupid listening to myself talk or listening to other people talk to me about themselves."[48] The old adage about movie deals being made on golf courses or in fashionable homes rather than studios didn't seem to be true anymore. Everything was tightening up—which meant more early nights for Curtis, and less obsequiousness.

Kaufmann had caused part of the change in his attitude. "She brought a genuine desire for learning into my life," he allowed. "I began to experience the true pleasure there was in listening to a symphony [after meeting her], or reading a good book." Such a transformation had made him less pushy, less grasping. He gave an example of a recent incident when the studio rang and asked him to come in and pick up a $50,000 check. Instead of going in, he asked them to mail it to him: "Ten years ago I picked up all my own checks even if they were for $100. I thought if I didn't get the check in my hand it would disappear. Now it doesn't matter."[49]

Three months after the party, Kaufmann gave birth to a child. It was a girl, and they named her Alexandra. Curtis had wanted a son. His face fell. "Sorry it's not a boy," she said. Her brother Gunther was also at the hospital, and he cried joyfully. She found herself kissing him but not Curtis, who was taken aback. When he asked her why she didn't kiss him as well, she replied, "He was the only one to cry."[50]

Kaufmann's parenting techniques were different than those of Curtis. Being from a different era and culture, she was more *laissez-faire*. One day Alex wouldn't take her baby food. Kaufmann was inclined to leave it at that but Curtis fed her every morsel. The result was that she threw up.[51]

Lew Wasserman was now running Universal, so it was time for Curtis to find a new agent. He wished Wasserman well, fully aware of what he'd done for him. "Lew got me out of Universal," he said. "Had I not done that I would have died as the King of the Bs."[52] Curtis replaced him with Irving "Swifty" Lazar. "The joke about Swifty," he said, "was that he was better known than a lot of his clients." He promptly earned Curtis $125,000 for his next movie, *The Great Race,* as well as a chunk of the profits.

Lazar, like Curtis, was a New York Jew from the wrong side of the tracks. Ambitious from a young age, he got his nickname from Humphrey Bogart after Bogart had watched him clinch three separate deals for him in just one afternoon.[53] "Everybody has two agents," went the Hollywood phrase, "his own and Irving Lazar."[54] "I rode into Hollywood," Lazar said, "when stars still dressed for dinner and people gave glittering parties with no connections to charities or to political causes."[55] His own parties were legendary, particularly his post–Oscar *soirées*.

A huge amount of money was spent on *The Great Race* ($12 million, to be exact), and it's all up there on the screen. And yet one can't help feeling that this "Boys with Toys" spectacular might have been better advised to put some of that cash into developing a credible script rather than taxing the viewer with almost three hours of motor mania.

Based on the first around-the-world automobile race held in 1908, which went from New York to Paris, it was a thrill-a-minute odyssey into adolescent lunacy, replete with as many verbal and visual gags as you could shake a monkey wrench at. Jack Lemmon and Natalie Wood costarred, with Peter Falk in a lesser role. Blake Edwards directed with his customary vigor, but when the budget soared, Jack Warner told him he was going to get rid of him.

Wood made no secret of the fact that its humor didn't appeal to her, a comment that didn't endear her to Edwards, according to her biographer Gavin Lambert. Lambert alleges that Edwards took his revenge by ignoring her in favor of Curtis and Lemmon when filming began.[56] This is as dubious as Lambert's previous allegation that Wood and Curtis didn't get along.

Wood's sister Lana claimed she didn't enjoy making the film because of an excess of male camaraderie on the set, chiefly instigated by Edwards, "a man she was not thrilled with."[57] This pointedly contradicted Curtis' version of events, which was that Wood liked Edwards enormously, so much so that when Warner fired him from the picture she threatened to "walk" as well unless he was reinstated.[58]

Lambert also alleges Wood tried to kill herself by taking an overdose of Seconal on the set of the film one night after an argument with Warren Beatty.[59] This is something one would expect Curtis to have known about if it took place. He didn't mention it in either of his autobiographies. James Robert Parish quoted Curtis as saying Wood was too career-minded, too "wrapped up in herself" and not as friendly as she used to be. He also has Curtis saying he hoped there would be a party when the film ended so they could set each other on fire.[60]

Curtis told a different story in his autobiography. Not only did they like each other, they even got physical in her trailer one day, making "crazy" love on the sofa: "We didn't say anything before, during, or after. It was perfect just the way it was." His use of the word "perfect" is unique here, as is his subsequent comment that Wood and himself stayed away from each other after the encounter because "I was happily married to Christine."[61] In this little vignette we have the "perfect" encapsulation of his ability to make cheating sound romantic. (He didn't mention anything about cavorting with Wood in his 1994 autobiography.)

Peter Falk relished the experience of appearing in a movie that had a set "the size of a football field."[62] By the end of the shoot he became a card-carrying funster, entering into the spirit of the climactic pie-fight like one to the manner born.[63] The elaborate nature of the fight, in which 2,357 pies were thrown, shot the film's budget up so high that Jack

The Great Race (1965) was Curtis' third film with Natalie Wood. She's pictured with him here in a scene from the multi-million-dollar madcap comedy which was helmed, again, by Blake Edwards. (As well as *Operation Petticoat*, Edwards had directed Curtis in *Mr. Cory* and *The Perfect Furlough*.) Like many Curtis movies, it fared better with the public than the critics, though by now he had developed a comic patter that seemed effortlesly infectious.

Warner banned Edwards from the set. This was unprecedented in cinema history. It was also senseless because it was costing them even more with everybody sitting around doing nothing."[64]

One writer charted Edwards' decline as beginning with *The Great Race*. He put this partly down to the fact that he had too much money to play with. The final cost of $12 million was a fortune at this time. The film didn't do anything like the kind of business that would justify such a budget.[65] Neither did the eponymous race itself justify that accreditation "great." The film had pace and verve but it failed to find a human interest level to drive the slapstick. One would have needed a Billy Wilder at the helm to have achieved that.

The critics hated it but its success at the box office made it one of the top ten grossers of 1965. What matter that it was little more than a low-rent version of *Those Magnificent Men in Their Flying Machines*? People were so busy laughing they didn't care. Neither did Curtis. But as was the case with *Some Like It Hot*, he was outgunned comedically by Lemmon. When this happened to him he tended to become derisive, as he'd been about Bobby Darin in *Captain Newman M.D.* He told a reporter he thought Lemmon was "really rather corny" in the film and not as funny as he thought he was.[66]

After Curtis finished *The Great Race* he was profiled by Sidney Skolsky of the *Hollywood Citizen-News*. Skolsky wrote the usual rags-to-riches style piece, creating a picture of a star who had more shoes than Imelda Marcos and a room where ranks of his suits hung three abreast. "He resides in a house that set him back $250,000," Skolsky informed his readers. "The dining-room table stretches out to twelve feet. It's being replaced because it's too small."[67] It wasn't bad for a man who only had $4.12 to his name when he first landed in Hollywood.

Despite the extravagance, Curtis' diet was frugal: "People eat two-thirds more food than they should." His main source of exercise was fencing; it had replaced the gym in his life. When the discussion moved to the fair sex he offered the view that the most attractive quality a woman could possess was intellect. He defined this — conveniently — as "an understanding of life ... and how to keep her man calm and happy."[68]

He was reunited with his old friend Jerry Lewis to make *Boeing Boeing*, a film as frothy as *The Great Race*, though on a much smaller budget. Lewis decided to play it straight for a change, which was the only original thing about the film. Curtis was a man simultaneously engaged to three air-hostesses, somehow managing to negotiate his three-timing by dint of their unorthodox timetables. It was partly filmed in Paris, but by now this city he once loved so much was beginning to lose its allure for him. Lewis also got on his nerves, stepping on his lines and engaging in the kind of pratfalls and grinning that he suddenly seemed too old for. Curtis found Lewis' hydraulic energy exhausting. He was also increasingly irked by his gargantuan ego. Lewis demanded top billing in the movie and got it. Curtis snarled, "Jerry would want top billing in the men's room."

After shooting was completed, Curtis visited Joseph Cornell, the famous box artist. He loved the effects Cornell achieved by cutting holes in his boxes and letting the light filter in to the curiosities he stored inside them. Cornell was also fascinated by movie stars, in particular actresses like Lauren Bacall and Hedy Lamarr. Curtis brought Kaufmann with him, and Cornell took some photos of her, presumably to use for his art. Curtis, being Curtis, also felt they might provide him with some "sexual excitement."[69]

Cornell was one of America's most famous box constructors. He began his collages in the 1940s, using commonplace artifacts from five-and-dime stores in New York as well as material from books and Victorian illustrations. An eccentric whose father died of leukemia when he was thirteen, he lived all his life with his mother. Though he professed to enjoy female company, he never married. He had many strange habits, like looking out of windows in a trance-like state even in the middle of a conversation. He also engaged in self-hypnosis.

He believed this helped his art. Diane Waldman remembered him sitting beside a stove one day to keep himself warm and then jumping away from it suddenly as he went into a daze and forgot where he was.[70]

He rarely entertained guests. An avid Christian Scientist, he saw the world primarily as a spiritual place. He believed religion provided a framework for his understanding of Surrealism.[71] He scoured shops for objects for his boxes, even taxidermy shops and pet stores. He bought everything from stamps to wine glasses to bracelets. Like Curtis he admired Harry Houdini. Also like Curtis, he had an invalid brother called Robert. Robert suffered from cerebral palsy. This made Cornell very protective of him. He was extremely sympathetic to his plight. He not only made boxes for him but also elaborate trains that Robert could operate by means of a pen or pencil he held in his teeth. This fascinated Curtis. "It was the most touching, incredible thing to watch," he said.[72] When Robert died, Joseph demonstrated his eccentricity by having a fit of laughing as he lay on his bed. He pulled a blanket over his head afterwards, apologizing with the words, "It was a comic aside."[73]

Curtis may have been right about the sexual excitement. Waldman held the view that his images of Bacall and Lamarr could have been examples of "repressed eroticism." Bacall he saw as possessing "Botticellian slenderness, with a touch of *jeune fille* awkwardness."[74] He was fascinated by Hedy Lamarr in *Come Live with Me*, writing of her as the "enchanted wanderer."[75]

Cornell opened Curtis' eyes to a world outside movies even as he was talking about stars like these. When Curtis was a child, somewhat like Cornell, he'd put his favorite possessions in cigar boxes under his bed. That quality of keeping mementos now found expression in a more formal manner. Each piece of box art Curtis constructed was like a snapshot of a period in his life. He was able to make a mosaic of his experiences thus far by putting them together. What he was doing was giving a visual narrative of his past, the way children sometimes drew cartoons on notebooks that were almost the same as the one on the page before, flipping through them to create the illusion of moving images.

The boxes were like objective representations of his brain, so many grab-bags of assorted memorabilia and bric-a-brac amassed over the years. Curtis offered this list of their possible contents: "Old letters, photos, keys, dice, marbles, timepieces, you name it—all carefully ordered with their own esoteric logic."[76]

In addition to making box art at this time, he continued to paint in the more traditional manner as well, inspired by the Old Masters:

> When I stand in front of a Picasso, Pablo is saying, "Now, Tony, look at the way I used that line and that figure. You notice that I put in the color after the line was made so it isn't solid where the line and color meet." Whereas Matisse says, "What I did was put in the color and then painted black on the outside of it so that the shape became more clear." Braque says, "Tony—bullshit. Why don't you take the figures and let them speak for themselves and then put the color in." These guys are talking to me personally like brothers and sisters. That's why I love being a painter.[77]

One of his peccadilloes was an avoidance of brown. He found it grounded him too much. It was "too close to the planet."[78]

Painting was also his way of improving on reality, particularly when he painted women who'd appeared with him onscreen. "I'd like to have seen Marilyn with a longer neck," he stated, "bigger bosoms, a smaller waist, ass not quite as big, legs a little big straighter. I would have given Natalie Wood longer arms, bigger knockers, longer legs."[79] He became a kind of plastic surgeon with his brushes and easels.

He was influenced by Matisse, not only in his painting but his upbeat philosophy of life. In later years Matisse became crippled — not unlike the wheelchair-bound Curtis — but still continued to paint. That perseverance brought tears to Curtis' eyes. It inspired him to keep on keeping on.

He also loved Van Gogh, mainly for his purity of purpose, the fact that he was so real, so ordinary. Curtis hated being called a celebrity artist. "That cheapens my work," he said.[80]

He liked to tell a joke about Van Gogh. After he dies, Van Gogh goes up to heaven. God sympathizes with him for cutting off his ear. He tries to console him by telling Van Gogh that the paintings he did when he was poor on earth are now going for multi-million-dollar sums. The outraged painter says, "Shit — I couldn't sell zip when I was alive" ... and then proceeds to cut off his other ear!

"How many people on this planet are Van Goghs?" Curtis asked a journalist once. "Imagine an abstract painter who's fucking nuts, who cuts off his ear, who lives with potato eaters when he could live better. Sells one painting his whole life. Imagine finding a nut like him in the Bronx."[81]

Curtis had a more mercenary attitude to acting, concentrating on films he felt would make money rather than raise consciousness. By now he seemed to have reached a resigned state of mind about his acting abilities, or lack of some. He said in 1965, "I just want to be as good an actor as I possibly can. I'm no Larry Olivier. I used to try to be like him and to be able to act like him and speak like him. But that, as they say, is absurd. I am what I am and I'm happy."[82]

He seemed to be mellowing gradually into middle age. "I'm forty," he announced, "and I have to dye my hair for the parts I play. So I know I'm getting on." He didn't recommend this: "There's nature, very kindly giving us grey hair to soften the wrinkles on the face and we're busy dying it dark again, which only points it up. The only secret I know for remaining youthful is to marry someone young, as I did."[83]

He was resigned to the fact that he was the Baron of Beefcake, "a jerk who crawled out of a trashcan" on First Avenue. No matter how famous he became he never forgot who he was. If he did, others reminded him. One day he bumped into an old friend from the Bronx who looked at him and said, "Bernie Schwartz! What have you been doing all these years?"[84] He liked these reality checks just as he liked to see his films on the Bronx marquees advertising "our Own Bernie Schwartz."

On June 3, 1966, Kaufmann walked into his bedroom to find him crying. She asked him what the matter was. He said, "I'm 42 today." "No, you're 41," she corrected, speaking with "the cruelty of someone who's much younger."[85] She was disgusted by his infantile attitude. She saw the incident as signaling "the beginning of the end" of the marriage — something of an overreaction, one would have thought.

As the marriage went downhill he became more and more of a loner. He spent a lot of his time in bed watching TV. Kaufmann taunted, "You don't know what it's like to be young." By now he'd had a hair transplant and was feeling insecure about himself. Kaufmann had also changed from being the pretty woman who liked to make small talk in elegant clothes. She was now a woman who preferred to discuss box art with someone like Joseph Cornell than movies with Curtis.[86]

Curtis' fourth daughter, Allegra, arrived in the summer of 1966. She was born into a home that had a cook, a gardener and two secretaries. She described it as "a palace where no one wore a crown."[87]

She was also born into a crisis marriage. Curtis and Kaufmann spent a lot of their time arguing with one another now. As a result, Allegra could never bear to look at them in *Taras Bulba* together, the intimacy of their scenes in the movie at total variance with what she witnessed in front of her each day.[88]

Allegra often thought she would have preferred Bernie Schwartz as a parent than the "phantom" figure of Curtis, a man who'd been given a false name and a false identity by Hollywood. She found it strange to think that at the age of twenty he was informed, "You're someone else," and he accepted it uncomplainingly, his only ambition being material success, having shed everything that happened to him on the streets of New York.[89]

When Kaufmann realized the marriage was beyond repair she had a nervous breakdown. Her weight plummeted and she found herself succumbing to panic attacks. To paper over the cracks of a looming meltdown they arranged to move into a new house, but this only made their distance from one another more palpable.[90]

Curtis' next film was another comedy, *Not with My Wife You Don't*. This time he was caught in a love triangle with George C. Scott and Virna Lisi. He knew Scott could have blown him off the screen with his pregnant pauses so he decided to play it uptempo and try to upstage him that way. Scott took the bait and camped along with him. Lisi played his wife in the movie but had a "hands-off" approach to Curtis, being all too well aware of his playboy reputation. The plot was mainly nonsense, but familiar nonsense to Curtis by now. He flattered the material with his laidback sense of comic timing.

After finishing the movie he and Kaufmann moved into a Mediterranean-style mansion in Holmby Hills, the former home of oil magnate Bill Keck. Situated on four acres of the most expensive land in California, it had 18 rooms as well as an Olympic-sized indoor pool inlaid with Byzantine tile. In the garage adjoining the house he kept a Rolls Royce, a Bentley, a Lincoln Continental, an Excalibur SS and a vintage Duesenberg. Considering Kaufmann didn't drive, that was quite a catalogue of vehicles.

He now made another trite comedy, *Arrivaderci Baby!* In Britain it was called *Drop Dead, Darling*, perhaps a more appropriate title. As David Shipman remarked, all of Curtis' recent comedies had "dropped dead" at the box office as well.[91] It was partly shot in Europe. The film signaled his uneasy descent into the realms of black comedy. A slightly more ponderous retread of the previous year's *How to Murder Your Wife* with Jack Lemmon and Virna Lisi, it had him marrying rich women for their money and then bumping them off to get the inheritance. All goes well when his first two spouses become safely transported to a better place, but his third wife (Rosanna Schiaffino) turns the tables on him by trying to murder *him*. And then they fall in love — as you do.

Curtis seemed nervous on the set. The director asked him to redo a scene in which he lay on a bed with the semi-nude Zsa Zsa Gabor, but he refused. This was out of character for him. "I can't retake it," he said. "That would be impossible." This was probably because her then-husband Herbert Hutner was watching. Hutner was ecstatic at Curtis' graciousness, according to Gabor. The irony was that Gabor was falling out of love with him at this point. His kindness was depressing her, she explained.[92]

It wasn't long before she dispensed with Hutner and went to the altar with her next husband, Joshua Cosden. The dress she chose for her wedding was the one she'd worn in the scene with Curtis in *Arrivaderci Baby!* "I don't think there is anything wrong with a woman who has been married before wearing white," she exclaimed. Curtis attended the wedding and warned, "Zsa Zsa, don't tell him you're marrying him in the same wedding dress you married me in six months ago." Gabor didn't listen.[93] Six months later she was divorced from Cosden as well.

Curtis found Gabor heavy duty, a powerhouse woman who was her own best publicist: "If Zsa Zsa Gabor had been Adolf Hitler's press agent," he said, "he would have been loved by everybody."[94]

One of the reasons Curtis made *Arrivaderci Baby!* was because Lew Wasserman encouraged him to go to Europe. Here again Wasserman was ahead of his time. Clint Eastwood had made *A Fistful of Dollars* for Sergio Leone in 1964 but it wasn't released in the U.S. until three years later. In Eastwood's view there was "a feeling that an American actor making an Italian movie was sort of taking a step backward."[95] But Leone's "spaghetti" westerns totally revitalized Eastwood's career.

Curtis didn't do as well with Swifty Lazar as he had with Wasserman. Lazar procured some lucrative contracts for him but there was never enough continuity. Also, the material was often shoddy. But Curtis couldn't refuse: he needed the money for child support and alimony for Leigh.

That was the main reason he found himself in *Don't Make Waves,* which offered him a percentage of the gross. He also got a "sweetener" for recommending Alexander Mackendrick to direct it. He felt he owed Mackendrick for giving him respectability in *Sweet Smell.* Mackendrick brought out the best in Curtis in this latest offering as well, though it shouldn't be mentioned even in the same breath as the earlier film.

Robyn Karney dubbed it *The Sour Smell of Failure.* Mackendrick himself thought it was absolute rubbish. So did Curtis, though he liked the book. He played a university professor in California who loses his job after being caught in a police raid at a student party. Thereafter he goes into the swimming pool business and lives in a house that's falling off a cliff. It sounded good in theory. There are some hilarious moments, but the expected chemistry with his costar (Claudia Cardinale) didn't really take off.

The film looked as if it was edited with a meat cleaver. It could have presented us with Curtis as an amiable version of Sidney Falco but chose instead to portray him as a sitcom caricature figure—"the accident-prone butt of fate, given to tumbling into swimming pools and banging his head on low ceilings."[96] Mackendrick thought it might have worked if Curtis was a viewer of the action rather than a participant in it. That way, the ludicrous situations could have had a wry perspective to them. But wryness is the job of the director rather than the star. Mackendrick was asking Curtis to do two jobs here. That was slightly unfair.

In its funnier moments it's an enjoyable satire of Californian values, or what passes for them. Here's Curtis in post–Sidney Falco mode, giving his best-of-everything speech: "You know what I want? A box of 25 Monte Cristo panatellas. I want a king-size vibrator bed. I want a 35mm Hasselblad, a Rolls-Royce convertible. I want driving gloves made from the underside of antelope ears. A bold man's cologne for the man who does something for women. A cashmere double-breasted jacket that's gonna get me there fast."

There are times when the film approaches Altmanesque parameters. Phillip Kemp cited the example of a swimming pool dangling 300 feet above a coastal highway, something Roger Banham referred to as "the heartbreak that ends the Angeleno dream."⁹⁷ We're veering close to the surreal here, but such moments are few and far between.

Curtis and Mackendrick seemed content to negotiate Clousseau-like slapstick routines that cut anything more significant off at the pass. If he was in Hollywood he might have had more leeway but a lot of money was riding on the film. He was handcuffed by budgetary constraints as well as a cast not too familiar with satirical subtexts. Neither was there any Burt Lancaster to rescue him this time by racking up the tension, or a Clifford Odets to feed him the kind of dialogue that would have made the film really pop. In the end it became a mish-mash of half-realized set-pieces and unresolved dilemmas. It could have been *M*A*S*H* or *The Graduate* but settled instead for an uneasy mix of *Baywatch* and *Gidget Goes Hawaiian*.

Sharon Tate was also in the cast. Curtis' infatuation with her is much funnier than his entanglement with Cardinale. If she wasn't married it might have continued offscreen.

He only got to know her slightly. The biographer of her husband, Roman Polanski, said an air of sexual possibility charged the set of the film, so much so that Tate bought a vibrator during the shoot. She entreated Polanski in a letter: "You should get one, it's really funny. Mine can't plug in on an English current but I must try it on you. It's also good for stiff necks."⁹⁸

Curtis followed *Don't Make Waves* with his seventh successive comedy, an Italian production dogged by controversy and bad dubbing. The wackily-titled *On My Way to the Crusades I Met a Girl Who ...* tells us everything we need to know about it. *A Funny Thing Happened on the Way to the Forum* was a recent success and it looked it was trying to cash in on this. In some theaters it was titled *A Funny Thing Happened on My Way to the Crusades*, which was close to plagiarism. In the UK, in a third title change (usually a sign of panic on the part of the distributors), it became *The Chastity Belt*. This was unwise as it drew attention to a salacious element in the plot. The censorship laws were stricter there, which meant that a half hour was lopped off the final cut before it was deemed acceptable viewing for the British public.

It was more boring than *risqué*, however, notwithstanding the central theme of Curtis making his wife (Monica Vitti) don the eponymous belt while he's off fighting Hugh Griffith in 11th-century Italy. Curtis didn't get on with Vitti, finding her to be something of a prima donna. "She was also sleeping with the cameraman at the time," said Curtis, "which meant she got all the best angles." Not that it mattered too much anyway, as the film (replete with bad dubbing) was one he would have preferred to forget.

Just as the "Arabian Nights rubbish" had given way to serious drama, such drama was now replaced by a sea of froth. He was probably being defensive when he declaimed to a reporter, "Comedy is the most honest way for an actor to make a living." An added benefit was that "people would rather laugh than cry." For Curtis the basic difference between comedy and drama was time. "The quickest way to change drama into comedy," he argued, "is simply to speed up the film."⁹⁹

Another reason for the comedies was to try and divert him from his offscreen problems. By now Bobby was institutionalized and had deteriorated further, partly due to the stress caused by his mother, who insisted on visiting him despite constant pleas from Curtis not to. "If I said nothing she might have gone less," he remarked. Bobby became violent with him on occasion and then slipped into semi-comatose states in which he hardly knew him. It was too painful to watch, so he scaled back on his visits to him. Curtis was also concerned that prolonged exposure to Bobby might result in his own fragile temperamnent becoming exacerbated. "Most of the Curtises are schizoid," he said. "It's handy for an actor because it means you can slip in and out of all these identities. Maybe the whole family should have become actors."

His problems with Kaufmann were now coming to a head as well. Having left the movies, her life of shopping and doing up the house fell somewhat short for excitement. She was irked as she watched Curtis ogling his costars on film sets in front of her. She suspected him of sleeping with them behind her back. Suddenly she knew how Janet Leigh must have felt during the shooting of *Taras Bulba* four years earlier.

After Allegra was born she expressed a wish to return to acting. Curtis wasn't in favor of this. Despite moving to the new house they still bickered constantly. She accused him of being a bully, while he saw her as a hypocrite. "A fridge made of marzipan," as he put it.[100]

His behavior became erratic. He appeared on *The Tonight Show* in a turtleneck shirt, with hippie beads around his neck. All he was missing was the flowers in his hair. He was also featured on the cover of the Beatles album *Sgt. Pepper's Lonely Hearts Club Band* alongside iconic figures like Einstein, Karl Marx and Marilyn Monroe. He got a buzz out of that. It was like being the Prince of Cool all over again. (Paul McCartney had dedicated one of the Beatles concerts to him when he met him during the filming of *The Chastity Belt*.)

Curtis was still looking at women young enough to be his daughters, or even granddaughters. He expressed an interest in Cher's younger sister Georgianne, then only sixteen. A columnist wrote, "Tony Curtis' dates keep getting younger and younger. Behind those psychedelic specs and those far-out mod clothes, he looks pretty much like a teenager. Which, of course, is probably his intent."[101] No matter how well he looked, though, his birth certificate said he was 42 years old, which meant Georgianne was 26 years his junior. If he continued at the present rate, a wit observed, he would one day end up dating an embryo. Said Cher, "Tony's fucked up but I love him." Curtis countered, "Take out the 'up' and you've got it!"

Work was still sporadic, and he continued to take the meager scraps. He had an uncredited part in Roman Polanski's *Rosemary's Baby* in 1968, playing an actor who phones Mia Farrow about a part in a movie which he doesn't get because John Cassavetes has put a spell on him. He wasn't seen, nor did Farrow know who she was talking to until the scene was over. It gave her a kick, and Curtis too. They became friends afterwards.

In August of that year, just as Polanski's career was beginning to take off, a pregnant Sharon Tate and a number of her friends were viciously murdered by Charles Manson and his gang, her blood spattering the walls of the Polanski mansion in an attack that was barbaric in the extreme. Curtis was devastated. "It was a random murder," he said. "It could have been any of us. We were shocked but also afraid. For a long time afterwards many of us looked over our shoulders every time we turned the key in our door."

13

Into Strangler Hell

As the sixties drew to a close, many movie icons began to look askance at the decade, wondering why it hadn't fulfilled the promise of the fifties. Elvis Presley, for one, was thoroughly disenchanted with the 30-plus sex-and-music movies he'd made mainly for the loot and was bracing himself for a reinvention on stage. Marlon Brando was similarly discomfited, having been labeled "box office poison" after one too many self-indulgent farragoes. Brando had made a string of classics in the fifties. Presley had also given his best performance in that decade, in *King Creole*, as Curtis noted.

Curtis' two most acclaimed movies, *Sweet Smell of Success* and *Some Like It Hot*, had also come from that decade. In the early sixties he'd widened his scope with more epic-oriented works like *Spartacus* and *Taras Bulba*, but as the decade went on he'd become mired in all those fluffy comedies. He developed such a patter in these that he could almost have phoned in his performances. But he was now hungering for something more stimulating than a man three-timing air hostesses, or an 11th century warrior worried about someone finding the key to his wife's vagina.

He found it in a book by Gerald Frank about a murderer who looked for all the world like a happily-married man, someone who killed without admitting that fact to himself, a schizophrenic who called up some comparisons with Curtis' own brother and mother—and perhaps even himself. It was called *The Boston Strangler* and dealt with the tortured mind and revolting acts of a basically inconspicuous maintenance man called Albert DeSalvo. Curtis would later reflect, "There's a little bit of the Boston Strangler in everyone."[1] The film was being directed by Richard Fleischer, with whom he'd worked on *The Vikings*.

By the time he made *The Boston Strangler*, he confessed, "The parts started falling apart. There were fewer and fewer good roles.... From 22 to about 37 I was lucky, but by the middle sixties I wasn't getting the kind of parts I wanted and it kind of soured me." At first he blamed the industry for this, but then he realized people weren't picking on him, that the root cause was in his own failure to come up to scratch: "You've got to not become paranoid. You've got to not become neurotic."[2]

Curtis had admired Frank's style in the book. It seemed to have been written more as tragedy than horror story. "Perhaps the doctors can cut out the corner of my brain that made me do those things," DeSalvo ponders on the last page, the previous ones concentrating more on his war with himself than his massacre of thirteen defenseless women.[3]

Curtis put on fifteen pounds for the role. He also put putty on his nose to make himself less handsome, and wore ankle weights in his shoes to give himself an awkward walk. The process was completed by thinning his hair to a "frizzy, parched scrub" and daubing his eyebrows with mascara. Then he photographed himself in front of a mirror and sent the pictures to Fleischer.

"I wanted to play DeSalvo so much I'd have spent three years in jail as compensation," he divulged to a reporter. He studied medical records on him, traveled around Boston investigating the locations of his crimes, and read every newspaper report on him he could get his hands on:

> It was a sort of purging for me. For years I've wanted to find myself, to assess what might have happened to me if I hadn't been taken up by Hollywood when I didn't have a syllable to rub against another. I might have been on the wrong side of the law myself. By doing this film I lost my anger. It isn't so much that I became sympathetic with DeSalvo but I got what I might call empathy with him.[4]

One would have thought empathy a stronger emotion than sympathy, but he continued: "I regret never having met him. I *became* DeSalvo. I could no longer believe in Tony Curtis." Further, "DeSalvo had remarkable qualities. I found out he could go into a room and fix every detail of it in his mind. He had the visual memory of a genius. It could have made him a superb architect or a painter."[5]

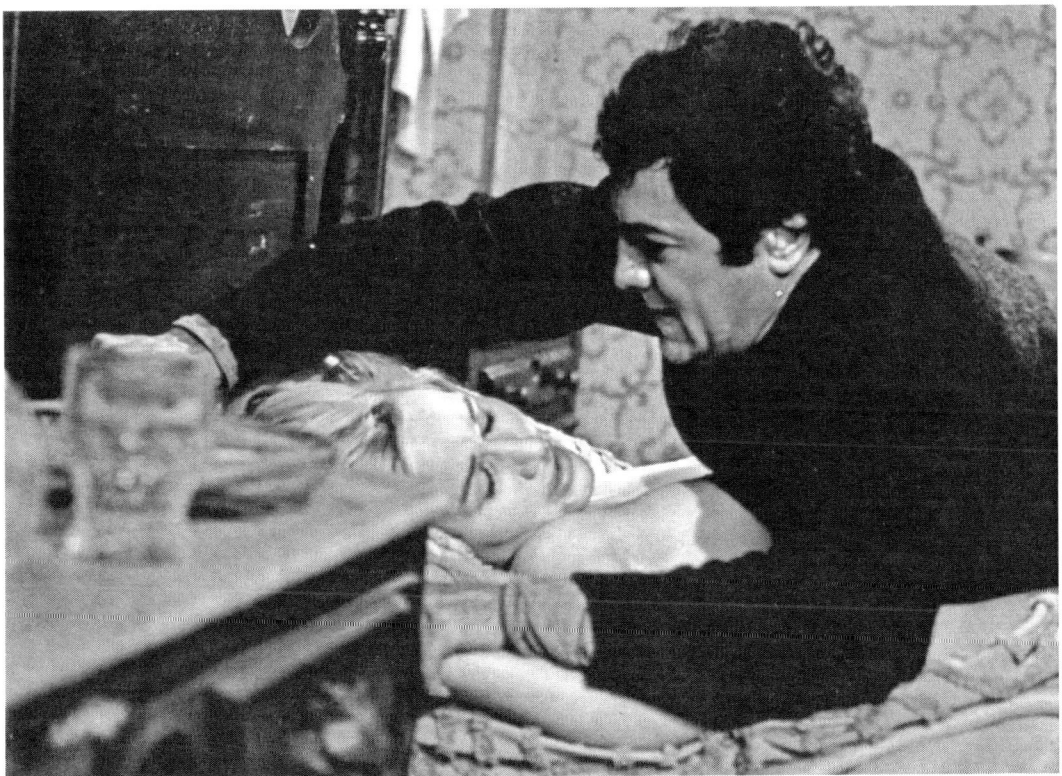

Curtis reestabished his credentials as a bona fide actor with a resounding performance in *The Boston Strangler* (1968), which both shocked and impressed his colleagues in the film industry. He was widely praised for the way he took on the guise of the psychotic killer Albert DeSalvo — here attempting to dispatch Sally Kellerman to the hereafter. The film, sadly, didn't lead to other offers that would continue such thespian dedication, and in the seventies he again descended into fulsome fare.

The putty nose gave him the appearance of a punch-drunk fighter. He then put in brown contact lenses to disguise his eyes. Now came the hard part: "I had to go on my knees to 20th Century–Fox to get the role." Was he confident? "I spent a fortune on head-shrinkers so I thought I knew a little bit about things that go adrift in a man's mind."[6]

Fleischer liked the new image but pulled Curtis up on one point: his fingernails were too clean.[7] This was duly dealt with. Nails suitably stained, went on his knees again and this time Fox said yes.

When I asked Curtis if the problems of his recent past might have helped his performance, he agreed.

> Not just the recent past—*all* my past. I've always felt conflicted inside myself. My body may have been in Hollywood but my mind was in the Bronx, or even Budapest. The more success I had, the less I felt worthy of it. It was a Trojan horse pulling me down. So I had an "in" with the character from the start. I drew on those thoughts for my key scenes.

Hearing him talk, I was reminded of how he'd criticized his parents for bringing Budapest to the Bronx with them; now he admitted to doing that too. The sins of the father were being visited on the son without him even realizing it.

Fleischer asked Terence Rattigan, the acclaimed British playwright, to write the screenplay. The director had high hopes he'd turn in a high quality script but Rattigan started to behave oddly at an early story conference that was attended by Fleischer, Robert Fryer, the film's producer, and Frank. The other three men discussed the story in general, but only one thing seemed to entrance Rattigan: the size of DeSalvo's penis. It was at this point Fleischer started to worry about whether he'd got the right man for the job.

Rattigan went off to an island to work on the script. After a few months he submitted a forty-page treatment. There was only one problem: it was written as a comedy! Further, the chief suspect for the crimes was a man called Darryl Zanuck. Was Rattigan trying to get himself sacked? It sounded like it. If he was, he succeeded. He was promptly replaced by Edward Anhalt.

Nobody could understand why Rattigan behaved so outlandishly. After he was dismissed from the film he wrote a letter to Fleischer telling him he found the job beyond him because Frank had already told the story so well. "I wouldn't have hired myself," he conceded, adding, "I invent. It is the only reason for my existence. When that minor gift leaves me I will leave the world."[8]

Fleischer couldn't understand why he took the commission in the first place if he felt unsuited to it. What had been his motivation, he wondered. Money? Work? To find out the size of DeSalvo's member? Money seemed the more likely option because even after admitting his treatment was abysmal he still held on to the rather large advance he'd been given. Fleischer tried to put the episode behind him and get on with the movie.

Curtis didn't appear until 45 minutes in. This lent added importance to his entrance. "It worked the other way too," he said. "It meant I had more to live up to. But I liked that. I was going for broke on this one."

He found the crew a pleasure to work with. They got on well with him too. Alex Rocco, his voice coach, went out to dinner with him one night. The restaurant was full. The proprietor suggested asking some of the other diners to leave, and Curtis was aghast. "What kind of fairness is that?" he asked. Then he walked out. Rocco was impressed.

Another day Curtis was talking about his contact lenses with a PR man on the film.

The man told him a story about someone in his office who'd dropped a contact lens on the floor. He had looked hilarious on all fours looking for it among a forest of legs. Everyone laughed except Curtis, who simply inquired, "Did he find it?"[9]

People on the set were relieved that he wasn't acting like a big "I Am." He was asked how he felt about the adulation accorded to movie stars like himself. Did he see it as love or blind adoration? His reply was interesting: "What's the difference whether the love is for me or for a movie star? You can feel the reaction of people toward you. That's a terrific sensation. You can feel that love. The fact that it's directed toward you is very beautiful."[10]

DeSalvo had a lot in common with Curtis. For one thing, he'd been beaten by a parent as a child. (In DeSalvo's case it was his father rather than his mother.)[11] He also ran away from street fights as a child, and discovered his manhood in "the service."[12] He was poor at school, like Curtis, but had an intuitive intelligence. When he married, his wife put him down in front of others, as Leigh sometimes did with Curtis.[13] She also refused him sex after their child had been born handicapped, fearing another pregnancy. "Our next baby might be born without arms," she cried.[14] Curtis never had a handicapped child, but at the time he made the film Kaufmann was refusing him sex. He found himself cruising the streets at night looking for some kind of stimulation. (He was taking drugs now as well.)

After shooting was finished each day, he went home to an unhappy Kaufmann. He suspected her of sleeping with Dean Martin's son Ricky, even though he never caught them in the act. This angered him. Even though he'd cheated on her too, at least he'd been discreet about it. As had been the case with Leigh, he saw this as an indemnification of sorts. His Eleventh Commandment had always been "Thou Shalt Not Get Caught."

There were times when he owned up to the mindgames he played in such situations: "Perhaps I had the paranoid fantasies that my wives were cheating on me in order to give myself an excuse to [cheat as well]."[15] He often said that he only became unfaithful when his wives lost interest in him. This may have been another rationalization.

By now he'd met the Boston model Leslie Allen. He was sleeping with her intermittently behind Kaufmann's back. She swept him off his feet, and she was also the right age: 23. Notwithstanding this, he was still possessive of Kaufmann. One night he lost his temper with her over Martin's son and told her to leave the house. She said she'd be more than happy to go. "Don't take any of my paintings with you," he warned. "I don't want your paintings," she snapped back. "All I want is my children."[16]

She got a divorce from him in Mexico without him knowing she was going there. She was given custody of Allegra and Alexandra. He was confused by this. Why hadn't she divorced him in the U.S. where she would have had a bigger claim on his money? "I never thought about alimony," she protested.[17] Curtis found this hard to credit. So many of his own problems had been caused by money, he seemed to think it was the only problem people could have, or the only thing departing wives could want.

Her divorce was granted on April 16, 1968. Four days later Curtis married Allen in the Sahara Hotel in Las Vegas. He seemed enraptured by her, as indeed he had been with his other wives in the early days of his marriages to them. The price he paid was losing his daughters. This was the one blight on his horizon now. He had access to them, but it could never compensate. He didn't play the role of the part-time father well when it wasn't on his terms. It had been the same with Kelly and Jamie when he lost them to Janet Leigh. "I had four daughters," he said, "but none of them felt like they were mine anymore. They were with me and then they were gone. I didn't have enough time to get close to them."

He tried to look on the bright side. *Strangler* was nearing completion. He was on top of his performance like a musician with a symphony, tweaking it and driving it, inhabiting it like a well-fitting suit.

Fleischer concentrated on DeSalvo's character rather than what he did, a wise decision. It became not so much a crime story as a psychological drama, giving Curtis the opportunity to delve into the motivation for his horrific acts. Getting him to confront the other person inside himself became the main fulcrum of the action. Was he insane or just an ordinary man driven over the edge by background and circumstance? Curtis normalized him even as he was acting out his inner torments in graphic form. When DeSalvo tried to strangle his wife towards the end, we felt more relief than fear; relief that he was finally coming to terms with the stranger inside himself, no longer in denial.

Curtis played DeSalvo with sensitivity. This wasn't the done thing with serial killers at this time. When he strangles women he looks more tortured than pleased. What we're watching is a man going through the motions of an addiction like any other addiction. He isn't in charge; another person is taking him over. Fleischer used a split screen for the climactic scene, a rather obvious device to denote DeSalvo's equally split personality. The rest of the film was more nuanced.

Henry Fonda played the policeman who brings DeSalvo to self-realization. Curtis had worked with him on *Sex and the Single Girl* but didn't find him too friendly there. This was more of the same. He didn't know why. Maybe he'd heard Curtis was difficult to deal with, or was having marital problems. "Or maybe he was just a pain in the ass," he joked.

"I took the film from him," Curtis insisted. "He can't have been expecting that because of his past — and because of my past. Maybe that made it harder to take. I was gaining on him." Fonda didn't even mention the film in his autobiography, another possible sign of defensiveness.[18]

There are many reasons why Curtis' performance was head and shoulders above anything he'd been doing for years. The most obvious one was desperation. He felt he was the Forgotten Man of Hollywood, somebody no one really considered anymore for serious parts. Then there was his strange empathy with the killer: "All of us are light and dark. The unique thing is that we can slip in and out of that in an instant. If you're sitting at home and the phone rings, depending on who's on it, another character in you will burst out."[19]

He was fascinated by the fact that DeSalvo killed thirteen times without being caught. "Try killing one person and getting away with it," he suggested. (DeSalvo might never have been caught if he hadn't confessed to another inmate in prison.)

Was there any special reason why Curtis devoted himself so much to the part? "I was living alone at the time. That had something to do with it. No parties, no nights out. Alone. Me and Albert."[20] (Considering he was canoodling with Allen at this time, perhaps he should have added, "Me, Albert and Leslie.")

Curtis wasn't nominated for an Oscar for the film. This outraged him and amazed his costars and director. People who'd acted with him in the past, like Natalie Wood, were also dumbfounded. What did he have to do to earn his acting chops — die on the set? Once tarred with the brush of anodyne idolatry, the critical fraternity refused to let him escape it: "When I started out I was pretty and made lots of movies, some not too good. Then later the intellectuals discovered I could act. But they never forgave me for that early career."[21]

Some critics were disparaging of the film. Michael Kerbel dismissed it as nothing more than "a slick thriller despite its psychological and sociological pretensions."[22] Such pretensions could be seen in the leadfooted style of its later segments, though a case can be made for this because of the atmospheric nature of the piece. The "jump" editing was also effective in exposing DeSalvo's unhinged psyche.

The role reestablished Curtis as a star to be contended with. The downside was a plethora of letters he received from "nuts" who said things like, "You're not the Boston Strangler, I am." He consoled himself by ringing up friends and saying, "Hello, this is Albert DeSalvo speaking!"

After appearing as DeSalvo he took out an option on the life story of another unappetizing character, the Chicago gangster Bugsy Siegel. "He's just as nasty as the Strangler," Curtis observed, "only he's dressed differently."[23]

The Boston Strangler changed his attitude toward acting: "After twenty years I think I've graduated.... In future I'll concentrate more on the subtleties of a character."[24] Little did he know then that DeSalvo was almost as good as it would get for him, the following decades offering him little but eccentric cameos or two-dimensional leads. A product of the studio system, he would find it difficult to breathe clean air outside it.

Asked if this depressed him, he replied, "After a while it didn't. I almost got a perverse sense of pleasure out of doing dumb movies after *Strangler*. My attitude [toward Hollywood] was 'Fuck you. If you didn't like me when I was good, let's see how bad I can be when I'm bad.'" Maybe it was hard to blame him. His attitude throws some light on his subsequent career choices.

Those Daring Young Men in Their Jaunty Jalopies was the first of these. Set in the 1920s and shot in various parts of Europe, it was a spoof about a 1500-mile car race. It was written by Jack Davies and Ken Annakin, who'd had some success with the already mentioned, *Those Magnificent Men in Their Flying Machines*. It was called *Monte Carlo or Bust* in the U.K.— the third of Curtis' films in two years to have alternate U.S. and U.K. titles. By now, as Tony Crawley commented, his movies were sporting more titles than stars.[25] He did the short-sighted klutz well, however, jumping in and out of cars, and scrapes, with bumbling confusion.

His costar was Susan Hampshire. The pair of them were almost killed in one scene when the brakes in the car in which they were traveling failed. Curtis was very angry about this over thirty years later when I asked him about it. "Those pricks in the studio told me gremlins were responsible," he blasted. "I said, 'Fuck you and your gremlins.'"

He got on well with Hampshire. He conceded in his first autobiography that he "might" have had sex with her. In his second one he was definite he had, a rare example of his memory improving as he grew older. As Hillary Clinton once remarked, "A man may forget where he parked his car but not whether he had sex." Whatever happened between them, it's unlikely it was anything more than a casual dalliance. When Curtis was giving out about the failure of the brakes to me he couldn't even remember her name, speaking of her as "that British actress"— not very flattering for a former lover.

Another forgettable romp was *Suppose They Gave a War and Nobody Came*, a film that had absolutely nothing to do with its title. Curtis was entertaining in it, playing a soldier with an eye for the ladies. His energy level played very well opposite the apparently drugged Brian Keith, one of his commanding officers. But as a satire of war or smalltown values, it left far too many holes.

Curtis is part of an army unit stationed at a hick town in Davis County during peacetime. It's Keith's job to improve relations between the soldiers and the townsfolk. When Curtis falls foul of the bullish sheriff (Ernest Borgnine) and gets himself locked up, Keith gets drunk and decides to wreck the jail by driving a tank through it. By this stage Curtis' on-again, off-again relationship with pretty waitress Suzanne Pleshette seems to have been forgotten about by the film's director, Hy Averback. The film ends with Keith "liberating" Curtis in a riotous scene that looks like it was salvaged from one of Burt Reynolds' road movies.

Taken at the level of amiable farce it passes muster, Curtis being at his most charismatic (and looking great as well). Some critics saw it as a subtle tract against the Vietnam war. This was to give it ideas beyond its station. When Keith is asked what he thinks he has proved by wrecking the town in the final reel, he replies, "Not a goddam thing." Many people felt the same about the film as a whole — with good reason.

Still sulking over being ignored by the intelligentsia for *The Boston Strangler*, Curtis seemed to be appearing in films like this almost as a protest. Leslie Allen told him to make as many movies as possible and he took her advice, a decision he would subsequently come to regret.

He travelled to London with her in the middle of 1969 and seemed ecstatic with her. "For the first time I feel completely fulfilled as a man," he burbled.[26] But, of course, he'd said something similar after marrying Leigh and Kaufmann. In fact, he'd probably said something similar after being with his first girlfriend, and his second, and his third. It was as if he needed to keep convincing himself that each period in his life was the best, as if by repeatedly telling himself he was ecstatic he would bring about the feeling by some kind of osmosis. He had a similar policy with his movies. Each time he finished one he talked it up as if it was his best, even if it was mindless twaddle.

He told Allen she was the only woman who ever understood "the real me." It was unusual that an intelligent person like her would buy this line from someone who'd talked hundreds of women into bed, but she did. She thought his previous marriages foundered because his other wives were too driven or too focused on their careers. Nothing could have been further from the truth. "No matter how close you are to someone," she theorized, "you just can't keep on surviving six month partings all the time." If she thought deeper about the circumstances of Leigh and Kaufmann she would have seen that these partings had nothing to do with the eventual collapse of the two marriages. Nonetheless, she felt the secret to being the third Mrs. Curtis was to accompany her man everywhere: "I sit there on the set working at my needlepoint. I've made so many pillows I've lost count."[27]

Allen and Curtis were concentrating on a healthy life together by eating sensibly. "We do chicken nicely on a spit," Curtis disclosed. "Steak, fish, not too much bread, fresh salads, fruit, a lot of water, good wine and a lot of kissing."[28] He kept the best ingredient till last. Knowing Curtis, there would have been tons of that for dessert.

Curtis now went to Istanbul to make an adventure film called *You Can't Win 'Em All*. "A turkey from Turkey" was his description of it to me when I asked him about it. However, he enjoyed the camaraderie with his costar Charles Bronson ("an actor who could do nothing very well," in his view). He and Bronson were soldiers protecting a train transporting gold bullion in 1922. Or is it just lead? Not too many people cared, least of all the cast. It was helmed by Peter Collinson, who had some quality works in his back catalogue, like *The Long Day's Dying*.

The film had two good things going for it — humor and authenticity of locale. Its most notable feature, Curtis thought, was the fact that Collinson "kidded the genre." The fact that Istanbul was the actual shooting location put it head and shoulders above those films where whole villages were built on studio backlots. "I made about ten films on one," he scoffed. "No matter how detailed they were, they always looked like Walt Disney."[29]

After *You Can Win 'Em All* completed shooting, Curtis had another lull in his career. In the absence of any better offers he went to Las Vegas and made an unwise attempt to become a nightclub performer, appearing at Caesar's Palace in a show where he told jokes, anecdotes and even sang, something he once vowed he'd never do. Ralph Pearl sniped that he wasn't just a lousy movie actor but "a lousy cafe entertainer as well."[30]

Pearl's barb didn't hurt him. "I'm not running anymore," he declared. "I can stand still and look around. I've been kissed by the gods." And if everything ended tomorrow? "Maybe I'd just go back to the Bronx and steal tires."

14

A Passionate Amoeba

After the career high of *The Boston Strangler*, Curtis had to deal with that inevitable moment that takes place in almost every performer's life — the moment when the phone stops ringing and one has to deal with the silence. Judy Garland used to shake it sometimes to make sure it was working. Other stars threw it against the wall or rang their agents to find out what was happening (or, more to the point, *not* happening).

Curtis couldn't figure out why his own phone wasn't ringing. He didn't accept the fact that failing returns on recent movies were the cause. "So my pictures were falling on their butts. *Everybody's* pictures fall on their butts. Robert Redford? I'd hate to show you some of the grosses on his recent ones. Paul Newman? He's had some bummers that would turn your hair blue."[1]

In later years his drug use caused movie offers to dry up. "I wasn't reliable enough. The word got out that I was 'using.' But everybody was using in those days."[2] His income at this time largely came from "residuals" from his old movies turning up on TV or in overseas theaters, but that couldn't tide him over forever. A new injection of capital — and enthusiasm — had to come from somewhere.

When he first got into movies, he said, people like Gary Cooper and Rosalind Russell told him, "You are now a prince." He thought it would last forever — once a prince, always a prince. But it didn't. A different order took root in the late sixties. The new wave of filmmaking was ushered in by the movie "brats"— people like Francis Ford Coppola and Martin Scorsese behind the camera, and Robert de Niro and Dustin Hoffman and a horde of others in front of it. Maverick and "indie" directors were also making their appearance, with edgier material. Drugs and sex became common themes as the demise of the studio system gave way to an "anything goes" ethos. Audiences suddenly didn't know what kind of films they were going to see any more, even if they knew the actors in them. Some stars of the old guard, like Burt Lancaster and Henry Fonda, were being cast against type in films like *The Swimmer* and *Once Upon a Time in the West*.

Curtis' daughter Allegra thought Curtis' main problem as he grew older was that he failed to shift gears and blamed Hollywood as a result. She thought he put an undue emphasis on his appearance and the changes that came into it as he got older. The aforementioned Robert Redford and Paul Newman had also lost some of their Adonis-like beauty as they aged, but they reinvented themselves in more character-driven roles. Why couldn't her father do that? Or why didn't he tap into some of that dry Jewish humor he shared with his former acting colleague Walter Matthau?[3]

Curtis had a hunch that television was where he needed to go, if not to salvage his career then at least to keep it ticking over until something better came along. Lew Wasserman had been extolling the merits of the medium since the forties when he first observed crowds of people standing mesmerized in front of store windows to watch the TV cartoons. (Wasserman boasted of owning one of only two television sets in California in 1940.)[4]

Television became a very real possibility to Curtis when an appetizing project now presented itself. It was an urbane comedy-drama that would have him appearing opposite Roger Moore, the pair of them fighting crime in luxurious locations around Europe. Each episode would last an hour.

The Persuaders was the brainchild of entrepreneur Lew Grade, the founder of Associated Television. He conceived it during a trip to the U.S. to meet the network bosses. They told him they had a slot available for a one-hour show running over 24 weeks. At this point a concept formed in Grade's fluid brain. He envisaged an American oil tycoon and a British peer gallivanting around the French Riviera in a series of humorous adventures: Curtis and Moore, respectively.

The idea met with resistance when Grade mentioned Moore's name. "No," they chorused, "he's been around much too long in *The Saint*. He's been over-exposed." Grade then made the following proposition: "What would you say if I could get Tony Curtis for the other role?" A hush came over the room. This was bigger game. Grade licked his lips as he heard the words, "You'll have a firm order for 24 episodes."[5]

He went to California the next day and phoned George Chasin, an agent who used to be with MCA, to see if he could get Curtis. Chasin was dubious. "Tony will never do television," he warned. Grade then asked him if he could speak to Curtis himself. He said he could but that it would be a waste of time. Nonetheless, later that day Chasin rang him to say Curtis had agreed to meet him at the Beverly Hills hotel. An hour and a half later the deal was done. Grade patted himself on the back for his powers of "persuasion."[6]

His next task was to get Moore roped in. Grade flew to London and approached him about it, but Moore said no. At this point Grade went to a cabinet and took out a check for a "substantial" amount of money. He waved it at Moore's head. "Roger, old boy," he teased, "this is to be getting on with." Moore must have been impressed with the figure because he jumped up from the sofa on which he was sitting and asked, "When do we start?"[7]

Moore had just spent seven years doing *The Saint* and wanted a break from television "for good behavior," but when Grade waved the juicy check in front of him that all changed. "When I was starting out," Moore revealed to a reporter, "I was told I must accept every job I was offered because if I wasn't working I wasn't truly an actor. And if I was fortunate to be offered two jobs at the same time, take the one that offered the most money."[8]

The series' budget was set at $3 million. Grade had already earned this amount by pre-selling the show in the U.S. No wonder he could be generous with Moore. (He always went for the big splash. One of his favorite sayings was, "All my shows are great. Some of them are bad, but they're all great.")[9]

Moore was excited about the chemistry he hoped to create with Curtis. He was looking forward to having a constant costar, in contrast to the relative loneliness of his "saintly" life. "For the first time in many years I would have a screen partner. It's very much like a game of tennis, and unless there's a firm surface, the ball doesn't bounce."[10]

He met Curtis in his home and they got along fine — except for Curtis' attitude toward smoking. When Moore asked him for a cigarette (one of his few vices was chain-smoking), Curtis was horrified. He only offered him one with great reluctance. Before he left the house Curtis presented Moore with a book. On its cover was a picture of something Moore thought looked like chewing gum but turned out to be a pair of lungs that had become diseased from the effects of smoking. He was shocked by the graphic nature of the image. When Moore started coughing blood sometime afterwards he was convinced he'd contracted lung cancer. All he had was a sinus infection, but the experience weighed on him so heavily he all but gave up smoking for life there and then.[11] Also weighing on his mind was Curtis' chilling comment as he puffed on the cigarette reluctantly offered when they met: "That's another minute outa your life, pal."[12]

This episode had an ironic footnote. When Curtis flew to the U.K., customs officers found an ounce of cannabis in his shaving kit at the airport. They immediately marched him off to the local police station and charged him. His lawyer argued that he wasn't a habitual user, having it in his possession merely because a friend gave it to him to ease the tension of the transatlantic flight. He got off with a fine of just £50. This was a tenable excuse because of his well-documented horror of flying, but those who knew him were aware he'd been a recreational user of cannabis for years.

The amount discovered may have been small, but its discovery had wide repercussions. The news was considered important enough to be featured in *The Book of Dates*.[13] Back in the U.S., Bob Hope referred to it in one of his stage acts: "Tony Curtis has been flying around London for three months, waiting to land."[14] Curtis thought to himself, "Why don't my *films* get this kind of publicity?"

News of his arrest even affected his daughter Jamie Lee, whose classmates teased her about it at school. "I can't forget this poem they used to say to me," she said. "Your father's Tony Curtis/And your mother's Janet Leigh/Your father just got busted/But your mommy is free.'" For Jamie Lee the poem carried a deeper meaning: she felt it gave vent to feelings of jealousy her classmates had towards her.[15]

Curtis was hit harder in the pocket than he was in court, as three American TV networks canceled the anti-smoking commercials he'd been doing prior to the bust.[16] It was doubly embarrassing for him because he was actually president of an anti-smoking organization in the U.S. It was called the IQ Club, IQ standing for "I Quit." He was also heavily involved with the American Cancer Society at this time and frequently lobbied for cigarette commercials to be banned from television. He put the situation in stark terms: "Smoking shortens your life by eight years. I love watching pro-football on television. If I smoke, I'll miss 400 games."[17]

He also had another reason for launching the campaign:

> I quit smoking about ten years ago. I had the example of my father. From the time he came from Hungary a cigarette was always dangling from his lips. He was one of those men who talked through the smoke. He developed lung cancer at 42, younger than I am now. They removed a lung and he lived several years, but it was a hellish life — the brain still young and eager in a body that didn't function. I think you carry what your father was on your back. I'm 44 but I figure I carry maybe 80 or 90 years of living around with me. Maybe it's my father that sent Leslie and me to the cancer society last year.[18]

Emanuel had been warned he'd be killing himself if he smoked after his operation, but he couldn't resist sneaking a few. Deprived of them, he climbed the walls in anguish. He

Like many stars frustrated over the fact that they weren't being offered big-budget features, Curtis turned to television to try and revive his career in 1970, costarring with Roger Moore (pictured with him here) in the adventure series *The Persuaders*. It ran for 24 episodes (1971–1972) and cast Curtis as the extrovert playboy Danny Wilde, solving crimes the police weren't able to, with the assistance of Roger Moore (left), who was cast as Lord Brett. It succeeded better in the U.K. than the U.S. and also precipitated a geographical move by Curtis to London, where he took up residence in the fashionable suburb of Belgravia with his third wife, Leslie Allen, having now split from Christine Kaufmann after many years of bickering. The butler above is unidentified.

also took his nerves out on his wife. Curtis thought a few joints of marijuana might relax him, and after some initial reluctance, "Manny" complied.[19]

Allen was disgusted by the cancellation of her husband's anti-smoking commercials. "Leave it to a man's countrymen to do him in,' she thundered. "60,000 people are going to die this year from lung cancer and nobody yet has died from less than an ounce of grass."[20] Curtis remained undaunted in his campaign even after these events. He also continued to smoke hash. Moore remembered him dragging on a "spliff" during an episode of *The Persuaders*.[21] One night Curtis saw Michael Caine chain-smoking at a party and was disgusted. He put his hand into Caine's pocket, took out Caine's packet of cigarettes and hurled it into the fire. He then gave Caine a "very detailed and convincing" lecture on the perils of smoking.[22]

After all the controversy, Curtis found it difficult to concentrate on *The Persuaders*. He also had some issues with Grade. For one thing, Curtis wanted Danny Wilde, the character he played, to dress in casual clothes. Grade felt these ill-befitted a successful businessman. Curtis argued that Wilde was more of a playboy than a businessman, and got his way.[23] Bob Baker, the show's producer, thought Curtis took the name of his character too literally and was capable of running too "wild" with the storylines.[24]

Curtis did a lot of improvising, unlike Moore, who played things straighter. Curtis felt superior to Moore, like many actors who go from the big screen to the small one. He didn't realize that in some quarters TV stars outstripped movie legends — particularly legends like Curtis who were temporarily out of favor. This was brought home to him in no uncertain terms one day when he found himself outside a casino in Monte Carlo with Moore. He spotted some Spanish tourists disembarking from a bus and walking towards them. "Goddam fans," he snapped, "I don't want to have to sign autographs." A moment later he saw them bypassing him for Moore. (Moore had become a household name in Spain from the success of *The Saint*.)[25]

Curtis threw a few tantrums over the long months of shooting. One day when he was called upon to wash his hands for a scene. He didn't want to remove a pair of leather gloves he'd become fond of, so he washed his hands with the gloves on.[26] Another day he threw a fit about his wardrobe. Moore listened to him bawling out the man responsible and said, "To think those lips once kissed Piper Laurie!"[27] Even Curtis had to see the funny side of that.

Many of the early episodes were shot in the south of France. Curtis had a chauffeur drive him to the set. Every morning the man asked the same question: "Where are we going today, Monsieur Curtis?" Because it was the same location each day, Curtis became infuriated with the driver and told him to shut up. On the last day of shooting the driver gave Moore an envelope containing a photograph of himself and a message saying, "This is for you, Mr. Moore, but not that prick Mr. Curtis." Moore was amused but later discovered Curtis had written the message himself, the driver not being aware of what was in the envelope.[28]

Curtis usually loved having a laugh at himself, but this wasn't the case during an episode that starred Joan Collins. Collins didn't get on with "Sooty," Moore's nickname for Curtis. Soon after meeting her, Curtis started going into one of his fairly familiar demolitions of Marilyn Monroe, describing her as "a pain in the ass. And, what's worse, a no-talent pain in the ass." This didn't go down well with Collins. She deeply admired the "sweet, naïve" star."[29]

Curtis had a scene with Collins which called on her to bend down behind a rock that was about to explode when villains shoot at it. She wanted to be sure the fall-out from the special effects explosion didn't damage her face, which she described as her "proverbial fortune." Curtis thought she was being overly cautious. When she continued to delay he bellowed, "Jesus Christ, just do the fucking scene. What's all the fuss? Anyone would think you're a fucking princess or something."[30] Her caution proved to be well-founded. A rehearsal of the scene resulted in a huge sheet of flame shooting out from the rock, which then exploded.[31] Curtis stalked off the set in anger.

His mood wasn't much better the next day when he had to drive her across a riverbed in a jeep. The scene had to be re-shot a number of times and she started to feel sick because of all the jerking around. Eventually she decided to walk to the starting point instead of having him drive her. When she got back to the jeep she lit up a cigarette and Curtis lost his temper. He fanned his hands in the air trying to expel the smoke. After she left the jeep for the fourth time he erupted. "You stupid cunt," he said, "what the fuck are you doing? Who the fuck do you think you are?" Nobody ever used the "C" word to her before, certainly not within earshot of a film crew. "What did you call me?" she said. He repeated it with a smirk. Still incredulous, she called out to the crew, "Did you hear that?" A voice replied, "Yes, and bloody rude it was too."[32] Collins took this as her cue to walk off the set until an apology was forthcoming.

Moore tried to pacify her in her trailer. "Roger," she wailed, "the son-of-a-bitch called me a cunt in front of the whole bloody crew." Her own choice of language was amusing in the circumstances. (One is reminded of Jack Nicholson's comment, "My mother never saw the irony in calling me a son-of-a-bitch.") Moore consoled her with, "There's only one cunt on this picture, Joanie, and that's Sooty."

He followed this with the putdown, "Hollywood actors can be a real pain in the butt," thereby making the incident into a Britain-versus-U.S. issue. "I'll make the idiot apologize to you," he promised. He went to Curtis, who offered the hilarious, "Hey, man, look, I'm sorry, really sorry I called her a cunt. Tell the cunt to accept my apologies." Collins gave a different version of events, saying Curtis was "abject with remorse."[33]

Curtis would have been the first to admit he had a quicksilver temperament but he was also very sensitive. "I'm not the same person I was 21 years ago," he told Michael Freedland, "but only in the same way as I'm not the same person I was 21 minutes ago."[34] Most people's fuses grow shorter with age and this man was no exception. He claimed that what initially annoyed him about Collins wasn't her leaving the jeep so much as doing her makeup inside it to get "into the mood" for the scene, *à la* Marilyn Monroe.[35]

During a later episode he was shocked to see her ask another actor, Robert Hutton, to leave his trailer so she could use the bathroom. Moore told him bluntly that the dictates of the series meant trailers had to be shared. He didn't see her as pulling rank. "This is a TV show," he explained, "we're all in it together. We don't make waves." Curtis tried to hide his disgruntlement with a *faux*–British concession: "Yes, dear sweet Roger, you're right. You're always right."[36]

Curtis thought *The Persuaders* worked better for Moore than himself because of its anglicized format. He also thought the series lacked "a spine." Every episode should have been different, in his view. It should have had the audience guessing what would happen next. "It was a cartoon," he reckoned, "a Batman. There were mythical men chasing mythical spies all over mythical countries with mythical daughters of mythical fathers turning chemicals into gold out of water."[37]

It was a hit in Europe but performed poorly in the U.S. In many ways it signaled the end of Curtis' career as a matinee idol, "milking the last drops of boyishness" out of him.[38] Tony Parsons summed up its iconic appeal: "The opening scene where they beat the crap out of each other remains tattooed forever on my heart."[39]

Why didn't it take off in the U.S.? Curtis felt it was a victim of bad timing. "The networks in America fucked it up," he opined, "They put it on Saturday night at 10 o'clock. The only ones up at that time are male nurses giving enemas."[40] Bob Baker thought it fell prey to another kind of timing: "I think part of the reason it didn't work too well in America was because it was a few years ahead of itself. Later we had *Moonlighting* and *Remington Steele*."[41]

Lew Grade attributed its failure to a more debatable root cause: "Roger and Tony didn't hit it off all that well. Apart from an understandable rivalry, Roger was annoyed at Tony's insistence that work should cease on the dot of 5 P.M. Roger was always willing to work late to finish filming a sequence but Tony had just got married and wanted to spend as much time as possible with his new bride. He couldn't wait to get home each day."[42]

That didn't mean Curtis didn't take the show seriously. Television, he told Michael Freedland, was "no different from making films for the cinema."[43] But he knew it was still a comedown for him. The fact that he signed up for it, wrote Peter Bradshaw, "tipped us off that his career was in its autumnal phase."[44]

The British broadcaster Barry Norman interviewed Curtis in October 1970 and found him extolling the merits of TV over movies.[45] He also talked about the way Moore and himself had spent many years "hardnosing" around Hollywood.[46] Two months later he showed he hadn't lost his sense of humor when he explained to Ray Connolly what *The Persuaders* was about: "It's a series of 50-minute melodramas, comedies and horror stories all laced together by two men, one an English lord and the other an American wiseguy. Roger Moore plays the wiseguy and I'm his Jewish mother."[47]

As was the case with Norman, Curtis engaged in a rant against cinemas: "They're pushing candy on you all the time when it's bad for your teeth. People are smoking cigarettes all the time too, which is bad for your lungs. Then on top of that they push a commercial, a short that's junk, and coming attractions that are rubbish [too]. All you wanted was to go and see some guy making it with some girl."[48]

When Connolly asked him how he felt about being busted for possessing pot the previous summer, Curtis threw a monkey wrench into the question, suggesting that it could have been a concerted plot by a tobacco company to halt his anti-smoking campaign — an interesting theory.[49] He said he himself gave up smoking eight years before. "My father died of a heart attack brought on by the fact that he had cancer. He was 58 when he died but looked as though he was 76. I watched him for 16 years after they took out his lung — an invalid who couldn't eat."[50]

Curtis branched out into a general reflection on being mistreated by the media for his work on screen: "Awful things were said about me. I really had atrocious reviews. Sure they hurt. Jesus, you're just doing your job.... David Susskind said on television that I was a 'passionate amoeba.' Why would a man want to say a thing like that? He debased me and made me look like a schmuck." Curtis didn't let Connolly go without having a poke at his own favorite target: the intelligentsia. Or, more particularly, those thespians who believed in going up their own rear ends for artistic catharses. "Everybody has to be so *aware* these days," he expostulated, "aware of themselves, aware of their senses. It's like masturbating in Macy's window."[51] There was no answer to that.

Another interview he did at this time was with the author Donald Zec. Zec described Curtis as being so ferociously friendly he hugged anything that came into his hotel room: "Men, dogs, animal, vegetable, or mineral." When Allen appeared on the scene, their embrace had "all the groping ardor of a mating of octopuses."[52]

Curtis had always been ultra-friendly. His extra good spirits on this occasion were down to his great expectations for *The Persuaders*. "Cassette television will revolutionize the movie business," he predicted. "Horse manure and the moguls killed off the old Hollywood. They were like ostriches putting their heads in the sand and their fingers in their ears hoping the crisis would blow over."[53] Notwithstanding the unfortunate mixed metaphor, his point held good.

He was humble enough to tell Zec that his career had been created by the movie machine rather than any talent he had. Describing himself as "a big bag of nothing put together with spit, glue and a couple of film stills," he was delighted to grab it with both hands. "When you've shined shoes, delivered papers, made broom handles and served in hamburger joints, 75 bucks a week and girls to go with it is no hardship."[54] Before the interview ended he went into ecstacies about Allen. "Leslie is more than a good wife," he beamed. "She's the most genuine thing I've ever known, and that includes men, women, cats, dogs and snakes."[55]

By now he'd bought a house in the Belgravia area of London. Himself and Allen lived an undemonstrative life there behind the scenes. He liked doing ordinary things with her — going for walks, listening to music, bargain-hunting on the High Street at weekends. "I think she puts on her oldest clothes and looks very poor because she always bargains well," Curtis joked. "But then I approve of that. If there's one thing that bugs me it's getting took. When I buy, I don't like people to know it's me. That's asking for trouble."[56]

He even hated paying rent. That was why he'd decided to buy the house. He also decided to do it up himself because "decorators cost the earth and never really give you a home. They just paper the walls with money for effect." But he wasn't parsimonious. He liked giving money to those that deserved it. His priority was people who'd come to his rescue in the past. "In my whole life there have been maybe six occasions when people have helped me out of pure kindness. As soon as I made it I singled those people out and repaid them ten times over. That was a marvelous feeling." It worked the other way too. When he became successful he got his revenge on his enemies — not by taking money from them but in other ways. "Oh, and that was sweet, settling old scores."[57]

He didn't know how long he'd be in London. "Five years, eight, maybe for always. My work makes me a gypsy but I like to get some roots down." He felt more respect coming his way in Britain than the U.S. "I feel I'm accepted better here. In America there are some who will always think of me as an upstart slob. Here I am what I am now."[58]

Curtis' first son, Nicholas, was born on the last day of 1970. "After five times I finally got it right," he chortled. Allegra thought of him as a Henry VIII character, "always in search of a wife who could give him a male heir to the throne."[59]

He regained custody of Alexandra and Allegra at this time, Kaufmann having been found to be remiss in some of her duties towards her children. For one thing, their teeth had been destroyed by junk food. Curtis also said their stomachs were distended "like the starving children of Africa."[60] She was given limited access to them at holiday times. Curtis also instigated proceedings to obtain legal custody of Kelly and Jamie from Leigh that year, and to have $100,000 that he gave her for child support returned to him. Because, he said, she hadn't used the money for that purpose.

Allegra felt Kaufmann was badly treated by Allen and Curtis. She thought the "bad teeth" accusation was little more than an excuse. As the new Mrs. Curtis, Allen wanted to present Curtis and herself to the world as kindly figures, to build up a family image. Curtis rowed in behind that aim. "He wouldn't have taken us if he was alone," Allegra charged. It was a media gesture. The press asked: Why did Christine let her children go?[61]

Kaufmann knew she didn't have a leg to stand on in any custody suit. The law in the U.S. was that the rights were given to the financially wealthier parent except in rare circumstances. Curtis had servants, a swimming pool, the money to put Alex and Allegra into the best schools. She herself, on the contrary, was "a nomad mother without roots." Curtis also argued that Allen wouldn't have to work to support the children so she could be a more hands-on parent. Kaufmann didn't dispute any of this. She felt Allen wanted the children more than he did. Neither did she think a tug-of-love court battle would do them any good. So she decided to give in gracefully. But she still felt her daughters were being "kidnapped" from her.[62]

Once Curtis and Allen had the children, they disposed of all the clothes and toys Kaufmann had bought for them. It was as if they were banishing all memories of her from their lives, or seeking to make Kaufmann feel even more insignificant.[63] A story about her mother packing dirty clothes for them on a flight to Sardinia once was given as "evidence" of her substandard mothering.[64]

In the following years Curtis frequently badmouthed Kaufmann, sometimes in completely over-the-top fashion. He once told a reporter she "deserved to be gassed." Fortunately for both of them, the remark never appeared in print.[65]

Allegra loved being with him in the basement of his Belgravia home. Here he hid from the world like a child, immersing himself in his paintings, his box art, his broken mirrors, his dried flowers, his cut-up postcards, his animal figures. "He always smelt of turpentine," she remembered. He loved charcoal and smeared it all over his fingers for her to see. These were the times she had him all to herself, sitting in his lap or painting with him on a big white sheet of paper on the floor. Sometimes he brought her to saunas where they'd both sweat profusely. Why would people want to sweat so much, she wondered. But like most children she liked to mimic the behavior of adults. In the evenings she'd have bubble baths with her father and Allen.[66]

One day Curtis received a gift of a book from Jamie. It was a collection of photographs of painters at work. He cried as he looked through it. He was easily moved to tears at times like this. Much more important than the book was the fact that it endorsed his identity as a painter for him in her eyes. It was a testament to that fact, and also to the fact that she was thinking of him.[67]

He returned to the States to do a Broadway comedy called *Turtlenecks*. Hugh Hefner was putting up some of the money for it. Curtis played a character who writes shows for the half-time slot at football games. He liked the play but wasn't too keen on having to learn pages of dialogue for almost every scene. Movies didn't demand such reliance on memory.

He was asked if Broadway was where over-the-hill movie actors went to die. He begged to disagree. Plays were where it was at now, not movies. Hollywood was "on its ass." Besides, he didn't need the money. As well as having a house in L.A. he had another one in London and a ranch in California. He also owned a percentage of a basketball team and a computer company. If the play succeeded, good and well. If not, that was okay too. Acting was now a "minor theme" in his life. Critics couldn't hurt him anymore. They always murdered him, so why should this be any different? He wasn't going to be like Marilyn Monroe, "being squeezed like a toothpaste tube."[68]

Hugh Hefner and Curtis had high hopes for *Turtlenecks* but it didn't take off, becoming yet another in a long string of disappointments for the beleaguered actor. An added humiliation was the fact that many people walked out during the actual performances. It played five weeks to poor houses in Detroit and then a fortnight in Philadelphia, where things failed to pick up. The title was changed to *The One-Night Stand* afterwards. This became strangely appropriate as it folded soon afterwards. Curtis licked his wounds and made a tail-between-the-legs return to Britain.

He found the English to be more sensitive than their American counterparts. "I don't know why," he admitted. "Maybe it's because it's such a small country it makes everybody introspective, throws everybody inside each other."[69] He told David Gillard, "England's a fine place to live but I like to fashion myself as a citizen of the world. I want to eliminate all those factors that separate us, like passports and color."[70]

He also wanted to eliminate ageism. "I'm a very dissatisfied person. I really resent the fact that I won't be in the Olympics. I just wish there were Olympics for 40-year-olds."[71] (He was actually 47.)

"I want to go out and help with the ecological problems of this world," he continued. "I want to contribute but I find I'm not allowed to enter those areas. The days of the adventurer are over. If you go on safari now you go with cameras and there's a toilet ten yards from the lions."[72] Gillard must have been wondering what was coming next in the rambling discourse. It turned out to be the movies. "I don't really want or need pictures anymore," Curtis declared. "When I started making movies in 1948 it was my life. I know I made some crappy [ones] at the beginning and people laughed. But they shouldn't have been laughing too much because I kept getting paid. Now when the job is over I just shake hands and walk away."[73]

In mid–1973 he announced his retirement from movies with this broadside against the industry: "I'm going to take no more crap from anyone. I've spent 25 years in the clink. I won't make a feature film for anyone except myself. I have paid the piper."[74]

He decided to spend the summer in London. He tried his best to entertain Jamie but she was aloof with him. She took his desertion of Leigh much worse than Kelly and carried her resentment into any time they spent together. Curtis always blamed Leigh for Jamie's alienation from him. Leigh denied she ever "knocked" him to Jamie, but he convinced himself she told Jamie he was "a rake, a drunk and a dope addict."[75]

At the end of the summer he reiterated his disenchantment with Hollywood's hypocrisy: "All the promises made by those nice guys in tailored suits behind walnut desks, smoking large cigars, telling you what a great movie you're going to make — I've had it with them. I don't want my sons to sit in front of a TV set twenty years hence and say 'Gee, how did you make a movie like that?'"[76]

From now on he was going to be in charge of the process. "If I ever make another film it will be totally me. Produced, directed, written and played by Tony Curtis." He had also started writing. "I figure: Why pay for scripts when I can write my own just as well?"[77]

Whenever an idea struck him it seemed to blot out everything that went before. It was as if he could wake up one morning and say "I'm going to be a writer" and that would be that. Goodbye Hollywood, hello the literati. Everything was exaggerated in his mind. There were never any half-measures; he would be ruthless in his excision of the past. "When I was a kid," he said, "I used to go to the movie house and watch the heroes fencing and doing the love scenes. And I thought, 'That's for me.' Then when I got to Hollywood I figured if being a movie star is being nice to Louella Parsons and doing silly publicity then I had to do it. Can you believe it?"[78]

We would indeed believe it because we'd seen it happen. He had climbed one mountain and found the view from the top disenchanting. He was now going to attempt to scale another one.

15
Faded Grandeur

Curtis let his body go in the seventies. This was partly due to the fact that he stopped making what he called "the physical movies." To get it back he started using "substances."[1] These kept his weight down. He also needed them to soak up the depression he felt over the fact that his career was going so badly.

The Dream Factory closed up shop for him when he left Leigh but it was as if it took until now for that fact to catch up with him — "like a delayed-action switch you pulled to stop a machine."

Hollywood had also started to take itself too seriously. Nobody, suddenly, had any time for "Tony Curtis films." Could he define these? No, it was just a sense he got. Was realism better? Yes and no. Yes because of obvious reasons, no because it meant people lost sight of why movies began in the first place — because of their magic. As Richard Widmark scoffed, "Hollywood got into trouble when the town started making films instead of movies."[2]

Drink and drugs immunized him to the pain he was feeling. They also filled him with delusions. He started to dress flamboyantly and behave eccentrically. He took to wearing things like army berets and doing interviews on the floors of hotel rooms.[3]

The last addition to the Curtis family, another boy, arrived in May 1973. He was called Benjamin. Curtis had a vasectomy after he was born. "I figured I'd contributed enough to the population of the planet," he reasoned.[4] The operation led to some amusing incidents. One night he was at the Sands Hotel with Frank Sinatra when a woman he'd been with said, "I've got something to tell you. I'm pregnant and the only one I've been with is you." Curtis replied, "Well boy did you get fucked because I've just had a vasectomy!"[5]

He bounced back from the *Turtlenecks* fiasco with an interesting performance as the Jewish mobster Louis Lepke, a man so ruthless he made Al Capone look like "chopped liver." Lepke had 200 killers on contract to him, declared Curtis, "all making ten to one hundred thousand dollars a year from their business. I wanted to know what was in his background, his environment, to make him that kind of man." Curtis was also intrigued by the fact that Lepke was "the only one of the kingpin gangsters of that era who died in the electric chair. He was so powerful none of the other guys tried to bump him off."[6]

He thought long and hard before he made the movie. *Lepke* was his first feature film in five years. His last one had been *The Boston Strangler*. They were both grim features, and both, in a sense, featured similar characters. Lepke was as vicious as Albert DeSalvo if not quite as unhinged. For Curtis they represented similar challenges because they were both equally pugnacious, both equally bitter. From an actor's point of view they gave him room to maneuver, to do things that weren't necessarily in the script.

Lepke was a Jew born in the New York slums, like Curtis, and he also dropped out of school to join street gangs. "Had things gone differently for me I could have been a Louis Lepke," he reckoned. Well, maybe not quite. Lepke was a man who "organized murders as if he was buying a ticket to board a train."[7] He grew so powerful in the 1930s as the self-styled king of the labor rackets he could effectively shut down a city by having the key union people rubbed out. He rarely pulled the trigger himself, paying as little as $25 for a hit, depending on the importance of the victim.

Said Curtis:

> I had a particular interest in Lepke because he infiltrated the garment trade. Most of the gangsters were into bootlegging and prostitution but he sidestepped those. He got into the bakery unions later. No more than Albert DeSalvo, they would probably never have caught him if he hadn't given himself up. He was promised a soft deal by the law but it didn't happen. They set him up for a fall.

The key scene of the movie for him was where Lepke is electrocuted. He refrained from entering the electrocution room before the scene was shot so he could replicate Lepke's surprise at seeing where he was going to die. He knew Lepke got into the chair arrogantly and without fear, so he did that. It was like Gary Gilmore's imprecation to his executioner in 1977: "Let's do it." "He showed no expression on his face," Gilbert Millstein remarked. "You might have thought he was at a soda fountain."[8]

Curtis was excited about *Lepke*. It was his *Godfather* movie. If Frank Sinatra could retire and then reappear, so could he. If it worked it could be his comeback vehicle. But it didn't, and it wasn't.

The reasons were many. Basically the film looks too bland. Curtis also looked too handsome. He was too tanned, too groomed. He looked as if he just came out of a Bel Air salon rather than Skid Row. Neither did he appear ethnic enough. We felt we were looking at the Curtis of the sex comedies. Reviews of it were thus lukewarm. Morten Ross described it as a big screen shoot-'em-up that hardly added to the art of cinema.[9]

Curtis' mother died while he was making the film. When he got the call to say she was suffering from heart failure he flew to the hospital in Culver City to be by her side, but as soon as he got to her ward and heard her calling him he stopped short. Suddenly all the memories of her demanding nature and her unremitting cruelty came flooding back, and he couldn't go into her room.

The nurse in charge was flummoxed. How could he have flown to see her and then leave the hospital when he was just a few feet from where she lay? Nobody could understand his anger but himself. "I walked out," he said, "and never went back." She died a week later, leaving all her money ($10,000) to Bobby.

Curtis had always told her that if she did that the state would appropriate it, and they did. Instead of feeling remorse for not seeing her, all he felt now was even more anger. "She did it deliberately," he wrote in his autobiography. "She knew how to stick it to me even in death."[10] In her defense, Curtis was a wealthy movie star and Bobby a patient in a psychiatric clinic who needed the best attention he could get. What mother wouldn't prioritize the latter?

This account of her death was from his second autobiography. In his first one he said his mother "gave" Bobby $10,000 "once," thereby implying it was a gift to him from when she was alive. He added that she knew "full well that Bobby, who was then a ward of state, would blow it all."[11] This is significantly different from having it taken from him by the state.

Curtis' drugtaking began in earnest with *Lepke*. "A woman working on the set said, 'Try this.' It was a packet of paper. I knew it was cocaine. I snorted it. I found instant energy and a craving for it. Before I knew it, I was hooked."[12]

One of his drug "buddies" at this time was the Rolling Stones guitarist Ronnie Wood. Wood also shared Curtis' interest in painting. They sketched one another, took cocaine and discussed (who else) Marilyn Monroe. "I'd chop up coke for myself on top of her photographs," Wood wrote in his memoirs, recalling nights when the two of them were stoned together, "and he'd mumble, 'You bitch. You bitch.'"[13] It was on one of these evenings that Curtis' bitterness about Monroe (which he tended to downplay in interviews) came out. He told Wood that when they were making *Some Like It Hot* she was the first person on the studio lot every morning and the last one off it at night "because she was fucking everybody."[14]

Curtis asked Wood to "house-sit" for him once when he was spending some time away from London. He showed him around prior to his departure, even giving him the use of his wine cellar.[14] That was his first mistake. His second was to leave over forty vintage wines there, all of which Wood and his cronies slurped back at their nightly parties when Curtis was away, except for a bottle of Chateau Petrus which they bountifully left. Curtis was enraged when he got back and found his precious supply gone. (He had been collecting the wines for years.) Wood offered to replace them but Curtis said that was impossible. Wood then said, "Tony, does this mean we're not friends anymore?" Curtis replied, "Ron, I love your company but I can't stand your hours."[15]

Depressed about his career, Curtis now started to turn his attention to literature. He'd started to write a novel and was high on it. "I really want to do everything. If some guy next to me writes a novel, why can't I?"[16] His working title was *Kid Andrew Cody and Julie Sparrow*. "It's about two brothers of the same father but different mothers," he explained. "They've been raised in different environments and they don't meet until late in life. One is connected with a Las Vegas casino; the other is an actor. I have a feeling it will be published in England."[17]

He related this news in an interview with Morton Ross. Ross was amused that he had a publisher already organized when he'd hardly put pen to paper. "First it's published," Ross commented dryly, "then it's a screenplay and soon a movie. He'll direct the movie and play the father of the two brothers."[18] (Though Curtis was about to join the literary world, he had no great love of writers.)[19]

When the conversation turned to acting, Curtis went on a familiar rant against Lee Strasberg's Academy: "What no instruction explains is that indefinable something, the reason why the eye of the audience is on one person in a scene."[20] There seemed to be a Freudian slip in an anecdote Curtis related to Ross about visiting the Actor's Studio in the early 1950s when a lecture was going on. Nobody knew he was in the room. In the course of the lecture the speaker talked about "our method in contrast to the Tony Curtis way." Curtis was livid. "You act by going out there and acting," he stressed, "not by learning how to stick your fingers down your throat to prepare yourself for a part."[21]

He now signed up for another TV series, *McCoy*, and was hopeful about its prospects.

"I think I can do something that may be a harbinger of the future of prime time television," he glowed.[22] This was a big claim for a series that turned out to be little more than standard fluff. He played a con man setting up stings to catch villains. Larry Hagman costarred with him in one episode, *The Big Rip-Off*. He loved Curtis' sense of fun but was amazed at his inability to remember his lines. The effects of his drugtaking were beginning to kick in. "You'd never guess he had slips of paper pasted everywhere," Hagman divulged. "We did one scene in a car and I held a flashlight so he could see them."[23]

Curtis bought a $12 million house in California after securing the series, which netted him a cool $75,000 per episode. He had a habit of buying houses to reward himself for snagging lucrative roles. There was also a possible health benefit, as he alluded to in an anecdote he related. "I once read about an eccentric old woman who was convinced she'd die unless she kept adding rooms to her mansion. She lived to be 95. One room for each year."[24] He promised to do his best to emulate her.

He went to the Cannes Film Festival in 1975 and felt he was back in the big time again:

> My feature films were playing every night on TV. I was followed everywhere. All of the big stars are there and I'm eating them up alive. That was a revelation. If you hang around Hollywood and listen to the doomsayers long enough you begin to feel fortunate you're even holding a Screen Actor's Guild card. You've got to get out, travel a little bit, see the sense of pleasure your films give people, be stopped in the street by crying women and quivering men.[25]

Rex Reed saw the situation differently, spiking Curtis' bubble with the acid-laced, "When a hundred photographers show up to mob Tony Curtis, you know the festival is in trouble." Curtis bridled at this kind of gratuitous abuse. "I stiff-arm it. Don't even get the trade papers. Columnists don't call me because they know I'll reject them."[26] A more likely reason was that he wasn't hot copy anymore.

He returned to his swashbuckling ways with a TV movie, *The Count of Monte Cristo*. This time, for a change, he was cast as a villain. It was supposed to be followed up with a role in the remake of *The Man in the Iron Mask*, but this didn't materialize. "I started to feel time was running out for me," he said. Where was the optimism of Cannes?

Now that he was fifty, age was a concern. "You begin to see the final curtain, you realize today isn't forever." That meant not placing too big an importance on big houses (or extended room space). He had given up cigars and cut down on the number of cars in his garage. It used to be up to six, along with "three Mexican gardeners and a cook who could improvise James Beard midnight suppers." For the episodes of *McCoy* he was less showy, more focused: "I go on the set carrying the standard mimeographed script under my arm." The production people were also shocked to discover he had no stand-in. "Years ago my stand-in had a stand-in!" he declaimed.[27]

Things weren't ideal on the home front by now. The relationship between Allen and his daughters wasn't good. Allegra wanted to tell Curtis Allen treated her badly when he was away, but she felt he really didn't want to know. "He had always gone into denial about potentially threatening scenarios, so he wrapped himself in silence."[28]

Allegra's happiest moments as she grew were when she'd watch him swimming in the pool every morning, or when he taught her to swim herself, or told funny stories at the dining table. She was less impressed with the way he walked around the house semi-clothed, or even naked, wallowing in the image of himself as a "Californian liberal." One day he wanted to drive her to school in his underpants but she wouldn't have it.

She didn't fare well from being juggled between Kaufmann and Allen. "Your mother is a hippie and a heroin addict," Allen told her in her role as Wicked Stepmother. Allegra didn't know whether to believe her or not, imagining her aggressiveness might have been caused by Allegra's pining for Kaufmann. Allen barked: "Just because she brought you into the world doesn't mean she's your mother."[29]

Allegra's mental condition deteriorated as she grew. She self-harmed and wet her bed. Curtis' "solution" was to give her a plastic sheet. He didn't delve into the cause of her malaise. His thinking was: How could anyone have problems if they're rich? He sent her to a psychologist, the quick fix solution. After a while she refused to go.

His inability to empathize with either Allegra or Alexandra continued as they grew into young women. Said Allegra, "He gave us things that didn't suit our ages."[30]

On a visit to Hugh Hefner in London once with Curtis, Allegra put perfume on her chest to impress him. She had seen Allen do this. But Allen didn't like it. "You behaved like a whore and you looked like a whore," was her reaction.[31]

Allegra asked Curtis why Allen was so aggressive toward her. "Leslie is just going through a phase," was his defensive response to the accusation. "He distanced himself from my tears and my sufferings," Allegra complained. She thought she'd have been better off with Kaufmann than Allen, which caused Curtis to snap, "I saved you from a mother who was incapable of being a mother." Allegra saw this as a cop-out. She didn't think he really cared. "My words just bounced off him."[32]

Kaufmann admitted to Allegra that she wasn't the perfect wife to Curtis. She said she divorced him because she had a yearning to act. "That yearning," she told the young girl, "cost you your childhood." Being with Curtis now meant she'd have better schooling.[33] (And probably better teeth.)

In 1976 Curtis played a supporting role in the movie adaptation of F. Scott Fitzgerald's final novel, *The Last Tycoon*. It told the story of the movie tycoon Monroe Stahr, loosely based on the studio *wunderkind* Irving Thalberg. Jack Nicholson wanted to play the lead role but Robert De Niro scooped it instead. Nicholson settled for the role of a Communist negotiator.[34] The film was directed by Elia Kazan.

Curtis played a faded movie star, Rodriguez. Harold Pinter wrote the screenplay so there were a lot of big names involved. Sam Spiegel, the producer, also managed to secure the services of veteran stars like Robert Mitchum, Jeanne Moreau, Ray Milland and Donald Pleasance.

Thalberg died at age 36. He had a huge ego, but he was prone to mistakes. One was imagining *Gone with the Wind* would be a flop.[35] As the film begins, the precocious mogul is trying to come to terms with the death of his wife, Minna Davis. Then he sees her lookalike in an English woman called Kathleen Moore and falls in love with her. Both of these parts were played by the newcomer Ingrid Boulting.

Fitzgerald was supposed to have thought up this idea from his own feelings about the gossip columnist Sheilah Graham, his partner when he died. Graham resembled Fitzgerald's wife Zelda in appearance.[36] This is how he described the moment when Stahr spots Moore in his book: "Smiling faintly at him from not four feet away was the face of his dead wife, identical even to the expression."[37]

De Niro jumped at the chance to work with Kazan, but Kazan felt Pinter's script was too sluggish. Spiegel didn't agree. De Niro's biographer, John Parker, etched in the madcap scenario: "There was an old-time Hollywood producer aged 75, hiring a one-time directorial ace aged 66, hiring a trusting young admirer. All three were working with a screenplay produced by a famous writer trapped by his own mystical structures and eccentricities in an attempt to make a comprehensible movie out of the unfinished work of an alcoholic genius."[38]

Apart from Pinter's screenplay, the main problem was Boulting. She'd had little or no experience before the camera. Spiegel had recommended Boulting to Kazan but was now having second thoughts about her. Kazan also disapproved of Boulting, but as time went on he felt he might be able to get a good performance out of her. Kazan was more dubious about the equally inexperienced Therese Russell in a lesser part, but Spiegel, who was trying to bed her at the time (unsuccessfully, as it happened), persuaded Kazan to give her a chance. As was the case with Boulting, Kazan felt he had work to do here.

Kazan's mother was dying as he took on the film. She was elderly, and her doctor expressed little hope for her recovery. Many days after shooting, Kazan visited her in the hospital. Each day he watched her sinking lower. Meanwhile, the film went on in fits and starts.

Kazan saw something of the intuitiveness of the young Brando in De Niro, but Spiegel felt he lacked star power. De Niro was underplaying, and Kazan worried about the fact that the love story wouldn't take off as a result. "Why the hell doesn't he take her?" Kazan's wife Barbara demanded, frustrated at De Niro's reticence around Boulting.[39]

Curtis' character was suffering from impotence. "Maybe this was a metaphor for my failing appeal at the box office," he joked. Rodriguez hadn't been in Fitzgerald's novel, so Curtis was doubly glad to have received the offer from Kazan to do it. "When Elia called me," he wrote in his autobiography, "it brought tears to my eyes because at that point I really thought my career was over."[40] Kazan confided to him that before he made the call he'd been warned that Curtis might be difficult. This enraged Curtis. "Obviously," he scowled, "those motherfuckers in that Strasberg School of Bullshit bumrapped every actor who didn't go through their system."[41]

De Niro suggested working on Sundays to nail the part. Such a suggestion didn't appeal to Curtis. Mitchum didn't like De Niro's fussiness either. He resented the way he took up so much of Kazan's time, "interpreting and analyzing his character almost line by line."[42] De Niro's demands raised Spiegel's blood pressure. "I have five and a half million dollars of my money invested in this fucking movie," he railed at Kazan, "and it's riding on this boy who's spoiling fast and is so willful and arrogant. I'm thinking of replacing him."[43] Boulting also continued to be a problem. "I was lost in the middle of all that madness," Curtis lamented. "For a while I felt like walking off the picture and leaving them all with their 18-carat egos. Maybe De Niro should have played Narcissus instead."

What Curtis didn't realize was that De Niro was suffering almost as much as he was. Spiegel continued to heap derision on him, accusing him of being a "petty larceny little punk" because the actor had asked for an increase in his expenses. All of these arguments took the life out of Kazan. He wrote in his diary, "I like to swing, to make things up as I go along in a scene. But the resilience has gone out of me, and the fun. A good professional job doesn't make a good film."[44]

The production cranked on like a car in fourth gear, but Curtis did well as the *angst*-ridden Rodriguez. Kazan was so happy with him he even let him direct one of his own scenes. This gratified him hugely.[45] Kazan advised him to become a director himself, so pleased was he with Curtis' work in the movie.[46] After Curtis did his last scene he brought Kazan a gift to thank him for his direction. Kazan, for some strange reason, refused it. Equally mysteriously, Curtis reacted to the refusal by saying to him, "Any man who would fuck his wife is an animal."[47] Was he annoyed at Kazan or merely being frivolous? He wasn't sure.

At the end of the prescribed shooting time, Kazan decided to film one more scene. He saw it as his signature to the film and indeed a valedictory to his career.[48] By doing so he was mirroring the life of Thalberg, the "doomed prince."[49] He was sad when it was over, but it hadn't gone the way he wanted. Neither were the reviews good when it went into release. Only Nicholson emerged with anything approaching a commendation.[50] Curtis received mixed notices for his performance. Some critics felt it was a brave career change. Others, like De Niro's biographer John Baxter, merely found him embarrassing.[51] Baxter misinterpreted the performance: it's Rodriguez who's embarrassing, not Curtis. He imbues the role with a kind of comic desperation by dint of his whispers and his halting delivery. It's a wonderfully camp cameo. It's a pity it didn't go on longer to give us some relief from the dull brooding of De Niro and Boulting.

Clive James went so far as to say Curtis overshadowed De Niro in the film, his cameo as the swashbuckling hero of silent movies who'd lost his confidence "work[ing] perfectly in two registers."[52]

When I asked Curtis how he'd gotten on with De Niro on the set, his answer surprised me. "Robert De Niro is a charming man but he doesn't give you much as an actor. He kept to himself a lot. I thought of him as introverted. There wasn't much chemistry between us." It was like a microcosm of what the movie was about, Stahr being isolated and Curtis as the fading *roué*. Two different generations were colliding, both onscreen and off it. Maybe, I suggested, De Niro's perceived introversion was simply an example of him trying to get in character. "You may be right," he allowed, "but I just saw it as bad manners. That is not the way I behave toward my costars. He came across as slightly rude but he may have had his reasons. As you can see from the way the movie performed, it might not have been a wise decision on his part." I sensed an anger behind his words, maybe even an element of glee that the prima donna had gotten his just desserts in the end. He had done exactly what he was asked. The result was a purported panegyric that played itself out like a mirage. Moore likened the activity of speaking Pinter's words to "blowing air into yeast when making bread."[53]

This was almost the last time Curtis would work for a high-quality director. In the following years he would make more dumb comedies, a demonic exploitation film, a film verging on soft porn, a sci-fi clunker, an assembly line whodunit, a Shakespearean disaster and various other films which were either desperate ploys to convince himself he was still employable or that he still had something to offer an industry that was bypassing him just as surely as it had bypassed Elia Kazan, Monroe Stahr and the impotent, pathetic Rodriguez.

16

Author Author

Curtis' performance in *The Last Tycoon* didn't win him an Oscar nod or raise his profile with other directors. "Sometimes it feels that if you treat that lot with disdain," he brooded, "they fall over themselves to be nice to you. George C. Scott tells them what they can do with their Oscar and they can't wait to hand him one. And Kate Hepburn, who doesn't want to know about Hollywood, she's only got to burp and they hand her an award."[1]

He thought a shift into writing might revive his reputation. He'd begun work on his novel between scenes of the Kazan movie and now took it up again in earnest. As with everything else he did in life, he threw himself into it 110 percent. "When I decided to start writing," he told an interviewer, "I picked up a couple of How-To books and couldn't believe the crap I read. Then Irving Lazar sent me a journal by Somerset Maugham that hooked me. It's called *A Writer's Notebook*."[2]

Curtis rarely read fiction himself, he went on, preferring to dip into *Scientific American* or "some theoretical discussion about Plato." (Only Curtis could go from science to philosophy in the blink of an eye and not see a disjunction.) As regards research for his book, he figured life itself would provide that: "Making all the movies I have has allowed me to experience twice the life of most people."[3]

He concluded the interview with a general overview of where he was at:

> I like my work in films and I like writing and painting, but what's most important to me is living. I take care of myself to enjoy life. You can't live well without being healthy. I eat simply — fresh orange juice with two raw eggs in the morning, never any lunch, maybe an apple in the afternoon and in the evening my dear wife will fix, say, chicken with rice and a big salad. What keeps me fit is an active sex life. I'm horny. I have no hang-ups about it. Also, art comes out of sexuality. Doesn't everything? It's another form of ejaculation, peak, renewal. Nothing can beat rubbing against someone's leg and boom ... a thousand colors flash.[4]

But it wasn't only his "dear wife" he was communing with, and the healthy diet was supplemented with some more exotic ingredients, like cocaine.

He had excessive expectations of how the novel would perform. At one point he actually felt he'd be able to retire from acting on the proceeds that would accrue from his literary exploits. "I'm going to turn myself into a writing factory," he promised.[5]

Kid Andrew Cody and Julie Sparrow was originally two separate novels. The first he intended to make into a film, with himself in the title role.[6] It was written in an impressionistic, stream-of-consciousness style. Curtis had always been fleet of foot. Now his writing testified to the fact that his brain also flitted willy-nilly from theme to theme and era to era. His wired literary persona hit the reader like a chainsaw in the solar plexus. Writing was a form of word-painting to him: "You become like litmus paper, using the colors you need to reflect the proper emotion and leave the rest to chance."[7]

He enjoyed writing the novel because he had control over the process. There was no director to defer to, no crew to engage with, no high daily costs of production to fret about if he didn't feel like turning up at his desk. He set himself daily limits of a few thousand words and adhered to this discipline. The fact that the material was largely autobiographical meant he didn't have to break into a sweat to blacken pages. He dangled his characters like marionettes but was also one of them. "That was the thrill," he said, "being both subject and object. I didn't know where they were going to go, where I was going to go. I was like God, a creator — but also a victim. My pen led me."

Was the book some kind of vicarious attempt to make up to his brother Julie for having ignored him on the day he died? Was it an attempt to give his slain sibling the kiss of life in print? Whatever it was, the writing was compulsively readable, a kind of Bret Easton Ellis meets J.D. Salinger. He trawled through the worlds of sex, dope, crime, gambling and showbusiness in search of some tenuous nirvana.

One of the most autobiographical parts of the book deals with the way he stands up to the school bully. This character is even given his real name, Webber, when he taunts the young Curtis — here called Julie — with names like "Jew kike" and "asshole Heb." Curtis doesn't give us the expectable bully/victim scenario, choosing instead to portray Webber as an interesting person, a "dark angel" possessing both "madness" and "earnestness." Julie flails out at him one day in general assembly, thereby ending his reign of terror in one fell swoop.[8]

The language Curtis employs ranges from hardboiled to Ed McBain–style journalese to off-the-wall flights of fancy. There are Runyonesque gambling forays, stints in Vegas: "There was more silicon in them there hills than there was in all the first-class seats in the new 707s."[9] In one sense the book reads like one long sentence, a kind of *Finnegans Wake* without the obfuscation. It's as rambling and inchoate as its characters.

The internal monologue was something else: so many heady incursions into the soul of a narrator ostensibly crass and cynical but somewhere between the lines betraying a bruised sensibility and even (whisper it) a longing to be loved. "The stewardess was tired, big-titted and just disagreeable enough to interest Julie," he wrote.[10] Elsewhere we have the same sense of mischief: "Julie, what I like about you is your sense of humor, which is non-existent." Lower down the same page we get this exchange: "Waxie, why are there so many Jews in the picture business?" "No other business would have us, Julie."[11] Clifford Odets would have been impressed.[12]

Curtis cleverly interweaves the themes that engaged and enraged him, like anti–Semitism, into a narrative that on another level plays itself out as a simple oedipal story: the search of a father for a son, or a son for a father. This was his own search through life as well. He wielded his pen like a machete. It was as if all the years of bad parts convulsed within him to create this inspired odyssey into Desolation Row.

"They all stayed together the whole weekend," he wrote at the end of one chapter, "sunbathing, making love, swimming, eating Chinese food, reading scripts, chatting, gossiping and loving. All five of them had an itch that needed soothing. Billie Jean Baby made pancakes. Monica made a *nicoise* salad. That evening, nude, they smoked grass and grilled some steaks. By Sunday at five-thirty he was all alone again."[13]

This sense of a dying fall permeates the book, undercut by the stylistic flourishes that act as a corollary and lift it almost to the level of epiphany. Curtis always stops one step short of this, playing his cards close to his chest for fear of losing the poker-faced persona of his narrator. "In Hollywood he was a flop," he writes, "in the rest of the world a movie star."[14] And again we think: Is this about himself? An autobiography before his autobiography proper? A kind of pre–Julia Phillips *You'll Never Snort Coke in This Town Again*?

The Phillips argot is strongly in evidence in passages like the following: "We'll take that afternoon plane; just tell the old lady you're out scouting locations. I'll cover you. Sit-down dinner parties given on the lawns of these houses covered over with a cellophane contraceptive to keep out the cold or keep in the hot, with burning gas heaters smelling of kerosene mixed with beef stroganoff, Chanel No. 5 and menopause No. 3."[15] This passage is repeated verbatim in his first autobiography.[16]

One is tempted to see the book as a tribute to his brother, even as an apology to him for being his "tormentor" rather than his "mentor," to use Curtis' own language. When I asked him if this was true he wouldn't be drawn. I then put the question another way, citing the example of Elvis Presley, the surviving member of twins at birth and a man who, it was said, felt guilty at having lived, as if he was somehow responsible for the death of the other twin. People have theorized that this guilt drove him to over-achieve, to carry the burden of two people inside him. Did Curtis feel he had to do the work of two people too? Was this infused into the guts of the book?

He replied:

> I felt I had to do the work of *three* people, because Bobby was gone from us as well. That put a lot of pressure on me. It accounted for many of the bad movies. But the book is about more than that, and maybe less than that. You're entitled to draw a connection but I didn't see it that way when I was writing it. That's for critics to argue about. Your subconscious takes over when you sit at your desk. It wasn't meant to be an expiation.

Just as Curtis had a certain sensitivity about being a "celebrity" artist, as if that gave him an unfair advantage over the opposition, he also felt that being a "celebrity" author might cause people to think he was only being published because of who he was. He believed his book was good enough to sell on its own merits, so he toyed with the idea of bringing it out under a pseudonym. But then he thought: "I did that to break into pictures." Why should he have to go through it all over again.[17]

The book was aggressively marketed and sold well, but the critics by and large panned it, one reviewer going so far as to say a chimpanzee at a typewriter could have done as good.[18] Though sales were reasonable, the publishers had expected more because of who he was. It was suggested that if he bought a substantial number of his own books to bump up sales he could end up on the best seller list. For Curtis this was a form of prostitution, and he gave the idea a definite thumbs-down.

Bloodied but unbowed, he went back to the "day" job and another spectacularly bad movie. *Casanova & Co.* was an ode to satirical hamfistedness, dealing with the great lover's attempt to cure impotence. Curtis played two parts. "A lot of it is acting opposite myself," he joked, "Fortunately I'm wonderful to work with."[19] It was made at the same time as Fellini's *Casanova*. This led to some confusion in the publicity department, but the similarity between the two movies ended there. It sank without trace.

Curtis finally fell prey to the film world's penchant for black magic when he agreed to star in the exploitative *The Manitou* in 1977. "That movie wasn't released," he scoffed, "it escaped. I would class it as the cruddiest piece of work I've done, and that's saying something. They tell me it has a cult following now. That usually only happens to really great films or really terrible ones."[20] This was one of the latter.

Dealing with the evil spirit of a 400-year-old Red Indian that becomes resurrected as a tumor on the neck of Susan Strasberg, *The Manitou* has her soliciting the advice of a former boyfriend (Curtis) who tries to keep a straight face during the next hour and a half of hokum. Love conquers all in the end, but careers have been killed by less amateurish films than this. When William Girdler, its director, was killed in a helicopter accident a few months after filming was completed it seemed to underline the baroque absurdity of it all.

The luster was beginning to disappear from Curtis' marriage to Leslie Allen by now, though he kept this fact under wraps when speaking publicly. In October 1977 he expressed the view that she was the finest woman he'd ever known, that the smartest move he'd ever made was marrying her, and that he was now enjoying life "more than I ever have before." That was a lot of superlatives, especially considering the tensions hidden behind the familiarly upbeat persona.[21]

He was on a high from the success of his book. It had sold 40,000 copies, and he was due $2.50 on each copy. This added up to a tidy figure. He was also working on a new novel now, writing it between scenes of *The Manitou*. The film's plethora of special effects suited him, his scenes being patchy and spread apart. "Instead of sitting around I decided to apply myself."[22] He dictated his narrative into a tape recorder which his secretary then typed up. He typed the dialogue himself. Additions were done on scraps of paper and then incorporated into the body of the text.

Doubleday publishers now approached him and offered a $50,000 advance for the novel, which was to be called *Starstruck*. He looked forward to writing about a world he knew so well in novelistic form. It was going to be totally about Hollywood.

Over the next few years he tinkered on and off with the book, looking on it as a way to craft an autobiography that wouldn't, as it were, name names. There would be actual people in it but that was just the shell. When it came to any tawdry revelations he might have he was going to change the identities of the perpetrators to protect the innocent — or, rather, the guilty.

The next movie he appeared in was one of his strangest. His costar was none other than the legendary Mae West. *Sextette* was West's last stage play and would also be her last film. Many people thought the dire camp comedy *Myra Breckinridge* would be her swan song but the indomitable diva had one more ace in the hole. She played a movie star married to an English aristocrat. She's on her honeymoon with him but there are a lot of her ex-husbands floating about, including Curtis, playing a Soviet diplomat.

He didn't really get to know West during the making of the film, but she told him she liked his accent and that impressed him. She also admired his style: "She said it in that sexy way of hers. It was like the most suggestive thing anybody ever said to me."[23] Even at 85 she was flirting.

Curtis appeared in *Sextette* mainly to be able to boast that he acted with West. "Cary Grant, whom I so admired, had worked with both Marilyn Monroe and Mae West. There aren't many who can claim that. I had worked with Monroe so now I wanted to work with

Mae West."[24] It was a daunting experience because of West's age: "We had to shoot one line at a time." Between scenes West had no interest in talking about anything contemporary, only the old days. But she didn't want her age mentioned. "She just refused to acknowledge that time was passing. That's how she coped with it."[25] Curtis regretted not having worked with her in her prime: "She made sex funny when it was this big taboo subject. It was easier for the rest of us to push the boat out but she was the first."[26]

He referred to *Sextette* as the most bizarre project of his life because of her. Her day began with her bodyguard driving her to the set at 11 o'clock, after which they'd start on her hair. "Then they'd take her into a kind of bathroom-cum-dressing room for her daily enema. Maybe by 1:15 they'd wheel her onto the set. I left for work when she started her enema. She had poor hearing, so when they wanted her to turn around in a scene, a prop man would lie flat on the floor with his arms stretched out around her feet. She was like *The Battleship Potemkin*."[27]

Curtis had been outraged at Marilyn Monroe for keeping him waiting so long between takes on *Some Like It Hot*. West inspired different feelings in him because of her infirmities. The hearing aid she wore led to some hilarious situations. One day the frequency was low and the signal became scrambled. As she tottered around the set on her high heels she didn't hear the director feeding her the dialogue she expected. Instead she got a traffic report from the local police station: "There's a 305 on Melrose and Fairway. Proceed with caution!"[28]

Asked if she looked 85, Curtis replied:

She could have been even more, but it didn't matter. You can't be ageist. I just took her as I found her. It broke me up listening to her speaking her lines out of her hair — where the hearing aid was. It was funnier than anything in the script. And then you had Ken Hughes [the film's director] in a booth with a loudspeaker and a bottle of Jack Daniels. Suddenly, Billy Wilder's problems with Marilyn were like a breeze. Ken said directing her was like trying to talk a plane down in a snowstorm.[29]

Joan Collins went to a party at West's house with some other cast members shortly after the film was completed. She was amazed to finally meet "'the ultimate fag hag," as she called her.[30]

Curtis next embarked on a sequel to the highly successful baseball movie *The Bad News Bears*, from 1976. Entitled *The Bad News Bears Go to Japan*, it continued the baseball theme but didn't have the fizz of the original. A more interesting diversion was his portrayal of one of his familiar washed-up film stars in the TV movie *The Users*, this time with the twist of a homosexual subtheme. He also appeared in a detective series called *Vega$*, playing a casino owner. He would appear in sixteen episodes of the series in the next few years. People accused him of spreading himself too thin but he needed to work to stave off feelings of depression — and desertion. He was taking more drugs now and they were playing havoc with his moods. Howard Johns summed up his career at this point by saying he was making films where he played "the buffoon instead of the best man, acted stupid instead of smart, and pretended the joke was on him when, in fact, he was often the whole joke."[31]

Curtis went to Israel in late 1978 to film *It Rained All Night the Day I Left*, an adventure story featuring him as a gunrunning mercenary who, as he described it, "doesn't want to grow old and is always chasing rainbows."[32] Israel doubled for Africa as the setting. It had a decent cast in Louis Gossett Jr. and Sally Kellerman but Curtis' lack of interest in the film was evident in almost every frame. It was hard to blame him. It was a fourth-rate effort, only slightly less confusing than its title.

His mood was dark on the set. He started to exhibit some diva-like qualities that appeared out of character. He accorded the film's director, Nicholas Gessner, only limited respect because of his lack of experience. Neither was he complimentary about the movie, commenting resignedly about it, "I had to accept the ugly reality that there are fewer parts to play now than before, that I couldn't be 25 forever."[33]

He was interviewed by Joan Borsten of the *Los Angeles Times*. Asked if Israel meant more to him than other countries because he was Jewish, he replied testily that it didn't. Neither had he come to Israel to rediscover his roots. "I adhered to my father's type of Judaism until I was bar mitzvah. [Then I] became a man and had a right to choose my own way. I avoid Jewish Hollywood not to be different, arrogant, coquettish or cute but because I choose to be the type of Jew who runs for his pen instead of his gun."[34] He thawed out towards Borsten after spotting another cast member, John Vernon. He kissed Vernon on the cheek with this commendation: "To know you is to love you." To Borsten he drawled, "I have a nice time living but I don't have the keys to paradise."[35]

Curtis snatched moments between scenes to write *Starstruck*, but his relationship with Gessner grew worse as the shoot continued. A war of attrition broke out between them, each circling one another like cagey fighters as they strove to convince the rest of the cast that they knew more about the movie (and movie-making in general) than the other. If the film itself had been good, such a fraught atmosphere could have been forgotten. But it was awful. Curtis marked time as he waited for the final scene to be shot so he could collect his check and say *adieu*—or, rather, *shalom*.

The experience left him with a sour aftertaste. He didn't like Israel, he didn't like the film company, and he didn't like Gessner. "Nobody seemed to know what they were doing," he griped, "so I became obstreperous."[36]

At this time his career was overshadowed by an unlikely rival: his daughter. In 1978 Jamie Lee sent shock waves throughout the U.S. with her star turn in the John Carpenter chiller *Halloween*. Her father thought she was trying to move too fast, and making some elementary mistakes as a result—like hiring a publicist and an agent: "All that should come later, after she's mastered her craft. First you make a product, then you sell it."[37]

Halloween became her trademark movie in much the same way *Psycho* became her mother's. After it was released a magazine published photographs of both movies side by side to highlight the comparison.[38] The irony was that Jamie didn't like horror movies at all. She was so sensitive she couldn't even watch the children's film *Oliver!* without covering her eyes because of the scene where Oliver Reed strangles Shani Wallis.[39]

Halloween spawned spinoffs like *The Fog*, *Prom Night* and *Terror Train*. The fact that Jamie was Leigh's daughter helped publicize such movies. She was never in denial about that. "Being the daughter of myself and Janet opened a door for Jamie," Tony allowed, "but she still had to walk through it. Being well-known gets you an audition; it doesn't always get you a part." She had to fight to be accepted. Said Jamie, "When I made the horror films, all the women's rights groups were after me because I was supposedly promoting violence against women. But I never took off my clothes, I never swore, I never smoked dope. I was the all–American girl who stood up for her values and fought back."[40]

Afterwards, when she played more edgy roles like that of the *Playboy* centerfold Dorothy

Stratten, she gained an unlikely acceptance from the people who originally reviled her. "I'm legitimate. I swear and I take off my clothes. But now the same women's groups are calling me and asking me to join their organizations. And all I can say is, 'Fuck you.'"[41]

Curtis thought his daughter was right to work in all kinds of movies, even lowbrow ones. "That's where the money is," he conceded, "you keep coming back to the craps table where you won more than you did before. That's the nature of the profession."[42] He called this "fuck you" money. For him it was like putting a dipstick into his car when it needed oil. He'd made many films in the past merely to pay the rent — or, in later days, the alimony. But he wanted to see her do more comedy. Like himself, she had a flair for it. He added bitchily, "She doesn't get it from her mother."[43]

Curtis' career nosedived as Jamie's rose. In 1979 he made *Title Shot*, a straight-to-video clunker that had him as a criminal using computers to try and predict the results of sporting events like boxing. It was third-rate dross, an unintentionally funny caper that seemed to sum up everything that was wrong about his life at this time. He played an oleaginous fixer, "a piece of garbage wrapped up in a $500 suit," as his character is referred to at one stage. The film basically came across like a particularly bad episode of a TV series. The lighting was poor and the script cliché-ridden. There was also an irritating drumbeat sound in the background of some scenes. It was presumably there to ratchet up the tension but instead merely had the effect of emphasizing the amateurishness of the direction.

Curtis' relationship with Allen had reached breaking point by now. He didn't come home many nights. When he did, she bore the brunt of his frustration.

Title Shot was made in Canada. While Curtis was there, Allen took Nicholas and Ben to a house they owned in Cape Cod. When Curtis finished the film he went back to Los Angeles, but only Nicholas and Ben were there. Allen had remained in Cape Cod. Nicholas told him she had a man there, that she'd been with him the whole time Curtis had been making the movie. After the immediate shock of the news, he accepted it.

From now on the pair of them were basically just marking time until they split up. "A part of me almost felt relieved," he admitted later. Perhaps they knew the marriage was over even before she went to Cape Cod. Prior to her departure he said with a rueful grin, "My wife tells me she needs space. I'm going to see that she gets it!"[44]

17

The Road to Perdition

"Hollywood is a funny place," Julia Phillips wrote in *You'll Never Eat Lunch in This Town Again*. "There are a lot of gorgeous young guys here. Some of them get to be stars and some of them get to be just another beautiful junkie."[1] Or, in the case of Curtis, they get to be both.

He split temporarily from Allen in 1979, holing up at Hugh Hefner's *Playboy* mansion to try and get his mind off her. There were women disporting themselves in various stages of undress everywhere he looked, but he was too depressed to enjoy them as he might have done a few years before.

He knew exactly where he stood with Hefner, which made their friendship one he could tap into at any time. "He'd give you a room," he said, "and there you were. There were all these beautiful girls roaming around and if you were clever and you had flair and you weren't a ding dong and you didn't make anyone feel unhappy you could have a relationship with [them] for a weekend or a week."[2]

He would always be grateful to Hefner for his kindness at this time. "Hef" didn't pass judgment on him about his drug use or anything else. He just gave him a place to stay for as long as he needed it. He could wake or sleep as he wished, or spend all day imbibing his substance of choice. He could drop out and tune in and forget about who he was. "Everyone needs to get back to the still center of themselves sometimes," he reflected, "and in that little room I took everything out of myself that shouldn't have been there and got back to where I was before I allowed people to destroy me."

He continued to work on *Starstruck* in his hideaway haven. "It's all about the Hollywood I knew as a Universal contract player," he said, "and to make it realistic I'm using real names alongside the fictional ones. So I have Clark Gable eating in the studio commissary with a reporter, and Fred Astaire and Cyd Charisse hurrying through their salads to get back to the set. I'm really enjoying this one."[3]

He ruled out the idea of ever writing his memoirs, despite tempting advances from publishers.[4] "Can you imagine me telling what happened in the steam room at the Sands in Las Vegas with Frank Sinatra? Or writing about my relationship with Marilyn Monroe."[5] At times it sounded like he was trying to build himself up to divulge the very things he promised he never would, like someone saying he had a secret but couldn't reveal it: An appetite was whetted.

In April he submitted the first draft of *Starstruck* to Doubleday. The experience of writing it had both exhausted and depressed him. "Truman Capote once said that finishing a book was like taking a child out behind a house and shooting it. I had an empty feeling too." He signed himself into a psychiatric hospital, feeling a nervous breakdown coming on. His past was catching up with him. "I was asked a question: Was I taking drugs because my marriage was breaking up or was my marriage breaking up because I was taking drugs. I couldn't answer that. It was like one of those 'Have you stopped beating your wife?' types of questions."

Asked about Allen, he didn't deny they'd experienced a "temporary split" but said everything was fine now. Yes he had moved out of the family home, but only to get some rest. This might have sounded okay if the place of rest wasn't the *Playboy* mansion. One's mind conjured up images of the particular type of "rest" that might be offered in this location, a type generally involving more than one person.[6] One of the people Curtis ran into at this time was the ill-fated *Playboy* bunny Dorothy Stratten. As mentioned, Jamie Lee would go on to play her in a TV movie, *Death of a Centerfold*, though the names of all the main participants were changed at Stratten's family's insistence.[7]

Allen was disparaging about Curtis as their marriage continued to implode. She met the artist Andy Warhol one day and told him she was "a rich society girl from Boston and how could she marry an actor and a Jew."[8] When Curtis read this in Warhol's published diaries he found it hard to forgive her, even if she was sozzled when she said it.

Another member of the jet set that he saw off and on at this time was Mick Jagger of the Rolling Stones. Jagger came to his house one day when Allegra was thirteen. He seemed unkempt to her, and she also noticed he had BO. "Does he never wash?" she asked Curtis. "Don't be so impudent!" he rebuked. It was as if he thought being a celebrity gave one the right to smell. There was always that double standard with him, that hunger to be in with the "right" people regardless of the number of ways they might fall short of acceptable behavior.[9]

The following year she lived with Curtis in a tacky apartment for a time. Kelly shook her head in disgust when she saw it. "You can't stay here," she said. But Allegra didn't want to live with Allen. She had a new boyfriend now and he treated her "like dirt."[10]

Curtis was desolate at this point of his life. He stayed in his room watching television for much of the day, only leaving to get drugs. He was freebasing cocaine by now, smoking it on a waterpipe for a bigger hit. "I would see a towel in the crack of the bathroom door," Allegra remembered. "He put it there to keep the fumes in." Then she'd hear the gurgling of the pipe as he sucked on it. When he came out he'd be in a good mood and she'd be glad of that, relating it to the father he'd been when she was a child. "I took him as he was," she said. "The important thing was that he was happy again." She didn't care how such happiness was reached. "Do you want a draw?" he would ask her sometimes. She'd refuse because "I had to look after him." When she told Kaufmann what was going on, Kaufmann said, "That's child abuse." Allegra didn't see it like this. "I took him under my wing," she said. "I protected him to win his love." She felt sorry for him because she knew he was trying to get off drugs and back to the easels that were gathering dust in the corner of the room. He disappeared for weeks but usually came back in the same condition as he departed: "His only luxury was coke."[11]

Between traumas he acted, taking the crumbs routinely dished out to him, the leavings from the rich man's plate. One such was *Little Miss Marker*. This was the fourth version of Damon Runyon's story to hit the screen. Curtis had been in the third version, *Forty Pounds of Trouble*, in 1963. He'd had the lead role then. Now he was in support mode as a mobster. Julie Andrews was the main female lead. She professed to have decided on it so she could work with the leading actor, Walter Matthau, a rather unique ambition considering he wasn't generally seen as ranking too high on women's list of favored costars.[12] Matthau's character (Sorrowful Jones) was hardly charismatic. Allan Hunter said he made Scrooge look "positively philanthropic."[13]

Curtis received far more kudos for his portrayal of David O. Selznick in *Movieola: The Scarlett O'Hara War*. By now he was trying to come to terms with a receding hairline, but it enhanced his resemblance to Selznick in the TV movie, for which he received an Emmy nomination.

He also got a part in Neil Simon's play *I Ought to Be in Pictures* in 1980, playing a screenwriter with drinking and gambling problems. It was being staged in Los Angeles and set for a Broadway run afterwards. Curtis was looking forward to being before a live audience again, playing the kind of character he knew best: a New Yorker on the skids. The play told the story of a young girl (here played by Dinah Manoff) who was abandoned by her father as a child and raised by her mother. When she grows up she visits her father and asks him to use his influence to help her in an acting career.

Simon thought of Curtis for the role of the father as soon as he finished writing the play. His reasons weren't straightforward. "Certainly he was not the greatest actor in the world," he grudged, "but he possessed a world of charm, sex appeal and humor."[14] This contradicts what Allan Hunter wrote in his biography of Walter Matthau. Here Matthau claimed Simon originally asked *him* to be in it, an offer he refused.[15] Simon called Irving Lazar, who was his agent at the time, as well as being Curtis'. Lazar, much to Simon's shock, told him he thought the play wouldn't turn out well with Curtis in it—a rare instance of an agent badmouthing his own client. Simon pricked up his ears at this and inquired if Curtis was having a problem with substance abuse. (There had been rumors about this for some time in the press.) Lazar refused to elaborate. He then went back on his own caveat by telling Simon that if he still wanted Curtis he would give him his whole-hearted recommendation.[16]

According to George Jacobs, Frank Sinatra's valet, Lazar had a "superphobia" about failure. "It smells worse than shit," he used to say, "and you can smell it from further away."[17]

Simon, amazingly, ignored Lazar's original reservations and plumped for Curtis. "I knew I was headed for trouble," he wrote in his memoirs. Against this, he also "knew" Curtis would be able to "charm the pants off a mannequin."[18] (Even when drugged?)

Simon met Curtis a few days later with the play's director, Herbert Ross. Simon knew he was nervous, and also that he was having difficulty learning his lines.[19] By the time of the first preview, Simon became worried, but there was compensation: "If we hired a more experienced stage actor, he probably wouldn't [have] come close to the charm and warmth that Tony was showing on the stage."[20]

The first preview passed without crisis. After it was over, Simon told Curtis he was planning some rewrites. This revelation enraged Curtis. He'd stretched himself to the pin of his collar to learn what was already there. "What do you mean, rewrites?" he asked. "I thought this was the play." Simon countered weakly, "Well, Tony, it's just the beginning. I can't write a play and get it all correct in one draft."[21]

Curtis' face turned white with horror. "No way," he replied. "Either we do it this way or we forget about it." With that sentence he signed his death warrant. Curtis said to me:

> That was the moment I knew I'd had it with these guys. I'd done my job, which wasn't easy for me, having to learn all those lines with the condition I was in with Penny and all that. And now they're saying "Scrap it, we'll start again from zero." I couldn't take that. No. Fuck you, Neil. Fuck you, Herb. This is Tony Curtis here. Remember me? I used to be a movie star. I ought to be in pictures. Shove it up your ass. [Curtis called Leslie Allen "Penny"]

Simon concluded, "It was clear to both of us that Tony was never going to make it to Broadway." To which one might add: He would have if you had let him. Curtis could have had a legal case against dismissal, having learned the script that was put before him. But they didn't sack him immediately. "We still had four weeks to play out in L.A.," Simon related, "and one never knew what miracles could happen in four weeks."[22]

One night during the play's run an unexpected visitor turned up in the audience: Curtis' former costar, Piper Laurie. They hadn't communicated since falling out in the early 1950s as Curtis was about to marry Janet Leigh. Laurie thought it was high time to patch things up. When she got to the theater, however, she was informed that she wasn't allowed to sit in the seat she'd booked, only one much further back. It was feared Curtis would see her in the audience. She wasn't told why he wouldn't have wanted to see her. Was it because it might affect his performance? Or, more ominously, that he didn't wish to see her at all? Laurie feared the latter. She had intended to go backstage and talk to him but changed her mind. She never saw him again.[23]

Maybe it was for the best. He wouldn't have been in any condition to see her anyway, quite apart from their problems in the old days. Maybe this was why he'd asked for her to be moved farther back from the stage.

Everything was beginning to get to him. Ross had been rude to him offstage. He even roared at him on occasion. Allen was also getting under his skin. Some nights he didn't go home to her after the show. Other nights he slept in his car outside the house, curled up in a fetal position like an infant.

One evening before a performance he heard through the grapevine that Ross and Simon were planning to have him replaced before the show got to Broadway. He blew a fuse. It was bad enough being canned; not being told face to face made it ten times worse. He thought Simon wanted him out because he'd negotiated a percentage of the profits.

The manner in which he exacted revenge for this latest slight was classic Curtis. During a matinee performance one day, towards the end of the first act, he let fly at Manoff with a string of words that weren't in the script. He ended with a choice "Fuck you!" before exiting stage left. The words were ostensibly directed at Manoff (he was in the middle of an argument with her at the time) but were really for the ears of Simon and Ross.

The audience gasped as he departed the stage. Manoff followed him, breaking down in tears in her dressing-room. When the stage manager knocked on Curtis' door he found him putting on his street clothes as he prepared to leave the theater.

Simon wrote in his memoirs, "I can't remember if Tony Curtis ever came back to finish the engagement," an astonishing statement considering the foregoing. How could a playwright forget which actor played the main role in one of his plays, particularly in such dramatic circumstances as these? He'd read Curtis' autobiography and perhaps felt validated in his decision by the fact that Curtis told his readers his marriage was falling apart at the time and also that he was doing a lot of coke. Perhaps this inspired Simon to take a final dig at him: "The next time an agent advises me not to take his client for a role, I would think over my answer much more carefully."[24]

The play was a hit on Broadway, earning Manoff a "Tony"(!) award, but when it was made into a film it performed abominably at the box office. Vincent Canby, of *The New York Times*, hated it. "Though it has the hyped-up-pacing one associates with Broadway," he harangued, "it seems longer than *Nicholas Nickleby*."[26] Curtis was quietly amused. "Let's just say I didn't lose any sleep over the fact that it bombed," he said to me, trying to suppress a smile.

He felt he was back on more solid ground later that year with *The Mirror Crack'd*, but this was really little more than an excuse to get former screen legends Elizabeth Taylor, Kim Novak and Rock Hudson together in a poorly-conceived Agatha Christie yarn. Natalie Wood had been offered the Taylor role first but refused it. According to her sister Lana, she "read the script, put it down and started swearing. She would not, she said, stoop to such shit."[27] Taylor got four times as much money for stepping into her shoes.[28]

It was set in England in the 1950s and dealt with the filming of a movie on Mary Queen of Scots (referred to as "Mary Queen of Sluts") with an assortment of faded stars. Taylor and Novak didn't get on so it was fitting that the dialogue between them was bitchy. Cue Taylor to Novak: "In that wig you could play Lassie. What are you supposed to be—a birthday cake? Too bad everyone's had a piece." Novak in reply: "Chin up—both of them!"

Curtis played the seedy producer of the film. He was hilarious in the few scenes he got to play, looking like the Rodriguez of *The Last Tycoon* four years on, albeit slightly more paunchy. He had a lot of funny lines and delivered them with great vigor, playing off Novak beautifully. It's a pity the film itself was a dud. He was in it too little to really make an impression.

There was a lot of media interest surrounding the production, mostly for the wrong reasons. The stars did well to avoid it, putting more or less of an embargo on interviews. Hudson was afraid he'd be quizzed about the gay rumors surrounding him (he'd already fended them off for a quarter of a century), and Taylor was aware people were saying her marriage to John Warner was on the rocks.[29] There were similar media concerns about Curtis and Allen.

Curtis refused to admit his marriage was in trouble in an interview he did with Roderick Mann on the set. "I still talk to Leslie," he informed Mann. "We're not separated, just apart at the moment, so who knows what might happen?"[30] This was wildly optimistic under the circumstances but Curtis was never one to spoil the media with revelations, even when they were *faits accomplis*.

Angela Lansbury was also in the cast, playing a character she would become identified with in time, the canny sleuth Miss Marple. Curtis steered clear of her on the set, still upset by her derogatory comment about him after *The Purple Mask*. She avoided him too. But she was glad to be reunited with Taylor. She had appeared with her many years before in *National Velvet*. "She was eighteen and I was eleven," Lansbury recalled, "and I was very conscious of the age gap."[31]

Curtis broke up with Allen for good after the film wrapped. He ran to Hugh Hefner again to lick his wounds, or have them licked for him by Hefner's bunnies. "There were boundaries," he said, "even at the *Playboy* mansion. Romances were to be conducted on the grounds, not taken to a hotel room or to someone's home." In other words, the merchandise didn't leave the premises. The friendship of Hef's bunnies was "more important to me than the sex," Curtis emphasized.[32] (But one doubts he objected to the sex.)

The divorce from Allen was bitter. He blamed her for the fact that he'd made so many bad movies when he was married to her, and for driving him to "insane feelings" about himself.[33] He checked himself into a drug rehab clinic in Pasadena amidst rumors that he'd threatened her life. Curtis completely discounted these rumors. He felt he was being manipulated by her lawyers. Allen countered that he was so drugged at times he wouldn't have remembered his threats. He said the year had been "a bitch" for him — and that Allen was another one. The doctors diagnosed him as suffering from severe melancholia.

"I was living through mental turmoil," he declared, "as I saw my life being ripped to shreds. But it's behind me now. It goes without saying that I miss my wife and my family but I've got a place of my own now in Bel Air and I'm gradually getting used to living alone. I used to be scared of the prospect but not anymore."[34] Cleaning out his system had brought humility. "When I was under drugs I thought I knew it all. What I see now I don't understand. The more I see, the less I know."

He was a grandfather now, Alexandra having given birth to twins. He liked the sense of the Curtis tribe expanding, "but if anyone starts treating me like a grandpa I'll be smashing plates on their head. I'll have to be a great-grandfather before I'm treated as an old dodderer."[35]

As the eighties went on he became more mellow, his painting helping him evaluate himself and his self-indulgent past. As a recovering drug addict he was philosophical about the nature of addiction: "It's a disease all of us have on different levels. Some people use too much sugar or too many credit cards, or they're addicted to loving, or hating, or working. It's a terrible, killing epidemic."[36] He was watching his diet now and taking long walks by the sea. He also swam a lot. He didn't like living alone, but he was nervous about committing to a woman again for any lengthy period of time.

Nothing much was happening on the film front. He was supposed to have played a hit man with a grudge against Kirk Douglas and Burt Lancaster in *Tough Guys*, but it didn't happen. (He'd made six films with Douglas and Lancaster, if one includes his bit part in *Criss Cross*.[37]) Instead he made *Balboa*. Looking more like an over-the-hill song-and-dance man than the corrupt realty operator he was supposed to be, Curtis seemed like a cross between Hugh Hefner and J.R. Ewing in this pilot for a projected mini-series. One of the few amusing lines in the script has him describing himself as a rich, would-be Prince Charming: "So you go out and buy yourself a Cinderella." The direction was clunky and the sets like something from a particularly bad episode of *Dynasty*. There was even a female narrator "explaining" the action in this empty paradise where you "park your yacht and flit around in your Ferrari." Here's Curtis in an exchange with his latest "squeeze," Jennifer Chase:

CHASE: "Do you ever think of anyone else when we're making love?"
CURTIS: "Uh-huh. Snakes, chickens, cats...."
CHASE: "Did the earth move?"
CURTIS: "No, it was the water bed."

Also in the cast was Sam Kanaly (a refugee from *Dallas*) playing a character who's now dating Curtis' ex (Carol Lynley) and investigating his bribery of politicians. It was retitled *Rich and Powerful* for the DVD release but bombed there too.

After completing *Balboa*, Curtis' drug abuse continued. In 1981 he had an unusual accomplice: his daughter Jamie Lee. She was making the TV movie *She's in the Army Now* and at the nadir of an excessive lifestyle. "When he was doing drugs," she confessed, "I also was doing drugs. We'd go over to his house and have [them]. It was that simple and it was that sick. It was that whorish."[38]

Later in the year Curtis visited Andy Warhol. He informed him he was giving up movies and devoting himself to art instead.[39] By now he was looking for any "out" from acting, writing providing the most obvious escape route. He'd just put the finishing touches to *Starstruck* and delivered it to Doubleday. He had high hopes for it but it was tackily written and lacked any form of order. His previous novel had been ambitious, even if the critics found fault with it. Here, in contrast, was a pretentious attempt at a potboiler.

Doubleday wanted him to rework it totally. He considered doing this for a while but in the end it proved too daunting a task so he said no. They then asked him to return the $50,000 advance they'd given him in 1977. Again he refused. They now began legal proceedings to retrieve the money. The case would rumble on for four more years.

He made two more TV movies in the interim: *Inmates: A Love Story* and *The Million Dollar Face*. Neither of them created any great stir but they kept his name before the public. This seemed to be about the height of his career ambitions by now. At the end of the year he met a new woman, Andria Savio. She was 38 years younger than him, which placed her roughly in the right age bracket for him. He told reporters he was in love with her and planned to marry her.

Some people imagine he did. Her name crops up in some biographical accounts of him as his wife. Savio believed his promises for a while but in time came to see them as publicity stunts to take the attention away from his problems.

His divorce from Allen was finalized in early 1982. Curtis now made another low budget movie, *Brain Waves*. The film had an interesting premise: A woman is knocked down after she gets her high heel caught in a trolley track and subsequently goes into a coma. Curtis is an experimental surgeon who's pioneered "the Clavius Process." This can bring about an electric brain transfer from a donor and hopefully return her to full health. The problem is that the donor in question has been murdered, so the recipient of the transfer remembers the moment of her violent death.

Can she identify her killer? All she remembers is two X marks on his wrist as he threw a transistor radio into a bath and electrocuted her. Her husband (Keir Dullea) begins a search for the killer. Curtis looks so ominous in some of the scenes one could even be forgiven for suspecting *him*. His face betrays his history of substance abuse here. Neither is his appearance helped by his receding hairline. The film has a kick in the tail, as the last scene features the killer with the X marks on his wrist being wheeled in for another brain transfer: obviously the person who receives this brain will also have memories of how *he* was killed (by falling off a cliff).

Curtis followed this with a Shakespearean film: *Othello—The Black Commando*. The title tells us all we need to know about the movie. He played Iago to Max Boulois' dark prince. It was deservedly crucified by the critics. The producers ran out of money before it was finished. Curtis was asked to bail them out by returning part of his fee in exchange for a chunk of the profits. He refused. "It was a panic call," he said afterwards. "I knew there wouldn't be any profits." He was right; the film died at the box office.

He was now hit with another shock when Christine Kaufmann released a set of nude photographs of Allegra to a magazine. She did so because she wanted to make "Tony Curtis" [sic] mad at her, because he would now see how beautiful his abent daughter had become. But why would this make him mad, one was entitled to inquire. Would he not be glad she was beautiful? The average father would only be "mad" that such beauty was being displayed to the world. In an article adjoining the photos, Kaufmann said she took Alexandra and Allegra from him because they wanted to be removed from their "drinking, drug-taking" father.[40] Curtis denied these charges strenuously.

His next undertaking was another ill-advised film, set in England but financed from Europe. It was called *Where Is Parsifal?* He played an inventor trying to market a laser machine that could save the world. Orson Welles was a magician he tries to interest in buying his invention. Welles had a great interest in magic in real life and had performed in many magic shows. He had once "sawed" his wife Rita Hayworth in half during one such show. She thoroughly enjoyed the experience, though Welles generally insisted men got much more from magic than women.[41]

Peter Lawford was also in the movie. He was as deeply into cocaine use as Curtis at this time. The main difference between them was that Curtis wanted to detox whereas Lawford seemed to have a death wish. His partner, Patricia Seaton, had tried to reform him but to no avail.[42]

Seaton's main reason for being on the set was to keep an eye on Lawford. She described the cast of the movie as "a rather pathetic gathering of brilliant losers — men who were major stars but who hadn't had a meaningful role in several years." It was being filmed in a dilapidated mansion which conjured up images of "a group of medieval diners throwing food around and wiping their hands on passing dogs during orgies."[43]

By the time he made the movie, Welles' brain was damaged from the pressure put on his heart by his obesity. Maybe this was why, on his way to England, he got on the wrong plane and ended up in France. A special plane had to be dispatched to Paris because his "several hundred pounds of weight" wouldn't fit into a normal first-class seat.[44] Afterwards he had to be conveyed by a London cab to the castle because he was too large to fit into a limousine. This wasn't an unusual circumstance for him. David Thomson wrote about him having been trapped in a car once and having to be cut out of it.[45]

Seaton was given the unenviable task of feeding Welles each day on the set. This was easier said than done since he ate like a horse as well as weighing almost as much as one. After Curtis had eaten his fill each day, Welles would only be warming up. Welles lived in the basement of the mansion because it was feared the stairs would collapse under his bulk were he to step on them. Seaton carried so much food for him on her tray that she had to walk sideways on the steps down to the basement to avoid hitting the walls. One day she happened to glance back after walking up the six steps of the stairs. The door opened and a hand shot out. Seaton wrote: "The plate was jerked inside so rapidly that it made a whooshing noise going through the air."[46]

Welles once said, "I was born to be fat." It didn't seem to bother him, despite the obvious difficulty in moving around or the dangers to his health. More often than not he was in good form. "He preferred being Falstaff than Hamlet," said Curtis. Curtis was once asked how Welles had become so fat. He replied that eating had replaced creativity in his life. "When young, thin and bankable, he had been able to make works of art. Now unable to direct, he passed the time by turning *himself* into a work of art."[47]

Curtis understood this. "There's something strangely comforting about being fat," he thought. "All you're worried about is your next meal. Job problems, family problems — all [become] secondary or nonexistent. You've just got to feed that one monster, your body. By the time you've finished eating and digested and gone to the toilet, it's time to start eating again."[48]

Welles considered having surgery to reduce his weight but was worried that an operation might be dangerous.[49] In another mood he saw gluttony as "a good deal less deadly than some of the other deadly sins because it's affirmative, isn't it? [It] may be a sin but a lot of fun goes into committing it."[50] He alluded to Curtis' point when he said, "Take my word for it — when responsibilities get to be almost unendurable, a man on a diet takes to his sugars and starches as an addict retreats to his opium pipe or a drunkard to his bottle."[51]

Welles died shortly after making the movie. So did Lawford, his body finally giving out on Christmas Eve 1984. His obituary notice carried the heading, "Kennedy In-Law Was Last to Speak to Marilyn Monroe."[52] As Curtis sighed afterwards, "It says everything about our business that that's all he was remembered for 22 years later — the fact that he was Marilyn's stooge."

18

Fighting the Demons

What would happen if Marilyn Monroe, Albert Einstein, Joseph McCarthy and Joe DiMaggio all shared the same New York hotel room on an otherwise ordinary day in 1953? That's the question the precocious British director Nicolas Roeg posed in *Insignificance*, a 1984 film that featured Curtis in one of the fewer later roles for which he was commended by the press. The above quartet weren't identified by name but rather as generalized characters: the Ballplayer, the Professor, the Actress and the Senator. Roeg described the film as "a real, mythical, melodramatic farce."[1]

Curtis played the Senator, the part loosely based on McCarthy. He saw him as a man who was both intense and glib, someone who could take anything that was given to him and turn it into something positive for himself.[2] Gary Busey was the Ballplayer and Michael Emil the Professor. Therese Russell played the Actress. Curtis was asked if she was as good as Marilyn Monroe. "Even better," he whooped. (The fact that she was married to Roeg at the time might have been a contributory factor to his enthusiasm.)

Based on a play by Terry Johnson, *Insignificance* was first performed at the Royal Court in 1982. Johnson said it was meant to be about the fact that what the characters were famous for was different from what they really were.[3] He wanted to strip away the carapace of image and find the ticking soul underneath. Roeg decided to take it into another direction, a semi-surreal one in which he would play with time and place, much as Einstein himself had while still preserving the solid structure of a beginning, middle and end.[4]

Roeg described the scenario as "a collision of myths." Accepted notions are reversed in his refracted world-view: "An Actress lectures on scientific theory, a Professor shows her his legs, a powerful Senator confronts his impotence, a Ballplayer displays his tenderness." It's the ultimate "What if" movie, taking talismanic cultural figures and giving them unexpected dimensions, making the extraordinary ordinary and the ordinary extraordinary. In Roeg's words, "Bubblegum heroes and basic fears, Hiroshima in New York, 24 frames a second.... Simple truths are put into the mouths of what appear to be clever people and wise things in the mouths of apparently dumb people. It's all about chance."[5]

Einstein famously speculated that God didn't play dice with the universe. But a film director could. Maybe this is best shown in the playful exchange between the Professor and the Actress when he asks her, "Is it early or late?" She replies, hilariously, "It's relative!"[6]

We hear DiMaggio's frustration in lines like, "Every time I turn my back there's a different man in my wife's room." It's also in his pained plea to the Professor, "Will you tell her the shape of the friggin' universe; I want to get her home." The Ballplayer doesn't expect to be talking to her about $e=mc^2$. "How was it for you?" would be a more expected query.

The Actress is like Aphrodite or Eve, "permanently offering the apple of temptation to the prince/king/man who would temporarily be allowed to enter the orchard of paradise and rule with her for a while."[7] That "for a while" is significant because what she's offering, in effect, is a poisoned apple, a transient bliss. The next morning the prince/king/man will be expelled from whatever Garden of Eden she conjures up and forced to deal with more diurnal truths.

Roeg saw the relationship between the Actress and the Ballplayer as epitomizing "detachedness." "Nobody knows a damn thing about anyone."[8] There was a split between their "insistent self-importance" and their lack of self-knowledge, "very dangerous in people with such power." They needed to cultivate a sense of insignificance, as the film's title suggested.[9]

The most obvious theme in the film is the disjunction between image and reality. We get the obscurity-craving Actress, the frightened Ballplayer, the confused Professor, the impotent Senator. Coupled with this is the manner in which these figures have been popularized and accessorized, "flattened into two dimensions rather than three," as Neil Sinyard put it, "the Actress on a calendar, the Ballplayer on a bubblegum card, the Professor with his theses, the Senator with his subpoenas."[10]

Roeg enjoys this playful mix of stereotypes and echoes, inversions and subversions, overtures and anti-climaxes. We may laugh or cry, fume or be immune. Any reaction is fair game in this dissonant mélange of bent souls craving some kind of relevance in a plastic cosmos as Armageddon looms. Roeg bends time like a celluloid Einstein, dangling his legendary marionettes before us like subangelic loners touching base with other subangelic loners, screaming from the balcony, whispering from the cave. In the end nothing really gets resolved but it's still been an interesting experiment, probably for that very reason.

Curtis' character suffered from impotence. "Maybe I should have taken out a patent on the condition at this stage," he suggested. He played down his preparation for the role. "I didn't need to research the legislative system, but when I put on that hat and that gray double-breasted suit, I *became* that senator."[11]

People felt Roeg chose him because of his relationship with Monroe in *Some Like It Hot*, but there was also another consideration: "Here's Sidney Falco thirty years on, having gained his glittering prize of power and too stupid to notice the price."[12]

He had some wonderful lines, like, "Did you know that according to the Law of Probability, you drink a glass of water and you drink a piece of Napoleon's crap? Perhaps even Mussolini, but more likely Napoleon's on account of he's been dead longer."

Curtis played down McCarthy's anti–Left tirades. McCarthy may have had the same relationship with communists as Buffalo Bill had with the North American bison, as one writer speculated, "but he did not create the fishing fleet. He was simply the masthead on the Cold War's ship of fools."[13] Far more interesting were his private vices, like his addiction to alcohol. Even at congressional hearings he had "frequent recourse to a bottle of cough medicine in a brown paper bag."[14] (One is conservatively guessing it wasn't cough medicine.)

"I didn't take the part because he was a right-wing son-of-a-bitch," Curtis insisted.[15] Instead, he looked for his inner vulnerability. "For all his machinations and madnesses, anger and deceitfulness, there was still a little boy in there, a child looking for guidance in life."[16]

Curtis professed not to know what the film was really about, but that made it better for him. It gave him room to maneuver. Roeg had a freeflowing directorial style. This contrasted with Billy Wilder, who was "'too Teutonic" for Curtis. "I prefer a director who lets you work things out for yourself."[17]

The Actress says to the Professor at one point, "A girlfriend and I played a game a few years back. We each made a list of the men it would be nicest to sleep with. You came third on mine." In Shelley Winters' autobiography she talks about playing such a game with Marilyn Monroe when they were rooming together, and Monroe mentioned Einstein. After she died, Winters spotted a framed photograph of him among Monroe's effects. On it was written, "To Marilyn with respect and love and thanks, Albert Einstein."[18]

Curtis thoroughly enjoyed making the movie, and the cast and crew enjoyed him too. Jeremy Thomas, the producer, described him as an "ironic, humorous, profound, highly natural person who had the most impeccable manners."[19] He also had eccentricity. Whenever Curtis had a closeup he used to put his hand on the camera and leave it there until "Action" was called. Thomas asked him why he did this. Curtis replied, "Because it loves me, baby."[20] Such affection was clearly mutual.

After *Insignificance* it was back to the small screen again for *Mafia Princess*, a telemovie in which he played the hoodlum Sam Giancana (whom he knew slightly in real life). He followed this with another TV movie, *Murder in Three Acts*, costarring Peter Ustinov. Ustinov told Curtis he'd get more rewarding work if he removed his hairpiece, but Curtis refused.[21] What Ustinov was overlooking was the fact that he himself was a character actor. Curtis wasn't, at least not yet. It would have been difficult to imagine Ustinov swinging from a rope to rescue a damsel in distress. Once bitten by the Screen Hero bug it was difficult to discard it even when time took away the traits that made it possible.

Curtis became closer to Jamie at this time. Like her father, she too was aware that the glitz and glamour of the old Hollywood had disappeared.[22]

Jamie proved invaluable to him in the summer of 1984 when he had the biggest scare of his life thus far. He collapsed in his Bel Air mansion and had to be rushed to the emergency room of the Cedars-Sinai hospital in L.A. He was diagnosed as having cirrhosis of the liver and internal bleeding. It was "Last Chance Saloon" time for him. He almost died.

At this time he was snorting cocaine mixed with a baby laxative. Sometimes he didn't know which was which. He cruised the streets looking for thrills, regressing to the life he'd lived as a poor kid from the wrong side of the tracks. He feared he'd be found dead in some alley. Some nights he slept rough. He was taking sleeping pills mixed with dexedrine, and drinking whiskey for breakfast to take the edge off coming down. He was also drinking at the parties he had to attend for PR purposes, and taking pills to knock himself out afterwards, especially if he had to be on a film set early the next morning, using uppers to get himself going.

The work he was doing was more often than not third-rate but it was better than nothing. Sometimes he rang producers asking them if they had anything for him, a sure sign of desperation. This never worked. If anything, it turned them against him. The word was out that he was "using." He thought most of his colleagues were as well, but he showed it more. When he looked at himself in the mirror sometimes he saw an old man looking back at him. He panicked, which made him take even more substances.

One day he went to an apartment to buy cocaine. The man selling it pulled out a handgun and left it cocked on his desk as the deal was done. Curtis "got the hell" out of the apartment fast. As he walked down the hall a girl approached him, telling him she'd give him oral sex if he shared some of it with her. This happened more than once. He was living in a netherworld of depravity and panic. "It was as if I died," he said chillingly, "only someone forgot to tell me about it."[23]

When he came out of the hospital, his attorney, Eli Blumenfeld, persuaded him to enter the Betty Ford Clinic to have himself cleaned out. His family also exerted pressure. He resisted their entreaties at first but eventually succumbed.

Deciding to check himself into the clinic was a life-changing experience for him. It was also a very humbling one:

> There I was, sitting with all these guys of 22, 18, 31, and the therapist says, "This is the only 58-year-old fuck-up you guys will ever see so you'd better take a good look." That shook me up quicker than anything, I can tell you. I was in a lot of pain. I was angry and frustrated. I didn't like the idea of getting old. I didn't like the idea that I wasn't getting those parts that I wanted anymore. I didn't like the idea that I didn't like my wife anymore. Whoever she was.[24]

Maybe these last three words are the most telling of all. They're shocking but also (being Curtis) very funny.

His time in the clinic probably saved his life. It also brought him down to earth by having him do things like wait on tables. But the most important thing it did was make him confront himself. In therapy he made a strong effort to explain his many excesses. A recurring theme seemed to be the cruelty of his mother and his resultant anger against her. Once he emptied himself of that anger it seemed to free up his mind, to cleanse it.

Jamie cemented her burgeoning affection for him at this time, despite having had little enough to do with him up until now. Maybe that was the key. "Because I didn't really have a relationship with him, he couldn't let me down. I just happened to be one of the last people who hadn't been disappointed too many times. For years I didn't know who Tony Curtis was as much as other people told me who he was."[25] Who he was, as it happened, was a man threatening to make his last exit on a Hollywood set. A man who'd taken one too many tumbles, smoked one too many joints. He was in need but found it hard to say that. He was running out of road and looked to a deserted daughter to push him where he needed to go.

The fact that Jamie had grown up with Janet Leigh was a constant worry to Curtis. He felt Leigh filled her with "stuff" about him. Many people would say she was entitled to. If she did, it didn't stick. She had always regarded her father as a rascal, but a likeable one. She commended him for his personality. "When he entered a room he sucked the air out of it," she allowed. In later years they bonded.

Curtis also advised her about her career. "Don't ever forget this will last forever," he warned.[26] He knew fame was non-reversible. Whatever a person did was out there to haunt them if they put a foot wrong — especially on celluloid.

Sometimes he feared she would punish him by writing a book about him. Joan Crawford's children had done it. He found the emergence of Childpower somewhat daunting: "Everybody's writing *Mommie Dearest*," he announced. "I'm going to write *Son and Daughter Dearest*!"[27] But those who talk tough are often pussycats and Curtis was no exception, his two autobiographies overflowing with glowing tributes to his children. (His detractors might say this was his compensation for being such a lousy father to them.)

His recovery wasn't instant. After he came out of the clinic he went back to substance abuse again. Like many addicts who behave themselves in rehabilitation centers, he found the real struggle began when he was back in his daily environment.

He broke up with Andria Savio in early 1985 and took up with a British girl called Debee Ashby. Ashby spent time with him at his Palm Springs home. There was speculation that this was more of a publicity stunt than anything else, a continuation of his "rehab."

"I saw more of his housekeeper, Charmaine," Ashby disclosed to *The Sun* in a kiss-and-tell article. Or rather a tell-but-no-kiss. "Tony wasn't looking for a sex kitten," the former Page 3 girl divulged, "he was more in need of a nursemaid." She said he was more interested in a hot water bottle in his bed than a mistress. "He used to call me to his bedroom, but only to fetch him tea or a snack. Out on the town he loved to have me on his arm and always wanted to buy me sequined low-cut tops to show off my figure. He loved other people to see me in that gear when I was with him, but in the twelve months I was seeing him he never once tried to seduce me."[28] This was said as a complaint rather than in relief.

During the two weeks she spent at his villa in Palm Springs the former stud didn't even kiss her. "I was 174,000 miles from home and totally alone. He could have tried anything but he was a perfect gentleman." She had informed him she wasn't a virgin, "so he knew I wasn't exactly sweet and innocent. But that didn't make any difference." Though his house was crammed with pictures of topless women, "I think that was part of the facade to fool his guests that he was a stud."[29]

One night Curtis poured his heart out to Ashby about his failed marriages and neglected children. She imagined his tears might be a form of foreplay but he didn't take it any further. "He kept asking me if I liked him. He said he couldn't tell anymore if people really [did], and he kept crying."[30]

The next morning he was back to himself again, doing thirty lengths in the pool in his "tiny" trunks and afterwards parading himself about for her delectation. "He was very proud of his body," she remarked, but hardly lustful for hers—despite the fact that what first attracted him to her was her 38DD breasts.[31]

Insult was added to ignominy for Ashby when she took the aging Lothario home to Hertshire to meet her parents. They found him to be a sweetheart, which wasn't quite the reaction she was looking for. It was in marked contrast to the reaction of Curtis' family to her. One night Jamie phoned him and Ashby answered the phone. Jamie was outraged and called her a slut, "another one of her father's young bits of stuff." Then she slammed the phone down.[32]

Ashby eventually left him, fed up with people thinking she was his lover when the relationship was merely platonic.

When an interviewer asked Curtis how he felt about her, a different perspective on their relationship emerged. "I was just getting over my drug period," he said, "and I invited this girl with big breasts to Palm Springs. Her mother, [who was also her] agent and manager, lurked in cars with telephoto lenses. They were working me like a slot machine in Vegas."[33]

Whatever about that, they were certainly viewing him very closely. Here's Ashby on his cocaine use: "That was probably what repressed his sexual appetite. There were lots of candles, strange tubes and little silver foil packages filled with coke around the house." In her favor she admitted he never tried to introduce her to it.[34] He was probably more inclined to ask her to try one of his hot water bottles.

Later that year Curtis was ordered to repay his $50,000 advance from Doubleday for *Starstruck* because it was deemed unpublishable in its present state. Doubleday's editor, Lisa Drew, was unequivocal in her condemnation of his draft, which she dismissed as being "junk, pure and simple"—if junk could ever be described as pure.[35] Curtis countersued for $150,000, contending that the publisher had failed to provide adequate editorial services. Both suits were dismissed but Doubleday appealed and won, the judge of the day (her name was Kaufmann, ironically) ruling that the termination was made in good faith and editing not really an issue.

It was a hard pill for him to swallow. He'd made many noises over the years about being a writer more than an actor and was looking forward to having his books transferred to the screen. *Kid Andrew Cody and Julie Sparrow* had flown off the shelves in its hardback run and he'd hoped to use the head of steam it built up for *Starstruck*. Sadly, he found it difficult to maintain the concentration he'd had eight years before with the earlier work. The court order, in effect, was the death knell to his writing career. (*Kid Andrew Cody* hadn't sold well in paperback, partly due to the fact that he didn't actively promote it.) He was also annoyed that Leslie Allen had received half of his Doubleday advance when they split up but wasn't asked to part with this when the final legal ruling was made.

He used the financial shock to explain his drug abuse. "I lived through the depths of depravity as I turned from amphetamines and barbiturates to acid, marijuana, angel dust. Then cocaine began slowly to raise its ugly head. Then heroin."[36]

If his career had pressured him into the substance abuse, so had women. His three failed marriages turned him into a depressive who lived in a constant state of fear that any woman in his life would only be interested in him for his fame and fortune. "Then when my money was gone I'd be discarded like a dirty old shoe. I'd be left to die in the streets, a broken-hearted old man."[37]

He described the time between 1984 and 1985 as "the best ten years" [sic] of his life because he'd overcome his twin addictions to drink and drugs. Drugs also gave him a skewed version of reality. "You think you're being witty when in fact you're a bore. You think you're being eccentric when in fact you're a little nuts."[38]

He moved from Hollywood to a home over 100 miles away in an area called Indian Wells. Los Angeles had been too oppressive: he was only a phone call away from people he didn't want to connect with. Rebuilding his life meant surrounding himself only with loved ones. He had reconciled with all his family, though Jamie was still upset with him. He had also reconciled with his past wives, even Janet Leigh, which was a surprise to him. He lived alone but saw women occasionally, like the ex-model Vivienne Lynn and the Italian actress Petra Scharbach. His drug hell hadn't bankrupted him—land he bought for $750 dollars an acre in his twenties was now worth $50,000 an acre—but he was cautious about being ripped off. Women who tried to wheedle money out of him found they couldn't cash checks he wrote because they had to be countersigned by his attorney beforehand.

His mental state was good, but there were certain things that still haunted him:

> The terrible thing about being alone is getting through the night. The early part of the evening is okay. You have a beautiful girl with you, you go out to dinner, see chums. But just before dawn is when the demons pop out of the cellar and dance around in your skull. [They] come

tip-toeing into my brain and when I won't give in they finally say, "What the hell," and go back to their little basement.[39]

He was philosophical about the fact that his career was dwindling. He never had grandiose notions about the business he was in, realizing that cinemas were often just convenience stores for audiences rather than places where dreams were nurtured. He said in Deauville in 1986, "When young people don't want to kiss their girl in the living room because their parents are looking, the best place to go is a movie theater. So the movie's not important. We think we're such great filmmakers when in reality our audience just wants to be alone."[40]

Cary Grant died that year too, marking the end of an era for Curtis. He had dearly wanted to be Grant as a young man. "Everybody wants to be Cary Grant," Grant joked, "even *I* want to be Cary Grant!"[41] Curtis had kept in touch with him all his life. When the aging star was ailing he visited him regularly, keeping Grant's mind off dark thoughts about health or mortality with his zippy tales of life in the fast lane.[42] Curtis also opened up to Grant about his own problems, in particular the dominating influence his mother had had on him. Grant had a saying, "The hand that rocks the cradle fucks the world," which Curtis loved to repeat.[43]

He was as upbeat as ever about life as a cocaine-free convert: "For the past year I have been rebuilding myself after twenty years of reaching out for a glass or a pill to make me feel good, and there is no question they did just that. Having a different woman all the time was part of the same system. And if a woman wasn't available, drugs eliminated the need for one."[44] In time, painting became a different kind of drug.

He exhibited his art in Hawaii in April 1987 and was interviewed by Lesley Salisbury in conjunction with it. His life, Salisbury wrote, was "as colorful as his canvases and as black as the macabre collections in his boxes." He was the man who had "three wives, six children and 32 girlfriends."[45] (Was that all?)

Gone was the tragicomic character who spent his time with a dollybird on his arm, dressed like "a latterday Cecil Beaton in floppy hat, velvet suit, flowing cravat and silver cane." In its place was a sober, buttoned-down middle-ager who knew the score. "I take long walks," he told Salisbury. "I make love as much as possible, and then I paint."[46]

He suffered a minor embarrassment later that year when he fell victim to a prank. Like many other famous people, he was conned by a hoax letter. It came from a woman calling herself Gerda von Nussink. She said she was rich and wished to donate her fortune to Curtis. Her reason? "For years I have been an admirer of your artistic ideas." Not only that, "I will always remember what your country did for us during the postwar period."[47] Gerda was actually a man. He had written the same letter to 100 celebrities to "prove" that rich people were as greedy as anyone else.

The film offers that came Curtis' way at this point of his life were almost as worthless as the hoax letter, but he still said yes to almost everything, from the fifth-rate on down — and for cutprice salaries. "If they offer me good parts," he promised, "I'm going to put on my trunks and gloves and kick the shit out of them."[48] This was fine in theory, but often the "shit" stayed in.

Sometimes he found himself in movies which were mostly awful but still had some redeeming qualities. *Midnight* (1989) was a piece of comedy horror sludge in which he played a TV mogul trying to steal the rights of a late night cult show from Lynn Redgrave.

Redgrave was excellent as a vampiress figure rising from her coffin nightly with a Bloody Mary in her hand as she proceeded to lambast delighted audiences. Curtis was very much a peripheral figure but he entered into the spirit of the material with an almost camp *mien*. He flattered the material with his blackly comic hamming.

He was willing to try anything. He even appeared in a Danish movie in 1989, the little seen *Walter & Carlo I Amerika*. Afterwards came *Lobster Man from Mars*, a spoof of fifties B-movies. He played a man trying to make a flop for a tax write-off. He admitted it was a direct ripoff of Mel Brooks' *The Producers*. By now he had more or less lost his chocolate box looks, so much so that when he was being interviewed about the film a journalist asked him if he played the lobster or the man. He grinned at the snipe but he wasn't amused.[49]

He advertised the film with typical Curtis verve: "I'm gonna have my own dress designer. I'm gonna wear mini-skirts. I'm gonna have a twenty foot tongue that I attack my enemies with."[50] He saw it as a male version of *Sunset Boulevard*.

Allegra thought he was going through a midlife crisis. "He had no identity apart from his life as a star," she supposed. He was also losing his hair by now, and having transplants. If he didn't have his hair, he believed, he would lose his livelihood too. It was all mixed in together.[51]

His problems with his children continued. Allegra had started up a jewelry business by now. She wanted to bring him in on it but he wasn't interested. Neither did he help her financially. Alexandra was in theater management but he didn't seem too interested in that either. He'd also fallen out with Benjamin and failed to sympathize with him over a car accident he had. "Dad's world revolved around Dad," Allegra accused. She went to a film festival with him once and was amazed at how entranced he became when he saw himself onscreen: a real-life Narcissus. Or was he too troubled inside himself to be able to give himself to his family anymore?

Something that upset him greatly at this time was the fact that Burt Lancaster suffered a massive stroke. Curtis was devastated at the news: that huge monolithic body had finally succumbed. He had always held Lancaster in high esteem, not only because of his acting but the work he did for Civil Rights and the underprivileged, most of which went uncredited. "Here's this great big aggressive guy that looks like a ding-dong athlete playing these tough guys," he praised, "and he has the soul of—who were those first philosophers of equality?— Socrates and Plato."[52]

Lancaster hung on for four more years. He was alert in his mind but not his body— the worst kind of situation for anyone who was accustomed to an active life. He resembled a silent screen star in his enforced isolation.[53] Curtis was distraught thinking about it all. It was time to take stock, to look at everything that had happened to all of them since fame hit. What was life all about at the end of the day? "Marriage, money, everything became small when someone's health failed," he remarked. He was grateful he still had that—just about.

His moods fluctuated. He also argued with his children, especially Allegra. One night after he'd been drinking he said to her, "It's time you got married. You're pretty." She told him she hadn't met the right man. He said she should marry a friend of his called Giacomo. She told him she wouldn't marry Giacomo if he was the last man on earth. Curtis blew up at this. "You insulted my friend!" he shouted at her. Then he shook her and threw her to the ground. "It was the only time he ever raised his hands against me," she said, "but that night he was beside himself with rage."[54]

Curtis wanted to set Allegra up with his friend Dodi Al Fayed. She was only 18 when she first met him. Curtis had been invited to his villa in Malibu. After the visit he said to her, "He's an important man. Phone him." When he was in L.A. he advised her to get close to him, or at least move in his circle. But Allegra wasn't really interested. He argued with her about this.[55] Their relationship deteriorated further when Allegra posed nude for *Playboy* in 1990. This angered him at the time, though he later accepted her right to do so.

Lesley Salisbury did a feature on Curtis' children in *The Times* in 1990. Jamie was quoted as saying, "I think he would love to have been royalty — Baron Curtis or something." Having been hardly three when he walked out on Janet Leigh, she never really knew him as a father. And now?

> Now, quite frankly, I have a weird relationship with him. It doesn't matter if, out of the blue, he calls and says, "I'm in town." I'll say, "Great, come on over and see your grandbaby." It used to make me more angry that he hadn't [seen] her than all the years he didn't come and see *me*. Now I don't care. He comes and goes. I'm very happy that he's my father. He has a lot of insight and a lot of funny stories and he's great company. We've worked it out.[56]

A part of Curtis felt trapped by his children, even trapped by their financial demands. He liked to say, "If I'd had a vasectomy when I arrived in Hollywood I would have been the wealthiest man in town." This may have been true but it begged a lot of questions. He didn't seem to understand what to do with children once he'd brought them into the world. Ben and Nicholas, for instance, had spent a few months in the *Playboy* mansion when they were growing up and he saw nothing remiss in that. "The boys loved it there," he remembered. "There were all these beautiful women around. The occasional glimpse of a naked lady diving into the swimming pool would just set their little hearts a-throb. It was so open and free. There was nothing salacious going on there."[57]

The fact that Allegra and Alexandra were tossed back and forth between himself and Kaufmann, or that they underwent many adolescent agonies, seemed to have washed over his head. "Children," he reproached, "don't realize that your life is as precious as theirs."[58] Did he not understand from his own troubled youth that they could also be irreparably damaged by neglect? Maybe he did, but he was so messed up in his own life he couldn't always do the right thing. "I stopped being a concerned father after Janet got together with Bob Brandt," he admitted. "The cattle call visiting rights thing got to me. After a while I stopped caring. The mountain had to come to Muhammad."

He gave an interview to Graham Fuller in 1991. He first came to Fuller's attention in *The Great Race,* which Fuller had seen as a child. Instead of watching Jack Lemmon play a double role, or Natalie Wood with her body dripping cream, Fuller was drawn to The Great Leslie in his white fencing outfit, his furtive charm winning him over.[59] Fuller began by asking Curtis why people had never really taken him seriously as an actor. Curtis' blunt reply summed up his frustration: "I had too much black hair and blue eyes. I was fucking too many good-looking women for anybody to be interested in any depth."[60]

He went on to talk about the highs and lows of his life in his usual frank manner. As the interview wound to a close he said to Fuller:

> I'd like to give you a little insight into what happened to me. When I came to California I rented a house on Franklin Avenue in Hollywood and it had a pool in it — a small, dirty pool. The water was really dirty. [Then] I went out to Universal. I went to an acting class and I came back and decided to take a swim. It was a brisk and chilly day. I jumped into the pool and it

was so cold and the water was dark and dirty underneath. So I got out of the pool and I went into the house and took a shower, got dressed, put on my shorts, came in here and met you and we started our interview. That's how quick that forty years went.[61]

It was a beautiful way of putting it.

This was his lead into why he didn't now want to become the token elder statesman of the movies. He still felt 17 underneath the skin so why shouldn't he act like it? He refused to play character parts because, even at 66, "I still want to end up with the girls."[62]

He talked to *The Telegraph* afterwards and some of his comments here were curious. Among his favorite films, for instance, he named *Insignificance*.[63] Asked if he was upset over never having won an Oscar, he replied, "Nothing hurts me deep inside. That is only one part of my life." But we know from subsequent interviews, and from his two autobiographies, that the Oscar lacuna in his CV hurt him very deeply. He was equally mystifying when, asked for his favorite costars over the years, he mentioned Marilyn Monroe, arguably his most problematic one.[64]

He was back in familiar mode when the subject of substance abuse came up. Did he blame Hollywood for these vices? "Hollywood had nothing to do with it, and don't call it a vice." The seeds of self-destruction were in all of us. "You know it's foolish to end your life at 35," he added, "because it's going to end at 85."[65]

The interview was being conducted in England. He was asked if he had fond memories of working there in the 1970s. The answer was an unequivocal yes because of the fun times he had with Roger Moore shooting *The Persuaders*. He added that his son Nicholas was also born in London. "He was born on December 31, just two hours before the New Year. Had he been the first child born in the New Year, the Queen would have sent him a cable saying 'Welcome to England.'"[66] (Reading this made it all the more poignant to reflect on the fact that in a few years Nicholas would become a victim of the same drug hell as his father when he overdosed on heroin.)

Curtis continued to appear in substandard movies. In 1991 he made *Prime Target*, playing a wisecracking Mafia don (not so much a Mob informant, as Michael Munn stated in his biography of Curtis, as an FBI one) being brought to court by a man who has to blow away a bevy of crooked cops to drive him there. He followed that with *Center of the Web*, a TV movie in which he also played a villain. This one had a surprise ending.

He made another TV movie, *Christmas in Connecticut*, in 1992. It was directed by Arnold Schwarzenegger, who went on to become a close friend of Curtis. It was a harmless comedy but Curtis was entertaining in it.

His brother Bobby also died that year, having signed himself out of the institution he'd been living in for so many years. He had no plans about where he would go, so he lived largely on the streets and slept rough. One night he was beaten to death in L.A. for no discernible reason. It was as absurd as everything else about his life. Curtis had always feared something like this might happen. "His illness overwhelmed him," he said, "it devoured his life."[67]

Bobby was just two months short of his 52nd birthday when he died. Curtis spoke of him as his "big secret." "When someone is so emotionally disturbed it's tragic," he said. "It's not like a broken leg you can fix." He hadn't seen him for a number of years but was speaking out now "because my painful story might help relatives of other disturbed people cope with their torment."[68]

Later that year he went to Budapest with Kelly to help out a charity he had set up to preserve sites of Jewish interest in Hungary. Called "The Emanuel Foundation" after his father, it was a cause dear to his heart. Kelly was equally devoted to it, being more anxious than her siblings to investigate her heritage.

On a date in 1992 that would forever be embedded on the American consciousness for all the wrong reasons, September 11 (9/11), Curtis met the woman who would become his fourth wife. Lisa Deutsch was a law graduate from L.A. He was immediately taken with her when he saw her at an alumni dinner. She was young, she was pretty, she had big breasts — what was not to love? He asked for her phone number that very night. She was entertained by him but also concerned by what appeared to be over-eagerness on his part. And, of course, there was a huge age gap between them. She was 33 years to his 67.

He rang her off the hook over the next few weeks and did all the things romantic suitors did. He behaved like a total gentleman to her and charmed her with his gentility and wit.

The age difference was the big stumbling block between them. This manifested itself one night when Curtis brought her to a party where a number of stars from his era were in attendance. He thought she'd be awed but instead she was indifferent. They meant nothing to her because they were outside her frame of reference. This should have given him cause for concern but it didn't. He continued to date her, becoming engaged to her after knowing her less than six months.

Her parents were conflicted about the relationship. The fact that they were Jewish made them less nervous of him than they might otherwise have been but her father, a lawyer, still wanted Curtis to sign a prenuptial agreement that would entitle Lisa to half his fortune if they divorced. Curtis refused, which took the luster off his romantic pronouncements to her. "I never thought she was a gold-digger," he said, "but you have to protect yourself."

Shortly after they married he published his autobiography, *Tony Curtis*. It was cowritten with Barry Paris and became a best seller. This wasn't surprising, as it was one of the most incisive books ever written about life in the movies, a kind of *Hollywood Babylon Revisited*.

It spared nobody's blushes, least of all his own. It wasn't salacious but steam still rose from the pages. He strode like a Colossus through the hoopla and the hype, the money men and the deal men, the sycophants and brown-nosers, the groupies and the drug-addicted, like himself, tenuously picking his steps from the ghettos of First Avenue to Hollywood's blandishments and back again. It was a sizzling page-turner, a delicious broadside against the industry that made and almost broke him, a double-edged paean to the Golden Age, to a miserable childhood, a stop-go career and a Prospero-like philosophy of middle age. The Great Imposter had become the Great Survivor, a man who beat the odds not once, as Ol' Blue Eyes intimated, but twice, before emerging from his drink/drug hell to swap the camera lens first for an easel and now a pen.

He went to Australia to promote it. A journalist called Susan Chendry interviewed him about it in Sydney. She seemed more interested in writing about his hair, which she described as "deserving a director's chair all of its own" and making him look as if he had a small animal on his head. As the interview ended, Chendry was still being bitchy, writing, "He and his hairstyle stand up to leave."[69]

He exhibited of his art in the Catto Gallery in North London shortly afterwards, the exhibition timed to coincide with the publication of the book. It was a personal event for him as well as a professional one. In one work, "French Impressionists," pages torn from a book stood alongside children's toys like dice and marbles. "I had a brother who was killed by a truck," he said, "and that's what we played with. He was nine, I was twelve and we used to shoot marbles. So marbles became a symbol to me. That marble looks as good now as then, [but] the kid that owned it is dead."[70]

He also did an interview with Eve Summers of *The Daily Telegraph* in conjunction with his exhibition, flirting with her as he usually did with younger female interviewers. "Feel my legs," he commanded, and she did, finding them "curvaceous." His hair was grey and his eyes a paler shade of their "once shocking blue," but he still looked "damned good" for his 68 years. "I love my looks," he trilled. "I get up some days and feel a bit lost, but then I go to the mirror and go, 'Mmmmm, what have I to be unhappy about? I could look like Danny De Vito.'"[71]

She asked him about his life and he gave a fast-forward account of his phoenix-like rise from the ashes of Hell's Kitchen. Before Hollywood it was the Navy that had saved him and afterwards the movies. "I thought God must be repaying me for all those bad days in New York City."[72] But then came the Fall, the early swashbuckling promise transmogrified into those vapid sixties roles which destroyed his credibility with directors, until eventually, after *Lepke*, he became a drug addict.

"You can easily slip into it when you're distraught, envious, angry, frustrated and unhappy, which is what I used to be. If being a movie star is really heaven on earth, like people say, then why did so many kill themselves?" Summers had no answer for him.

"Life is for living," he concluded. "It's not just about a reflection on a screen. That's just a fantasy. You spend your whole life developing a reputation and one afternoon, at 47, you fall over a table and there you are — forgotten but not gone."[73]

19
Rendezvous in Dublin

Dublin was Curtis' last port of call in the promotional tour for his book. I was asked by the *Sunday Independent* to interview him so I turned up one Friday morning at the Shelbourne hotel, where he was staying, wondering if the man would live up to the writer — or actor. The first thing he said to me as he walked towards me in the lobby of the Shelbourne Hotel was straight and to the point: "I'm fucking freezing!" I liked him immediately.

There had been a problem with the heating the evening before and he'd been awake for most of the night as a result. He looked remarkably well for his 68 years but was wringing his hands in his distressed state. "Some like it hot," I remarked. I'm sure it wasn't the funniest quip he'd ever heard but he acted like it was.

The idea was that we'd have breakfast together as he chatted about his life and career. "Don't worry if you get nothing out of him," my editor had consoled me as she gave me the gig. "Next week we can do someone else instead." Little did she suspect that for the next few hours he would barely pause for breath as he treated me to the richness of his personality.

He led me into the dining room like a grand lord admitting a guest to his mansion. There was a hush as he entered. Hollywood royalty had arrived. There were mildly reverential nods from some of the diners, which he acknowledged with a slightly upraised hand. When we sat down he ordered a Diet Coke and some decaffeinated coffee. The drug addict of yore had done an about-turn. It was all about health now. Though he was tipping seventy he could have passed for a decade younger, maybe even more. He still had that boyish swagger, that soldierly bearing. With his vegetarian diet and his Schwarzenegger-style exercise regime he seemed to roll back the years. Only the grey hair — still in a quiff— betrayed his vintage. He was shirtless, wearing only a vest under his black jacket, which I suspected was Armani. ("Armani or your life!" was one of his favored one-liners.) He wore Levis jeans as well. These were equally rejuvenating.

He swallowed a blood pressure tablet with a glass of water. "This is the only drug I take now," he smiled. I decided to begin by asking him about his art exhibition in London. Was painting as important to him as it had ever been? "Even more so." How many did he sell at the Catto? "32. Not bad, eh?" Could he remember when he'd first started painting? He stroked his chin. "I don't ever remember *not* painting. It's a passion that goes back a long way."

As he sipped at his coffee I noticed the delicacy of his painter's hands. There was even something effeminate about them, and about himself, despite his muscular frame. I wasn't sure what to talk about first. He seemed personable, but there were always those first few awkward moments with any interviewee where one wondered how to start the ball rolling.

Jamie had been in the papers over the past few days so I thought I'd ask him how they were getting on now after all the years of friction. "We've buried our differences," he said simply. "I've behaved in ways she didn't appreciate over the years but now we're all in a different place." One article I'd read had him saying he wanted to play her mother in a movie. Was this true? "Of course it is. One thing's for sure — I'm not going to play her father!" Was he joking? I couldn't be sure.

Jamie had been quoted as saying, "I used to dream of being normal. When I moved out of our home in Benedict Canyon, I went to a little house in the San Fernando Valley. That was my dream — a home in suburbia."[1] The article was making the point that every abnormality in her life thus far was actually normal to her because she'd grown up in such an abnormal world.

The reformed hellraiser in a more reflective mood in Dublin between interviews. By now he was a recovering drug addict and enjoying the simple life again after so many decades of excess. "The only drug I take now," he quipped, "is my blood pressure pill." He had also recently married again, to Lisa Deutsch, though the marriage collapsed shortly afterwards. Photo by Brian Farrell.

How did he feel about that? "Film stars aren't special," he said. "That's the first thing we have to get straight. Jamie was speaking about growing up in a house where people like Frank Sinatra and Sammy Davis were dropping in regularly. These aren't necessarily special people. We're all just doing a job."

I thought of what his friend Kirk Douglas once said about trying to juggle fame with family life: "My boys would turn on the television and watch their father kill a handful of Romans. Then they'd look around the room and see Tony Curtis sitting there, and Burt Lancaster over there, and maybe Gregory Peck coming through the door."[2]

"I think you're special," I said, and he thanked me, putting his palms together in a kind of prayer gesture. He buttered a slice of toast to have with his coffee. In my briefcase I had a copy of his novel. I had been reading it over the past few days in preparation for meeting him. I remarked on the similarity of themes between the novel and his autobiography.

He thought for a moment and then said animatedly:

A novel is an autobiography and an autobiography is a novel. I'm dovetailing reality and fantasy. Let me give you an example. When I was sixteen I saw Cary Grant in a submarine film called *Destination Tokyo*. As soon as I was seventeen I went into the Navy because of that movie. I came back, went to an acting school, and the next thing I know I'm getting any kind of part I want. So one day I say I want to do a service comedy in a submarine and I'd like Cary Grant to be the captain. And, would you believe, that's exactly what happened. Then it flipped around again in 1977 when Jamie Lee appeared in a TV series based on that movie. So tell me, which is reality and which is fantasy? Doesn't that intrigue you? Call it fortune or call it destiny, I don't care. It's inexplicable.

He related a story that was in his book about a night he was in the Mocambo restaurant on Sunset Boulevard. He was looking at a set of cages that had canaries in them. He was always in awe of how they could survive the smoky atmosphere. Then one night he saw one falling from its perch in front of him and dying. A moment later a waiter took it away and replaced it with another one. In that instant the mystery was solved for him. Nobody but him witnessed it. "That canary falling became a symbol," he said to me, "a symbol of fame and how short fame is. One day you're there in the Mocambo and then, boom, you're gone and the new Tony Curtis, or whoever, is on your perch. Knowing that helped me deal with things when my career wasn't going the way I wanted it to."

He told me his philosophy of life was always to over-reach himself, to keep pushing himself beyond his limits. "When I was growing up in the Bronx there were these steps outside where I lived. One day I'd jump down four steps, then five, then six, until I couldn't make it anymore. But then I'd try seven and fall. Was that dumb? I wasn't sure."

"Look at a sparrow in flight, he continued, "If you keep your eye on it, nothing can disturb you. It's like Zen." I was confused. What did he mean? "You have to go beyond the target," he said. "That's the way I live my life. I go beyond the target and make fantasy into reality." Was he still referring to *Destination Tokyo*? "In a way. I met Cary Grant because of that movie. But before that I played him in another movie, *Some Like It Hot*. Do you see how convoluted everything is? Not many people understand that."

He was on a roll now. "It's like that ivory ball the Chinese used to have. They cut the ball inside, inside, inside." He made a chopping motion with his hand. "Like a Russian doll?" I hazarded. "Yeah, but they never took it apart. They started with just a small piece of ivory. Can you imagine? And then somehow they made another ball on the inside, and another one, and another. How intricate. Isn't it intriguing how the human condition can dive in and out of itself like that?"

He talked about his career as an identity-changer: "Films give me the privilege of being anyone I want to be. I don't want to be trapped in Bernie Schwartz' body. I don't want to be a Hungarian American Jew. I don't want to be Ferdinand W. DeMara, who became many people." As soon as he got a script, he said, he immediately started to work out how he might play it. "They say a statue is inside a block of stone for a sculptor. I feel the same about my performance being inside a page. Not that all of them were great. But at least I put my own spin on them."

Which character could he identify with most from his back catalogue?

I feel I've been all the characters I've played in my movies. I've always had a split personality. It runs in the family all the way from my mother to myself to Bobby. I was able to change from

Bernie Schwartz to Tony Curtis faster than most people could change their shirts. It probably went back to my heritage. Budapest was inside me just as it was inside my parents. That made a life of acting easy, maybe even inevitable. It also made *The Great Imposter* my most obvious role. When I walked into a room as Fred W. DeMara and performed operations on people, or pulled their teeth out, I was him for that time just as I was Albert De Salvo or anyone else I played.

I felt we were getting into Method territory here. But Curtis had always professed to abhor Method acting. All his life he'd espoused the art of simplicity. Was there not a contradiction here? "No, because I get where I'm going in different ways to Method actors, more direct ways. And I don't take my work home with me like they do:"

He wrote a lot about Marilyn Monroe in his book. I asked him if it was as big a thrill to act with her as it had been with Grant? "No," he replied, "because we knew each other starting out. That changes things." (I wasn't aware at this point that he'd had an affair with her in 1949.)

I quoted a famous line of hers to him: "Hollywood is a place where they offer you $10,000 for a kiss and ten cents for your soul." He replied, "Marilyn would have known about both of those options." So which had she taken? "Maybe one leads to the other," he suggested, "though who am I to talk? Men don't get abused the same way as women for sex."

Had she driven him mad during her hysterical episodes between scenes in *Some Like It Hot*? He nodded. "These are the pressures of the profession." What about Mae West, another icon he relished appearing with precisely for her iconic status. How had he coped with her delays on the set of *Sextette*? Did it bother him that she had to have an enema every morning before she was able to appear in a scene, or have her wig put on?

> I don't want to denigrate either of these women. If you had to have an enema, you had to have an enema. If you had to wear a hairpiece, you had to wear a hairpiece. That's the business we're in, making things right for each other. Did you know Mario Lanza had to lose forty pounds for a role once? Everybody has something. Actors sell dreams and they usually come with a price tag. If you wanted brighter teeth you got 'em fixed. If you wanted to be taller you wore lifts. Unless you're someone like Michael J. Fox, who's making a point about being a little guy in a big world. A lot of these things are immaterial unless they bother you.

Would he agree that, by and large, people were as big as they thought they were? "For sure. Napoleon was four foot one and he had three generals who were six foot two looking down on him. They were taking orders from him." He added, perhaps in jest, "I think Michael J. Fox would have been perfect for Napoleon."

We got on to the subject of the "small man syndrome"—i.e. the fact that many short men in history (like Napoleon and Hitler) became dictators. Were we all engaged in a war against a central fault we had in some way? "Only if we get opposition on account of it. If we're brought up good-looking in a world of ugliness, for example, we might get to hate our good-lookingness and want to be ugly like everyone else. In that way maybe a small man can become obsessed about being a tall man." (I took his point, but somehow I found it hard to get my head around the fact of someone like Curtis hating his "goodlookingness.")

I asked him how much it bothered him not being taken seriously as an actor because of his appearance. He replied:

Everyone is in the movies because of the way they look. That can work for or against you, or maybe both. Danny De Vito is in movies because he's short, Arnold Schwarzenegger because of his muscles. Al Pacino is in movies because of that power-driven look he has. It all goes back to your appearance in the end. I may give out about the fact that I didn't get enough meaty roles but if I'm honest with myself I have to admit that I probably wouldn't have got past the gate if I wasn't handsome. And I don't say that arrogantly.

What about his mother taking lumps out of him as a child because of those handsome features — how much did that hurt? He put his hands over his face in contemplation and I wondered if I'd hit a nerve. The room seemed to become quiet around us, the clacking of trays and cutlery suddenly stopped. He waited a while before he answered, making me feel as if I was in a scene from a movie. "More than you'll ever know," he said finally.

I wondered if he was motivated to crawl out of his parents' impoverished situation as a result of ugly situations like this? "I'm sure I was," he mused, "even if I didn't see it in that way at the time." What about his father's thwarted ambitions to be in showbusiness — did that play a part in the young Bernie Schwartz wanting to be an actor? "I never equated it to that." And if he hadn't been handsome, would that have ruled out acting for him? "I don't know what I would have done if I didn't look the way I look. Had I looked differently perhaps I would have gone in another direction, maybe even crime, because I was around those types of people a lot growing up. But when I got off the ground I found acting to be the most effortless way of becoming successful. That's the way it happened, but that doesn't mean it's the only way it could have happened."

Much of his autobiography focused on this theme of chance, the fact of one guy making it and another not, often for inexplicable reasons. He said:

> I was kept on at Universal because of my fan mail but it could have worked the other way. They took a lot of us on and bumped a lot of us off. It was the law of averages. Throw enough dirt at a wall and some of it will stick. We all became rivals that way, juggling against one another for face time. I got two minutes in a film called *Criss Cross* and I made them count. The letterboxes were jammed with mail from women who thought I was hot. The film is now remembered for that. Who remembers Burt Lancaster in it now, or Yvonne De Carlo? That's why I say it's all chance. I could have died in that movie, or even had my scene canned. Who presides over these things, what God of motion pictures? Your guess is as good as mine.

He told a story in his autobiography about saying to Marlon Brando one day when he was rooming with him, "Marlon, I wonder what would have happened if you'd have turned left down Barham Boulevard and gone to Universal to be the son of Ali Baba, and I'd turned right and become Stanley Kowalski?" Brando replied, "Then I'd have been stuck with 'Yondah lies the castle of my faddah,' and you'd have been yelling 'Ste-l-l-a-a!'"[3] The anecdote jibed with the general theme of chance that filled the book.

Was life both inside and outside the movies largely down to random events rather than a Grand Plan, I wondered. I gave the example of John F. Kennedy's assassination, which he'd mentioned in this context in his book. If Kennedy's car hadn't slowed to a snail's pace on that horseshoe bend in Dallas in 1963 would he have survived, or would the people who contacted Lee Harvey Oswald to wipe him out have got him some other way?

"I've never bought into that line of thinking. I don't believe there was any conspiracy in the Kennedy assassination. It's always been my belief that Oswald acted alone." I presumed he didn't think there was any conspiracy in the death of Marilyn Monroe either. "Absolutely not. Marilyn wasn't murdered by the Mafia or the CIA or anyone else. What secrets was she going to spill — the size of Kennedy's dick?" Did he believe she was planning to commit suicide? "No. She took those pills and then started calling people on the phone to help her. She'd taken pills before and been revived. But this time she called Peter Lawford, who was the last guy in the world she should have called because he was as drunk as she was that night."

I asked him what he thought she said in the phone call to Lawford.

Probably the stuff she said to him on most of her other calls to him around that time, which was why he didn't take her seriously enough, and why ultimately she died. She wanted to cry on his shoulder about the way she'd been tossed between the Kennedy brothers like a piece of meat. He knew she was "on" something by the drugged sound of her voice, but that wasn't unusual for her. Her threats of suicide weren't unusual either. She was ringing him in a desperate cry for help but he didn't recognize it. I can't blame him for that, even though she'd tried to do herself in not long before in the Cal-Neva Lodge. It was like the boy who cried wolf. "Here's Marilyn again, telling us she's going to pull the plug." So he didn't really listen to her. He had her on hold. He was trying to think of some way to offload the call. He rang his manager, Milt Ebbins, and told him he was thinking of calling in on her. Ebbins told him it wouldn't look good as the president's brother-in-law, so he dropped the idea. That was his big mistake and it ate into him. Some people say it killed him eventually. I don't know about that, but I know about guilt from my own life....

Did he think Monroe could have been saved that night?

Probably yes, but she'd have tried it again. Marilyn was in too much pain. She needed to be out of it. She'd had her time. I didn't see it as too big a tragedy, to be honest. They blew it up afterwards because of who she was. I can understand that. I didn't see it that way because I was closer to her. Not as close emotionally as I might have liked but in the sense of being part of her life in some way through a lot of it. That colors your perspective.

Did the negative feelings he'd had about her from her tantrums on *Some Like It Hot* form part of that perspective?

Undoubtedly. Let me tell you, I was more afraid of Marilyn in that movie than I was of George Raft. She knew she had the power to kill any take. Because she was Marilyn. But it hurt. Some days it affected the way I related to her. Which made her even more nervous. It was a vicious circle. Sometimes you just wanted to go with the bad take because so many other things were at stake. It was almost like Marilyn was a co-director, even though she was half-way off the rails. Maybe you could have made a funnier picture about *that*.

He spoke about his initial reluctance to appear in drag. "It was easier for Jack [Lemmon]," he said, "because he wasn't as much of a prettyboy as I was. His history had been in more zany roles so he was really just carrying that on. I was different. I had an image to protect." Did he mean as a sex symbol?

Not quite. Just the crossdressing idea in itself. It wasn't as prevalent then as now. When Dustin Hoffman did it in *Tootsie* it was a kind of Method thing. Then you had Robin Williams playing it for laughs in *Mrs. Doubtfire*. Jack was more like Robin in his approach, and I suppose I was more like Dustin. I wanted to be seen as a real woman but I realized afterwards that that was the wrong attitude.

Was he sore about the fact that Lemmon got an Oscar nomination for the film but he didn't? "You're damn right I was. They should have given me a Best Actress nomination as well!"

He admonished Monroe too:

The Actor's Studio stuffed her head with bullshit. The people running these places should know who they're dealing with. Undoubtedly they do some people some good, but with Marilyn they took away her natural gift for comic timing. After a conversation with Paula Strasberg she tended to question everything. "What am I doing here? Who am I? What's that jug doing on the table?" Jack and me were going, "Marilyn, just say the fuckin' line — please?"[4]

I asked him the $64 dollar question: Had he really said kissing Monroe was akin to kissing Hitler? "It was a throwaway line because she pissed everyone off on the set. It was no big deal." As a Jew, was Hitler a special hate figure to bring up? "I didn't think of it in those terms. It came out without my preparing it. Since then nobody has let me forget it. The Sob Sisters of my profession love to pick up on something like this and jump all over it. I've suffered more for that line than any other one in my whole career, with the possible exception of 'Yondah lies the castle of my faddah.'"

The "Sob Sisters" reference led me to the subject of gossip columnists. I mentioned a story to him that I heard about Louella Parsons seeing Hope Lange having lunch with Don Murray one day and saying to Lange, "How dare you be here! In my column I say you're off in Mexico having an affair with Glenn Ford." He laughed loudly at this. "I get it. It's like, 'How dare you not be unfaithful.' We have that a lot in the gutter press. Hollywood is built on innuendo. The true stories never really cut it, comparatively speaking."

Had the media been kind to him generally? "If you asked me that question a few years ago I would probably have said no, but if you asked it two decades ago I might have said they were overly kind. Maybe it all evens out in the course of a career. I played the game with Louella and Hedda at the start because that was what you did, what everyone did. Later on I drew back a bit. I had to." Why was that? "Different things. The break-up with Janet and so on. I didn't blame them. They had a job to do and they gave me publicity when I needed it. But it's a double-edged sword. At the end of the day these people don't really care what happens to you. It took me years to come to that awareness. By the time I did, a lot of damage had been done."

In what way? "In a hundred different ways. When I started out, for instance, people made fun of my haircut and my accent. That hurt me. It took me years to get over it." What about the Method idea of "using the difficulty"? He frowned. "I don't get what you mean." I seemed to remember someone telling him he could make hay out of the publicity surrounding his thick Bronx accent. He laughed again. "Okay. People did say that to me. Shelley Winters said it. Hugh Hefner said it. But you have to be careful about things like that. It can go wrong. They were hitting me at a weak point. It's okay to be casual about it now when it doesn't matter anymore, but it did then. After *Son of Ali Baba* there were times I thought I'd never work again."[5]

He talked about other people who'd been brought down by bad publicity — Brando, Elvis, his friend Rock Hudson after he got AIDS in the 1980s. "They compared me to Elvis when I got to Hollywood first," he said. "One critic wrote, 'Tony Curtis is the worst actor to appear in movies since Elvis Presley.' Why do people say things like that? What this cocksucker didn't realize was that I *admired* Elvis' acting ability." Did that help? He burst out laughing again. "Not really!"

I asked him how he thought the publicity machine affected Marilyn Monroe. "The way it affects all of us. Good cop, bad cop." Did he feel she was the beneficiary of an excessive degree of sympathy from the media after she died?

In my view she was. She became the tragic heroine of all time, didn't she? Marilyn fell into the genre of the poor, unsuspecting, emotionally-prone darling girl who'd been raped and abused by the industry and so she died. Bullshit. That had nothing to do with it. I agree with Billy Wilder, who said it wasn't Hollywood that killed Marilyn but rather that it was the Marilyns of this world that were killing Hollywood. The fact of the matter is that she went out and did everything she had to do to become successful. I know she did. She lived with Joe Schenck and a whole slew of other guys. Schenck was head of Twentieth Century–Fox and she lived with him in his house, a house I ended up owning.[6] As soon as she started to make it she started getting even with every guy that ever took advantage of her. And even the guys that didn't take advantage of her, she started getting even with. So when I met her on the *Some Like It Hot* set she was a different person, a vindictive, angry, frustrated girl.

What did he think had caused the change?

Who knows? She'd had a terrible time doing *The Prince and the Showgirl* with Laurence Olivier. Maybe that had something to do with it. There was a lot of controversy about that. Then she started getting hung up on the people from the acting school. She was also starting to lose her looks, and that had to hurt. This was Marilyn Monroe, after all. Not since the forties had she had to work at getting men interested in her. And then there was all the Kennedy stuff. I don't know how much of that was true. Whether it was or not, Jack Lemmon and myself caught the end of it on *Some Like It Hot*. Things got even worse when Paula Strasberg turned up on the set. What a tragedy that was for all concerned!

Watching Monroe conferring with Strasberg after almost every take did Wilder's head in. Said Curtis, "It made me feel a bit better to know I wasn't the only one going barmy." I mentioned a quote I read somewhere in which Wilder said that there were more books written about Marilyn Monroe than World War II, "and the comparison doesn't end there." This amused Curtis greatly. He now provided another Billy Wilder quote for me, one about the exacting film critic Judith Crist. "Getting a kind review from Judith Crist, Billy told me one day, was a bit like having your neck massaged by the Boston Strangler." (Wilder had even less time for Ms. Crist than he had for Monroe.)

Since we were sharing quotes, I thought I'd give him another one I'd read. It was Fred Allen's "You can take all the sincerity in Hollywood, put it in the navel of a fruitfly, and still have room for three caraway seeds and a producer's heart." I was trying so hard to remember the words that I didn't deliver them well, but he still laughed heartily. He punched his fist onto the table twice for good measure, knocking his cup off its saucer in the process. Some diners looked over at us and he put up his hand to them to apologize. He was making me feel like the entertainer even though I had fluffed the line.

I'd started to like Curtis a lot by now, despite the bad reports I'd read on him over the years for his philandering. Who was any of us to judge? I tried to put all my preconceptions of him on hold and just let the interview go where it would. The more we talked, the more questions came up in my mind. It wasn't like work because he was so forthcoming. If it was work to him, he certainly didn't show it. He seemed to get particularly excited talking about Marilyn Monroe so I continued firing questions about her at him. In a way she seemed to epitomize both the glamour and hellishness of his own life. I asked him if her beauty made her tantrums easier to take, or did it work the other way.

Marilyn was the most beautiful woman in the world when she was at her best, but the drink and the pills took that away from her. And age. She couldn't accept that. In later years I understood it, but in 1958 I didn't get it as well as I do now. Maybe I didn't sympathize enough. Billy and myself tore our hair out — well, Billy didn't have much hair to begin with — and Jack too at times, but he was usually more amused by her, or curious to know what was driving her. I didn't ask myself these questions. I just wanted to get the scene done.

He talked about how difficult it is to please everyone in the business — your costars, the director, the cameraman, the crew, the tea lady. Maybe the miracle was that any good films got made at all. Then there was all the backstabbing that went on:

> You get done over so many times you harden up. It's like Marlon Brando says in *On the Waterfront*: "Do it to him before he does it to you." You have to think that way to survive. When I came to Hollywood first I expected an honest day's work for an honest day's pay but it doesn't work like that. You have to read the small print — or get your agent to do it. If you're lucky he'll break your fall.

The way he saw it, the film business was a crapshoot. "Listen," he said, sitting forward, "I have an agent who once said to me, 'I'm 99 percent right in everything I do, which is turn people down.'" Was that Swifty Lazar?

> Yes. I said to him, "How do you figure that?" He said, "It's obvious. Out of every 100 scripts I get I say no to 99 of them, and I'm usually right. If I say yes to one, that can be a mistake. The trick is knowing which one to say yes to. But only one in 100 makes good." If we all knew which one that was, we'd all be rich. It's like in a casino. Only one guy out of a hundred beats the bank, but they still say "Everybody wins" and we believe it. That's what drives movies too, that illusion."

He went further, claiming life outside movies was a crapshoot too. "I believe there are 100 people for every job on this planet. Wouldn't you agree? How many people would like to be that waiter we're looking at, for instance. How many people would like your job in the newspaper you work for, or mine in the movies?" (His one-in-a-hundred job somehow seemed better than mine.)

"So we're all a bit like that canary in Mocambo," I suggested. "Exactly! But you have to beat the odds. That's what Frank Sinatra said he liked about me. And he should have known. He was a gambler." I had been aware of this quote. One night Sinatra was asked who his favorite actor was and he replied, "Tony Curtis, because he beat the fucking odds." Sinatra could equally have been speaking of himself, another street urchin who learned the laws of survival early and turned them to his advantage.

Curtis went back to the theme that had opened our discussion, the fact that every movie he made had some kind of ambition attached to it, right from the moment he decided he wanted to be in a film with Cary Grant. It didn't stop there:

> I made *The Mirror Crack'd* purely to be able to kiss Elizabeth Taylor's hand. There was just that little sliver of hope driving me. For *Sextette* it became the expectation of a moment with Mae West. The film didn't have to be a classic. It was who was in it. Not that these women were any more extraordinary than any other women. I just knew I wanted to meet them and that was the only way to do it. Then you do it and it's there forever in some vault. Every day someone somewhere is watching it and living it through me, or watching me living it through them, or whatever.

In his book he wrote about the fact that in "1237" years from now somebody on Jupiter would have a microchip with every movie ever made on it. Did he still believe this? "Of course I do. Do you not feel it's gonna be like that? In 2000 years time, or 3000 years, some Algoonagon from the planet Philoclaca" — he was obviously making up these words as he went along — "will have a chip and every movie ever made will be on it. And they'll slip it into a machine and click onto a certain year and see what movie they want." His eyes lit up at the possibilities: "1956: *Trapeze*. 1959: *Some Like It Hot*. 1962: *Taras Bulba*." I was amused at him trotting out the names with a kind of childlike glee. "They'll watch the movie and then they'll say, 'That's how those humans lived in those days on that planet.' Thinking like that makes me feel good about the process. That's the trigger you have." (Such a "machine" would almost be in existence before he died, what with iPods and so on; civilization would hardly need to wait 2000 years for the pleasure.) "We shall see what we shall see, Sidney," I said, quoting a line of J.J. Hunsecker's from *Sweet Smell of Success*, and he chortled again. "Burt would love you for that!"

We had been talking for a number of hours but he still seemed to have more in the tank. His drive amazed me. "I won't say everything in my life is wonderful now," he continued. "Nobody ever gets to that point, but I think I know where the dangers lie now. I know what I can deal with and what I can't deal with. Lisa helps me a lot. And whatever else I do — my paintings, this movie coming up with Scorsese." He was speaking about *Naked in New York*. It was only a small part, but he was still, as he put it, "in the game."

He seemed to be lost in some inner reverie suddenly. He said:

I'm trying to get back to a peaceful part of myself but it's not easy. Everywhere you look there's dissent. Why should we have to fight with each other? That's the demise of this life, and a lot of it comes from religion. Most of the wars in the world have been fought because of religion. It's absurd. I try to stay away from areas of friction now, away from areas where I feel I can't compete. That way I don't have the envy my parents had.

Could he say, like Edith Piaf, "*Je ne regrette rien*"? He paused for a moment, then answered:

You know what it's like? If I knocked everything off the table we're sitting at and you photographed it and everything spewed all over the place and then we ran the film backwards and it went ... [he made a whirring sound] back to exactly the way it was, that's what I'd like to see, to see you and me and everybody go [he made the whirring sound again] back to the purity we essentially are. We're so bogged down and inhibited by our pains and angers and other people's inputs to us that it takes us too long to get to where we want to be.

I asked him about his brother Bobby, who'd spent most of his life incarcerated in an institution and whose death in 1992 at the age of 52 only merited a footnote in his book. "I didn't even know who he was when I visited him," he said sharply. "I don't even know the circumstances he died in. And I'm not sure I want to."

He talked about the demons of his past, his drink and drugs hell, about losing his friends. "I was in a bad way. I would wake up at 4 A.M. and think: Who am I? But that's all past now. Big fucking deal — excuse my language. The beat goes on. I don't fret about these kinds of things anymore."

Had he any idea how he got into the mess he did with alcohol?

I was getting bad parts in dumb movies and I started to wonder what it was all about. The drink came to my rescue like an old friend, but only for a while. I couldn't cope with the hangovers. I was on uppers to get me through the day and then I'd wind down with other drugs. It was an insane treadmill.

Bad marriages, bad movies, getting on in years, I could pick a thousand reasons, but at the end of the day it comes back to yourself. Why did I goof? Why did I not try harder? Why did I not turn left with Marlon? Why is the sky blue? Why is the grass green? The short answer is I don't know. Maybe it was a case of too much too soon and I wasn't able to handle it. I never thought of myself being famous. Even though I wanted to be Tony Curtis all my life, Bernie Schwartz kept coming back to haunt me.

Was there any self-destructiveness in his family? "My father suffered from depression, and I have a lot of him in me, and a few slivers of my grandfather as well. And maybe even a little bit of my great grandfather, whom I didn't know at all." I remarked that he didn't write about the latter man in his book. "He was a prick, excuse me. He was a terrible man. He tried to hit my father once and I never forgot that."[7]

He refused to pass the buck, however. We got our basic genes from our lineage "but after that our personalities begin to take on their own emphases. Were you and I able to conceive a way of being produced without being tainted and tinted by our families or by a previous society and culture, we could access much more without pain, anger, avarice, envy. But we're born into that. What I'm trying to do in my life is get back to zero and become the man I want to be."

We talked about his relationship with his mother. Apart from the physical abuse, he said it became annoying in a different way when he was famous. She continually pressed him to "do something for Bobby." Because Julie was gone and Bobby institutionalized,

> I was expected to do the work of three sons. I was torn apart. I did a lot of movies for no other reason than that she was screaming down some phone line at me. I wasn't together enough in myself that I could stand up to her or divorce her from my mind. That's what caused me to make bad movies. I couldn't concentrate. I'd be doing a picture but my mind would be a million miles away. I'd be thinking of my family, or maybe a girl that told me she was pregnant when she wasn't, or getting into a marriage I didn't want to because people were telling me it was for the best.

I told him I didn't want to reopen old wounds, that he didn't have to talk about these things if he didn't want to. "It's okay," he said, "I've opened up the wounds myself in the book. I can deal with things now that I mightn't have been able to a few years ago. It helps me to understand myself."

His eyes lit up suddenly. "Did you know I was the last person to see Julie alive?" I nodded. "I visited him in the hospital after he was knocked down. He was unconscious but I talked to him at his bedside. I was the last person he heard. I found out later that even when you're in an unconscious condition your hearing doesn't abate. It's the last element to go. So he must have heard me standing there. That made me feel a little better."

Even though he was putting a brave face on it, I sensed a sadness in him that he didn't want to acknowledge. He seemed to go quiet as people started to file out of the dining area. He had finished many coffees but I'd barely touched mine, too busy listening — and hoping my little cassette recorder was picking up his outpourings.

Before we wrapped up I decided to ask him if he was happy with his career generally. The question seemed to annoy him. He snapped:

> Listen, I did a lot of movies to pay the rent, okay? Everybody does it. Some pictures I did because I needed money for child payments. Name me someone who didn't. Paul Newman? Marlon Brando? It doesn't matter how good you are. None of these motherfuckers has the right to point the finger at anyone else. Who's bullshitting who? Why am I the whipping boy? I don't even relate to that question. Whatever my reasons, every movie I ever made had a purpose and a plan and a reason. I have six children and I never missed a payment. Never.

Pride hung on his lips as he said the last word.[8]

Before we left the dining room he signed his novel for me. He also drew a sketch of a hand holding a pyramid on it. He didn't explain what it meant and I didn't ask. Was it Hollywood's Tower of Babel? A metaphor for chance? In a way it was more intriguing not to know.

I remarked on the fact that he'd dedicated the novel to Leslie Allen, the woman he was married to when he wrote it. This comment drew a blank. I'd like to have talked more about her but he seemed evasive on this score, muttering half under his breath, "She turned out to be deceitful so that's enough about that."

I asked him which of his past wives he was most friendly with. He looked perplexed at the question. "Most of the women I'm friendly with I haven't been married to." He then added, "Apart from my present wife, of course." His relationship to Lisa Deutsch was based on trust: "It doesn't have the baggage I brought to most of my other marriages." What kind of baggage? "Mainly my suspiciousness. At times this bordered on paranoia." I commented on the fact that Lisa once said it would take her her whole life to understand Curtis. Would he take that as a compliment? "I think so. We're working hard on the relationship." I couldn't understand the logic here. If things were as good as he claimed, why did the relationship need work?

His autobiography was on the table and I thumbed through it. He said it was on the best seller list in the U.S. I said I thought it was one of the best I'd ever read on the dizzy madness of Hollywood, that I didn't see it as in any way salacious. "I wasn't interested in talking about who I went to bed with just for the sake of it," he said. "We've had enough of those. It's frank but not too explicit." In fact, it was both.

"You should write more," I suggested. He said he would: "Nothing too complicated." Would it be a kiss-and-tell?' "No." "Not like the kind of book Sidney Falco would write?" He smiled. "Send me your article when it comes out," he said.

I found myself asking him how his friends were, people like Burt Lancaster and Dean Martin. "Burt had that terrible stroke. Dean is fine. He goes out every night. There are rumors about him being an introvert, but they're not true."[9]

He got up from the table and stretched. I felt I'd come out of some kind of trance. He looked around him for the waiter as he took up the bill. "Could you put a tip on this?" he asked.

As he spoke I couldn't help thinking about one of his first parts in movies where he delivered a telegram to Barbara Stanwyck in *The Lady Gambles* and waits for her to tip him. I also thought of Sidney Falco's streetwise advice in *Sweet Smell of Success*: "Leave a tip in every hatcheck room in town."

We moved out to the next room to have some photographs taken. I asked if I could be with him in one. "Definitely," he assured. He sidled in close to me. "Here we are at last," he whispered, as if I was his lover. "Are you who I think I am?" I said, a reference to a running line in his book about the complexities of one's identity. He repeated the line as if he hadn't heard it before, "Are you who I think I am!" Suddenly he looked like a dazed child caught in the klieg lights of Hollywood for the first time.

So what did the future hold for the latterday matinee idol? "I just want to keep on keeping on. I never thought of tomorrow when I was young, so why should I start now? My philosophy of life has always been clearcut: I do things instead of obsessing about them. As I say in the book, it's not about 'To be or not to be,' it's just 'Be.'"

The snaps were taken and hands were shook. The camera equipment was folded up.

19. Rendezvous in Dublin

Curtis with the author at Dublin's Shelbourne Hotel in 1994. He had just written his autobiography and was touring Britain and Ireland to promote it, as well as promoting a collection of his art, which had started to sell for lucrative sums in various galleries (photograph Brian Farrell).

A publicist floated by. A pretty young lady kissed him on both cheeks, whispering something about somewhere else he had to be. Suddenly we were finished. He gave me a firm hug and a high-five. "Goodbye, Tony," I said. It was the first time I'd used his name.

As we re-entered the lobby, a man came towards him that he took to be a fan. He put his hand out to shake it but it turned out to be just some security person who wanted to whisper something in his ear. I thought I saw his face fall as the outstretched hand was ignored. It was only a small detail but it showed how eager he still was to be wanted, and maybe how sensitive he was too.

I watched him disappear into the bowels of the hotel. He was surrounded by an array of journalists lining up for his next cattle call, the faint trace of a limp reminding me that he was only fifteen months short of the Biblical span.

That night he appeared on a television program, *The Late Late Show*, hosted by Gay Byrne. Jeremy Irons had been interviewed before him. When Curtis was introduced he said a brief hello to Byrne and then went over and shook hands individually with Irons and the other guests. I had never seen this done before in all the years I'd been watching *The Late Late Show*. Byrne looked stunned. Then he went down to the audience and shook hands with some people there too. It felt like Elvis Presley was in the building. There was that sense of warmth, of touching base with a larger-than-life presence.

He said to Irons, "You were in a movie I liked where you played twins."[10] Irons was embarrassed that the main guest of the night was talking about him. He replied, "You were in *Some Like It Hot*!" It was like: "Shut up!"

Byrne immediately launched into a discussion of Curtis' fondness for sexy women, into the way he portrayed himself as his costars' "Kissing instructor" in so many studios to get up close and personal with them. "Do you want me to show you how to kiss?" he asked Byrne playfully. "The first thing you do is keep your mouth shut."

In deference to the country he was in, he told a yarn about having Irish heritage, about thinking his real name was Bernie O'Schwartz. When he was young, people kept saying to him, "Oh Schwartz, come here." That was his little joke.

Byrne wasn't to be deflected from his intention to interrogate him about women. "Your sex needs are very intense," he pressed. Curtis looked at his watch. "What time is it?" he asked, and the audience erupted into laughter. A chastened Byrne remarked, "I'll come back to that later," whereupon Curtis replied, "You can come back to it anytime you like!"

Byrne asked him about his alcohol and drug hell. He said he was nine years sober now, that alcoholism was a disease curable only by abstinence. He emphasized the fact that one had to dearly want that abstinence before it was achievable. He quoted a line from Marilyn Monroe as she sipped a martini in *Some Like It Hot*: "I can stop any time I want to, only I don't want to." It was an important nuance.

So how had he slipped into his addictions? "There was no joy or pleasure in my life. I was losing my grip on reality. Drugs elevated all my feelings. Cocaine could make a coward think he was a brave man, or a dumb man imagine himself to be intelligent."

He talked about how he'd wrecked himself in matters of the heart and head. "We all bring madness to relationships." But that was all past now. He obeyed a strict health regimen, walking thirty minutes a day and working out with dumbbells ("The weights, not the people!"). He also ate a lot of pasta.

It was a long way away from the Curtis who came within a whisper of pressing the self-destruct button when he was freebasing cocaine. Withdrawal was the worst part; it was like two rusty pieces of metal scraping on each other. The perceived solution was to "use" again. At his worst he kept a loaded pistol in his house.

His mind was all over the place in his dark years. "I felt I was being checkmated in a chess game." He would put gasoline in the tank of his car and forget to put the cap back on. "I drove a Pontiac Trans-Am with a silver eagle on it, but I had nowhere to go." He had so little sense of personal worth he sometimes slept in his car, feeling like a hobo. He could easily have gone lower but somehow he hauled himself back from the precipice "I embrace each moment now," he announced, "at 68 years of age. The sky is blue at 2, at 22, at 82, up to the last breath we take...."

He spoke of movies as being like illusions. "I dream a lot, and sometimes I wonder if dreams are the reality or if reality is the preparation for dreams. We wake up to take care of business because you can't sleep for 24 hours." Movies, for him, tapped into this need. "The first movies we saw were like dreams too. We pay money for two hours of a dream, or a memory."

The audience was transfixed as he shared his convictions with them, opening up in the way he had with me earlier in the day. They were also aware how different he was from the stars we were generally presented with, spouting bromides about their last excursion into cosmetic surgery in Silicon Valley, or how many millions their last movie grossed.

Before he finished he was asked to relate a last funny story about his life. He chose one he'd told me earlier about his mother, about the time he was suddenly starting to make money in the movies and so could afford to send her on a holiday. He had her collected from the Bronx in a limo, then transported to Paris by TWA, then brought to Budapest to meet old acquaintances from her youth, and finally to Hollywood. It was all "Mrs. Schwartz this" and "Mrs. Schwartz that," and she lapped it up. She had hardly been out of the Bronx before, but she became so carried away with all the attention that was being lavished upon her that she felt like a superstar. As she was being strapped into the plane for the last leg of her journey she looked up at the air hostess and inquired, without any trace of a tongue in her cheek, "Excuse me, are there any other celebrities on board?"

20

Meltdown

When Curtis got back to the U.S., the problems he'd been having with Lisa got worse. She was working too hard, he thought, and drinking too much as well. One night she came home drunk, and he refused to let her into his room. She slept in the downstairs bedroom instead. Afterwards she took to being out more than in. This was a reversal of the usual pattern of his disintegrating marriages where he tended to gallivant and his wives house-hatched. They split up soon afterwards.

The parting from Lisa wasn't as traumatic as that with his other wives, probably because the marriage was so short. He put it down as a bad call, letting his eyes rule his heart. But worse was to come....

One day soon afterwards when he was working out at a gym in L.A. he became dizzy. When he went to the doctor he was informed he'd just had a silent heart attack. He was rushed to the hospital and two days later the surgeons took a vein out of his leg and used it to replace a blocked artery. He recovered quickly because of his general fitness but it was still a wake-up call for him. He knew he'd been burning the candle at both ends. "You can't fuck with your body at 68," he said afterwards. "The book tour took it out of me."

No sooner was he over this than he received another crippling blow, one which made him feel near-suicidal. On July 2, 1994, his 23-year-old son Nicholas was found dead from a drug overdose at the house of a friend in Massachusetts. Curtis couldn't comprehend the news. He adored Nicholas, "the artistic one." How could he be gone? Why hadn't he come to him if he needed help? What had happened to him?

In some ways he never quite recovered from his son's death. Nicholas was arguably his favorite child, the one he identified with most. He also had huge guilt issues about the fact that he'd been a poor father to him because of the deterioration of his relationship with Leslie Allen when Nicholas was hardly out of the cradle. Curtis always believed these early years in Nicholas' life formed his personality. The fact that he was continually being shunted between himself and Allen deprived him of any sense of stability. He became that all-to-frequent Hollywood statistic: The Shared Custody Child. In Curtis' view, that meant he had "two homes and none."

Curtis wrote about Nicholas' talent for art and music in his autobiography. More significantly, he added that he dropped out of school and turned inward in pursuit of these aims.[1] In this we may see the blueprint for the boy's downward spiral. He had too much time to think and not enough routine. That might have worked for some people but it didn't for him.

Nicholas was reported as having died of a mysterious seizure. Curtis believed his death was accidental but that didn't mitigate the tragedy. Maybe it made it worse. As well as drugs, he'd had a problem with alcohol. (Many of the mourners at his funeral were from Alcoholics Anonymous.)

Curtis rarely spoke about how Nicholas' death affected him. This was unusual for such a garrulous man. If asked about him he usually paused and then directed interviewers to the next question. The fact that he had a drug problem himself compounded his guilt. Billy Wilder said to him once, "He learned it from you, Tony."[2] This was like a dagger in his heart.

On the positive side, Nicholas' death brought Curtis closer to his other children. Jamie said, "I understand him better now. Perhaps not as a father but as a man."[3] At the funeral he looked his age for the first time, the strain etched on his face. Lisa and Jamie had him between them, their arms around him.

Allegra was afraid his heart wouldn't stand the strain of seeing Nicholas in his coffin. He cried like she'd never seen him cry before. He went over to Allen and they stood in silence and embraced. Afterwards he threw himself over the coffin like somebody in a movie. When he told Allegra he felt responsible for Nicholas' death, she said, "No, Dad, you didn't inject the drugs into his arm." Jamie shielded him from the paparazzi as they closed in on him.[4] It was one of the few times in his life when he spurned media attention.

A week after the funeral he managed to drag himself to a preview of Jamie's new film, *True Lies*. She was costarring with Arnold Schwarzenegger.[5] He'd been looking forward to the event before Nicholas died, but now it was just an ordeal to be gotten through.

Schwarzenegger hadn't wanted Jamie to be in the movie at first. It called for her to play a mother but he didn't see her as mother material. He was persuaded by James Cameron, the director, to give her a chance to prove him wrong. Cameron feared he might resent having his arm twisted and take it out on Curtis on the set but as things worked out they got on brilliantly.[6] Schwarzenegger went on to become good friends with Jamie and also her father. This was evidenced by his appearance at Nicholas' funeral.

A few weeks later Curtis was spotted out on the town with a dizzy blonde. Could he have been over the trauma of Nicholas already? Was he being unfaithful to Lisa? These were the questions journalists were asking. An interview with him that was published in the *Sunday Times* contained some worrying comments by him about marriage. "It's a business," he said, "a business so huge there are attorneys that deal in only that subject: prenuptial agreements, communal properties." So why had he gone into it so often? "Well, you get a car and it's not the color you want but you still buy it. Listen, a marriage can only last so long, then you kick into another gear and it lasts another length of time, and then another gear." There seemed to be a Freudian slip in his admission that "Women don't have to be in my bed now. My ideal would be if I had a nanny 24 hours a day. I just like to have someone round if I get sick or something. They can't just sit around waiting for you to talk to them." Was it possible to have a woman as a friend? "Only if she's ugly!"[7] he chortled.

Other stories appeared in newspapers and gossip magazines in the following months that had him "tomcatting" in Las Vegas and elsewhere. Traumatized by Nicholas' death and given intimations of mortality as a result of his heart scare, he was quoted more than once as saying, "Life's too short." Meaning, in Curtis-speak, life was too short for monogamy.

He turned 69 in June. He admitted there were some cracks in the marriage to Lisa but he said he was trying to iron them out. He loved his wife but she was driving him up the wall because she wanted him to stay in nights. The leopard couldn't change his spots. In July he attended a video convention in Las Vegas and hit all the hotspots nightly. He stayed a week and also bought a new Limited Edition Firebird to complete the image of "Bachelor Tony." Busty women hung on his arms. Arrowing in on seventy, he was still the hot rod who could pull the chicks. But he wanted to play it both ways. Quizzed about Lisa, he praised her to the hilt as being a caring and upright person. (Her only problem seemed to be her wish to continue being Mrs. Curtis — a minor detail in his eyes.)

"I spent my life looking for love," he said. "Maybe my mother took me off the tit too soon and I never recovered from that." The irreverent tone continued when he said his taste in women had changed over the years: "The older I get, the younger I like 'em."

He didn't just try and sweet-talk women into bed with such adolescent banter; he genuinely enjoyed their company. "I fell in love every day," he said once. "They say I've had a thousand women. I don't know about that, but I do know that what was important wasn't just the physical aspect — it was the intimacy."[8]

There are those who would say that if he put as much effort into his marriages as he did into his books and films he mightn't have had to go up the aisle four times before he met Ms. Right. Gloria Swanson said she worked harder on her autobiography than her marriages because "You can't divorce a book." Maybe Curtis was a man after her heart. Or maybe he just liked variety.

"I wouldn't be caught dead married to a woman old enough to be my wife," he joked.[9] And elsewhere: "Marriage is very difficult. Very few of us are fortunate enough to marry multi-millionaire girls with 39 inch busts who have undergone frontal lobotomies."[10]

Lisa wasn't even born the first time he went to the altar. He shared the following thought with a journalist: "I'm working on this marriage more than I ever did on the others. I'm having to learn not to bring to it all the garbage I had from my other relationships, the fears and pain when I didn't trust these other women. Otherwise I'm going to ruin it."[11]

One of the women he was seeing at this time was a porn star with the unlikely name of Danyel Cheeks. (She showed them to the camera often enough — at both ends). Some of her movie titles were so raunchy, the newspapers documenting her dalliances with Curtis around Vegas couldn't even name them. They'd met a year previously at the Annual Video Software Dealer's convention but sparks didn't fly until they bumped into each other again in July 1994 at Club Paradise in Las Vegas. Curtis was unburdening himself of the pain of Nicholas' death and Cheeks gave him a sympathetic shoulder to cry on. "Tony is just a beautiful, beautiful person," Cheeks gushed. "I love being with him."[12] He filed for divorce against Deutsch the following month.[13]

Curtis met Jill VandenBerg, the woman who would become his fifth wife, in a Los Angeles restaurant in 1995.[14] He was dining alone but she had company. It was only when he was halfway through his meal that he realized how beautiful (and well endowed) she was. When he did he went up to her table, oblivious to the fact that she was in the company of another man. "I was so smitten I couldn't see straight," he said. "I got up like a robot, walked over to her table and waited for this guy she was with to introduce me, knowing that if he didn't I would finally turn to her and say, 'Hello, my name is Tony.' And that's what I did."[15]

The fact that a 69-year-old man would approach a beautiful woman 44 years his junior in a restaurant meant that he was either very brave, very foolish or very lonely. It also meant that he'd lost nothing of the *chutzpah* that had lured hundreds of women into his bed over the past half-century. After telling her his name, she replied, "I know who you are. You worked with Marilyn Monroe." She'd always been fascinated by Monroe and even modeled a bathing suit the actress had worn once. She had also bought some rare photographs of Monroe from the sixties on eBay at exorbitant prices.

Curtis asked her what she did for a living. "I run a riding school in San Diego," she replied. He said he was familiar with San Diego. Then came the crunch question: "May I have your number?" He was amazed that he had the gall to do this right under the nose of the man she was with, though he appeared to be unperturbed.[16] (It emerged later that he was only a casual acquaintance.) Before he left the restaurant he said to the man, "How is your wife?" to embarrass him. VandenBerg overheard the comment and they had a laugh about it. Curtis wasn't proud of doing things like this but he still didn't stop doing them. VandenBerg didn't know whether to be shocked or amused. Curtis rang her to ask her out ten minutes after meeting her. They started dating afterwards and very soon became close. One night when he was feeling lonely he asked her to move in with him.

Neither of them were unduly concerned about the huge age difference between them. As was the case with many of his previous relationships with younger women, in many ways VandenBerg felt *she* was the more mature party, especially when Curtis came out with statements like, "I always wanted to be Tony Curtis, and I still want to be Tony Curtis when I grow up."[17]

People accused her of being a gold-digger, of being with him for what she could get out of him. She thought that theory rubbish, saying they simply got on well together and that he amused her greatly with his eccentric humor.

After he started living with her he distanced himself from his children. Christine Kaufmann huffed, "No one has a chance with Jill's big breasts."[18] Allegra referred to her as his "white trash beauty." She believed Jill manipulated him. Few invitations were issued from them for her to visit. On the odd occasion that she called, she found it difficult to connect with him. She thought he hid behind VandenBerg — and behind his silly jokes. For her he had become his image: a film star rather than her father. "He tried to love me beyond the facade of Tony Curtis," she contended, "but didn't succeed."[19]

Allegra noticed that VandenBerg only had photographs of Curtis as a young man in her room, pictured with people like Marilyn Monroe. She saw this as significant. Had she dreamed herself into the role of Monroe? Was it the youthful Curtis she really wanted?[20]

She found VandenBerg embarrassing with her impossibly high heels, her plunging necklines, an array of dresses that were so low they were hardly on her at all. VandenBerg was only three years older than Allegra herself. "She had something of Anna Nicole Smith about her," she thought, with her peroxide blond hairstyle.[21]

In April 1995 Andrew Duncan met Curtis in a Los Angeles hotel. He was awed by him, describing Curtis as "a walking monument to the unfairness of life." He should have been dead, Duncan surmised, as a result of his wild escapades, his multiple marriages, and a drug and alcohol addiction that would have killed lesser men. Curtis didn't object to that overview of his life. Dressed in a black Mao jacket which he wore over a colorful T-shirt, he beamed, "Looking good is the best revenge.... I feel great, but when I look in a mirror I feel better. I'm so vain I think the world was made just for me."[22]

He talked about the abuse he had received from his mother: "I never knew if she was going to kiss me or slap me."[23] He said he hated listening to his parents bickering. So constant was this that one day when he saw his mother kissing his father on the cheek he was shocked. "I went to my room and sobbed. I was so pissed off. I wasn't ready for them to like each other. They'd brainwashed me into thinking life is a horrible experience. And they were acting like children. Why put me into a position where I didn't know what to expect?"[24] That all changed when he grew up and discovered that women liked him. "When I hit 'em, their legs buckled. I didn't even have to say, 'I love you.'"[25]

When Duncan asked him about Marilyn Monroe, he was blunt. "I'm not putting her down, but why is Marilyn any more important in my life than any other woman? I knew girls who made her look like a guy and they were gone in the blink of an eye. They ended up in Vegas as hookers. Or they married and lived in the Valley. Or committed suicide."[26] Perhaps inevitably, the conversation veered towards the breakdown of his marriage to Lisa. He thought he put too much emphasis on sex: "All of us love breasts because we've been weaned on them."[27]

Would he go back to movies? Hardly. He didn't care too much for the new crop of stars. "They don't look as if they're having a good time. Everyone is so uptight." Neither were directors offering him leading roles any more, "and I don't want parts as doctors, lawyers or fathers." These were usually cardboard cut-out characters who spent their time sitting in chairs saying to their daughters, "Don't do that."[28]

He didn't fear age but he didn't want to end up in a wheelchair like a lot of his friends: "You spend seventy years kicking shit out of the enemy, finessing your way through, and all of a sudden you've got a motorized machine and you can't pick up girls anymore." He mentioned his recent open heart surgery, lifting up his shirt to show the scar which the operation had left on his chest. "Very painful," he remarked. "They cut through bone, tendon, muscle. It frightened me. I could easily have gone."

He started flirting with the waitress who was serving them. When she moved away he whispered to Duncan, "If it was just being kind to an old man I would have abdicated long ago, but I see them thinking 'Mmmm.' It makes guys go apeshit when they see how I operate." Had he any secret in this regard? "Dough, looks, a nice car and some reputation get you a table in any restaurant in the world. That means a lot to an impressionable young woman with a 42D cup. I rest my case."[29]

He appeared at the Bafta Awards in London's Palladium soon afterwards, wearing an unusual combination of double-breasted suit and fuzzy brothel creepers. He also "wore" VandenBerg, who was described as being "attached to his left elbow." Sixty-nine going on 17, he was determined to bring some L.A. kitsch to stuffy old England.[30]

His next movie was *The Continued Adventures of Reptile Man and His Faithful Sidekick Tadpole*, an outrageous offering in which he played a character who used to be a sixties TV crimefighter. He's been living off the glory of that since, donning foam rubber costumes for appearances at conventions and suchlike with Tadpole (his erstwhile sidekick) to carry on the dream. One day he even tries to stop a robbery at a convenience store. It could have been a farce but Curtis managed to infuse it with some truly touching moments, giving us a latterday Prospero unwilling to renounce his crown — a bit like himself in real life in many ways.

In the finale he leaps from the top of a skyscraper because, as Tadpole informs us,

"Superheroes don't take the elevator." Miraculously he survives the drop. He ends up in a mental hospital but is still full of life. Curtis gave everything to the part, going from trash to pathos and back again, often in the same scene. It was made on a shoestring, giving it the look of an Ed Wood feature or a Roger Corman one. This was a pity. If money was spent on it, it could have revived his career. But he just wasn't bankable anymore.

He went to Cannes to promote it. Some people thought he was past it; others paid homage to his stature in the industry. As ever, he flirted with the women sent to interview him in front of VandenBerg. "I'm one of the handsomest men in the world," he told journalist Dalya Alberge after kissing her hand and showering her with the Curtis charm. Her article was titled: "Kissed by the Man Who Kissed Monroe."[31] It was sad to think that he was still living off that, and that his latest offering would be almost laughed off the screen by a generation of filmgoers too young to appreciate Curtis or the movie's irony.

Catherine Ostler resisted few attempts to poke fun at him when interviewing him for *The Mail on Sunday*. His toupee she described as "an obedient furry mammal

Even in old age Curtis still sported his trademark quiff. "There may be snow on the roof," he joked, "but the fires are still burning below." They were too, right up to his eighties, as he continued to grow old disgracefully and with great vigor.

glued to his bald pate." On his arm, "or rather towering two heads above him," was the woman who hoped to be his fifth wife. "She must weigh about fourteen stone," Ostler wrote, "most of it above the waist."[32]

She reminded her readers that Curtis would soon be seventy. His presence in Cannes, for her, was a poignant reminder of the transitory nature of celebrity.[33] (Transitory? After 45 years?) She found it pathetic that the sometime dreamboat was now trying to sell himself as a hasbeen in a lizard suit. It's a pity she didn't realize that, even by her own estimation, nobody would be more qualified to empathize with the plight of "Reptile Man."

The film was pilloried by younger audiences. They wanted to see the new stars. Curtis made one of his grand entrances wearing white shorts and a white jacket as he docked at a pier in one of Dodi Al Fayed's yachts. As he did so, the words "Who is he?" were heard echoing across the water. The plight of Norma Desmond in *Sunset Boulevard* came to mind. "I'll pose for you anywhere, darling," he chirped to a female photographer, but for once the feistiness seemed misplaced, even offensive. "He still behaves like a matinee idol," Ostler hissed, "but he looks like a Chelsea pensioner."[34]

Back in the States he learned that Lew Wasserman was selling Universal for $350 million.[35] He still had warm feelings for Wasserman, even if their relationship between them had cooled since his divorce from Leigh. "Losing my friendship with Lew has always been one of my great regrets," Curtis admitted. "I see him out at restaurants or industry functions and he's perfectly cordial. I gave him a beautiful painting of mine once and I got a nice note back from him, but I never get invited to the house. That's all right, though. Life is like that. You can't make an omelette without breaking an egg."[36]

Leigh followed Curtis to the writing desk that year when she produced a blockbuster novel about the inner workings of Hollywood. Called *House of Destiny*, it was never going to be a contender for the Pulitzer Prize but it was a pageturner, a sizzling yarn that moved like a train. Telling the story of two men forming an empire between them, it was territory she knew like the back of her hand and she never let you forget that, even being so bold as to include herself in it: "They were so adorable, all of them.... That Kirk Douglas is a real hunk. And Janet Leigh's new husband is soooo handsome."[37]

One wonders at the advisability of such self-referential tidbits, or an incursion into sauciness that seems decidedly out of character later on.[38] Elsewhere in the book she namechecks *The Vikings*.[39] She even mentions herself and Curtis in the context of a John F. Kennedy rally.[40] Occasionally one can detect Curtis' voice in remarks like, "We can't turn back the clock to tent shows or nickelodeons or silents, but we can and should go back to what those creators always tried to give us — entertainment!"[41]

In the course of her promotion for the book she was asked if she missed movies. She replied, "I loved acting but it was only a job. Your family is forever. Hollywood changed a lot because of the transition away from the studio system. It became more corporate, and for me that took some of the magic away."[42] She was now 68 and still happily married to Bob Brandt. She was asked if the marriage to Curtis was a mistake. "We matured in different ways," she replied. Her interviewer suggested Curtis mightn't have matured at all. "Maybe he hasn't aged as gracefully as he might have," she conceded. She thought part of his problem was his attitude toward money. "He said, 'If I earn a million, I'll spend a million.' But you can't do that. You have to pay taxes and save so that when you don't earn a million you can still eat. He didn't want to deal with that reality."[43]

He certainly wasn't earning "a million" at the present time, either from his acting or his writing. His former *Persuaders* costar Joan Collins had a run-in with Random House publishers in 1996 which interested him as it bore many parallels to his altercation with Doubleday. They'd given her a $4 million advance to write two novels but then withdrew it when the manuscripts were deemed sub-par. Collins sued for the money and, with the help of Swifty Lazar, won a jury decision in her favor. Curtis was left feeling that if he'd played hardball with Doubleday over *Starstruck* he might have been the beneficiary of a similar judgment. Collins created a literary precedent that went beyond the issue of the actual quality of a particular book. Her argument would have suited Curtis. As she said herself, "They hadn't insisted that I produce the next *War and Peace*."[44]

Curtis was interviewed for *GQ* magazine in Spago's restaurant later that year, leaving nobody in any doubt that he'd lost any of his old roguishness. "I like you," he assured his interviewer, "You don't want to know how big my dick is and you don't want to know who I fucked and who I didn't fuck." Then he added conspiratorially, "Although just between you and me, my friend, I fucked them all." After which he emitted that trademark whinnying laugh that cascaded around the room.[45]

"Am I not a miracle?" he asked rhetorically as he became carried away by his own outrageousness. "Look at me. Look at the scars I got." He was referring to a whole life of pain. Scars, he said, speaking of himself in the third person, were where they "dug out his prostate, where they cracked open his sternum and garlanded his heart with a vein snatched from the length of his leg, where for years he ransacked his nose with all the major pollutants, where his crazy mother put his balls through the wringer, where his beloved little brother got run over by a truck, where his other little brother went nuts and wound up picking garbage off the streets of Hollywood, and where, dear God, he lost his son."[46]

When VandenBerg walked into the restaurant he told her she was looking younger than ever. This excited him. "Can you imagine me walking into Spago with a 70-year-old woman?" he speculated. "Fuck that. There's something about a woman just making her way in the world—the smell, the taste, there's a juice there that's very important." There was also the trophy element: "Beauty is America's lottery. Celebrity is America's royalty."[47] The article was entitled "The Last Swinger." Curtis came across as a curly-headed scoundrel having fun with a pneumatic lady whose breasts were so big they seemed to traverse separate postal zones.

Curtis saw himself as one of the last living legends. Only a handful remained from the "old" Hollywood. If they weren't dead they were in poor health. Frank Sinatra was one such. Sinatra was in his eighties now and showing signs of dementia. It hurt Curtis to think of "the Chairman of the Board" as being debilitated. He'd had a long time at the top, like Lancaster, and was suffering like him now, unable to comprehend the fact that his power was gone. Intense men often burned out: it seemed unfair to see them rust away like this. Curtis visited him as often as he could, having a soft spot for old people. His daughter Tina remembered him "cradling and kissing" Sinatra "as a son would a father."[48]

Sinatra's health continued to fail in the following months. Eventually he got to the stage where he could only eat ice cream. Curtis became distressed about him. In Allegra's view he became more concerned about him than he was about his own children: "He was almost like a woman taking care of a sick husband," she averred. Curtis usually brought VandenBerg with him on his visits to Sinatra. Allegra once asked him if Sinatra liked VandenBerg. He replied, "I think he was consoled when I told him I didn't need any Viagra."[49] When Sinatra died in 1998, Curtis said, "Frank was the last of the greats. I suppose I'll be next. It's a pity we don't start out old and then become young."

Fears of his own decrepitude were staved off by him focusing on his strengths, his upbeat spirit. He outlined a screen scenario he was contemplating: "The most perfect romantic movie I would love to make would be me with a 23-year-old girl. It's her first time and his last time. Two people who meet at just the right time in their lives. Time is not a dilemma. That is what I would call a great movie."[50] (But what if the woman was 71 and the man was 23? He wouldn't consider this variation.)

He made three movies in 1998—*Stargames, Louis and Frank* and *Play It to the Bone*— but none of them did any business at the box office. Somebody seemed to be trying to tell him something but he refused to listen. He would continue making phone calls and continue being rebuffed until they carried him away. And yet he insisted on telling reporters, "I don't give a fuck about Hollywood. I ate it and spat it out. I have a new life now." It was like somebody trying to convince himself he was over a lover but still plying her with flowers and extravagant declarations of undying love. "In his later years," Tom Teicholz observed, "the swagger he employed to play the Shell Oil millionaire in *Some Like It*

Hot seemed to have become absorbed into his public persona."[51] Put simply, he became "a character."

He occasionally took this to an extreme, getting himself over-dressed and overly made up like a regenerated Liberace, plugging poor films at Cannes and making pronouncements about everything from Viagra to vasectomies to anyone who thrust a microphone in his face. He was shameless and blameless, a rebel without a pause. He might have secured more acting roles, but one got the impression many directors were afraid to call him for fear of how he might interpret, or misinterpret, a part. On talkshows he was delightfully irreverent and had to have his expletives bleeped out. But he was still great value for money. If people had heard his stories a hundred times before there was always a new twist to them. Even if there wasn't, his enthusiasm in relating them was infectious. He said things like, "I'm the greatest cocksman to ever come down the pike, man," like some sophomore crowing from the top of a dunghill, or notching up bedposts in a locker-room contest, apparently unaware that genuine studs didn't boast of their conquests, or at least not this baldly. Was he still back in the world of *Casanova & Co.*, circa 1977?

As the decade wore on he came to be seen either as a benign elder statesman or a ham who'd outstayed his welcome. While waiting for the phone to ring (usually it didn't) he busied himself with his canvases and some personal appearances to accept film awards or to open festivals. Geoffrey McNab likened him to someone who'd stumbled out of a John Waters movie.

Others were less kind, feeling he'd had his day in the sun and now it was time to move over, darling.[52] Anyone who knew "Toniola," however, was aware he could never do that. He would wear purple, speak softly and carry a stick. Only sissies folded their tents. If he wanted to go to the opening of an envelope, wild horses wouldn't deter him.

21
Picasso of the Desert

Curtis married VandenBerg in November 1998, the walk down the aisle having become his "personal treadmill." She was asked to sign a prenup and was distressed about this for a while. But in the words of one observer, "Her prenuptial tears vanished when Tony slipped a diamond-studded ring on her finger." Curtis himself was effervescent: "I'm good looking, [I've] got a beautiful girl, I'm known all over the place, I drive a Trans Am, I buy Armani clothing. Oh God, be still my heart. That can't be all bad, can it?"[1] One could have been forgiven for imagining *him* to be the twentysomething rather than his bride.

The venue was the MGM Grand, 29 floors above the Las Vegas strip in the hotel's high roller suite. There were only 75 guests. Curtis' friend Kirk Kerkorian footed the bill. Three days after the civil ceremony the newlyweds left for a three-week tour of London, Paris and Switzerland. It was around the time of astronomical expansion. Curtis joked, "If John Glenn can go to the moon, I can go on a honeymoon."[2]

VandenBerg always denied she married him because of who he was. The money wasn't a factor, she insisted, and neither was his age. She felt women had taken advantage of him in the past. "I think I gave him some security," she opined.[3]

Curtis was more content with her than he'd been with any of his previous wives. They did most things together but for once he didn't feel suffocated. He liked to go in to Vegas now and again and "spiff it up" on the dance floor with his black suit and cowboy hat. Still playing the Casanova, he professed never to use Viagra, insisting (in a variation on a song lyric by Paul Simon) that there were "50 ways to please your lover."[4]

In 1999 Giles Whittell described him as an anti-ageing activist who "stares across the gulf between his ravaged being and his youth with the militant unconcern of a tightrope walker." Maybe, but it was a resignation hard won. He lived in a community that looked salubrious, Whittell remarked, but was, in effect, "a developer's dream of crammed-in, faux-baronial condominiums."[5]

Curtis didn't care either way. The structure didn't matter to him. He didn't need 18 rooms anymore. Such things were only important when he was a young man in a hurry, with Janet Leigh or Christine Kaufmann. How did he feel about these women now? Would he have done anything different to hold the marriages together? It was unlikely. "There must have been 27 other girls I cared for more than these wives."[6] He liked to bury the past each day. To be perfect was to have changed often. Houses, movie roles, spouses. Now he was with a good one. In a house with less gaudy luxury. As long as he had room to daub his canvases, everything was cool.

In February 2000 he gave the *Hollywood Reporter* a personal guide to eating, drinking and having fun in Hollywood. He liked to dine at Spago Hollywood with Jill, he said, and afterwards wander over to Tower Records across the street and pick up the latest Smashing Pumpkins album or some classic ballads from the sixties and seventies. He also liked going to the Rainbow on Sunset Boulevard. "Upstairs they have a private dining room and bar where you can hang out, and in the downstairs dining room there's always an electricity. What I like is that you can see all ages. If you've had dinner elsewhere it's ideal for a late-night drink. I get a charge out of it."[7] It was hard to believe this was a 74-year-old man talking.

The Gonga Room on Wilshire Boulevard was another popular haunt. He liked to salsa dance with Jill there. "It's contagious—go once and you can't get enough. And you dress any way you want." He also got a chance to practice his Spanish there. One was never too old to learn.[8] "Gallery hopping" led him to the Gagosian Gallery in Beverly Hills: "Not your typical stuff, but ultracontemporary." When he was in the mood for music, the Roxy was where it was at. "I feel good getting lost in the crowd," he explained. (It was hard to believe this.) Another hobby was ferreting out car wash emporiums. His favorite was between Santa Monica and Olympic Boulevard on the west side of Sepulveda. How did Jill keep up with him?

The pair of them moved from Hollywood to Las Vegas in 2001. They didn't like being in an environment where everyone was in competition with everyone else. (In such a context, maybe Curtis' 2002 film *Reflections of Evil*—a black comedy that doubled as a satire of the film world—was appropriate). They moved into a white stucco one-story Italian-Spanish ranch house with a swimming pool in the back. It also had an artist's studio for Curtis. He was glad to be away from the hurly-burly of Hollywood. The town carried too much negative energy for him. "On a single movie set you would have eighty workers," he recalled.[9] Some of them came to work with "built-up" anger and envy. "A lot of them verbalized their anger. They didn't hit me but I always felt afraid."[10]

The house looked small on the outside but this was deceptive. It was a huge residence that also boasted panoramic views of a golf course, some downtown hotels and the outlying desert. It was a painter's paradise.

Curtis enjoyed living in Vegas even if it didn't have the allure it used to have. Shirley MacLaine said it didn't need stars any more. If that was so, its lighter air suited him. He resembled an old casino shark sitting out the years with his easels and horses and fine wife. Sinatra was gone. So were Dean Martin, Sammy Davis Jr. and all the rest of the Rat Pack who'd made it their own when the cash registers were ringing. Now they'd all cashed in their chips.

Curtis had many friends there, like the stuntman Dean Shendel and entrepreneur Kirk Kerkorian, who, he claimed, practically *owned* Vegas. Larry King once said of Kerkorian, "He'll live forever. And if he doesn't, he'll buy heaven and sell shares."[11] Curtis liked his punchy attitude toward life. In some ways Kerkorian was like the new Sinatra to him.

If the edge of danger was gone from Las Vegas, so were the mad spending sprees and reckless nights. One could make a home there now. As Barry Manilow observed, "It used to be a place for hookers once. Now it's a place for hookers and their children!" The pace of living was relaxed too. Curtis wasn't tagged as an out-of-work actor but instead — euphemistically — as being "between jobs." If Hollywood wanted him it knew where to find him. Another reason he moved from L.A. was because too many of his friends had died there and he didn't want to be "confronted by ghosts."[12]

In interviews he was as incorrigible as ever. One of his favorite subjects was still sex, as Chris Hewitt of *Empire* magazine learned when he dared to address that subject, learning that, at 22, Curtis had "a constant hard-on."[13] For some people this was too much information, as was his confession in his autobiography that many of his early sexual experiences took place in his trousers, or that he suffered from premature ejaculation in his youth.[14] "My idea of foreplay," he once bragged, "was, 'Hi, I'm Tony Curtis.'" It was difficult to know if he was being tongue-in-cheek at times like this. Even at 75, he informed Hewitt, he was "still carrying a little something in my pants." Some of his other faculties were more impaired but that didn't bother him unduly. He admitted to being "a little deaf" but added, "I rather like it. I've heard everything now that anyone said or did so I don't have to listen so intently anymore." It would have bothered him more to lose his libido, however: "I tell ya, there isn't a guy I know that wouldn't love to jump on a beautiful woman without knowing her name."[15]

How did he feel modern movies differed from those of yore? The allure of the Dream Factory was gone. Pre-war movies were his favorites. "Those pictures carried a great sense of who we were and what we were. When you see a film made in the late thirties you know it's the late thirties. It doesn't try and bullshit you into thinking it was yesterday."[16]

Hollywood had undervalued him all his life but it was pointless to carp. "I don't want anything eating my stomach because all those bad guys are gone now. What am I gonna do — scream at the sky?"[17] It would have been a waste of energy, energy best kept for his painting, or what lust for life remained.

Later that year he talked to Bill Borrows from *Maxim* magazine. The conversation drifted over the decades. As ever, he managed to encapsulate a half century of agonies and ecstacies into bite-sized chunks of wit and some near-forensic self-analysis. His opener was the scene-stopping "I'm not really interested in movies," by which he meant he wasn't really interested in making any new ones — because all he was being offered was junk. "I'm not going to do the cameos this business wants. I get five or six scripts every month. 'Can you come in and do two days here?' Fuck you. Are you kidding me? I've got too many nice movies out there to end up as a bit player on some series on television. Not for me. William Shatner?"[18]

Now that Borrows was assured he wouldn't be appearing as a Dalek in *Star Trek: The Sequel*, he asked him to elaborate on his acting career. Curtis replied by saying he didn't understand terms like "acting." He preferred to offer a speculative scenario to Borrows that illustrated his instinctive approach: "I'm trying to impart some information to you. It could be that if I do, you're gonna give me $1000. It could be that if I don't do it right, you're gonna kill me. If I do it right you'll let me see your daughter. You can't fool that fucking screen."[19] He talked about his meltdown in the mid-seventies. Freebasing cocaine had "kind of smoothed everything out" and he was happy now with Jill. She trusted him so much she didn't even mind him chatting to other women. Girls were "nice to be around" because they weren't "belching or scratching all the time."[20]

Shortly before the interview took place, Curtis had been in receipt of a plethora of awards: The Chevalier Order of Arts and Letters, a Lifetime Achievement Award in Frankfurt, a Donatello Italy and a BAFTA. The one glaring omission on that list was an Academy Award. That was hardly likely now, nor a Life Achievement Award from Hollywood either.

"If they were ever to offer me any award I would not take it. Where were you when I needed you? Fuck 'em, feed 'em fish." In America, he contended, "You have to die before they say something nice about you. But I ain't going."[21]

Lew Wasserman died on June 3, 2002.[22] Curtis would never forget how influential the wily agent was in his early years, negotiating deals where he earned a "chunk" of his major movies. "I still retain those rights," he said, "so I'm always generating some income on them." Wasserman was a father figure to him, just as Burt Lancaster and Cary Grant had been, in the absence of any real direction from his birth father. "I trusted him and every piece of advice he ever gave me implicitly."[23] "To be on your job and be there right up until the end is a mitzvah," was his final tribute to the Svengali figure who would now join all the other movie legends in that big studio in the sky.[24] "Too many funerals," he sighed. "That's my social life these days."

He felt in good shape himself apart from still being slightly deaf in one ear. (He put it down to too many years listening to gunshots and explosions on movie sets.) He took a tablet every day for his blood pressure, and also a Prozac, "which helps to straighten out those bends in the river and stop me lingering on the past." He wasted a lot of time in the past, but now he was "centered," his life being uncomplicated with "Jilly," their seven dogs, and Fluffy, their white cat. He had a good relationship with his six children but perhaps an even better one with his grandchildren. "I ship the little ones out here for a week or two whenever there's a holiday coming up."[25]

Painting was his most important hobby now, along with box-making. The boxes were perhaps more personal. "There's a Marilyn one, a Diana one — Dodi Fayed was my finest friend — and several to do with me, though there's no ego involved. I've shown them at the University of Las Vegas but I don't have the heart to sell them." At this stage of his life emotion was more important than money. "I've spent $30,000 on a Picasso but the cost isn't the point. I also love a little model of me in *The Persuaders* made by a fan, which I keep in my bedroom."[26]

Each day he went into Las Vegas to eat, usually donning one of his cowboy hats and the inflatable Armani jacket. He was always applauded when he walked into the casinos. He loved that. "I'm not one of those actors who can't handle fame." Last thing at night he unwound by reading in bed. "At the moment it's a biography of Einstein." He felt very fulfilled with his life. He was looking forward to appearing in a musical version of *Some Like It Hot* but was adamant that there would be no pathos in it, no sense of *déjà vu*. "I'll just be enjoying myself."[27]

It was being staged on Broadway. He played Osgood, the role that Joe E. Brown had essayed in the movie. He embarked on singing and dancing lessons to prepare himself for the role and was hugely excited about it. "Ten years from now," he promised, "I'll probably play Sugar."[28]

George Wayne interviewed him for *Vanity Fair* and asked him how many films he'd made. "120," he replied. Wayne countered, "I thought it was 130." "Fifteen of these," he said, "were child support payments."[29] (The mathematics were questionable but the point held good.) When Wayne quizzed him about the tragic life of Marilyn Monroe, Curtis took a familiar tack. "The biggest woman star in the business and she was living like a bag woman. There was no one to look after her. Where were all her friends? Why wasn't anyone with her after she'd tried to kill herself a few times before?"[30]

Wayne asked him if he'd made "whoopee" with Monroe. The world already knew he did from his 1998 book. "We were 'on' for a few months," Curtis replied. "We were in our twenties. There was nothing special or unique about it." So how many of his leading ladies had he bedded altogether? "Every leading lady except one — Jack Lemmon." (With wit like this, the man could have carved out a second career as a stand-up comic. Did he prepare these one-liners beforehand or did they just come out? Either way, they made him any interviewer's dream.)

Wayne tried to make him feel his age by asking him, "What's the first thing to go at 75?" Curtis never liked this kind of negativity. Shifting the conversation away from a tasteless remark by Wayne about the possibility of a "testicle tuck," he instead suggested he was considering having a different type of plastic surgery performed. "In a year or two I plan to do a little facial work. I had to have some work done on my nose for a deviated septum from too much cocaine."[31] This was much more to Curtis' liking, being a septuagenarian junkie rather than a candidate for an old folks home. Osgood would have been proud.

Curtis was only onstage for eighteen minutes. "That's enough for me," he said. "It's not supposed to be heavy lifting."[32] An audience of over 2500 cheered him on the show's opening night as he sang, "We cannot hope for youth or for a crown of curls/ But naughty old men need naughty young girls," lines Joe E. Brown must dearly have wished he'd had in the original. For Curtis the Osgood character was about more than hanky panky with lasses half his age, especially when he settles for Daphne at the end. "I think Osgood has had so many affairs with beautiful women," he remarked, "he's happy to have this spiky person who fights back and walks all over him. Maybe he's relieved to have found companionship." In this sense, maybe the famous endline 'Nobody's perfect' is his way of telling Daphne, 'Just be my friend.'"[33] Curtis saw it all as adding a neat coda to his career. Scott Fitzgerald once wrote that there are no second acts in American lives but the 77-year-old Curtis seemed to give the lie to that adage, singing and dancing his way through the show in a manner that set out to prove Fitzgerald — and Father Time — wrong.[34]

Some Like It Hot was running in tandem with a Broadway version of Curtis' second most acclaimed film, *Sweet Smell of Success*. He hadn't gone to see this even though he had a studio for his artwork in New York. Maybe it hurt too much to think of Burt Lancaster. "We kept in touch until the last week of his life," he said. "I would make these silly home movies of myself clowning around and send them to him. His wife said, 'Keep sending them! He loves this stuff.'" Almost a half century after the groundbreaking movie, Sidney Falco was still trying to please J.J. Hunsecker by his frantic antics.[35]

Janet Leigh produced another novel that year, *The Dream Factory*. Like *House of Destiny* it was a mainstream blockbuster written in a breezy style. Hardly surprisingly, it was again about Hollywood, except this time starting back in the 1930s. As was the case with *House of Destiny*, she didn't fail to mention herself, or rather her car.[36] The film *My Sister Eileen* received a mention as well.[37] She wrote about the assassination of John F. Kennedy in her previous novel and here she did again, this time going into more detail about its aftermath.[38]

Curtis didn't go into Leigh's achievements as a novelist in either of his books, or indeed anything at all about her after their divorce. This seemed to be the way he dealt with all the women in his life. If a parting was in any way bitter he didn't like to dwell on it. I remembered that when I mentioned to him that his novel had been dedicated to Leslie

Allen he grew momentarily grumpy and said, "That's enough about that." This surprised me, as it was the one time he showed even the tiniest degree of petulance.

By now Allegra had a son, Raphael, but Curtis didn't show too much of an interest in him, locked as he was into his relationship with VandenBerg. In 2003 he called Allegra from Budapest and asked her to bring Raphael to see him over there. (He was engaged in some promotional work for the President of Hungary at the time, giving a lecture on how much his homeland meant to him.) Allegra was thrown. Could he not see the boy in Nevada?

Curtis and VandenBerg set up a charity in 2003. It was called the Shiloh Horse Rescue Foundation and was devoted to saving the lives of slaughter-bound horses. By now she needed another dimension to her life. She'd become bored with being what she called "the bimbo wife." One could only shop or schmooze so much.

The fact that she rescued "old stallions from knacker's yards" led to more than one gag about Curtis himself being another one.[39] She got the inspiration from watching Oprah Winfrey on TV one day. Winfrey was hosting a show about realizing one's dreams. VandenBerg had always wanted to do something for horses. She looked up a website that featured details of the torture that condemned horses went through. That was the moment her charity was born. ("Shiloh" is Hebrew for "place of peace.")

She went to auctions and outbid the people she called "killers" to procure the horses. Then she brought them to her ranch. She also lobbied for the passing of laws that would prevent their illegal transport across the border. Some of the horses she brought to Shiloh Rescue weren't in danger of dying; they just needed food and medication — what VandenBerg called "rehab."

She'd been fascinated by horses all her life, believing them to have similar personalities to dogs. As a child she made jumps for her pet dogs as if in preparation for this latest obsession. Curtis always liked horses too, at least after those early experiences at Universal where he found it hard to ride them. "A horse understands if you're uncomfortable," he said. "It can also sense if you're not a nice person. It will move away from gruff people." He said he felt "like a king" whenever he went up on one but he also had anxiety and a fear of falling. It was this combination that made for excitement when he sat in the saddle.[40] (This outpouring contrasts sharply with what he said in an old *Photoplay* interview: "I don't dig any animal.")[41]

"We don't have any children," he stated. "Maybe they're a substitute. Who knows? It's not worth analyzing. The point is, it feels good to be around them. It fulfills our lives and we do something for them too. Everybody wins."

It was Curtis' fortune that made it possible. He bought the land and the buildings and took care of the running expenses when donations didn't cover them. But VandenBerg was insistent she didn't spend his money frivolously. "All it costs to save a horse is $8. If I decide not to buy a pair of shoes I can save three of 'em." Parts of Shiloh looked elaborate, but one could save a horse's life by corralling it to a shed with duct tape and some baling twine. Everything after that was a bonus.[42]

She saw herself in the tradition of the Marilyn Monroe character from *The Misfits* who became distressed over the horses being sold for dog food. She felt her life mirrored Monroe's, not only because of the way she looked (and, of course, being involved with Curtis) but also because of the theme of that film. Curtis also said she *kissed* like Monroe. (With VandenBerg it could be said he got the reincarnation of Marilyn without the neuroses.)

On his 79th birthday he was asked for the secret of his longevity. "I watch my diet," he said, "I take long walks, and I make love as often as possible." Despite the crises of his past he was in a good place now with his painting and the occasional movie, like the just-completed *Pizza with Bullets* and the aptly-titled *Love Is a Survivor*.

The year 2005 was significant for him for two reasons: an award and a temporal landmark. In April he was given a Lifetime Achievement Award at the Jules Verne Film Festival in Paris. ("Only when I leave America," he speculated, "do I realize how famous I am."[43]) In June he hit eighty. It would have been a culture shock for some but he used the occasion to do something very characteristic: he posed naked for *Vanity Fair* magazine. He said the shoot made him feel "released," an unusual admission for someone who'd been exposing himself in some form or another for the past half century.[44] He was in a wheelchair now.

Even in his wheelchair he insisted on going out on "dates" with Jill. He entered casinos through the invalid doors and enjoyed people oohing and aahing over him. He spoke to everyone. He was always just "Tony." He had dinner at a restaurant called Picassos (where else would a painter go?), and then he might take Jill to a show before going home to swim in his pool. Could anyone beat that for a lifestyle?

He was "eighty fucking years old," but he didn't feel like dying. In fact, he didn't feel any different to how he felt at thirty. Okay, so his feet hurt and he didn't pee on time and his eyes and ears weren't what they used to be, but he had all his main faculties, and "I have no disease that's going to kill me — not yet anyway."[45]

He admitted he hadn't been a good father. "I was never around when my kids were growing up. I was divorced from their mothers so I didn't get to know them very well." A few of them he liked, a few he had no relationship with. But his grandchildren came in to his studio and he played with them, perhaps trying to make up for lost time with their parents.[46]

He was a good husband to Jill because he was finally ready for marriage when he met her: "My first four marriages taught me how to do the fifth." Some people didn't need five tries, some people didn't even need two, but Curtis did. In fact, he still looked at girls even yet, "so I've gotta be careful."[47] Once a rake always a rake. As for his career, he spoke like someone just starting out. When a reporter asked him in 2006 at what point did he know he'd "made it," he replied, "In my profession you never really feel that."[48]

He was presented with a Lifetime Achievement award from the staff of *Empire* magazine in March 2006 in association with Sony Ericcson. It should have come from the American Film Institute but he was still gratified to receive it. Roger Moore presented it to him, 36 years after sharing a TV screen with him.[49] They both looked as if they had a picture in the attic. Given half an offer, one got the impression both of them would have been all too willing to hit the French Riviera for another dollop of *The Persuaders*.

"In the end," a philosophical Curtis concluded, "time is the most precious commodity. We don't really learn how to use it well until we've used most of it up. But better late than never. Enjoy each day. Enjoy each encounter, each discovery, each person. Enjoy each sunset."[50]

Painting made his days go round. He mooched around his studio putting things in boxes and then taking them out again, arranging and rearranging the mosaics of his life like a puppetmaster dangling marionettes. In the old days he'd had to make time to do his paintings but now he thought of little else. The Museum of Modern Art in New York (MOMA) had just bought one of them for $25,000. "You never know with those guys," he joked to John Patterson. "MOMA's got a really big basement for hiding things in."[51] (The reference to the basement was probably a play on Norman Bates' "Momma" from *Psycho*.)

He resisted the temptation to take himself too seriously, his only concession to an artistic demeanor being the self-parodic "So now I dress like Picasso all the time. I wear striped shirts and shorts no matter what the weather."[52] He looked a bit like him too, the weight he'd gained over the years making him seem smaller in stature. The the bald pate rounded off the Buddha look.

In 2007 he did the voice of God in a short film called *Blacksmith and the Carpenter*. The following year he made his last movie, *David and Fatima*, saying his lines from the wheelchair. (He spent most of his time in the wheelchair now but didn't like to admit this.) The following year Harrods invited him to London to launch an exhibition of his paintings and "Vanity Curtis" surprisingly appeared *sans* toupee. The famous quiff was no more. He accepted his baldness but brought a Stetson for some of the photographs. "Just because it's cold on the roof doesn't mean there isn't a fire down below," he guffawed. He was in good spirits. He rose briefly from his wheelchair to pose with his friend Mohamed Al Fayed, the owner of the store. How did he stay so healthy? It was primarily down to a good diet, but he also did "exercise and stuff."

Petronella Wyatt interviewed him for *The Mail*. He opened the discussion by saying, "It's such a relief to be sitting here with you without feeling sexually roused."[53] An offended Wyatt thought: "If he wasn't 82 and recovering from a mild illness, I think I might slap him." At which point Curtis backtracked with a chastened, "Don't get me wrong. I've been sick for most of my life in my head. I was insecure with women so I wanted to go to bed with them all."[54] She accepted his apology for the unintended slight.

Wyatt saw him as a contradiction. "He's a streetfighting boy from the Bronx," she wrote, " yet he hand-kisses like a count in an Austrian operetta." He put such a contradiction down to his youth, a youth that saw him starved of the love he craved, his mother beating him mercilessly instead: "If I didn't finish my soup she would throw me against the wall." Wyatt wondered if he mightn't have a warped Oedipus complex. Curtis was more than up to the taunt. "I *am* Oedipus," he riposted.[55]

When she asked him about Marilyn Monroe on the set of *Some Like It Hot* he said she "nearly choked me to death by deliberately sticking her tongue down my windpipe." Would he consider making more movies? He thought not: "Actors today achieve nothing, nor do they have any glamour. They seem more interested in adopting babies than [making] films."[56] The films were terrible too. He preferred to stay at home with Jill. "This time it's not about her body. It's about talking, communicating." So what about his satyriasis? "It's a relief that it doesn't bother me anymore. I feel finally free." As for his future, he chose Norma Desmond's line from *Sunset Boulevard*: "When my time comes, I'm ready for my close-ups, Mr. DeMille."[57]

Steve Friess interviewed him later that year. His second autobiography, *American Prince*, had just been published, and Friess was shocked by the number of people he had insulted in the book. Did he feel bad about labelling Shelley Winters "obnoxious," for instance, or Danny Kaye "vicious"? He was unrepentant. "What was I going to do ... make everyone happy? What you have is my life." It was a non-question in his view.[58] When Friess asked him about his future he said he planned to reinvent himself as "an 85-year-old man who can do anything and everything."[59]

His appetite for adventure certainly made it look like that. In June 2009 he went to Los Angeles for an event called "The Magic of Tony Curtis." It was held at the Million Dollar Theater. Being the 50th anniversary of *Some Like It Hot*, that film was being screened at the theater alongside *Houdini* on a double bill. Also in attendance was the escape artist Curt Lovell, who replicated Houdini's water torture stunt after the film was shown. Curtis was in fine form for the trip down Memory Lane, entering into the spirit of the occasion with a merry "I'm 84 years old and still kicking sand."[60]

The following month he appeared at the Clark County Library in Las Vegas. The library had a theater *in situ* and a collage of his kissing scenes was shown. He enjoyed this enormously. Asked afterwards who was the best kisser he had encountered in his career he replied inimitably, "Me!"[61]

He arrived at the event in his self-propelled wheelchair. This, he stressed, was "merely a convenience." At one point of the evening he stood up to dance a little rhumba. He did a Q&A after the collage, talking about his first flight from New York to L.A. to attend an interview for Universal. Jack Warner had been on the flight, which "had to be a good omen."[62] His life had been a compendium of many serendipitous moments like this.

Charming as ever, he told the packed gathering he loved everything about Las Vegas, even the clouds. Having been greeted with a standing ovation when he first appeared, he was now given a rapturous round of applause by the locals. They were more accustomed to celebrities talking about the neon of Vegas than its dark clouds. But that was Curtis. As Dolly Parton liked to say, you couldn't have the rainbow without the rain. And painters liked clouds. The light and dark of his life gave it that chiaroscuro.

After the Q&A he signed copies of his book for the many who attended it for that reason. One of those in attendance, Megan Edwards, was delighted to see that he also added a little drawing above his signature. It was of a cat and bore the inscription "Always ready."[63] This also sounded like an apt description of the man.

In August 2009 he did an interview with *Vanity Fair* magazine which threw up some surprising revelations. He listed Arnold Schwarzenegger, for instance, as the person he most admired. If he were to be reincarnated, he said he thought it would be as the son of Ali Baba. (No doubt this was tongue-in-cheek.) His favorite writers he listed as Fyodor Dostoevsky and Charles Schulz, probably the first and only time those two individuals would ever be mentioned in the same breath. His favorite hero of fiction was Tarzan (not Anthony Adverse), and the way he would like to die was "Alone." There was no surprise, though, in his reply to being asked what was his idea of perfect happiness: "Top billing!"[64]

He accepted the reality that his life was winding down, conveying that fact in a graphic image: "I'm like a ship in the ocean. The water in front is so calm you can practically take a bath. It's only when a 5000-ton ship hits it that the water splashes away and creates the wave."[65]

Allegra visited him off and on. They had a good conversation in a restaurant one night where he opened up to her about his childhood, but she still found it hard to break through the shell of his image to get at the real man. Before she left he pressed a $100 bill into her hand. "Always have money in your pocket," he exhorted. She was amused at the paltry sum he'd given her. In light of his overall wealth it was a joke.

She saw him as selfish to the end of his days: "His toothaches were always more important than my toothaches." Neither had his infantile nature receded. "He needed children to enable him to be a child himself because he hadn't been able to be a child as a child."[66]

On her last phone call with him he asked, "Are you depressed?" He knew she suffered from low feelings just like he did. She didn't know what to say to him. Should she be angry? Forgiving? Remote? Cher had once said to her, "Tony is all fucked up; make allowances for him." She tried to but it was difficult because he kept pushing her away, kept telling her everything was all right when it wasn't. There were too many defense mechanisms, too many barriers, too many lies. "Do you need anything?" he said then. He meant money, but it was really his love she was seeking.[67]

He died on September 29, 2010. Few people were surprised at the news. He couldn't speak or eat in his last days. As well as lung problems, he had a part of his intestines removed. COPD (Chronic Obstructive Pulmonary disease) was listed as the official cause of death. On his last night he had a panic attack and was given a tranquillizer. He fell into a sleep and didn't come out of it. "I didn't cry," Allegra said when she heard he'd gone, "I wailed." She phoned Jamie to tell her but Jamie's reaction was surprisingly cold: "It doesn't matter. He was a shitty father."[68]

When I asked him what were his feelings about religion, I received this reply:

> Frank Sinatra said he was for anything that got you through the night — prayer, a woman, or Jack Daniels. I've tried all three. Different things work at different times. Religion for many people is like the one-armed bandit at the casino. You want the three cherries all the time, then when things are going well you forget it. You get back to the mean s.o.b. you always were ... until the next time you're in trouble. What's that quote? "There are no atheists in the trenches." I've been there. We don't know what's down the pike. You just grab the moment. Your life is the sum of all your experiences and out of that maybe you deserve an eternity. Maybe.[69]

Did he believe in eternity himself? "The short answer to that is I don't know. I'd like to, that goes without saying. We all need something bigger and more mystical than ourselves. There's also a lot more to be gained by believing. There's everything. And a lot to be lost by not believing. It goes in circles." Which was he more drawn to if pushed to it? He paused. "In one way I find myself able to 'believe' in a non-believer more. There's nothing in it for a non-believer to not believe, if you will. In that sense, they come to their conclusion the hard way. A believer has the *need* to believe and that could color it. But that's not to say I don't believe. A lot of thoughts go through my mind each day in every direction." He paused again. "The miracle of life would make you imagine there has to be someone pulling the strings. The problem is, why does he pull the wrong ones so often." He smiled and then added, "Or she!"

What about movie immortality? He waved his hand. "That's just an expression writers use. As Woody Allen says, 'I'd prefer to achieve immortality by not dying.'" (For the record, Curtis thought Mia Farrow was "nuts" to hook up with Allen because of the age gap — a view that blithely ignored the age gaps he himself embraced with most of his wives.)

He was buried with a selection of his favorite possessions: his trademark Stetson, an Armani scarf and a copy of the novel that inspired both his name and career, *Anthony Adverse*. The coffin was draped with the American flag. After the funeral a montage of some of his films was shown. The assembled gathering hooted as he was shown in a *Flintstones* episode as "Stoney Curtis." VandenBerg reminded people that they should remember his life rather than his death. He was, she said, "a once-in-a-lifetime man." Pallbearer Gene Kilroy added, "He had a way of making everybody feel like they were *Spartacus*."

Newspapers from around the world carried laudatory tributes. The British talkshow host Michael Parkinson was quoted as saying, "He was a great guest, wonderfully indiscreet, very bright and didn't take himself too seriously."[70] Tony Parsons labeled him "the first rock 'n' roll star," writing that "even before James Dean he brought the grease and danger of the new music to Hollywood.... One look at his sly, cheeky grin and you could easily believe that man could spend his life being famous, bedding some of the most beautiful women on the planet and still die a happy man. I imagine he'll be buried with a grin on his face."[71]

Parsons paid tribute to his fighting qualities when he said, "Just as love of the bottle could never claim the soul of Sinatra, so no white powder could ever really sink its fangs into Tony Curtis. He liked the ladies too much for that."[72]

Geoffrey McNab felt that there was something "wonderfully far-fetched" about him. "His life story would have seemed outlandish even in a Saul Bellow or Philip Roth novel about a Jewish-American journey through the 20th century."[73] McNab thought of him as one of those movie stars fans couldn't help but warm to. He *made* them love him. "They liked him in his good movies and they liked him in his bad movies too." Jeremy Thomas, who'd worked with him on *Insignificance*, went a step further with this tribute: "As soon as you went to the cinema you saw Tony Curtis. You grew up with Tony Curtis. If you're my age, Tony Curtis has always been there."[74] And, as he often added himself, he always would be.

The Evening Standard quoted Curtis as saying he went into acting for "the girls and the money," presumably in that order.[75] Many obituaries listed him as being married to Andria Savio, a fairly common error that showed the laziness of the research involved. Most of them carried the same clichés about a man who was spearheaded into swashbuckling roles before falling prey to routine comedies, rehabilitating himself with roles as a crossdresser and a slimy press agent, and then descending into a drink and drugs hell and telling people that kissing Marilyn Monroe was like kissing Hitler. Sometimes it was easy to microscope a life into 800 words—at least if people didn't care what they were writing about.

The general view of the critics was that he had had only two high points in his career, the "reptilian" Sidney Falco in *Sweet Smell of Success* and the "sublimely harassed" Josephine in *Some Like It Hot*. "His other successes," Mario Reading charged, "have always seemed variations on those themes. But the two films revealed a genuine and surprising talent given his inauspicious beginnings as part of Universal's soul-destroying star production line."[76] One can empathize with Reading's view of the studio's cattle call regime but it's a trivialization of his career to look at his 140-plus movies as "variations" of two films which weren't even similar in the first place. How could an obsequious press agent in New York's journalistic cosmos compare with a demure crossdresser doubling as a Shell magnate to escape the Mob? These were the bromides trotted out frequently in staid denunciations of Curtis' career.

Alexander Mackendrick said an unusual thing about him once: "He has vanity but no ego." Curtis knew what he meant. "I'm the type of guy who has to keep checking himself in the mirror. That's vanity but it's also insecurity. I know people who don't look at themselves from one day to the next. They may not be beautiful but they're secure in who they are." As for ego, "Take Burt Lancaster or Kirk Douglas. These are ego-driven guys. Or Marlon." Curtis was different. "I don't propel myself; I'm propeled."[77]

When the eagles are silent, the parrots begin to jabber. Curtis was hardly cold in his grave when a catfight regarding his estate began. It was the old story: he'd left all his money—

an estate valued at $60 million — to VandenBerg. Family members were understandably aggrieved as he'd always promised to provide for them. On the other hand, VandenBerg had been with him for many years now and she'd nursed him as well as loved him. It wasn't unprecedented for the estates of aging millionaires to go solely to their last spouse.

Kelly and Alexandra were rumored to be taking legal action to contest the will, which was written just five months before his death. Christine Kaufmann feared he could have written it under the influence of painkillers, which "make you really stoned." Her belief was that, deep down, Curtis was a nice Jewish father. "And nice Jewish fathers do not disinherit their children."[78]

Giving VandenBerg "absolute power," as the will stated, to take possession of his estate — which comprised homes in Hollywood, Nevada and Hawaii as well as cash — angered Kaufmann. She thought the money would disappear quickly in VandenBerg's sanctuary. "Jill has lots of three-legged horses to take care of," she noted, "which are very expensive." Kaufmann stressed the fact that she wasn't "picking" on her because she admired her for staying with Curtis. "But Tony promised to take care of the children and we all want to know what happened to that promise."[79]

Ben was reported to be so incensed at not getting anything that he refused to attend his father's funeral. At the other end of the scale, Jamie remained tightlipped about the matter but was privately reported as stating that it would be futile to sue because she believed VandenBerg had already spent most of the money. (The relationship between Curtis and Jamie never really sorted itself out, despite his protestations to the contrary. As late as 2006 he was accusing her of being jealous of him and struggling with her career.)[80]

Many of his personal belongings were put up for auction in August 2011, including artwork by Picasso, Andy Warhol and himself. The sailor jacket he wore during the kissing scene with Marilyn Monroe in *Some Like It Hot* also went under the hammer, as did ceramics and prints he owned by Braque and Chagall, a Fabergé cigarette case, and a rosewood flute given to him by Frank Sinatra.

Would he have been pleased by this? Hardly. "Tony always said he was an artist first and an actor second," proclaimed Darren Julien of Julien's Auctions, following this up with the non-sequitur, "I think he would love the exhibition we created. He's looking down now and hoping the items find a good home because he truly loved these pieces."[81] But if he did truly love them, surely he would have wanted them in his own home where his family could continue to admire them privately?

One can imagine him smiling down on all of this from movie heaven because he was always humble about himself behind the *bragadocchio*. "There wasn't any great novel," he said once. "I didn't write a great song. I didn't give a great performance in a movie. I came along with a hairstyle and jeans, into perpetuity."[82]

So how did he get to make movies and have children and paint and write books?

"I don't now," he admitted, "I must have been quite a fellow."[83] He was. And quite a lady too.

Film and Television Listing

Movies

Criss Cross (1949)
City Across the River (1949)
The Lady Gambles (1949)
Johnny Stool Pigeon (1949)
Francis (1950)
I Was a Shoplifter (1950)
Winchester 73 (1950)
Sierra (1950)
Kansas Raiders (1950)
The Prince Who Was a Thief (1951)
Son of Ali Baba (1952)
Flesh and Fury (1952)
No Room for the Groom (1952)
Meet Danny Wilson (1952)
Houdini (1953)
The All-American (1953)
Forbidden (1953)
Beachhead (1954)
Johnny Dark (1954)
The Black Shield of Falworth (1954)
So This Is Paris (1954)
Six Bridges to Cross (1955)
The Purple Mask (1955)
The Square Jungle (1955)
The Rawhide Years (1956)
Trapeze (1956)
Mister Cory (1957)
The Midnight Story (1957)
Sweet Smell of Success (1957)
The Vikings (1958)
The Defiant Ones (1958)
Kings Go Forth (1958)
The Perfect Furlough (1958)
Some Like It Hot (1959)
Operation Petticoat (1959)
Who Was That Lady? (1959)
The Rat Race (1960)
Spartacus (1960)
Pepe (1960)
The Great Imposter (1961)
The Outsider (1961)
Taras Bulba (1962)
Forty Pounds of Trouble (1962)
Captain Newman M.D. (1963)
The List of Adrian Messenger (1963)
Wild and Wonderful (1964)
Goodbye Charlie (1964)
Sex and the Single Girl (1964)
Paris When It Sizzles (1964)
The Great Race (1965)
Boeing Boeing (1965)
Not with My Wife You Don't (1966)
Arrivaderci Baby! (1966)
Chamber of Horrors (1966)
Don't Make Waves (1967)
The Chastity Belt (1967)
The Boston Strangler (1968)
Rosemary's Baby (1968)
Those Daring Young Men in their Jaunty Jalopies (1969)
Suppose They Gave a War and Nobody Came? (1969)
You Can't Win 'Em All (1970)
Lepke (1975)
The Last Tycoon (1976)
Casanova & Co. (1977)
The Manitou (1977)
Sextette (1978)
The Bad News Bear Go to Japan (1978)
Title Shot (1979)
It Rained All Night the Day I Left (1980)
Little Miss Marker (1980)
The Mirror Crack'd (1980)

Brain Waves (1982)
Othello: The Black Commando (1982)
Where Is Parsifal? (1983)
Insignificance (1985)
King of the City (1985)
Balboa (1986)
Midnight (1989)
Lobster Man from Mars (1989)
Prime Target (1991)
Center of the Web (1992)
The Mummy Lives (1993)
Naked in New York (1993)
The Immortals (1995)
The Continued Adventures of Reptile Man (1997)
Hardball (1997)
The Blacksmith and the Carpenter (2007)
David & Fatima (2008)

Television

The Young Juggler (1960)
The Persuaders (1971–2)
The Third Girl from the Left (1973)
The Count of Monte Cristo (1975)
McCoy (1975–6)
The Users (1978)
The Scarlett O'Hara War (1978)
Inmates: A Love Story (1978)
Vega$ (1978–81)
The Million Dollar Face (1981)
Portrait of a Showgirl (1982)
The Fall Guy (1983)
Mafia Princess (1986)
Murder in Three Acts (1986)
Charlie (1989)
Tarzan in Manhattan (1989)
Thanksgiving Day (1990)
Christmas in Connecticut (1992)
A Perry Mason Mystery (1994)
The New Adventures of Superman (1996)
CSI: Crime Scene Investigation (2005)

Chapter Notes

Chapter 1

1. *Empire*, March 1994.
2. *Photoplay*, September 1955.
3. Ibid.
4. *American Weekly*, August 24, 1952.
5. *Cue*, August 2, 1958.
6. *The Guardian*, April 18, 2008.
7. *Esquire*, January 2006.
8. Doug McClelland, ed., *Star-Speak: Hollywood on Everything* (Boston: Faber and Faber, 1987), p. 103.
9. *Sunday Times*, March 6, 2004.
10. Michael Parkinson, *Parky's People* (London: Hodder and Stoughton, 2011), p. 35.
11. *Sunday Times*, March 6, 1994.
12. *Interview*, 1991.
13. *Saturday Evening Post*, July 25, 1959.
14. *Photoplay*, September 1955.
15. *Sunday Times*, March 6, 1994.
16. *The People*, August 23, 1970.
17. *Milwaukee Journal*, March 31, 1963.
18. *Redbook*, March 1957.
19. *Time Out*, May 30–June 5, 1985.
20. *Redbook*, March 1957.
21. *Interview*, 1991.
22. *American Weekly*, August 24, 1952.
23. James Robert Parish, Don E. Stanke, et al., *The Swashbucklers* (New Rochelle, NY: Arlington House, 1976), p. 575.
24. *L.A. Daily*, March 29, 1952.
25. *Photoplay*, May 1955.
26. *American Weekly*, August 24, 1952.
27. *Photoplay*, May 1952.
28. *L.A. Daily News*, March 29, 1952.
29. *Photoplay*, May 1952.
30. *Time Out*, March 16–23, 1994.
31. Allan Hunter, *Tony Curtis: The Man and His Movies* (Edinburgh: Paul Harris Publishing, 1985), p. 8.
32. Parkinson, *Parky's People*, pp. 35–6.
33. Tony Curtis, *Kid Andrew Cody and Julie Sparrow* (London: W.H. Allen, 1997), p. 53.
34. *Cowboys and Indians*, January 2011.
35. *Interview*, 1991.
36. Ibid.
37. *Saturday Evening Post*, July 25, 1959.
38. *Photoplay*, August 1954.
39. Tony Curtis, with Barry Paris, *The Autobiography* (London: Heinemann, 1994), p. 37.
40. *Redbook*, March 1957.
41. *Saturday Evening Post*, July 25, 1959.
42. *Photoplay*, May 1952.
43. *The Autobiography*, p. 37.
44. *Photoplay*, August 1954.
45. *Interview*, 1991.

Chapter 2

1. *Hollywood Citizen News*, June 12, 1965.
2. *L.A. Times*, February 18, 1951.
3. *Sunday Times*, April 20, 2008.
4. *Photoplay*, September 1955.
5. *Saturday Evening*, July 25, 1959.
6. *Interview*, June 1991.
7. Ibid.
8. Clive James, *Cultural Amnesia: Notes in the Margin of My Time* (London: Picador, 2007), p. 150.
9. *Redbook*, March 1957.
10. *Cue*, August 2, 1958.
11. Peter Manso, *Brando* (New York: Hyperion, 1994), p. 101.
12. When he was twelve, Curtis was introduced to a girl who gave kissing lessons at the back of his school for that price. This may be where he got the idea of being a self-styled "kissing instructor" on the Universal lot years later. See *Photoplay*, January 1957.
13. *Photoplay*, February 1951.
14. *Picture Show*, August 11, 1952.
15. Maurice Silver, *I Wish I'd Said That* (London: Robson, 1999), p. 119.
16. *Photoplay*, May 1957.
17. *Motion Picture*, July 1951.
18. *L.A. Examiner*, July 8, 1951.
19. Tony Curtis, with Peter Golenbock, *American Prince* (London: Virgin, 2008), p. 91. Here it's just an unidentified "somebody."
20. Curtis, with Paris, *The Autobiography*, p. 70.
21. Curtis, with Golenbock, *American Prince*, p. 90.
22. *Chicago Tribune*, June 28, 1964.
23. *L.A. Herald Examiner*, February 29, 1964.
24. *L.A. Daily News*, March 29, 1952.
25. *L.A. Examiner*, July 8, 1951.
26. *American Prince*, p. 91.
27. *L.A. Herald-Examiner*, March 3, 1964. Warner was more amused with Curtis than offended by him. "Jack didn't hold it against me," he admitted. Years later he made a film with Warner Bros., *Sex and the Single Girl*.
28. *Herald-Examiner*, February 29, 1964. Curtis gave a different version of the story in *American Prince*. In that version it's David O. Selznick who's perturbed by his funny walk in the card-enhanced shoes, not Goldstein. See *American Prince*, p. 91.

Chapter 3

1. *Photoplay*, November 1969.
2. Hunter, *The Man and His Movies*, p. 9.
3. Ibid.
4. Shelley Winters, *Shelley* (London: Granada, 1980), p. 100.
5. Curtis doesn't mention this in either of his autobiographies. He didn't like the way Winters claimed to have "made" him.

6. *Shelley*, p. 100.
7. Ibid. The line was from *Son of Ali Baba*.
8. Clive Hirschhorn, *The Universal Story* (London: Octopus, 1983), p. 156.
9. Phyllis Gates, *My Husband Rock Hudson* (London: Headline, 1998), p. 58.
10. John Izod, *Hollywood and the Box Office: 1895–1986* (London: Macmillan, 1986), p. 150.
11. Piper Laurie, *Learning to Live Out Loud* (New York: Crown Archetype, 2011), pp. 51–2.
12. Ibid., pp. 47–8.
13. Thomas Schatz, *The Genius of the System: Hollywood Filmmaking in the Studio Era* (London: Faber and Faber, 1998), p. 467.
14. Andrew Dowdy, *Films of the Fifties* (New York: William Morrow and Co., 1975), p. 173.
15. Izod, *Hollywood and the Box Office*, pp. 158–9.
16. Gary Edgerton, *American Film Exhibition and an Analysis of the Motion Picture Industry's Market Structure, 1963–1980* (London: Garland Publishing, 1983), pp. 141–2.
17. *Saturday Evening*, July 25, 1959.
18. *Sunday Express*, September 9, 1962.
19. Boze Hadleigh, ed., *Hollywood Bitch* (London: Robson, 1999), p. 118.
20. *Weekend*, November 24, 1951.
21. Curtis, with Paris, *The Autobiography*, p. 86. He said he was on the MGM lot merely to take some photographs but it's more likely he was there to have his speech improved, the reason he gives in *American Prince* (see p. 94). It's curious why he changed the story—unless he was embarrassed by the reason given in *The Autobiography*.
22. Hunter, *The Man and His Movies*, p. 12.
23. *Daily News*, March 29, 1952.
24. Geoff Tibballs, *First Jobs of the Famous* (London: Sphere, 1991), pp. 54–5.
25. *L.A. Mirror*, October 13, 1958.
26. *Picturegoer*, July 4, 1957.
27. *Motion Picture*, January 1952.
28. *GQ*, April 1996.
29. *Sunday Times*, April 20, 2008.
30. *The Guardian*, April 18, 2008.
31. *The Jill and Tony Curtis Story*, French Connection Films, 2004.
32. *Sunday Times*, April 20, 2008.
33. Curtis didn't reveal he'd had an affair with Monroe in his 1994 autobiography, only his 2008 one.
34. Charlotte Chandler, *Nobody's Perfect* (New York: Simon and Schuster, 2002), p. 200.
35. *Motion Picture*, June 1950.
36. *Time Out*, May 30–June 5, 1985.
37. Daily minutes, Universal Studios, December 2, 1949.
38. *The Guardian*, April 18, 2008.
39. Ibid.
40. *L.A. Times*, January 25, 1999.
41. *GQ*, April 1996.
42. *Time Out*, March 16–23, 1994.
43. *Motion Picture*, June 1950.
44. Barbara Sinatra, with Wendy Holden, *Lady Blue Eyes* (London: Hutchinson, 2011), p. 67.
45. Boze Hadleigh, ed., *Hollywood Babble On* (New York: Birch Lane Press, 1994), p. 189.
46. *Photoplay*, September 1955.
47. *Daily Sketch*, July 4, 1962.
48. *Saturday Evening Post*, July 25, 1959.
49. *The Guardian*, October 1, 2010.
50. *Hollywood Citizen News*, October 6, 1969.
51. *Photoplay*, January 1966.
52. *Orange County Register*, January 14, 2009.
53. *Photoplay*, September 1955.
54. Curtis, *American Prince*, p. 101.
55. David Shipman, *The Great Movie Stars* (London: Angus and Robertson, 1972), p. 104.
56. John Boorman and Walter Donohue, eds., *The Director's Cut* (London: Faber and Faber, 2006), p. 57.
57. Shipman, *The Great Movie Stars*, p. 104.
58. Doug McClelland, ed., *Forties Film Talk: Oral Histories of Hollywood* (Jefferson, NC: McFarland, 1992), p. 190.
59. *Photoplay*, September 1955.
60. *Motion Picture*, January 1951.
61. Peter Harry Brown and Pat H. Broeske, *Down at the End of Lonely Street* (London: Arrow, 1998), p. 25.
62. Schatz, *The Genius of the System*, p. 468.
63. Winters, *Shelley*, p. 296.
64. Schatz, *The Genius of the System*, pp. 470–1.
65. David Grove, *Jamie Lee Curtis: Scream Queen* (Albany: Bear Manor Media, 2010), p. 11.
66. Connie Bruck, *When Hollywood Had a King* (New York: Random House, 2004), p. 114.
67. Dennis McDougal, *The Last Mogul: MCA and the Hidden History of Hollywood* (New York: Crown Publishers, 1998), pp. 152–3.
68. Ibid., pp. 153–5.
69. Arthur Miller, *Timebends: A Life* (London: Methuen, 1988), p. 462.
70. Curtis liked the fact that there were never any papers on Wasserman's desk when he did business. "It's like the way a duck paddles," he said, "all the action is under the surface."
71. Matthew Bernstein, *Walter Wanger: Hollywood Independent* (Berkeley: University of California Press, 1994), p. 320.
72. Ibid.
73. Parish and Stanke, *The Swashbucklers*, pp. 578–9.
74. Janet Leigh, *There Really Was a Hollywood* (New York: Jove, 1984), p. 124.
75. Curtis, with Paris, *The Autobiography*, p. 98.
76. *Cowboys and Indians*, January 2011.
77. Ibid.
78. Boorman and Donohue, *The Director's Cut*, p. 58.
79. Curtis, with Golenbock, *American Prince*, pp. 119–20.
80. *Motion Picture*, January 1951.
81. Ibid.
82. Curtis often misspelled this as "Kertiz."
83. Edward Lucaire gives this as Curtis' "favorite" novel in his book *Celebrity Trivia* (New York: Warner, 1980, pp. 131–2). Many other accounts of his life also do. It wasn't so much his favorite book as the only one he read while he was in the Navy.
84. *Coronet*, June 1968.
85. Parkinson, *Parky's People*, p. 37.
86. *Empire*, April 1994.
87. *Photoplay*, November 1969.
88. Alanna Nash, *Baby, Let's Play House* (London: Aurum, 2010), p. 193.
89. Ibid., p. 51.
90. Ibid., p. 211.
91. *Herald Tribune*, August 19, 1957.
92. Boorman and Donohue, *The Director's Cut*, p. 58.
93. *Motion Picture*, May 1951.
94. Debbie Reynolds, with David Patrick Columbia, *My Life* (London: Pan, 1989), pp. 84–5.
95. David Bret, *Elizabeth Taylor: The Lover and the Legend* (Edinburgh: Mainstream, 2011), p. 254.
96. Stephen Farber and Marc Green, *Hollywood Dynasties* (New

York: Delilah Publications, 1984), p. 126.
97. Leigh, *There Really Was a Hollywood*, p. 121.
98. *Daily Telegraph*, April 16, 1996.
99. *Saturday Evening Post*, July 25, 1959.
100. Leigh, *There Really Was a Hollywood*, p. 125.
101. *Motion Picture*, June 1950.
102. Ibid.
103. Ibid.
104. Peter Hay, *Movie Anecdotes* (New York: Oxford University Press, 1990), p. 39.
105. *Daily News*, October 4, 1950.
106. Ibid.
107. Ibid.
108. Tony Curtis, with Mark A. Vieira, *Some Like It Hot: Me, Marilyn and the Movie* (London: Virgin, 2009), p. 39.
109. Darwin Porter, *Brando Unzipped* (Staten Island, NY: Blood Moon Productions, 2005), p. 313.
110. Winters, *Shelley*, p. 197.
111. Curtis, with Paris, *The Autobiography*, p. 324.
112. *Sunday Express*, September 9, 1962.
113. *Interview*, 1991.
114. Curtis, with Paris, *The Autobiography*, p. 82.
115. Joan Collins, *Second Act* (London: Boxtree, 1996), p. 152.
116. Marlon Brando, with Robert Lindsay, *Songs My Mother Taught Me* (London: Century, 1994), p. 79.

Chapter 4

1. *Motion Picture*, July 1951.
2. Ibid.
3. Ibid.
4. Curtis, with Paris, *The Autobiography*, p. 102.
5. Laurie, *Learning to Live Out Loud*, p. 73.
6. Ibid.
7. Donald Zec, *Some Enchanted Egos* (London: Alison and Busby, 1972), p. 242.
8. Universal Studios Committee Meeting Minutes, January 12, 1951.
9. *Photoplay*, April 1951.
10. *Saturday Evening Post*, February 9, 1952.
11. *Photoplay*, January 1966.
12. *Cosmopolitan*, February 1961.
13. *L.A. Times*, February 18, 1951.
14. *Motion Picture*, February 1952.
15. Laurie, *Learning to Live Out Loud*, p. 95.
16. Ibid., pp. 95–6.
17. Leigh, *There Really Was a Hollywood*, p. 137.
18. Laurie, *Learning to Live Out Loud*, p. 96.
19. *L.A. Examiner*, August 5, 1951.
20. Laurie, *Learning to Live Out Loud*, p. 97.
21. Alanna Nash, *Elvis Aaron Presley: Revelations from the Memphis Mafia* (New York: HarperCollins, 1995), p. 96.
22. Winters, *Shelley*, p. 101.
23. Curtis, with Golenbock, *American Prince*, p. 108.
24. Winters, *Shelley*, p. 286.
25. Tab Hunter, with Eddie Mueller, *Tab Hunter Confidential: The Making of a Movie Star* (Chapel Hill, NC: Algonquin Books, 2005), p. 242.
26. Robert Wagner and Scott Eyman, *Pieces of My Heart* (London: Hutchinson, 2009), p. 76.
27. *Interview*, 1991.
28. Aubrey Malone, *Sacred Profanity* (Santa Barbara, CA: ABC-CLIO, 2010), p. 38.
29. James, *Cultural Amnesia*, p. 150.
30. *Time Out*, May 30–June 5, 1985.
31. *Hollywood Citizen*, October 6, 1969.
32. *Motion Picture*, January 1952.
33. Laurie, *Learning to Live Out Loud*, p. 73.
34. Michael Munn, *Tony Curtis: Nobody's Perfect* (London: JR Books, 2011), p. 67.
35. Curtis, with Paris, *The Autobiography*, p. 100.
36. Laurie, *Learning to Live Out Loud*, p. 91.
37. Winters, *Shelley*, pp. 305–10.
38. Laurie, *Learning to Live Out Loud*, p. 94.
39. Deana Martin, with Wendy Holden, *Memories Are Made of This* (London: Pan, 2005), p. 31.
40. *Photoplay*, May 1969.

Chapter 5

1. Daily minutes, Committee Meeting, Universal Studios, June 20, 1951.
2. Will Haygood, *In Black and White: The Life of Sammy Davis Jr.* (London: Aurum, 2005), p. 161.
3. *Photoplay*, December 1951.
4. Boorman and Donohue, *The Director's Cut*, p. 51.
5. James Robert Parish and Ronald L. Bowers, *The MGM Stock Company: The Golden Era* (London: Ian Allen, 1973), p. 439.
6. Ibid.
7. *Photoplay*, September 1955.
8. *Architectural Digest*, March 2006.
9. Ibid.
10. *Saturday Evening Post*, July 25, 1959.
11. *TV Times*, April 4, 1987.
12. *Photoplay*, January 1966.
13. *Motion Picture*, April 1952.
14. *Photoplay*, February 1954.
15. *Hollywood Citizen News*, September 16, 1951.
16. *American Weekly*, August 24, 1952.
17. *Redbook*, March 1957.
18. *Photoplay*, February 1955.
19. *Screen Parade*, February 1952.
20. *American Weekly*, August 24, 1952.
21. *Interview*, 1991.
22. *Saturday Evening Post*, February 9, 1952.
23. *Motion Picture*, April 1952.
24. *Photoplay*, April 1954.
25. Allegra Curtis, *Ich Und Mein Vater* (Munich: Langen Muller, 2011), p. 207.
26. *GQ*, April 1996.
27. *Hollywood Citizen News*, November 9, 1951.
28. *L.A. Times*, November 9, 1951.
29. *Photoplay*, March 1979.
30. *Game*, December 1975.
31. *Saturday Evening Post*, January 17, 1953.
32. *Star Weekly*, November 1, 1952.
33. *Screen Parade*, December 1952.
34. *Star Weekly*, November 1, 1952.
35. Hunter, with Mueller, *Tab Hunter Confidential*, p. 125.
36. Ibid.
37. *Photoplay*, June 1952.
38. Leigh, *There Really Was a Hollywood*, p. 166.
39. *Daily News*, October 20, 1952.
40. *Hollywood Citizen News*, August 11, 1952.
41. *Motion Picture*, January 1953.
42. Brooke Kamin Rapaport, *Houdini, Art and Magic* (New Haven, CT: Yale University Press, 2010), p. 39.
43. Gordon Gow, *Hollywood in the Fifties* (New York: A.S. Barnes and Co., 1971), p. 163.
44. Ibid., pp. 163–4.
45. Curtis, with Golenbock, *American Prince*, pp. 139–40.

46. William Kalush and Larry Sloman, *The Secret Life of Houdini* (London: Pocket Books, 2007), pp. 508–10.
47. Ibid., pp. 511–5.
48. Ibid., ix.
49. *Sunday Times*, March 6, 1994.
50. *New York Times*, July 3, 1953.
51. *Chicago Daily Tribune*, September 11, 1953.
52. E.L. Doctorow, *Ragtime* (New York: Penguin, 1996), p. 8.
53. *Chicago Tribune Magazine*, November 8, 1953.
54. McDougal, *The Last Mogul*, p. 164.
55. Ibid., p. 274
56. Bruck, *When Hollywood Had a King*, pp. 471–2.
57. McDougall, *The Last Mogul*, pp. 151–2.
58. Ibid., p. 156.
59. Bruck, *When Hollywood Had a King*, p. 249.
60. *Motion Picture*, October 1953.
61. Leigh, *There Really Was a Hollywood*, pp. 171–2.
62. Robyn Karney, ed., *The Movie Stars Story* (London: Octopus, 1984), p. 162.
63. *Screenland*, April 1957.
64. Hirschhorn, *The Universal Story*, p. 219.
65. Wendy Leigh, *True Grace: The Life and Death of an American Princess* (London: JR Books, 2008), p. 180.
66. Nigel Cawthorne, *Sex Lives of the Hollywood Goddesses* (London: Prion, 1997), pp. 214–5.
67. *The Independent*, October 1, 2010.
68. *Photoplay*, November 1954.
69. Izod, *Hollywood and the Box Office, 1895–1986*, p. 146.
70. Dowdy, *Films of the Fifties*, p. 157.
71. Wagner, with Eyman, *Pieces of My Heart*, p. 83.
72. Robert Hofler, *The Man Who Invented Rock Hudson* (New York: Carroll and Graf, 2005), p. 24.
73. Robin Cross and John Marriot, *The World's Greatest Hollywood Scandals* (London: Hamlyn, 1989), p. 152.
74. *Confidential*, May 1955.
75. Hofler, *The Man Who Invented Rock Hudson*, xx.
76. Fred Otash, *Investigation Hollywood* (Chicago: Henry Regnery, 1976), p. 35.
77. Gates, *My Husband, Rock Hudson*, p. 87.
78. Curtis, with Golenbock, *American Prince*, p. 113.
79. Gates, *My Husband, Rock Hudson*, p. 87.
80. *Empire*, April 1994.
81. Hunter, *The Man and His Movies*, p. 56.
82. Curtis deals with this matter in both of his autobiographies. See *The Autobiography*, p. 126, and *American Prince*, p. 166.
83. Angela Lansbury, *A Life on Stage and Screen* (Secaucus, NJ: Citadel, 1999), p. 94.
84. *Photoplay*, November 1969.
85. *Screenland*, April 1957.
86. *Irish Independent*, October 1, 2010.
87. *Saturday Evening Post*, July 25, 1959.
88. *Hollywood Reporter*, July 20, 1957.
89. Curtis, with Golenbock, *American Prince*, pp. 167–8.
90. *Photoplay*, September 1955.
91. Jerry Lewis, with Herb Gluck, *Jerry Lewis in Person* (New York: Pinnacle Books, 1982), pp. 170–1.
92. Ibid., p. 171.
93. *Saturday Evening Post*, February 9, 1952.
94. Lewis, with Gluck, *Jerry Lewis in Person*, pp. 171–2.
95. Parish and Stanke, *The Swashbucklers*, p. 593.
96. *Architectural Digest*, March 2006.
97. *Hedda Hopper's Hollywood*, October 1, 1956.
98. Ibid.
99. *Photoplay*, December 1956.
100. Maurice Zotolow, *Billy Wilder in Hollywood* (New York: Limelight Editions, 1996), p. 147.
101. *Sunday Express*, October 10, 1965.
102. McDougal, *The Last Mogul*, p. 292n.
103. Ibid., p. 310.
104. *Sunday Express*, October 10, 1965.
105. Miller, *Timebends*, p. 534.

Chapter 6

1. Leigh, *There Really Was a Hollywood*, p. 189.
2. Kate Buford, *Burt Lancaster: An American Life* (London: Aurum, 2000), p. 175.
3. Ibid., p. 152.
4. *Photoplay*, December 1955.
5. Leigh, *There Really Was a Hollywood*, p. 192.
6. *Sunday News*, August 24, 1958.
7. *Hollywood Citizen News*, August 30–September 5, 1969.
8. *Modern Screen*, December 1955.
9. James, *Cultural Amnesia*, p. 150.
10. *American Life*, p. 153.
11. *Photoplay*, September 1955.
12. Curtis, with Paris, *The Autobiography*, p. 130.
13. Curtis, *American Prince*, p. 175.
14. *Photoplay*, December 1955.
15. Curtis, with Golenbock, *American Prince*, p. 174.
16. Oliver Reed, *Reed: All About Me* (London: W.H. Allen, 1979), pp. 212–3.
17. Ibid., p. 213.
18. Gary Fishgall, *Against Type: The Biography of Burt Lancaster* (New York: Scribner, 1995), p. 139.
19. Ibid.
20. *Sunday Express*, October 10, 1965.
21. *Picturegoer*, July 4, 1957.
22. Ibid.
23. *Hollywood Citizen News*, October 6, 1969.
24. *Beverly Hills Citizen*, December 3, 1957.
25. Fishgall, *Against Type*, p. 150.
26. *Hollywood Reporter*, May 12, 1978.
27. Leigh, *There Really Was a Hollywood*, p. 214.
28. Howard Johns, *Hollywood Celebrity Playground* (Fort Lee, NJ: Barricade Books, 2006), p. 306.
29. Curtis with Golenbock, *American Prince*, p. 152.

Chapter 7

1. Graydon Carter, ed., *Vanity Fair's Tales of Hollywood* (London: Penguin, 2008), p. 80.
2. John Brady, ed., *The Craft of the Screenwriter: Interviews with Six Celebrated Screenwriters* (New York: Simon and Schuster, 1981), p. 193.
3. Philip Kemp, *Lethal Innocence: The Cinema of Alexander Mackendrick*. (London: Methuen, 1991), p. 142.
4. Sam Kashner and Jennifer Macnair, *The Bad and the Beautiful: A Chronicle of Hollywood in the Fifties* (London: Little Brown, 2002), p. 225.
5. Mark Denning, ed., et al., *Empire Film Guide* (London: Virgin, 2007), p. 956.
6. Kemp, *Lethal Innocence*, p. 148.
7. Kashner and Macnair, *The Bad and the Beautiful*, p. 227.
8. Ibid., p. 234.
9. Shaun Considine, *Mad as Hell: The Life and Work of Paddy Chayefsky* (Lincoln, NE: iUniverse, 2000), p. 198.

10. Carter, *Vanity Fair's Tales of Hollywood*, p. 96.
11. Fishgall, *Against Type*, p. 162.
12. Kashner and Macnair, *The Bad and the Beautiful*, pp. 230–1.
13. Ibid., p. 231.
14. *Sunday Independent*, October 3, 2010.
15. Buford, *An American Life*, p. 2.
16. Ibid., p. 181.
17. Kashner and Macnair, *The Bad and the Beautiful*, p. 231.
18. Buford, *An American Life*, p. 181.
19. Kemp, *Lethal Innocence*, p. 153.
20. *Boston Phoenix*, June 5, 1979.
21. Carter, *Vanity Fair's Tales of Hollywood*, p. 95.
22. Karney, *The Movie Stars Story*, p. 164.
23. Kemp, *Lethal Innocence*, p. 148.
24. *Sight and Sound*, Autumn 1967.
25. James, *Cultural Amnesia*, p. 151.
26. Alexander Ballinger and Danny Graydon, eds., *The Rough Guide to Film Noir* (London: Penguin, 2007), p. 34.
27. David Shipman, *Caught in the Act: Sex and Eroticism in the Movies* (London: Elm Tree Books, 1985), p. 125.
28. Frank Miller, *Censored Hollywood: Sex, Sin and Violence on Screen* (Atlanta, GA: Turner Publications, 1994), p. 169.
29. Kemp, *Lethal Innocence*, pp. 160–1.
30. Interview, 1991.
31. Kashner and Macnair, *The Bad and the Beautiful*, p. 237.
32. Carter, *Vanity Fair's Tales of Hollywood*, p. 99.
33. Kemp, *Lethal Innocence*, p. 160.
34. *Saturday Review*, July 6, 1957.
35. *Evening Standard*, July 11, 1957.
36. *The Observer*, July 14, 1957.
37. Buford, *An American Life*, p. 183.
38. Fishgall, *Against Type*, p. 166.
39. Ibid., p. 165.
40. *The Scotsman*, October 29, 1962.
41. *Films and Filming*, August 1985.
42. Kashner and Macnair, *The Bad and the Beautiful*, p. 231.
43. Paul Simpson, ed., et al., *The Rough Guide to Cult Movies* (London: Haymarket Publishing, 2004), p. 173.
44. *Irish Daily Mirror*, October 1, 2010.
45. Interview, 1991.
46. *The Guardian*, October 1, 2010.
47. Interview, 1991.
48. James, *Cultural Amnesia*, p. 151.
49. Interview, 1991.
50. David Thomson, *A Biographical Dictionary of Cinema* (London: Secker and Warburg, 1980), p. 125.
51. Kemp, *Lethal Innocence*, p. 144.
52. Haygood, *In Black and White*, p. 33.
53. Joe Eszterhas, *The Devil's Guide to Hollywood* (London: Duckworth Overlook, 2007), p. 359.
54. Carter, *Vanity Fair's Tales of Hollywood*, p. 103.
55. Buford, *An American Life*, p. 3.
56. Kemp, *Lethal Innocence*, p. 147.
57. Neil Sinyard, *The Films of Richard Lester* (London: Croom Helm, 1985), p. 65.
58. Mark Borowski, *The Fame Formula*. (London: Sidgwick and Jackson, 2008), p. 309.

Chapter 8

1. *Hollywood Citizen News*, September 11, 1958.
2. *Hedda Hopper's Hollywood*, August 3, 1958.
3. *Photoplay*, October 1960.
4. Michael Munn, *Kirk Douglas* (New York: St. Martin's Press, 1989), p. 71.
5. Kirk Douglas, *The Ragman's Son: An Autobiography* (London: Simon and Schuster, 1988), p. 283.
6. *Photoplay*, November 1969.
7. *Photoplay*, January 1966.
8. *Empire News Sunday Chronicle*, July 7, 1957.
9. *Photoplay*, November 1957.
10. Munn, *Kirk Douglas*, pp. 71–2.
11. Douglas, *The Ragman's Son*, p. 284.
12. Richard Fleischer, *Just Tell Me When to Cry* (London: Souvenir, 1994), p. 144.
13. Ernest Borgnine, *My Autobiography* (London: JR Books, 2012), p. 124.
14. *L.A. Times*, August 3, 1958.
15. Buford, *An American Life*, p. 165.
16. Fleischer, *Just Tell Me When to Cry*, pp. 153–4.
17. Ibid., pp. 151–2.
18. *Empire Film Guide*, p. 1047.
19. Ibid.
20. *Daily Variety*, April 25, 1963.
21. Ibid.
22. Michael J. Mann, *How to Be a Movie Star: Elizabeth Taylor in Hollywood* (London: Faber, 2009), pp. 271–2.
23. *Daily Variety*, April 25, 1963.
24. *Picturegoer*, July 4, 1957.
25. Ibid.
26. Tom Santopietro, *Sinatra in Hollywood* (New York: St. Martin's Press, 2008), p. 244.
27. Gavin Lambert, *Natalie Wood: A Life* (London: Faber, 2004), p. 202.
28. Curtis, with Paris, *The Autobiography*, p. 149.
29. Lambert's view becomes more difficult to credit when we read in Curtis' book *American Prince* that he and Wood made passionate love one day in her trailer during the shooting of *The Great Race* seven years later (see pp. 252–4.)
30. Michael Munn, *Hollywood Rogues* (London: Robson, 1991), pp. 144–5.
31. *Saturday Evening Post*, March 23, 1968.
32. *Modern Screen*, July 1964.
33. *Photoplay*, January 1966.
34. Curtis, with Paris, *The Autobiography*, p. 194.
35. *Photoplay*, February 1959.
36. Grove, *Scream Queen*, p. 8.
37. Joey Berlin, ed., *Toxic Fame* (Detroit: Visible Ink Press, 1996), pp. 343–4.
38. Sammy Davis Jr. and Burt Boyar, *Why Me?* (London: Sphere, 1991), pp. 71–2.
39. Ibid., pp. 72–3.
40. Kashner and Macnair, *The Bad and the Beautiful*, pp. 206–7.
41. Tim Adler, *Hollywood and the Mob* (London: Bloomsbury, 2007), p. 130.
43. Ibid., p. 75.
44. Ibid., p. 79.
45. Cross and Marriott, *The World's Greatest Hollywood Scandals*, p. 88.
46. Douglas, *The Ragman's Son*, pp. 177–8.
47. Stanley Kramer with Thomas M. Coffey, *A Mad, Mad, Mad, Mad World* (London: Aurum Press, 1997), p. 149.
48. Ibid.
49. *USA Today*, October 14, 2008.
50. Ken Wlaschin, *The World's Great Movie Stars* (London: Salamander Books, 1979), p. 210.
51. Sidney Poitier, *The Measure of a Man* (London: Simon and Schuster, 2000), p. 102.
52. Ibid., pp. 102–3.
53. Ibid., pp. 103–5.
54. Sidney Poitier, *This Life*

(London: Hodder and Stoughton, 1981), p. 246.
55. Kramer, with Coffey, *A Mad, Mad, Mad, Mad World*, p. 15.
56. Poitier, *This Life*, p. 247.
57. Gow, *Hollywood in the Fifties*, pp. 100–1.
58. *Empire Film Guide*, p. 256.
59. Stefan Kanfer, *Somebody: The Reckless Life and Remarkable Career of Marlon Brando* (London: Faber, 2008), p. 160.
60. Ibid.
61. Mark Harris, *Scenes from a Revolution* (Edinburgh: Canongate, 2009), p. 114.
62. The film received a number of other nominations as well, winning Oscars for Best Cinematography and Best Original Screenplay.
63. *The Telegraph*, September 30, 2010.
64. *L.A. Herald Examiner*, July 6, 1975.
65. Peter Bogdanovich, *Who the Hell's in It?* (London: Faber, 2004), p. 451.
66. John Harkness, *The Academy Awards Handbook: Who Won What When* (New York: Pinnacle Books, 1994), p. 152.
67. *L.A. Mirror*, October 13, 1958.
68. Hunter, *The Man and His Movies*, p. 14.
69. Leigh, *There Really Was a Hollywood*, p. 264.
70. *Newsweek*, June 30, 1958.

Chapter 9

1. Don Widener, *Lemmon: A Biography* (London: W.H. Allen, 1977), p. 166.
2. Laurence Maslon, *Some Like It Hot: The Official 50th Anniversary Companion* (London: Pavilion, 2009), p. 43.
3. John Eastman, *Retakes: Behind the Scenes of 500 Classic Movies* (New York: Ballantine, 1989), p. 315.
4. *Empire Film Guide*, p. 902.
5. Marie Clayton, *Marilyn Monroe: Unseen Archives* (London: Parragon, 2005), p. 262.
6. McDougal, *The Last Mogul*, p. 248.
7. Gloria Steinem, *Marilyn: Norma Jeane* (New York: Signet, 1988), p. 101.
8. Zolotow, *Billy Wilder in Hollywood*, p. 202.
9. Maslon, *Some Like It Hot: The Official 50th Anniversary Companion*, p. 72.
10. Widener, *Lemmon: A Biography*, pp. 166–7.
11. In some scenes she had a "morning after" look resulting from her increasing pill intake.
12. Eastman, *Retakes*, p. 314.
13. Zolotow, *Billy Wilder in Hollywood*, p. 257.
14. *New York*, June 6, 1973.
15. Barbara Leaming, *Marilyn Monroe* (London.: Orion, 1998), pp. 313–4.
16. *Empire*, 2001.
17. Chandler, *Nobody's Perfect*, p. 210.
18. Ibid., pp. 212–3.
19. Ibid., p. 211.
20. Ibid., pp. 211–2.
21. *Empire Film Guide*, p. 902.
22. *Saturday Evening*, July 25, 1959.
23. Leigh, *There Really Was a Hollywood*, p. 251.
24. *The Telegraph*, September 30, 2010.
25. Michael Freedland, *Some Like It Cool: The Charmed Life of Jack Lemmon* (London: Robson Books, 2003), p. 77.
26. *The Telegraph*, September 30, 2010.
27. Sarah Churchill, *The Many Lives of Marilyn Monroe* (London: Granta, 2004), p. 71.
28. Shelley Winters, *Shelley II: The Middle of My Century* (New York: Pocket Books, 1990), p. 241.
29. Churchill, *The Many Lives of Marilyn Monroe*, p. 71.
30. Widener, *Lemmon: A Biography*, p. 170.
31. Zolotow, *Billy Wilder in Hollywood*, p. 258.
32. Ibid.
33. Ibid., p. 257.
34. Ibid., p. 262.
35. Guus Luijters, ed., *Marilyn Monroe: In Her Own Words* (London: Omnibus Press, 1990), p. 63.
36. Chandler, *Nobody's Perfect*, p. 213.
37. Maslon, *Some Like It Hot: The Official 50th Anniversary Companion*, p. 151.
38. Widener, *Lemmon: A Biography*, p. 170.
39. Bryan Forbes, *Actors on Actors* (London: Aurum, 1995), p. 15.
40. Widener, *Lemmon: A Biography*, p. 170.
41. Baltake, *Jack Lemmon: His Films and Career*, p. 97.
42. Parkinson, *Parky's People*, pp. 56–7.
43. Zolotow, *Billy Wilder in Hollywood*, pp. 261–2.
44. Matthew Smith, *Victim: The Secret Tapes of Marilyn Monroe* (London: Arrow, 2004), p. 22.
45. *Vanity Fair*, November 2008.
46. Zolotow, *Billy Wilder in Hollywood*, p. 262.
47. Donald H. Wolfe, *The Assassination of Marilyn Monroe* (London: Little Brown, 1998), pp. 317–8.
48. James Bacon, *Hollywood Is a Four-Letter Town* (New York: Avon, 1976), p. 136.
49. Zolotow, *Billy Wilder in Hollywood*, p. 321.
50. Wolfe, *The Assassination of Marilyn Monroe*, pp. 320.
51. Ibid., pp. 317–8.
52. Curtis, with Vieira, *Me, Marilyn and the Movie*, p. 121.
53. Miller, *Timebends*, p. 466.
54. Curtis, with Vieira, *Me, Marilyn and the Movie*, p. 90.
55. Monroe told James Bacon Montand he reminded her of DiMaggio (see Bacon, *Hollywood Is a Four-Letter Town*, p. 142).
56. Curtis, with Vieira, *Me, Marilyn and the Movie*, pp. 184–6.
57. Eastman, *Retakes*, p. 314.
58. Cameron Crowe, *Conversations with Wilder* (London: Faber and Faber, 1999), p. 159.
59. Ibid.
60. Leaming, *Marilyn Monroe*, p. 315.
61. Parkinson, *Parky's People*, p. 56.
62. J. Randy Tarraborelli, *The Secret Life of Marilyn Monroe* (London: Sidgwick and Jackson, 2009), p. 308.
63. Wilder reckoned she added approximately $750,000 to the film's $3 million budget.
64. Hay, *Movie Anecdotes*, p. 71.
65. Bob McCabe, ed., *The Rough Guide to Comedy Movies* (London: Rough Guides Reference, 2005), p. 141.
66. Ted Jordan, *Norma Jean: A Hollywood Love Story* (London: Pan, 1990), pp. 226–7.
67. Eastman, *Retakes*, p. 314.
68. *Motion Picture*, May 1951.
69. Maslon, *Some Like It Hot: The Official 50th Anniversary Edition*, p. 83.
70. James Naremore, *Acting in the Cinema* (Berkeley: University of California Press, 1988), p. 218.
71. *Coronet*, June 1968.
72. *Premiere*, June 2001.
73. Curtis, with Vieira, *Me, Marilyn and the Movie*, p. 111.
74. Chandler, *Nobody's Perfect*, p. 218.
75. Gary Morecambe and Martin Sterling, *In Name Only: A Biography of Cary Grant* (London: Robson, 2001), p. 244.
76. *The Times*, April 3, 1999.
77. Natasha Fraser-Cavassoni,

Sam Spiegel: The Biography of a Hollywood Legend (London: Time Warner, 2004), p. 251.
78. Morecambe and Sterling, *In Name Only*, p. 115.
79. Crowe, *Conversations with Wilder*, pp. 37–8.
80. Ibid., p. 156.
81. Ibid., p. 145.
82. *GQ*, April 1996.
83. Chandler, *Nobody's Perfect*, p. 209.
84. Jeremy Pascall and Clyde Jeavons, *A Pictorial History of Sex in the Movies* (London: Hamlyn, 1975), p. 128.
85. *Game*, September 1975.
86. Taraborelli, *The Secret Life of Marilyn Monroe*, p. 308.
87. John Kobal, *Marilyn Monroe: A Life on Film* (London: Hamlyn, 1974), p. 25.
88. Luijters, *Marilyn Monroe: In Her Own Words*, p. 64.
89. *Premiere*, June 2001.
90. Wolfe, *The Assassination of Marilyn Monroe*, p. 321.
91. Bacon, *Hollywood Is a Four-Letter Town*, p. 135.
92. Michael Caine, *The Elephant and Hollywood* (London: Hodder and Stoughton, 2010), p. 377.

Chapter 10

1. *The People*, August 23, 1970.
2. *Photoplay*, October 1969.
3. Munn, *Nobody's Perfect*, pp. 160–1.
4. Many people claim it was *Cat on a Hot Tin Roof* that was the other half of the double bill that night.
5. Zolotow, *Billy Wilder in Hollywood*, p. 203.
6. *Empire Guide*, p. 903.
7. Leaming, *Marilyn Monroe*, p. 315.
8. *Time Out*, May 30–June 5, 1985.
9. Robyn Karney, ed., *Cinema Year by Year: 1894–2003* (London: Darling Kindersley, 2005), p. 421.
10. Baltake, *Jack Lemmon: His Films and Career*, pp. 97–9.
11. Karney, *The Movie Stars Story*, p. 163.
12. *L.A. Herald Examiner*, June 5, 1977.
13. *Time Out*, May 30–June 5, 1985.
14. James, *Cultural Amnesia*, p. 152.
15. Ibid.
16. *Evening Standard*, March 3, 1994.
17. *The Guardian*, October 1, 2010.

18. Roy Pickard, *The Oscar Movies from A-Z* (Middlesex: Hamlyn, 1982), p. 161.
19. Frank Walsh, *Sin and Censorship: The Catholic Church and the Motion Picture Industry* (New Haven and London: Yale University Press, 1996), p. 291.
20. Vito Russo, *The Celluloid Closet: Homosexuality in the Movies* (New York: Harper and Row, 1987), p. 7.
21. Rebecca Bell-Metereau, *Hollywood Androgyny* (New York: Columbia University Press, 1985), pp. 10–11.
22. *The Celluloid Closet* (Polygram, 1995).
23. Clayton, *Marilyn Monroe: Unseen Archives*, p. 293.
24. Luijters, *Marilyn Monroe: In Her Own Words*, p. 66.
25. Wolfe, *The Assassination of Marilyn Monroe*, p. 322.
26. Zolotow, *Billy Wilder in Hollywood*, pp. 265–6.
27. Ibid., 266–7.
28. Wolfe, *The Assassination of Marilyn Monroe*, p. 323.
29. Miller, *Timebends*, p. 476.
30. Ibid.
31. Morecambe and Sterling, *In Name Only*, p. 245.
32. Lynn Haney, *Gregory Peck: A Charmed Life* (London: Robson, 2003), p. 292.
33. Ronnie Wood, *Ronnie* (London: Macmillan, 2007), p. 165.
34. Leigh, *There Really Was a Hollywood*, p. 254.
35. *Photoplay*, November 1969.
36. Grant had an obsession with Jennifer. For a detailed account of their relationship see Charles Higham's *The Lonely Heart* (New York: Avon Books, 1989), pp. 316–33.
37. Morecambe and Sterling, *In Name Only*, p. 140.
38. *The Celluloid Closet* (Polygram, 1995).
39. Interview, 1991.
40. Chandler, *Nobody's Perfect*, p. 218.
41. Parkinson, *Parky's People*, pp. 36–7.
42. Graham McCann, *A Class Apart: A Biography of Cary Grant* (London: Fourth Estate, 1996), p. 109.
43. Marc Eliot, *Cary Grant: A Biography* (New York: Harmony, 2004), pp. 322–3.
44. Hirschhorn, *The Universal Story*, p. 261.
45. *The Guardian*, October 1, 2010.
46. *Saturday Evening Post*, July 25, 1959.

47. Curtis, with Golenbock, *American Prince*, p. 218.
48. Munn, *Nobody's Perfect*, p. 165.
49. McDougal, *The Last Mogul*, p. 205.
50. Ibid., p. 314.
51. Ibid., pp. 250–1.
52. Higham, *The Lonely Heart*, p. 306.
53. Hunter, *The Man and His Movies*, p. 17.
54. *Saturday Evening Post*, July 25, 1989.
55. *Photoplay*, January 1957.
56. Hunter, *The Man and His Movies*, p. 13.
57. Michael Freedland, *Dean Martin: The King of the Road* (London: Robson, 2005), p. 105.
58. This was a myth he liked to play up. It belied his fine sense of comic timing.
59. Neil Norman and Jon Barraclough, *Insignificance: The Book* (London: Sidgwick and Jackson, 1985), p. 60.
60. Nick Tosches, *Dino: Living High in the Dirty Business of Dreams* (London: Minerva, 1993), p. 326.
61. Ibid., p. 317.
62. Ronald L. Davis, *The Glamour Factory: Inside Hollywood's Big Studio System* (Dallas: Southern Methodist University Press, 1993), p. 243.
63. Brown and Broeske, *Down at the End of Lonely Street*, p. 104.
64. Munn, *Nobody's Perfect*, p. 170.
65. Curtis, with Golenbock, *American Prince*, p. 184.
66. Cross and Marriott, *The World's Greatest Hollywood Scandals*, p. 108.
67. M.J. Trow, *Spartacus: The Myth and the Man* (Gloucestershire: Sutton Publishing, 2006), p. 9.
68. Rock Brynner, *Yul: The Man Who Would Be King* (Glasgow: Fontana, 1990), p. 127.
69. Munn, *Kirk Douglas*, p. 80.
70. Douglas, *The Ragman's Son*, p. 314. The killing is really a merciful one as the victor knows he's going to be crucified by the Romans.
71. John Baxter, *Stanley Kubrick: A Biography* (London: HarperCollins, 1997), p. 129.
72. Gene Philips, ed., *Stanley Kubrick: Interviews* (Mississippi: Jackson University Press, 2001).
73. Baxter, *Stanley Kubrick*, p. 131.
74. Ibid.
75. Ibid., pp. 124–5.
76. Trow, *Spartacus: The Myth and the Man*, p. 16.

77. Wagner, with Eyman, *Pieces of my Heart*, p. 234.
78. Donald Spoto, *Laurence Olivier: A Biography* (New York: HarperCollins, 1993), p. 347.
79. Douglas, *The Ragman's Son*, p. 318.
80. Leigh, *There Really Was a Hollywood*, pp. 258–9.
81. Dawn B. Sova, *Forbidden Films* (New York: Checkmark Books, 2001), p. 278.
82. Baxter, *Stanley Kubrick*, p. 139.
83. *The Celluloid Closet* (Polygram, 1995).
84. *Empire*, December 2001.
85. Trow, *Spartacus: The Myth and the Man*, p. 164.
86. Simon Callow, *Charles Laughton: A Difficult Actor* (London: Methuen, 1987), p. 252.
87. Peter Ustinov, *Dear Me* (Middlesex: Penguin, 1978), p. 275.
88. Callow, *A Difficult Actor*, p. 253.
89. Ustinov, *Dear Me*, p. 275.
90. Charles Higham, *Charles Laughton* (London: W.H. Allen, 1976), pp. 245–6.
91. Callow, *A Difficult Actor*, p. 255.
92. Trow, *Spartacus: The Myth and the Man*, p. 82.
93. Aubrey Malone, *Censoring Hollywood* (Jefferson, NC: McFarland, 2011), p. 119.
94. For an examination of this theme, see Donald Spoto's *Laurence Olivier: A Life* (New York: HarperCollins, 1993), pp. 277–8.
95. Russo, *The Celluloid Closet*, p. 120.
96. Curtis, with Golenbock, *Me, Marilyn and the Movies*, p. 57.
97. Wagner, with Eyman, *Pieces of My Heart*, p. 234.
98. *Empire*, December 2001.
99. Munn, *Kirk Douglas*, pp. 84–5.
100. *Metro Weekly*, August 22, 2002.
101. Malone, *Sacred Profanity*, pp. 21–3.
102. *Empire*, December 2001.
103. Douglas, *The Ragman's Son*, p. 332.
104. Curtis, *The Autobiography*, p. 181.
105. Ustinov, *Dear Me*, p. 274.

Chapter 11

1. *The Dick Cavett Show*, ABC, June 8, 1972.
2. Leigh, *There Really Was a Hollywood*, p. 261.
3. Ibid., p. 263.
4. Ibid., pp. 262–5.
5. John Russell Taylor, *Hitch* (London: Faber, 1978), p. 237.
6. Curtis, *The Autobiography*, p. 196.
7. Grove, *Scream Queen*, pp. 15–16.
8. Peter Keough, ed., *Flesh and Blood: The National Society of Film Critics on Sex, Violence and Censorship* (San Francisco: Mercury House, 1995), pp. 297–8.
9. David Thomson, *The Moment of Psycho* (New York: Basic Books, 2009), p. 24.
10. Charlotte Chandler, *It's Only a Movie: A Personal Biography of Alfred Hitchcock* (London: Simon and Schuster, 2005), p. 312.
11. Leigh, *There Really Was a Hollywood*, p. 279.
12. Ibid. p. 279.
13. *Cosmopolitan*, February 1961.
14. Robert Crichton, *The Great Imposter* (London: Pan, 1963), p. 220.
15. Ibid., p. 18.
16. Ibid., p. 219.
17. Hirschhorn, *The Universal Story*, p. 265.
18. Anthony Summers and Robbyn Swan, *Sinatra: The Life* (London: Transworld, 2005), p. 273.
19. Fred Kaplan, *Gore Vidal: A Biography* (London: Bloomsbury, 1999), pp. 479–80.
20. Summers, *Sinatra: The Life*, p. 275.
21. Tosches, *Living High in the Dirty Business of Dreams*, p. 330.
22. Curtis, with Paris, *The Autobiography*, pp. 191–2.
23. Curtis, with Golenbock, *American Prince*, p. 226.
24. George Jacobs and William Stadiem, *The Last Word on Frank Sinatra* (London: Macmillan, 2004), p. 118.
25. Curtis, with Golenbock, *American Prince*, p. 219.
26. Hirschhorn, *The Universal Story*, p. 269.
27. *Photoplay*, May 1955.
28. *There Really Was a Hollywood*, p. 283.
29. Grove, *Scream Queen*, p. 18.
30. Leigh, *There Really Was a Hollywood*, p. 281.
31. Brynner, *Yul*, p. 147.
32. Ibid., pp. 147–8.
33. Ibid., p. 148.
34. Curtis, *Ich und Mein Vater*, p. 20.
35. Hunter, *The Man and His Movies*, p. 93.
36. Parish and Stanke, *The Swashbucklers*, p. 613.
37. Brynner, *Yul*, pp. 148–9.
38. *L.A. Times*, January 5, 1962.
39. Ibid.
40. Ibid.
41. Curtis, with Golenbock, *American Prince*, p. 235.
42. *Daily Sketch*, July 4, 1962.
43. *Photoplay*, June 1962.
44. Leigh, *There Really Was a Hollywood*, p. 295.
45. Ibid., p. 296.
46. Ibid.
47. Ibid., pp. 296–7.
48. *The Mail*, April 18, 2008.
49. *The Guardian*, April 18, 2008.
50. *News of the World*, June 8, 1986.
51. Douglas Thompson, *Hollywood People* (London: Pan, 1995), p. 129.
52. Eddie Fisher, with David Fisher, *Been There, Done That* (London: Arrow, 2000), p. 122.
53. *Photoplay*, March 1963.
54. *L.A. Herald Examiner*, October 25, 1962.
55. Curtis, *Ich und Mein Vater*, pp. 201.
56. *Photoplay*, May 1963.
57. *Photoplay*, December 1962.
58. Christine Kaufmann, *Mein Doppelleben* (Gladbach: Bastelubbe, 2005), pp. 63–4.
59. Ibid., pp.70–3.
60. Curtis, *Ich und Mein Vater*, p. 103.
61. *Sunday Times*, March 6, 1994.
62. Curtis, with Paris, *The Autobiography*, pp. 206–7.
63. *Daily Sketch*, July 4, 1962.
64. *Films Review*, January 1979.
65. Grove, *Scream Queen*, p. 20.
66. Farber, *Hollywood Dynasties*, p. 128.
67. *Hello*, October 11, 2010.
68. Curtis, with Golenbock, *American Prince*, p. 299.
69. *Sunday Tribune*, March 20, 1994.
70. *The Mail*, April 18, 2008.
71. *Empire*, December 2001.
72. *Daily Sketch*, July 4, 1962.
73. *Sunday Express*, September 9, 1962.
74. *Chicago Tribune*, June 28, 1964.
75. *Daily News*, May 7, 1963.
76. Miller, *Timebends*, p. 461.
77. Patrick McGilligan, *George Cukor: A Double Life* (London: Faber, 1992), pp. 265–6.
78. Curtis, with Paris, *The Autobiography*, p. 220.
79. Curtis, with Golenbock, *American Prince*, p. 241.
80. Shaun Levy, *Paul Newman: A Life* (London: Aurum, 2009), 1993.

83. Ibid. He did, though, appearing as a Mexican bandit in *The Outrage* opposite Laurence Harvey a few years later.
84. Daniel O'Brien, *Paul Newman* (London: Faber and Faber, 2004), p. 112.
85. *Hollywood Reporter*, June 14, 1961.
86. *Newsweek*, February 27, 1961.
87. Ibid.
88. Hugh Hefner Papers, June 6, 1991.
89. Steven Watts, *Mr. Playboy: Hugh Hefner and the American Dream* (Somerset, NJ: John Wiley and Sons, 2008), p. 164.
90. *L.A. Mirror*, May 1, 1961.
91. John Austin, *Hollywood's Babylon Women* (New York: SPI Books, 1994), p. 7.
92. Zolotow, *Billy Wilder in Hollywood*, p. 272.
93. Curtis, with Vieira, *Me, Marilyn and the Movie*, pp. 216–7.
94. *Vanity Fair*, November 2008.
95. Parkinson, *Parky's People*, p. 55.
96. Berlin, *Toxic Fame*, p. 24.
97. Chandler, *Nobody's Perfect*, p. 219.
98. Leigh, *There Really Was a Hollywood*, p. 294.
99. Janet Leigh, *House of Destiny* (Don Mills Ontario: Mira, 1995), p. 429.
100. Ibid., pp. 473–5.
101. Kaufmann, *Mein Doppeleben*, p. 83. It's interesting that Curtis is watching JFK's funeral in *The Boston Strangler* when we first see him.
102. Summers, *Sinatra: The Life*, p. 293.
103. Sinatra with Holden, *Lady Blue Eyes*, p. 84.
104. Grove, *Scream Queen*, p. 21.
105. Boorman and Donohue, *The Director's Cut*, p. 80.

Chapter 12

1. Alexander Walker, *Sex in the Movies* (Middlesex: Penguin, 1966), pp. 236–7.
2. Curtis, *Ich und Mein Vater*, p. 22.
3. Molly Haskell, *From Reverence to Rape: The Treatment of Women in the Movies* (Chicago: University of Chicago Press), p. 300.
4. Barry Paris, *Audrey Hepburn* (London: Orion, 1998), pp. 91–2.
5. Donald Spoto, *Enchantment: The Life of Audrey Hepburn* (London: Arrow, 2007), p. 172.
6. Ibid., p. 173.
7. *American Movie Classics Magazine*, August 1998.
8. Curtis, with Paris, *The Autobiography*, pp. 209–10.
9. Michael Seth Starr, *Bobby Darin: A Life* (MD: Taylor Trade Publishing, 2004), pp. 124–5.
10. Ibid., p. 140.
11. *Milwaukee Journal*, March 31, 1963.
12. Ibid.
13. William R. Meyer, *Warner Brothers Directors* (New York: Arlington House, 1978), p. 198.
14. McGilligan, *George Cukor: A Double Life*, p. 266.
15. Walker, *Sex in the Movies*, p. 249.
16. Reynolds, with Columbia, *My Life*, pp. 265–6.
17. Emanuel Levy, *Vincente Minnelli: Hollywood's Dark Dreamer* (New York: St. Martin's Press, 2009), pp. 349–50.
18. Ibid., pp. 350–1.
19. Ibid., p. 352.
20. Elaine Tyler Mae, *Homeward Bound* (New York: Basic Books, 2008), p. 99.
21. Maureen Dowd, *Are Men Necessary?* (New York: Berkeley Books, 2005), p. 170.
22. Jennifer Scanlon, *Bad Girls Go Everywhere: The Life of Helen Gurley Brown* (New York: Oxford University Press, 2009), xii.
23. Helen Gurley Brown, *Sex and the Single Girl* (New York: Bernard A. Geis, 1962), p. 237.
24. Ibid., p. 25.
25. Kenneth C. Davis, *Two-Bit Culture: The Paperbacking of America* (Boston: Houghton Mifflin, 1984), p. 242.
26. Betsy Israel, *Bachelor Girl* (London: Aurum, 2003), p. 181.
27. Brown, *Sex and the Single Girl*, p. 7.
28. Ibid.
29. *New Yorker*, February 29, 1964.
30. *Miami Herald*, February 3, 1966.
31. Scanlon, *Bad Girls Go Everywhere*, p. 113.
32. Tracy Daugherty, *Just One Catch: A Biography of Joseph Heller* (New York: St. Martin's Press, 2011), p. 268.
33. Lambert, *Natalie Wood: A Life*, p. 202.
34. Scanlon, *Bad Girls Go Everywhere*, p. 113.
35. Daugherty, *Just One Catch*, p. 269.
36. Walker, *Sex in the Movies*, p. 240.
37. Ibid.
38. Michael Kerbel, *Fonda* (New York: Pyramid Publications, 1975), p. 114.
39. Johns, *Hollywood Celebrity Playground*, p. 294.
40. Lambert, *Natalie Wood: A Life*, p. 202.
41. Robert Sellers, *Bad Boy Drive* (London: Preface Books, 2009), p. 69.
42. *New York Times*, December 26, 1964.
43. Lambert, *Natalie Wood: A Life*, p. 202.
44. *L.A. Herald Examiner*, February 29, 1964.
45. Nash, *Baby, Let's Play House*, p. 211.
46. Brown and Broeske, *Down at the End of Lonely Street*, p. 300.
47. *Coronet*, April 1964.
48. Ibid.
49. Ibid.
50. Kaufmann, *Mein Doppeleben*, p. 89.
51. Ibid., p. 93.
52. Interview, 1991.
53. Bruck, *When Hollywood Had a King*, p. 79.
54. Irving Lazar, with Annette Tapert, *Swifty: My Life and Good Times* (New York: Simon and Schuster, 1995), p. 7.
55. Ibid., p. 13.
56. Lambert, *Natalie Wood: A Life*, pp. 209–10.
57. Lana Wood, *Natalie* (New York: Dell, 1984), pp. 112–3.
58. Curtis, with Paris, *The Autobiography*, pp. 251–2.
59. Lambert, *Natalie Wood: A Life*, pp. 215–9.
60. Parish and Stanke, *The Swashbucklers*, p. 619.
61. Curtis, with Golenbock, *American Prince*, pp. 252–4.
62. Peter Falk, *Just One More Thing* (London: Hutchinson, 2006), p. 108.
63. Ibid., p. 109.
64. Widener, *Lemmon: A Biography*, p. 208.
65. Richard Stirling, *Julie Andrews: An Intimate Biography* (London: Portrait, 2007), p. 175.
66. Freedland, *Some Like It Cool*, p. 111.
67. *Hollywood Citizen News*, June 12, 1965.
68. Ibid.
69. Curtis, with Golenbock, *American Prince*, p. 256.
70. Diane Waldman, *Joseph Cornell: Master of Dreams* (New York: Harry N. Abrams, 2002), p. 7.
71. Ibid., p. 17.
72. Curtis, with Paris, *The Autobiography*, p. 300.

73. Waldman, *Joseph Cornell*, p. 8.
74. Ibid., p. 134.
75. *View*, December 1941–January 1942.
76. *Not Born Yesterday*, May 2007.
77. *Sunday Tribune*, March 20, 1994.
78. *Empire*, December 2001.
79. Interview, 1991.
80. *View News*, September 19, 2004.
81. *Esquire*, January 2006.
82. Hunter, *The Man and His Movies*, p. 14.
83. Ibid., p. 16.
84. *New York Times*, October 1, 2010.
85. Curtis, *Ich und Mein Vater*, p. 24.
86. Ibid., p. 31.
87. Ibid., pp. 23–4.
88. Ibid., pp. 20–1.
89. Ibid., p. 30.
90. Kaufmann, *Mein Doppeleben*, p. 99.
91. Shipman, *The Great Movie Stars*, p. 107.
92. Zsa Zsa Gabor, *One Life Is Not Enough* (London: Headline, 1992), pp. 186–7.
93. Ibid., pp. 191–3.
94. *Empire*, April 1994.
95. Patrick McGilligan, *Clint: The Life and Legend* (London: HarperCollins, 1999), p. 144.
96. Kemp, *Lethal Innocence*, p. 222.
97. Banham Reyner, *Los Angeles: The Architecture of Four Ecologies* (London: Allen Lane, 1971), p. 54.
98. Christopher Sandford, *Polanski* (London: Arrow, 2009), p. 133.
99. *Photoplay*. May 1967.
100. *The Mail*, March 31, 2011.
101. *Coronet*, June 1968.

Chapter 13

1. Jonathon Green, *The Dictionary of Contemporary Quotations* (London: Pan, 1980), p. 399.
2. Interview, 1991.
3. Gerold Frank, *The Boston Strangler* (London, Sydney: Pan, 1977), p. 414.
4. *Daily Sketch*, June 27, 1969.
5. Ibid.
6. Hunter, *The Man and His Movies*, p. 16.
7. *L.A. Times*, July 13, 1969.
8. Fleischer, *Just Tell Me When to Cry*, p. 322.
9. *Coronet*, June 1968.
10. Ibid.
11. Frank, *The Boston Strangler*, p. 361.
12. Ibid., p. 398.
13. Ibid., p. 401.
14. Ibid., p. 358.
15. *Sunday Times*, March 6, 1994.
16. Curtis, *Ich und Mein Vater*, p. 34.
17. Kaufmann, *Mein Doppeleben*, p. 107.
18. Howard Teichman, *Fonda: My Life* (New York: Signet, 1982).
19. *Empire*, December 2001.
20. *Game*, December 1975.
21. *Films and Filming*, August 1985.
22. Kerbel, *Henry Fonda*, p. 131.
23. *Evening News*, June 26, 1969. Curtis never got around to making the biopic of Siegel. Barry Levinson directed it in 1991. It was called *Bugsy* and starred Warren Beatty in the title role. Curtis hated it.
24. Ibid.
25. *Game*, December 1975.
26. *L.A. Times*, June 27, 1969.
27. *L.A. Times*, July 13, 1969.
28. Ibid.
29. *Hollywood Citizen News*, October 6, 1969.
30. Parish and Stanke, *The Swashbucklers*, p. 628.

Chapter 14

1. *TV Guide*, November 29, 1975.
2. *The Times*, September 2, 2006.
3. Curtis, *Ich und Mein Vater*, p. 85.
4. Bruck, *When Hollywood Had a King*, p. 113.
5. Lew Grade, *Still Dancing* (Glasgow: Fontana, 1988), pp. 262–3.
6. Ibid., p. 263.
7. Ibid., pp. 263–4.
8. *Hello*, January 23, 2012.
9. *The Observer*, September 6, 1981.
10. Gareth Owen and Oliver Bayan, *Roger Moore: His Films and Career* (London: Robert Hale, 2002), p. 59.
11. Ibid., p. 60.
12. Michael Munn, *The Kid from the Bronx* (London: W.H. Allen, 1984), p. 162.
13. Gerard Masters, *The Book of Dates* (London: Pan, 1990), p. 21.
14. Roger Moore, *My Word Is My Bond* (London: Michael O'Mara, 2008), p. 194.
15. Farber, *Hollywood Dynasties*, p. 128.
16. Munn, *Hollywood Rogues*, pp. 98–9.
17. *L.A. Times*, December 25, 1969.
18. Ibid.
19. *Photoplay*, October 1969.
20. *L.A. Times*, June 1, 1970.
21. Moore, *My Word Is My Bond*, p. 234.
22. Caine, *The Elephant and Hollywood*, pp. 157–8.
23. Owen and Bayan, *Roger Moore: His Films and Career*, p. 61.
24. Ibid., p. 62.
25. Moore, *My Word Is My Bond*, p. 196.
26. Ibid., pp. 198–9.
27. Munn, *Nobody's Perfect*, p. 221.
28. Moore, *My Word Is My Bond*, p. 195.
29. Collins, *Second Act*, pp. 211–2.
30. Ibid., p. 212.
31. The special effects team had used too much gunpowder.
32. Collins, *Second Act*, pp. 213–4.
33. Ibid., p. 214.
34. *Photoplay*, March 1971.
35. Curtis, with Golenbock, *American Prince*, p. 283.
36. Moore, *My Word Is My Bond*, pp. 196–7.
37. Hunter, *The Man and His Movies*, p. 156.
38. Interview, 1991.
39. *Irish Daily Mirror*, October 1, 2010.
40. *The Times*, September 9, 2006.
41. Owen and Bayan, *Roger Moore: His Films and Career*, p. 63.
42. Grade, *Still Dancing*, p. 264.
43. *Photoplay*, March 1971.
44. *The Guardian*, October 1, 2010.
45. *Daily Mail*, October 10, 1970.
46. Ibid.
47. *Evening Standard*, December 17, 1970.
48. Curtis's anti-cinema tirades were obviously attempted rationalizations of his new television "career."
49. *Evening Standard*, December 17, 1970.
50. Ibid.
51. Ibid.
52. Zec, *Some Enchanted Egos*, p. 243.
53. "Some ostrich!" Zec speculated.
54. Zec, *Some Enchanted Egos*, p. 242.
55. Ibid., p. 243.
56. *The People*, August 23, 1970.
57. Ibid.
58. Ibid.
59. Curtis, *Ich und Mein Vater*, p. 50.
60. Ibid., p. 42.
61. Ibid., pp. 42–4.

62. Kaufmann, *Mein Doppeleben*, pp. 131–2.
63. Curtis, *Ich und Mein Vater*, p. 60.
64. Kaufmann, *Mein Doppeleben*, p. 133.
65. Ibid., p. 184.
66. Curtis, *Ich und Mein Vater*, pp. 68–70.
67. Ibid., p. 75.
68. *New Yorker*, June 6, 1973.
69. Boorman and Donohue, *The Director's Cut*, p. 47.
70. *Radio Times*, August 24, 1972.
71. Ibid.
72. Ibid.
73. Ibid.
74. *The Times*, June 25, 1973.
75. *Tube*, May 26, 1980.
76. *Sunday Telegraph*, August 19, 1973.
77. Ibid.
78. Ibid.

Chapter 15

1. *Empire*, December 2001.
2. *Hollywood Reporter*, April 17, 1984.
3. *The Telegraph*, September 30, 2010.
4. *News of the World*, June 8, 1986.
5. *The Times*, September 9, 2006.
6. Hunter, *The Man and His Movies*, p. 18.
7. *The Real Godfathers*, Green Umbrella DVD, 2010.
8. Ibid.
9. *L.A. Herald Examiner*, July 6, 1975.
10. Curtis, with Golenbock, *American Prince*, pp. 285–6.
11. Curtis, with Paris, *The Autobiography*, p. 275.
12. *Sunday Times*, April 4, 2008.
13. Wood, *Ronnie*, p. 166.
14. Ibid.
15. Ibid.
16. *L.A. Herald Examiner*, July 6, 1975.
17. Ibid.
18. Ibid.
19. "You'll find more dingbats among them than actors," he alleged.
20. *L.A. Herald Examiner*, July 6, 1975.
21. Ibid.
22. Ibid.
23. Larry Hagman, *Hello Darlin'* (London: Simon and Schuster, 2009), p. 186.
24. *TV Guide*, November 29, 1975.
25. Ibid.
26. Ibid.
27. Ibid.
28. Curtis, *Ich und Mein Vater*, p. 59.
29. Ibid., p. 47.
30. He once presented her with a garish plastic necklace, which disgusted her.
31. Curtis, *Ich und Mein Vater*, p. 48.
32. Ibid., pp. 49–50.
33. Ibid., p. 51.
34. Dennis McDougal, *Five Easy Decades* (Hoboken, NJ: John Wiley and Sons, 2008), pp. 192–3.
35. Otto Friedrich, *City of Nets* (London: Headline, 1987), pp. 16–17.
36. Kendall Taylor, *Sometimes Madness Is Wisdom* (London: Robson, 2002), p. 324.
37. F. Scott Fitzgerald, *The Last Tycoon* (London: Penguin, 2001), p. 33.
38. John Parker, *Robert de Niro: Portrait of a Legend* (London: John Blake 2009), p. 99.
39. Elia Kazan, *A Life* (New York: Anchor, 1989), pp. 779–80.
40. Curtis, with Golenbock, *American Prince*, p. 288.
41. Curtis, with Paris, *The Autobiography*, p. 250.
42. Parker, *Portrait of a Legend*, p. 100.
43. Ibid., p. 101.
44. Kazan, *A Life*, pp. 768–75.
45. Curtis, with Golenbock, *American Prince*, p. 288.
46. Munn, *Nobody's Perfect*, p. 239.
47. Kazan, *A Life*, p. 778.
48. Ibid., p. 781.
49. Neal Gabler, *An Empire of Their Own: How the Jews Invented Hollywood* (London: W.H. Allen, 1989), p. 221.
50. Barbara and Scott Siegel, *Jack Nicholson* (London: Angus and Robertson, 1990), p. 84.
51. John Baxter, *De Niro: A Biography* (London: HarperCollins, 2003), p. 148.
52. James, *Cultural Amnesia*, pp. 151–2.
53. Fraser-Cavassoni, *Sam Spiegel*, p. 352.

Chapter 16

1. *L.A. Times*, April 3, 1977.
2. *Hollywood Reporter*, May 12, 1978.
3. Ibid.
4. Ibid.
5. *L.A. Times*, April 3, 1977.
6. Hunter, *The Man and His Movies*, p. 154.
7. Ibid.
8. Curtis, *Kid Andrew Cody and Julie Sparrow*, pp. 59–60.
9. Ibid., p. 260.
10. Ibid., p. 286.
11. Ibid., p. 256.
12. On page 168 we actually get the expression "sweet smell of success."
13. Curtis, *Kid Andrew Cody and Julie Sparrow*, p. 284.
14. Ibid., p. 276.
15. Ibid., p. 168.
16. Curtis, with Paris, *The Autobiography*, p. 110.
17. *L.A. Times*, April 3, 1977.
18. *Not Born Yesterday*, May 2007.
19. Munn, *The Kid from the Bronx*, p. 185.
20. Malone, *Sacred Profanity*, p. 280.
21. *Photoplay*, October 1977.
22. Ibid.
23. Charlotte Chandler, *She Always Knew How: A Personal Biography of Mae West* (London: Pocket Books, 2009), p. 259.
24. Maurice Leonard, *Mae West: Empress of Sex* (London: HarperCollins, 1991), p. 390.
25. Ibid.
26. Malone, *Censoring Hollywood*, p. 61.
27. Kashner and Macnair, *The Bad and the Beautiful*, pp. 335–6.
28. *The Late Late Show*, RTE 1, March 19, 1994.
29. Malone, *Censoring Hollywood*, p. 61.
30. Collins, *Second Act*, pp. 221–6.
31. Johns, *Hollywood Celebrity Playground*, p. 253.
32. *L.A. Times*, January 9, 1979.
33. Ibid.
34. Ibid.
35. Ibid.
36. *The Times*, May 22, 1979.
37. Parish and Stanke, *The Swashbucklers*, p. 635.
38. Grove, *Scream Queen*, p. 113.
39. Ibid., p. 16.
40. Farber, *Hollywood Dynasties*, p. 139.
41. Ibid.
42. *Empire*, December 2001.
43. Ibid.
44. *Tube*, May 26, 1980.

Chapter 17

1. Julia Phillips, *You'll Never Eat Lunch in This Town Again* (New York: Random House, 1991), p. 12.
2. *Hugh Hefner: Playboy, Activist and Rebel*, Phase 4 Films, 2010.

3. Hunter, *The Man and His Movies*, pp. 154–5.
4. *L.A. Times*, May 22, 1979.
5. Ibid.
6. Ibid.
7. Peter Bogdanovich, *Killing of the Unicorn* (London: Futura, 1985), p. 163.
8. Pat Hackett, ed., *The Andy Warhol Diaries* (London: Pan, 1992), pp. 363–5.
9. Curtis, *Ich und Mein Vater*, pp. 91–3.
10. Ibid., pp. 92–3.
11. Ibid., pp. 94–8.
12. Stirling, *Julie Andrews*, p. 267.
13. Allan Hunter, *Walter Matthau* (London: W.H. Allen, 1984), p. 155.
14. Neil Simon, *The Play Goes On: A Memoir* (New York: Touchstone, 2002), pp. 153–4.
15. *Walter Matthau*, pp. 159–60.
16. Lazar, *Swifty: My Life and Good Times*, pp. 196–201.
17. Jacobs and Stadiem, *The Last Word on Frank Sinatra*, p. 21.
18. Simon, *The Play Goes On*, p. 154.
19. Ibid., pp. 154–5.
20. Ibid., p. 155.
21. Ibid.
22. Ibid.
23. Laurie, *Learning to Live Out Loud*, pp. 97–8.
24. Simon, *The Play Goes On*, p. 157.
25. *L.A. Times*, June 3, 1980.
26. Hunter, *Walter Matthau*, p. 168.
27. Wood, *Natalie*, p. 269.
28. Bret, *Elizabeth Taylor*, p. 230.
29. Ibid., pp. 230–1.
30. *L.A. Times*, June 3, 1980.
31. Lansbury, *A Life on Stage and Screen*, p. 207.
32. Curtis, with Golenbock, *American Prince*, p. 302.
33. *Orange County Register*, January 14, 2009.
34. *Sunday Express*, June 29, 1980.
35. Ibid.
36. *U.S.*, February 10, 1986.
37. These were *Criss Cross*, *Trapeze*, *Sweet Smell of Success*, *Vikings*, *Spartacus* and *The List of Adrian Messenger*.
38. Grove, *Scream Queen*, p. 315.
39. Hackett, ed., *The Andy Warhol Diaries*, p. 520.
40. Hunter, *The Man and His Movies*, p. 21.
41. David Thomson, *Rosebud: The Story of Orson Welles* (London: Abacus, 2001), p. 253.
42. Patricia Seaton Lawford, with Ted Schwarz, *Peter Lawford* (London: Futura, 1990), pp. 212–4.
43. Ibid., p. 221.
44. Ibid., pp. 222–4.
45. Thomson, *Rosebud*, p. 412.
46. Lawford, with Schwarz, *Peter Lawford*, p. 223.
47. Peter Conrad, *Orson Welles* (New York: Faber and Faber, 2004), p. 322.
48. Curtis, with Paris, *The Autobiography*, p. 267.
49. Thomson, *Rosebud*, p. 412.
50. Ibid., p. 390.
51. *Orson Welles*, p. 323.
52. James Spada, *Peter Lawford: The Man Who Kept the Secrets* (New York: Bantam, 1992), p. 521.

Chapter 18

1. Norman, *Insignificance: The Book*, p. 123.
2. Ibid., p. 60.
3. *Monthly Film Bulletin*, August 1985.
4. *The Guardian*, August 8, 1985.
5. Norman, *Insignificance: The Book*, p. 55.
6. Time is a strong sub-theme in the film. The Professor's watch, for instance, is stuck at 8:15, the moment the H-bomb went off in Nagasaki.
7. Norman, *Insignificance: The Book*, p. 14.
8. *Monthly Film Bulletin*, August 1985.
9. Neil Sinyard, *The Films of Nicolas Roeg* (London: Charles Lefts and Co., 1991), p. 96.
10. Ibid., pp. 97–9.
11. Interview, 1991.
12. *Time Out*, May 30–June 5, 1985.
13. Norman, *Insignificance: The Book*, p. 22.
14. Ibid., p. 36.
15. *Films and Filming*, August 1985.
16. *TV Times*, April 4, 1987.
17. *Films and Filming*, August 1985.
18. Winters, *Shelley*, p. 294.
19. *The Independent*, October 1, 2010.
20. Ibid.
21. Munn, *Nobody's Perfect*, p. 271.
22. Farber, *Hollywood Dynasties*, p. 138.
23. Curtis, with Golenbock, *American Prince*, pp. 303–5.
24. *Time Out*, March 16–23, 1994.
25. *TV Times*, April 4, 1987.
26. Berlin, *Toxic Fame*, p. 326.
27. McClelland, ed., *StarSpeak*, p. 54.
28. *The Sun*, September 1, 1994.
29. Ibid.
30. *The Telegraph*, September 30, 2010.
31. *The Sun*, September 1, 1994.
32. Ibid.
33. *Radio Times*, April 22–8, 1995.
34. *The Sun*, September 1, 1994.
35. *New York Times*, April 5, 1985.
36. *The Mirror*, August 13, 1985.
37. Ibid.
38. *News of the World*, June 8, 1986.
39. Ibid.
40. Tony Crawley, ed., *Chambers Film Quotes* (Edinburgh: W&R Chambers, 1991), p. 30.
41. *The Times*, December 15, 1986.
42. Eliot, *Cary Grant*, pp. 375–6.
43. Higham, *The Lonely Heart*, p. 334.
44. McClelland, ed., *StarSpeak*, p. 20.
45. *TV Times*, April 4, 1987.
46. Ibid.
47. Douglas, *The Ragman's Son*, p. 443.
48. *The Telegraph*, September 30, 2010.
49. *The Mail*, April 18, 2008.
50. *The Independent*, May 25, 1995.
51. Curtis, *Ich und Mein Vater*, p. 24.
52. Buford, *An American Life*, p. 267.
53. Ibid., pp. 340–1.
54. Curtis, *Ich und Mein Vater*, pp. 172–5.
55. Ibid., 175–7.
56. *The Times*, July 28–August 3, 1990.
57. Ibid.
58. Ibid.
59. Interview, 1991.
60. Ibid.
61. Ibid.
62. Ibid.
63. *The Telegraph*, January 29, 2012 (original interview reprinted on this date).
64. Ibid.
65. This was prescient as he was exactly that age when he died.
66. *The Telegraph*, January 29, 2012.
67. *Daily Mail*, November 28, 1992.
68. Ibid.
69. *Evening Standard*, March 3, 1994.
70. *The Independent*, March 25, 1994.
71. *Daily Telegraph*, March 14, 1994.

72. Ibid.
73. Ibid.

Chapter 19

1. Farber, *Hollywood Dynasties*, p. 138.
2. Munn, *Kirk Douglas*, p. 190.
3. Curtis, with Paris, *The Autobiography*, p. 99.
4. Curtis quoted Billy Wilder on this point in his last book: "Before going to the Actor's Studio [Marilyn] was like a tightrope walker who doesn't know there was a pit she could fall into. After the Strasbergs got to her, she thought of nothing *but* the pit." (*Me, Marilyn and the Movie*, p. 163.)
5. *Son of Ali Baba* is the film containing the line "Yonder lies the valley of my father, the Caliph."
6. The gossip columnist James Bacon once told Curtis he'd slept with Monroe in this house as well. Curtis was alleged to have been incredulous at the revelation. See *Hollywood Is a Four-Letter Town*, p. 126.
7. He finally mentioned this incident in his second autobiography. See *American Prince*, pp. 23–4.
8. Christine Kaufmann disputed this in her autobiography, claiming he didn't always make his child maintenance payments promptly. See *Mein Doppelleben*, p. 117.
9. Barbara Sinatra debunked this view, claiming Martin never recovered from the death of his son Dino in a plane crash in 1987, causing him to close in on himself so much he refused to even talk to anyone, including Frank Sinatra. See *Lady Blue Eyes*, p. 302.
10. He was referring to Irons' 1990 film *Reversal of Fortune*.

Chapter 20

1. Curtis, *The Autobiography*, pp. 308–9.
2. Aubrey Malone, *On the Edge* (Dublin: Solar Publications, 1999), p. 165.
3. *Hello*, October 11, 2010.
4. *Daily Mail*, May 14, 1994.
5. Curtis, *Ich und Mein Vater*, pp. 156–9.
6. Laurence Leamer, *Fantastic: The Life of Arnold Schwarzenegger* (London: Sidgwick and Jackson, 2005), p. 245.
7. *Sunday Times*, March 6, 1994.
8. *Irish Sun*, October 1, 2010.
9. Jarski, *Hollywood Wit*, p. 269.
10. Tamara Starr, ed., *In Her Master's Voice: 5000 Years of Putdowns and Pinups* (London: Penguin, 1991), p. 168.
11. *Sunday Tribune*, March, 20, 1994.
12. *Mail on Sunday*, August 28, 1994.
13. This was his shortest marriage, lasting a mere eighteen months after a gap of nine years from his previous one.
14. Both Curtis and his biographer Michael Munn mistakenly give the year as 1996.
15. *The Times*, April 3, 1999.
16. *Vanity Fair*, 2002.
17. *Empire*, April 1994.
18. Curtis, *Ich und Mein Vater*, p. 197.
19. Ibid., pp. 202–4.
20. Ibid., p. 227.
21. This image was Curtis' idea.
22. *Radio Times*, April 8–22, 1995.
23. Ibid.
24. Ibid.
25. Ibid.
26. As did Monroe, of course.
27. *Radio Times*, April 8–22, 1995.
28. Ibid.
29. Ibid.
30. *Evening Standard*, April 24, 1995.
31. *The Times*, May 16, 1995.
32. *Mail on Sunday*, May 24, 1995.
33. Ibid.
34. Ibid.
35. McDougal, *The Last Mogul*, p. 515.
36. Ibid. p. 311.
37. Leigh, *House of Destiny*, p. 247.
38. Ibid.
39. Ibid., p. 334.
40. Ibid., pp. 353–4.
41. Ibid., p. 507.
42. *Daily Telegraph*, April 16, 1996.
43. Ibid.
44. Collins, *Second Act*, p. 3.
45. *GQ*, April 1996.
46. Ibid.
47. Ibid.
48. Tina Sinatra, with Jeff Coplon, *My Father's Daughter* (New York: Simon and Schuster, 2000), p. 267.
49. Curtis, *Ich und Mein Vater*, pp. 137–8.
50. *L.A. Times*, January 25, 1999.
51. *The Jewish Journal*, October 8–14, 2010.
52. *The Independent*, October 1, 2010.

Chapter 21

1. *Upfront*, November 23, 1998.
2. *The People*, July 5, 1999.
3. *The Jill and Tony Curtis Story*, French Connection Films, 2004.
4. *Cowboys and Indians*, 2008.
5. *The Times*, April 3, 1999.
6. Ibid.
7. *Hollywood Reporter*, February 25, 2000.
8. Ibid.
9. *New Yorker*, June 3, 2002.
10. Ibid.
11. Christina Binkley, *Winner Takes All* (New York: Hyperion, 2008), p. 7.
12. *Empire*, December 2001.
13. Ibid.
14. Curtis, *The Autobiography*, p. 55.
15. *Empire*, December 2001.
16. Ibid.
17. Ibid.
18. *Maxim*, September 2001.
19. Ibid.
20. Ibid.
21. Ibid.
22. This was Curtis's 77th birthday. By another strange coincidence, his first day on the Universal lot had been his birthday as well.
23. McDougal, *The Last Mogul*, p. 205.
24. Ibid., p. 523.
25. *Radio Times*, April 13–19, 2002.
26. Ibid.
27. Ibid.
28. *USA Today*, June 5, 2002.
29. *Vanity Fair*, June 2002.
30. Ibid.
31. Ibid.
32. *New York Times*, October 6, 2002.
33. Ibid.
34. *Parade*, December 15, 2002.
35. Ibid.
36. Janet Leigh, *The Dream Factory* (Don Mills, Ontario: Mira Books, 2002), p. 207.
37. Ibid., p. 118.
38. Ibid., pp. 284–8.
39. *The Times*, September 9, 2006.
40. *The Jill and Tony Curtis Story*.
41. *Photoplay*, March 1955.
42. *The Jill and Tony Curtis Story*.
43. *Vanity Fair*, June 2005.
44. Ibid.
45. *Esquire*, January 2006.
46. Ibid.
47. Ibid.
48. *Architectural Digest*, March 2006.
49. *Film News*, April 2006.
50. *Not Born Yesterday*, May 2007.

51. *The Guardian*, April 18, 2008.
52. *Architectural Digest*, March 2006.
53. *The Mail*, April 18, 2008.
54. Ibid.
55. Ibid.
56. This is probably a reference to Angelina Jolie.
57. *The Mail*, April 18, 2008.
58. *USA Today*, October 14, 2008.
59. Ibid.
60. *L.A. Times*, June 1, 2009.
61. *Las Vegas Review Journal*, July 22, 2009.
62. Ibid.
63. Ibid.
64. *Vanity Fair*, August 2009.
65. *Hartford Courant*, October 1, 2009.
66. Curtis, *Ich und Mein Vater*, p. 86.
67. Ibid., pp. 233–5.
68. Ibid., pp. 14–15.
69. Malone, *Sacred Profanity*, p. 209.
70. *Irish Daily Mirror*, October 1, 2010.
71. Ibid.
72. Ibid.
73. *The Independent*, October 1, 2010.
74. Ibid.
75. *Evening Standard*, September 30, 2010.
76. Mario Reading, *The Movie Companion* (London: Constable and Robinson, 2006), p. 84.
77. *Time Out*, March 16–23, 1994.
78. *The Mail*, March 31, 2011.
79. Ibid.
80. *The Times*, September 9, 2006.
81. BBC News, Entertainment and Arts, August 10, 2011.
82. *Time Out*, March 16–23, 1994.
83. *The Times*, April 3, 1999.

Bibliography

Adler, Tim. *Hollywood and the Mob.* London: Bloomsbury, 2007.

Anger, Kenneth. *Hollywood Babylon.* London: Arrow, 1986.

Bacon, James. *Hollywood Is a Four-Letter Town.* New York: Avon, 1976.

Ballinger, Alexander, and Danny Graydon, eds. *The Rough Guide to Film Noir.* London: Penguin, 2007.

Baltake, Joe. *Jack Lemmon: His Films and Career.* Secaucus, NJ: Citadel, 1977.

Basinger, Jeanine. *The Star Machine.* New York: Vintage, 2009.

Baxter, John. *De Niro.* London: HarperCollins, 2003.

_____. *Stanley Kubrick: A Biography.* London: HarperCollins, 1997.

Bell-Metereau, Rebecca. *Hollywood Androgyny.* New York: Columbia University Press, 1985.

Berlin, Joey, ed. *Toxic Fame.* Detroit: Visible Ink Press, 1996.

Binkley, Christina. *Winner Takes All.* New York: Hyperion, 2008.

Bogdanovich, Peter. *The Killing Unicorn.* London: Futura, 1985.

_____. *Who the Hell's in It?* London: Faber and Faber, 2004.

Boorman, John, and Walter Donohue, eds. *The Director's Cut.* London: Faber and Faber, 2006.

Borkowski, Mark. *The Fame Formula.* London: Sidgwick and Jackson, 2008.

Brady, John. *The Craft of the Screenwriter.* New York: Simon and Schuster, 1981.

Brando, Marlon, with Robert Lindsay. *Songs My Mother Taught Me.* London: Century, 1994.

Bret, David. *Elizabeth Taylor: The Lady, the Lover, the Legend.* Edinburgh: Mainstream, 2011.

Brown, Helen Gurley. *Sex and the Single Girl.* New York: Bernard A. Geis, 1962.

Brown, Peter Harry, and Pat H. Broeske. *Down at the End of Lonely Street.* London: Arrow, 1998.

Bruck, Connie. *When Hollywood Had a King.* New York: Random House, 2004.

Brynner, Rock. *Yul: The Man Who Would Be King.* Glasgow: Fontana, 1990.

Buford, Kate. *Burt Lancaster: An American Life.* London: Aurum, 2000.

Caine, Michael. *The Elephant and Hollywood.* London: Hodder and Stoughton, 2010.

Callow, Simon. *Charles Laughton: A Difficult Actor.* London: Methuen, 1987.

Chandler, Charlotte. *It's Only a Movie: A Personal Biography of Alfred Hitchcock.* London: Simon and Schuster, 2005.

_____. *Nobody's Perfect: A Personal Biography of Billy Wilder.* New York: Simon and Schuster, 2002.

_____. *She Always Knew How: A Personal Biography of Mae West.* London: Pocket Books, 2009.

Churchill, Sarah. *The Many Lives of Marilyn Monroe.* London: Granta, 2004.

Clayton, Marie. *Marilyn Monroe: Unseen Archives.* London: Parragon, 2005.

Collins, Joan. *Second Act.* London: Boxtree, 1996.

Conrad, Peter. *Orson Welles.* New York: Faber and Faber, 2004.

Considine, Shaun. *Mad as Hell: The Life and Work of Paddy Chayefsky.* Lincoln, NE: IUniverse, 2000.

Crawley, Tony, ed. *Chambers Film Quotes.* Edinburgh: W&R Chambers, 1991.

Crichton, Robert. *The Great Imposter.* London: Pan, 1963.

Cross, Robert, and John Marriott. *The World's Greatest Hollywood Scandals.* London: Hamlyn, 1989.

Crowe, Cameron. *Conversations with Wilder.* London: Faber, 1999.

Curtis, Allegra. *Ich Und Mein Vater.* Munich: Langen Muller, 2011.

Curtis, Tony. *Kid Andrew Cody and Julie Sparrow.* London: W.H. Allen, 1977.

_____, with Peter Golenbock. *American Prince.* London: Virgin, 2008.

_____, with Barry Paris. *The Autobiography.* London: Heinemann, 1994.

_____, with Mark A. Vieira. *Some Like It Hot: Me, Marilyn and the Movie.* London: Virgin, 2009.

Daugherty, Tracy. *Just One Catch.* New York: St. Martin's Press, 2011.

Davis, Kenneth C. *Two-Bit Culture: The Paperbacking of America.* Boston: Houghton Mifflin, 1984.

Davis, Ronald L. *The Glamour Factory: Inside Hollywood's Big Studio System.* Dallas: Southern Methodist University Press, 1993.

Davis, Sammy Jr., with Burt Boyar. *Why Me?* London: Sphere, 1991.

Didion, Joan. *The White Album.* New York: Farrar, Strauss and Giroux, 2009.

Doctorow, E.L. *Ragtime.* New York: Penguin, 1996.

Douglas, Kirk. *The Ragman's Son: An Autobiography.* London: Simon and Schuster, 1988.

Dowdy, Andrew. *Films of the Fifties.* New York: William Morrow and Co., 1975.

Eastman, John. *Retakes: Behind the Scenes of 500 Classic Movies.* New York: Ballantine Books, 1989.

Edgerton, Gary. *American Film Exhibition and an Analysis of the Motion Picture Industry's Market Structure, 1963–1980.* London: Garland Publishing, 1983.

Eliot, Marc. *Cary Grant: A Biography.* New York: Harmony, 2004.

Eszterhas, Joe. *The Devil's Guide to Hollywood.* London: Duckworth Overlook, 2007.

Evans, Robert. *The Kid Stays in the Picture.* London: Aurum, 1994.

Falk, Peter. *Just One More Thing.* London: Hutchinson, 2006.

Fisher, Eddie, with David Fisher. *Been There, Done That.* London: Arrow, 2000.

Fishgall, Gary. *Against Type: The Biography of Burt Lancaster.* New York: Scribner, 1995.

Fitzgerald, F. Scott. *The Last Tycoon.* London: Penguin, 2001.

Fleischer, Richard. *Just Tell Me When to Cry.* London: Souvenir, 1994.

Forbes, Bryan, ed. *Actors on Actors.* London: Aurum, 1999.

Frank, Gerold. *The Boston Strangler.* London: Pan, 1977.

Fraser-Cavassoni, Natasha. *Sam Spiegel.* London: Time Warner, 2004.

Freedland, Michael. *Dean Martin: The King of the Road.* London: Robson, 2005.

_____. *Some Like It Cool: The Charmed Life of Jack Lemmon.* London: Robson, 2003.

Friedrich, Otto. *City of Nets.* London: Headline, 1987.

Gabler, Neal. *An Empire of Their Own: How the Jews Invented Hollywood.* London: W.H. Allen, 1989.

Gabor, Zsa Zsa. *One Life Is Not Enough.* London: Headline, 1992.

Gates, Phyllis. *My Husband Rock Hudson.* London: Headline, 1998.

Gow, Gordon. *Hollywood in the Fifties.* New York: A.S. Barnes and Co., 1971.

Grade, Lew. *Still Dancing.* Glasgow: Fontana, 1988.

Grove, David. *Jamie Lee Curtis: Scream Queen.* Albany: Bear Manor Media, 2010.

Hackett, Pat, ed. *The Andy Warhol Diaries.* London: Pan, 1992.

Hadleigh, Boze, ed. *Hollywood Babble On.* NY: Birch Lane Press, 1994.

_____. *Hollywood Bitch.* London: Robson, 1999.

Haney, Lynn. *Gregory Peck: A Charmed Life.* London: Robson, 2003.

Harkness, John. *The Academy Awards Handbook: Who Won What When.* NY: Pinnacle, 1994.

Harris, Mark. *Scenes from a Revolution.* Edinburgh: Canongate, 2009.

Haskell, Molly. *From Reverence to Rape: The Treatment of Women in the Movies.* Chicago: University of Chicago Press, 1987.

Hay, Peter. *Movie Anecdotes.* New York: Oxford University Press, 1990.

Haygood, Will. *In Black and White: The Life of Sammy Davis Jr.* London: Aurum, 2005.

Higham, Charles. *Charles Laughton.* London: W.H. Allen, 1976.

Hirschhorn, Clive. *The Universal Story.* London: Octopus, 1983.

Hofler, Robert. *The Man Who Invented Rock Hudson.* NY: Carroll and Graf, 2005.

Hunter, Allen. *Tony Curtis: The Man and His Movies.* Edinburgh: Paul Harris Publishing, 1985.

_____. *Walter Matthau.* London: W.H. Allen, 1984.

Hunter, Tab, with Eddie Mueller. *Tab Hunter Confidential: The Making of a Movie Star.* Chapel Hill, NC: Algonquin Books, 2005.

Israel, Betsy. *Bachelor Girl.* London: Aurum, 2003.

Izod, John. *Hollywood and the Box Office, 1895–1986.* London: Macmillan, 1988.

Jacobs, George, and William Stadiem. *The Last Word on Frank Sinatra.* London: Pan, 2004.

James, Clive. *Cultural Amnesia: Notes in the Margin of My Time.* London: Picador, 2007.

_____. *Fame in the 20th Century.* London: Penguin, 1993.

Johns, Howard. *Hollywood Celebrity Playground.* Fort Lee, NJ: Barricade Books, 2006.

Jordan, Ted. *Norma Jeane: A Hollywood Love Story.* London: Pan, 1990.

Kalush, William, with Larry Sloman. *The Secret Life of Houdini.* London: Pocket Books, 2007.

Kanfer, Stefan. *Somebody: The Reckless Life and Remarkable Career of Marlon Brando.* London: Faber and Faber, 2008.

Kaplan, Fred. *Gore Vidal: A Biography.* London: Bloomsbury, 1999.

Karney, Robyn. *Cinema Year by Year: 1894–2003*. London: Dorling Kindersley, 2005.

———, ed. *The Movie Stars Story*. London: Octopus, 1984.

Kashner, Sam, and Jennifer Macnair. *The Bad and the Beautiful: A Chronicle of Hollywood in the Fifties*. London: Little Brown, 2002.

Kaufmann, Christine. *Mein Doppelleben*. Gladbach: Bastelubbe, 2005.

Kazan, Elia. *A Life*. New York: Avon, 1989.

Kemp, Philip. *Lethal Innocence: The Cinema of Alexander Mackendrick*. London: Methuen, 1991.

Keough, Peter, ed. *Flesh and Blood: The National Society of Film Critics on Sex, Violence and Censorship*. San Francisco: Mercury House, 1995.

Kerbel, Michael. *Fonda*. New York: Pyramid Publications, 1975.

Kobal, John. *Marilyn Monroe: A Life on Film*. London: Hamlyn, 1974.

Kramer, Stanley, with Thomas M. Coffey. *A Mad, Mad, Mad, Mad World*. London: Aurum, 1997.

Lambert, Gavin. *Natalie Wood: A Life*. London: Faber, 2004.

Lane, Anthony. *Nobody's Perfect: Writings from* The New Yorker. London: Picador, 2004.

Laurie, Piper. *Learning to Live Out Loud*. New York: Crown Archetype, 2011.

Lawford, Patricia Seaton, with Ted Schwarz. *Peter Lawford*. London: Futura, 2009.

Lazar, Irving. *Swifty: My Life and Good Times*. New York: Simon and Schuster, 1995.

Leamer, Laurence. *Fantastic: The Life of Arnold Schwarzenegger*. London: Sidgwick and Jackson, 2005.

Leigh, Janet. *The Dream Factory*. Don Mills, Ontario: Mira, 2002.

———. *House of Destiny*. Don Mills, Ontario: Mira, 1995.

———. *There Really Was a Hollywood*. New York: Jove, 1984.

Leigh, Wendy. *True Grace: The Life and Death of an American Princess*. London: JR Books, 2008.

Leonard, Maurice. *Mae West: Empress of Sex*. London: HarperCollins, 1991.

Levy, Emanuel. *Vincente Minnelli: Hollywood's Dark Dreamer*. New York: St. Martin's Press, 2009.

Levy, Shaun. *Paul Newman: A Life*. London: Aurum, 2009.

Lewis, Jerry, with Herb Gluck. *Jerry Lewis in Person*. New York: Pinnacle Books, 1982.

Lucaire, Edward. *Celebrity Trivia*. New York: Warner, 1980.

Luijters, Guus, ed. *Marilyn Monroe: In Her Own Words*. London: Omnibus Press, 1990.

MacLaine, Shirley. *My Lucky Stars*. New York: Bantam Books, 1996.

Malone, Aubrey. *Censoring Hollywood*. Jefferson, NC: McFarland, 2011.

———. *On the Edge*. Dublin: Solar Publications, 1999.

———. *Sacred Profanity*. Santa Barbara, CA: ABC-CLIO, 2010.

Mann, Michael J. *How to Be a Movie Star*. London: Faber and Faber, 2009.

Manso, Peter. *Brando: The Biography*. New York: Hyperion, 1994.

Martin, Deana, with Wendy Holden. *Memories Are Made of This*. London: Pan, 2005.

Maslon, Laurence. *Some Like It Hot: The Official 50th Anniversary Companion*. London: Pavilion, 2009.

May, Elaine Taylor. *Homeward Bound*. New York: Basic Books, 2008.

McCabe, Bob, ed. *The Rough Guide to Comedy Movies*. London: Rough Guide Reference, 2005.

McCann, Graham. *A Class Apart: A Biography of Cary Grant*. London: Fourth Estate, 1996.

McClelland, Doug, ed. *Forties Film Talk: Oral Histories of Hollywood*. Jefferson, NC: McFarland, 1992.

———. *StarSpeak: Hollywood on Everything*. Boston: Faber and Faber, 1987.

McDougal, Dennis. *The Last Mogul: MCA and the Hidden History of Hollywood*. New York: Crown, 1998.

McGilligan, Patrick. *Clint: The Life and Legend*. London: HarperCollins, 1999.

———. *George Cukor: A Double Life*. London: Faber, 1991.

Meyer, William R. *Warner Brothers Directors*. New York: Arlington House, 1978.

Miller, Arthur. *Timebends: A Life*. London: Methuen, 1988.

Miller, Frank. *Censored Hollywood: Sex, Sin and Violence on Screen*. Atlanta, GA: Turner Publications, 1994.

Moore Roger. *My Word Is My Bond*. London: Michael O'Mara, 2008.

Morecambe, Gary, with Martin Sterling. *In Name Only: A Biography of Cary Grant*. London: Robson, 2001.

Munn, Michael. *Hollywood Rogues*. London: Robson, 1991.

———. *The Kid from the Bronx*. London: W.H. Allen, 1984.

———. *Kirk Douglas*. New York: St. Martin's Press, 1989.

———. *Nobody's Perfect*. London: JR Books, 2011.

Naremore. James. *Acting in the Cinema*. Berkeley: University of California Press, 1988.

Nash, Alanna. *Baby, Let's Play House*. London: Aurum, 2010.

———. *Elvis Aaron Presley: Revelations from the Memphis Mafia*. New York: HarperCollins, 1995.

O'Brien, Daniel. *Paul Newman*. London: Faber and Faber, 2004.
Otash, Fred. *Investigation Hollywood*. Chicago: Regnery, 1976.
Owen, Gareth, with Oliver Bayan. *Roger Moore: His Films and Career*. London: Robert Hale, 2002.
Paris, Barry. *Audrey Hepburn*. London: Orion, 1998.
Parker, John. *Robert De Niro: Birth of a Legend*. London: John Blake, 2009.
Parish, James Robert. *Hollywood's Great Love Teams*. New York: Arlington House, 1974.
_____. *The MGM Stock Company: The Golden Era*. London: W.H. Allen, 1973.
_____, et al. *The Swashbucklers*. New Rochelle, NY: Arlington House, 1976.
Parkinson, Michael. *Parky's People*. London: Hodder and Stoughton, 2011.
Philips, Gene, ed. *Stanley Kubrick: Interviews*. Mississippi: Jackson University Press, 2001.
Pickard, Roy. *The Oscar Movies from A–Z*. Middlesex: Hamlyn, 1982.
Poitier, Sidney. *This Life*. London: Hodder and Stoughton, 1981.
_____. *The Measure of a Man*. London: Simon and Schuster, 2000.
Porter, Darwin. *Brando Unzipped*. Staten Island, NY: Blood Moon Productions, 2005.
Rapaport, Brooke Kanin. *Houdini: Art and Magic*. New Haven, CT: Yale University Press, 2010.
Reading, Mario. *The Movie Companion*. London: Constable and Robinson, 2006.
Reed, Oliver. *Reed: All About Me*. London: W.H. Allen, 1979.
Reynolds, Debbie, with David Patrick Columbia. *My Life*. London: Pan, 1989.
Russo, Vito. *The Celluloid Closet*. New York: Harper and Row, 1987.
Sandford, Christopher. *Polanski*. London: Arrow, 2009.
Santopietro, Tom. *Sinatra in Hollywood*. New York: St. Martin's Press, 2008.
Scanlon, Jennifer. *Bad Girls Go Everywhere: The Life of Helen Gurley Brown*. NY: Oxford University Press, 2009.
Schatz, Thomas. *The Genius of the System: Hollywood Filmmaking in the Studio Era*. London: Faber and Faber, 1998.
Schreck, Nikolas. *The Satanic Screen*. Creation Books, 2000.
Sellers, Robert. *Bad Boy Drive*. London: Preface Books, 2009.
Shipman, David. *Caught in the Act: Sex and Eroticism in the Movies*. London: Elm Tree Books, 1985.
_____. *Great Movie Stars*. London: Angus and Robertson, 1972.
Simon, Neil. *The Play Goes On: A Memoir*. New York: Touchstone, 2002.
Simpson, Paul, ed., *The Rough Guide to Cult Movies*. London: Haymarket Publishing, 2004.
Sinatra, Barbara, with Wendy Holden. *Lady Blue Eyes*. London: Hutchinson, 2011.
Sinatra, Tina. *My Father's Daughter*. New York: Simon and Schuster, 2000.
Sinyard, Neil. *The Films of Richard Lester*. London: Croom Helm, 1985.
_____. *The Films of Nicolas Roeg*. London: Charles Letts and Co., 1991.
Sova, Dawn B. *Forbidden Films*. New York: Checkmark Books, 2001.
Spada, James. *Peter Lawford: The Man Who Kept the Secrets*. New York: Bantam, 1992.
Spoto, Donald. *Enchantment: The Life of Audrey Hepburn*. London: Arrow, 2007.
_____. *Laurence Olivier: A Biography*. New York: HarperCollins, 1993.
Starr, Michael Seth. *Bobby Darin: A Life*. Maryland: Taylor Trade Publishing, 2004.
Starr, Tamara, ed. *In Her Master's Voice: 5000 Years of Putdowns and Pinups*. London: Penguin, 1999.
Steinem, Gloria. *Marilyn: Norma Jeane*. New York: Signet, 1988.
Stirling, Richard. *Julie Andrews: An Intimate Biography*. London: Portrait Books, 2007.
Summers, Anthony, and Robbyn Swan. *Sinatra: The Life*. London: Transworld, 2005.
Taraborelli. Randy J. *The Secret Life of Marilyn Monroe*. London: Sidgwick and Jackson, 2009.
Taylor, John Russell. *Hitch*. London: Faber and Faber, 1978.
Taylor, Kendall. *Sometimes Madness Is Wisdom*. London: Robson, 2002.
Thomson, David. *A Biographical Dictionary of Cinema*. London: Secker and Warburg, 1980.
_____. *Rosebud*. London: Abacus, 2001.
_____. *The Moment of Psycho*. New York: Basic Books, 2009.
Tibballs, Geoff. *First Jobs of the Famous*. London: Sphere, 1991.
Tosches, Nick. *Living High in the Dirty Business of Dreams*. London: Minerva, 1993.
Trow, M.J. *Spartacus: The Myth and the Man*. Gloucestershire: Sutton Publishing, 2006.
Wagner, Robert, with Scott Eyman. *Pieces of My Heart*. London: Hutchinson, 2009.
Waldman, Diane. *Joseph Cornell: Master of Dreams*. New York: Barry N. Abrams, 2002.
Walker, Alexander. *Sex in the Movies*. Middlesex: Penguin, 1966.
Walsh, Frank. *Sin and Censorship: The Catholic Church and the Motion Picture Industry*. New Haven, CT: Yale University Press, 1996.
Watts, Steven. *Mr. Playboy: Hugh Hefner and the*

American Dream. Somerset, NJ: John Wiley and Sons, 2008.

Widener, Don. *Lemmon: A Biography.* London: W.H. Allen, 1977.

Winters, Shelley. *Shelley.* London: Granta, 1980.

_____. *Shelley II: The Middle of My Century.* New York: Pocket Books, 1990.

Wlaschin, Ken. *The World's Great Movie Stars.* London: Salamander Books, 1979.

Wolfe, Donald H. *The Assassination of Marilyn Monroe.* London: Little, Brown, 1998.

Wood, Lana. *Natalie.* New York: Dell, 1984.

Wood, Ronnie. *Ronnie.* London: Macmillan, 2007.

Zec, Donald. *Some Enchanted Egos.* London: Allison and Busby, 1972.

Zolotow, Maurice. *Billy Wilder in Hollywood.* New York: Limelight Editions, 1996.

Index

Page numbers in **_bold italics_** indicate illustrations.

acting, opinion on 29, 91, 93, 115, 152, 156, 215
acting debut 12
addiction, opinion on 173
Adler, Stella 29
affection for father 88
age, opinion on 153, 208, 219
Alberge, Dalya 209
Albert, Eddie 120
alcoholism 202
Al Fayed, Dodi 185, 209, 216
Al Fayed, Mohamed 220
alienation from mother 6, 40, 155, 180
The All-American 46
Allen, Fred 196
Allen, Leslie 140, 147, 174, 200, 205, 217–8; advises Curtis on career 142; birth of Benjamin 154; birth of Nicholas 151; marital problems with Curtis 164; marries Curtis 139; refuses to pay back Doubleday advance 182; splits with Curtis 168, 172–3; travels to London with Curtis 142; treats Allegra badly 157–8; unfaithful to Curtis in Cape Cod 167
Allen, Woody 222
American Cancer Society 146
American Prince 220
Anderson, Michael 122
Andrew, Geoff 35, 89
Andrews, Julie 170
Andrews, Lois 32
Anhalt, Edward 138
Annakin, Ken 141
Anthony Adverse 25, 222
anti-semitism 6, 10, 110
The Apartment 115
appearance 6, 22, 25, 41, 49, 144, 184, 188, 193, 207, 220
Arbuckle, "Fatty" 96
Arden, Eve 80
Arrivaderci Baby! 132
Ashby, Debee 181
Associated Television 145
Astaire, Fred 168
athletic ability 8, 52, 54, 60
audition, first 15
autobiography 187
Averback, Hy 142

awards 215–6, 219
Axelrod, George 121–2

Bacall, Lauren 129–30
background, poverty-stricken 5–7, 19, 28, 39, 47, 92, 129
Bacon, James 83, 87
The Bad News Bears 165
The Bad News Bears Go to Japan 165
Baker, Bob 147, 149
Balboa 173
Baldwin, James 75
Banham, Roger 134
Barbette 80–1
Barrett, Rona 112
The Battleship Potempkin 165
Baxter, John 95, 160
Baywatch 134
Beachhead 46
The Beatles 135
Beatty, Warren 127
"beefcake" 30, 48, 55
begging experiences 8
Bell-Metereau, Rebecca 89
Bellow, Saul 223
Ben-Hur 89, 99
The Best of Everything 123
Betty Ford Clinic 180
The Big Rip-Off 157
billing 6, 162, 74, 107, 129, 221
birth 5
The Black Shield of Falworth 47
The Blacksmith and the Carpenter 220
Blauner, Steve 120
Blumenfeld, Eli 180
Blyth, Ann 19, 20
Boeing Boeing 129
Bogart, Humphrey 9, 127
Bonnano, Margaret Wander 49
The Book of Dates 146
Boone, Pat 121
Boone, Richard 66
Borgnine, Ernest 51, 67–9, 142
Borkowski, Mark 66
Borrows, Bill 215
Borscht circuit 15
The Borscht Circuit 15
Borsten, Joan 166
The Boston Strangler 136–43, **_137_**, 144, 154; cathartic effect of film on Curtis 137; critical neglect of film

140–2; desperation of Curtis for role of strangler 137, 140; identification of Curtis with role 136–7; life as inspiration for role 138; preparation of Curtis for role 136–7; similarities of Curtis to Albert DeSalvo 139; strangler "normalized" by Curtis 140
Boulois, Max 174
Boulting, Ingrid 158–9
box art 129–30, 216
Boyd, Stephen 99
Bradshaw, Peter 65, 89, 150
Brady, Scott 26, 30
Brain Waves 174
Brando, Marlon 22, 25, 40, 48, 136, 193, 195, 197, 199, 223; considered for *Defiant Ones* role 73; as role model for Curtis 125; rooms with Curtis 28; seen by Curtis as epitomizing the "Method" 28–9; wins Oscar 51
Brandt, Robert 111–3, 185, 210
Breakfast at Tiffany's 104
Bridget Goes Hawaiian 134
Britain, opinion on 151
Brodeny, Oscar 27
Bronson, Charles 143
Brown, Helen Gurley 123–4
Brown, Joe E. 82, 90, 217
Bruck, Connie 46
Brynner, Rock 95
Brynner, Yul 95, 107–8
"buddy-buddy" roles 99
Buford, Kate 60
Buono, Victor 45
Burton, Richard 42
Busey, Gary 177
Byrne, Gay 201–2

Cabot, Susan **_34_**
Cagney, James 9, 51
Caine, Michael 87, 147
Calhoun, Rory 48
Callow, Simon 96–8
Cameron, James 205
Canby, Vincent 172
Cannes Film Festival 157
Capone, Al 154
Capote, Truman 168–9
Captain Newman, M.D. 120, 129

247

Cardinale, Claudia 133–4
Carpenter, John 166
cars 25, 102, 114, 132
Casanova 163
Casanova & Co. 163, 212
Cassavetes, John 29, 135
Cat Ballou 67
Catch-22 123
Catto, Max 52
celebrity, opinion on 163
Center of the Web 186
Chagall, Marc 224
Chandler, Charlotte 84, 117
Chandler, Jeff 30, 35, 55, 106
Charisma 3–4, 13, 142, 150, 180, 196, 209, 221
Charisse, Cyd 168
Chase, Jennifer 173
Chasin, George 145
The Chastity Belt 134–5
Chayefsky, Paddy 59
Cheeks, Danyel 206
Cher 135
Cherry Lane Players 15
Chicago Daily Tribune 45
childhood preparation for career 9, 12
child-like nature 120–1, 125, 221–2
Christmas in Connecticut 186
City Across the Water 21–2
Clash by Night 83
Cleopatra 69
Clift, Montgomery 22, 29
Clinton, Hillary 141
Clyde, Vander 80
Cohn, Harry 73
Colliers 58
Collins, Joan 148–9, 165, 210
Collinson, Peter 143
Come Live with Me 130
commendation: for *Some Like It Hot* 89
Confidential 48
Connolly, Ray 150
consideration for others 22, 138, 139
The Continued Adventures of Reptile Man and His Faithful Sidekick Tadpole 208–9
Cooper, Gary 144
Coppola, Francis Ford 144
Corman, Roger 208
Cornell, Joseph 129–31
Cosdan, Joshua 132–3
Cosmopolitan 57
cosmopolitanism 153
The Count of Monte Cristo 157
The Country Girl 47
Crain, Jeanne 30
Crash Dive 12
Crawford, Joan 81, 180
Crawley, Tony 141
Crichton, Michael 102
Criss Cross 19–20, 24, 173, 193
Crist, Judith 196
Cristal, Linda 77
critics, opinion on 21, 75, 77, 139–40, 150, 152, 157, 195
Crosby, Bing 47
Crowe, Cameron 83–5
Crowther, Bosley 56, 108, 120

Cukor, George 114, 121
Curtis, "Anthony" (original screen) **20**, 22, 24
Curtis, Alexandra 117, 139, 158, 184, 185; birth 126; disappointment of Curtis that she's female 126; gives birth to twins 173; rejoins Curtis after Kaufmann loses custody 151; will of Curtis 224
Curtis, Allegra 111, 139, 144, 151, 169, 184–5, 205, 207, 211, 218, 221, 222; birth 132; bonds with Curtis at his London home 152; disapproves of Jill VandenBerg 205; "juggled" between Leslie Allen and Christine Kaufmann 157–8; nude photographs of her circulated 175; poses for *Playboy* 185; prefers "Bernie Schwartz" to Curtis 132; reaction to death of Curtis 222
Curtis, Benjamin 154, 167, 184, 185, 224
Curtis, Jamie Lee 72, 107, 152, 153, 180–2, 185, 190, 191, 205; birth 88; cannabis arrest 146; childhood memories of Curtis 113; death of Curtis 222; drugtaking experiences with Curtis 174; first meeting of Curtis with Janet Leigh 26; "ghost" parenthood of Curtis 113; horror movie career 166; reconciliation with Curtis 185, 190, 224; supports Curtis when he collapses 179; will of Curtis 224
Curtis, Jill *see* Vandenberg, Jill
Curtis, Kelly 50–1, 88, 106, 107, 111, 153, 169, 186–7, 224
Curtis, Nicholas 167, 185–6, 204–5; birth 151; death 186, 204; funeral 205
Curtis, Raphael 218
custody of children 139, 151, 185

Daily Telegraph 188
Dallas 173
D'Amato, "Skinny" 220
Darin, Bobby 120–1, 129
Dassim, Jules 94
Daves, Delmer 71
David, Saul 123
David and Fatima 220
Davies, Jack 141
Davis, Sammy, Jr. 66, 72–3, 190, 214
deafness 215, 216
Dean, James 22, 25, 29, 223
Dear Ruth 15
death 222; of father 88; Julius 10–11; of mother 155
Death of a Centerfold 169
De Carlo, Yvonne 19–21, 36, 193
decline 119, 136, 140, 149–50, 208
defensiveness 158
The Defiant Ones 3, 72–7, **76**, 99, 125
Demara, Ferdinand Waldo 102
De Niro, Robert 144, 158–60; friction with Curtis 159–60
Derek, John 30
DeSalvo, Albert 136, 138–41, 154–5

desperation 179
Destination Tokyo 12, 191
Deutsch, Lisa 187, 190, 200, 205, 206; drinking problem 204; engaged to Curtis 187; marriage problems with Curtis 204–6; worries about age gap 187
The Devil's Disciple 65
De Vito, Danny 188, 193
Diamond, Izzy 83
Diana, Princess 216
Dickinson, Angie 120
Dietrich, Marlene 54
Di Maggio, Joe 79, 83, 177
Divorces: Christine Kaufmann 139; Leslie Allen 174; Lisa Deutsch 206; Janet Leigh 112
Dr. Jekyll and Mr. Hyde 14
Doctorow, E.L. 45
Donahue, Troy 119
Don't Make Waves 133–4
Dostoevsky, Fyodor 221
Doubleday 164, 174, 182, 210
Dougherty, Jim 83
Douglas, Kirk 24, 29, 72, 72, **97**, 121, 190, 210, 223; controlling personality 69; as costar 68–9, 95; insults Curtis 22; and *Spartacus* 94–100; and *Tough Guys* 173; and *The Vikings* 67–9
Dowdy, Andrew 18, 48
Dracula 99
The Dream Factory 217
dreams, opinion on 202
Dreiser, Theodore 30
dress sense 98–9, 129, 133, 147
Drew, Lisa 182
Drop Dead, Darling 132
Dru, Joanne 46
drug-taking 139, 144, 146, 154, 156–7, 165, 168–9, 173–4, 179, 181–2, 188, 189, 202, 217
Dullea, Keir 174
Duncan, Andrew 207–8
Durbin, Deanna 18
Duvall, Robert 120
Dylan, Bob 112
Dynasty 173

"Eastern" films 30–6
Eastwood, Clint 133
Ebbins, Milt 194
eccentricity 154, 211–2
education 6, 13
Edwards, Blake 56; clumsiness of 77; *The Great Race* 127–8; *Operation Petticoat* 90; rejects Curtis for *Breakfast at Tiffany's* 104–5
Edwards, Megan 221
Einstein, Albert 135, 177, 179, 216
Eliot, Marc 92
Ellis, Bret Easton 162
Elmer Gantry 102
Emil, Michael 177
emotional nature 152, 205
Empire magazine 215, 219
Empire Players 15
Enright, Ray 25
Errigo, Angie 78, 80

The Evening Standard 64, 223
eviction from home 7
Ewing, J.R. 173
extravagance 19, 25, 27, 39, 102, 106–7, 129, 210

fabricated events 10–11, 15, 54, 83, 104, 114–5, 141, 148–9
Fairbanks, Douglas 37, 67
Falco, Sidney: as generic term 65
Falk, Peter 127
fame, opinion on 40, 49, 121, 144
fan mail 20, 22, 30, 37, 41, 92, 193
Fanfaren der Liebe 127
fantasies 9
Farrow, Mia 135, 222
Fast, Howard 94, 95
father figures 72, 216
fear of flying 53–4, 68, 107–9, 146
fear of girls 14–15
Feiffer, Jules 90
Fellini, Federico 163
Films and Filming 70
Finnegans Wake 162
Finnigan, Joseph 120
first kiss 14
Fisher, Eddie 39, 110–1
A Fistful of Dollars 133
Fitzgerald, F. Scott 158
Fitzgerald, Zelda 158
Fleischer, Richard 68–9, 136–8, 140
Flesh and Fury 40–1
The Flintstones 222
flirting in old age 208, 209
Flynn, Errol 9, 23, 50
The Fog 166
Fonda, Henry 140, 144
Forbidden 46
Ford, Glenn 195
Forty Pounds of Trouble 119, 169–70
Fosse, Bob 49–50
Fox, Michael J. 192
Francis 23
Franciscus, James 105
Frank, Gerald 136, 138
Freedland, Michael 150
Freeman, Mona 41
Friess, Steve 220
Frym, Marco 49
Fuller, Graham 185
funeral 222–3
A Funny Thing Happened on the Way to the Forum 134

Gable, Clark 48, 51, 168
Gabor, Zsa Zsa 132–3
gang membership 9–10
Gardner, Ava 35
Garfield, John 29
Garland, Judy 144
Gates, Phyllis 17–18, 48
Gavin, John 101–2
gay rumors 48
Georgianne (daughter of Cher) 135
Gessner, Nicholas 166
GI Bill of Rights 14
Giancana, Sam 179
Gideon, Norma 111
Gigi 75

Gillard, David 153
Gilmore, Gary 155
Girdler, William 164
The Gladiators 95
Goddard, Paulette 29
The Godfather 155
The Golden Arrow 35
Golden Boy 15
Goldstein, Bob 15, 16, 18, 19, 25
Goldstein, Leonard 32
Gone with the Wind 158
Goodbye Charlie 121–2
Gordon, Michael 22
Gossett, Louis, Jr. 165
gossip columnists, opinion on 112, 157, 195
Gow, Gordon 44–5, 75
Grable, Betty 30
Grade, Lew 145, 147, 149
The Graduate 134
Graham, Sheilah 158
Granarte 92
grandfather 173
Grant, Cary 9, 12, 29, 41, 51, 89, *91*, 119, 191, 197, 216; costars with Curtis in *Operation Petticoat* 90–2; Curtis' fascination with 9, 13, 90–1; death of 183; impersonated by Curtis in *Some Like It Hot* 84–5; as role model for Curtis 13, 89–92
Grant, Jennifer 90
gratitude 151
The Great Impostor 102, **103**, 192
The Great Race 126–8, **128**, 185
The Greatest Story Ever Told 35
Greenberg, Abe 21, 56
Griffith, Hugh 134
guilt 10–11, 92, 111, 205
Gunga Din 13, 14, 84

Hagman, Larry 157
hair 15, 20, 23, 25–6, 54, 179, 184, 187, 220
Halloween 166
Hampshire, Susan 141
Harris, Julie 81
Harris, Radie 112
Harrison, Robert 48
Harrison, Susan 57, 63–4, 66
Harvey, Laurence 117–8
Have Gun, Will Travel 66
Hayes, Ira 105–6
Haygood, Will 37
Hayworth, Rita 175
heart attack 204, 208
Hecht, Harold 57, 65, 67, 115
Hecht-Hill-Lancaster 52, 58, 60, 67
Hefner, Hugh 102, 115–6, 123, 152, 158, 168, 172–3, 195
height 192
Heller, Joseph 123–4
Hemingway, Ernest 117
Hendrix, Wanda 24–5
Hepburn, Audrey 119–20
Hepburn, Katharine 161
The Herald-Examiner 15
Heston, Charlton 99
Hewitt, Chris 215
Higham, Charles 92

Hill, James 52, 59, 63
Hitchcock, Alfred 101–2
Hitler, Adolf 10, 86, 133, 192, 195, 223
Hoffman, Dustin 144, 194
Hoffman, Irving 57, 59
Hoffman, Joseph 124
Holden, William 47, 119–20
Hollywood: arrival in 17; debut 19–21
Hollywood Citizen-News 129
The Hollywood Reporter 214
homosexuality, opinion on 48, 99
Honigsbaum, Mark 75
Hope, Bob 78, 146
Hopper, Hedda 12, 33, 48, 50, 67, 100, 195
horses, opinion on 218
Houdini 42–5, **43**, **44**, 130, 221
Houdini, Harry 42, 45
house moves 5, 50, 67, 132, 151, 182, 214
House of Destiny 117, 210, 217
How to Make Love and Like It 124
How to Murder Your Wife 132
Howe, James Wong 59, 61–2
HUAC (House Un-American Activities Committee) 59, 94
Hudson, Rock 23, 48, 55, 119, 172, 195
Hughes, Ken 165
humility 131, 138–9, 150–1, 173, 224
Hunter, Allan 170
Hunter, Tab 23, 35, 41, 119
Hutner, Herbert 132–3
Hutton, Robert 149
Hyams, Joe 90
Hyer, Martha 56

I Ought to Be in Pictures 170–1
I Was a Shoplifter 23
identity, opinion on 207
identity change as actor 191–2
image 41, 69, 110, 117; opinion on 207; trendy 135, 157
improvisational ability 148
infidelity 47, 50, 53–4, 56–7, 109, 127, 135, 139
in-law tensions 33, 40, 112
Inmates: A Love Story 174
insecurity 24, 49, 75, 115, 121, 136, 220, 223
Insignificance 177–9, 186, 223
investments 92, 152, 157
IQ Club 146
Irons, Jeremy 201–2
It Rained All Night the Day I Left 165–6
Izod, John 18

Jacobs, George 170
Jaffe, Rona 123
Jagger, Mick 169
James, Clive 25, 53, 160; on articulation of Curtis 35; on charm of Curtis 13; compares Alexander Mackendrick to Max Ophuls 62; praises Curtis for *Some Like It Hot* 89; praises Curtis for *Sweet Smell of Success* 65

Johnny Dark 46
Johnny Stool Pigeon 22–3
Johns, Howard 165
Johnson, Sam 94
Johnson, Terry 177
Jolie, Angelina 37
Jones, Shirley 102
Jones Memorial Settlement House 12
Jordan, Ted 84
Judaism, opinion on 166
Julien, Darren 224
juvenile delinquent roles 22, 48

Kanaly, Sam 173
Kanin, Garson 93
Kansas Raiders 24, 26
Karney Robyn 89, 133
Kashner, Sam 60, 61
Kaufmann, Christine 107–9, **108**, 113–4, 117, 119, 120, **122**, 127, 129, 142, 158, 207, 213; age difference to Curtis 111; alimony 139; attitude to marriage 112; birth of Alexandra 126; birth of Allegra 132; childhood 112; custody of children 139, 151–2; divorces Curtis 139; on drug use of Curtis 169; marital problems with Curtis 131–2, 135; marries Curtis 112; mother's disapproval of Curtis 112; nude photographs of Allegra 175; parenting problems 151–2; will of Curtis 224
Kaufmann, Gunther 126
Kaye, Danny 78, 98, 220
Kazan, Barbara 159
Kazan, Elia 28, 158–60
Keith, Brian 142
Kellerman, Sally **137**, 165
Kelly, Grace 47, 80
Kemp, Philip 59, 62, 65–6, 133–4
Kennedy, Eunica 104
Kennedy, Joe 104
Kennedy, John F. 72, 102–4, 116–7, 196, 210, 217; assassination of 117, 193; congratulates Curtis on *The Great Impostor* 104
Kerbel, Michael 141
Kerkorian, Kirk 213, 214
Kerr, Deborah 111
Key Witness 66
Kid Andrew Cody and Julie Sparrow 161–3, 164, 182
The Killing Frost 52
Kilroy, Gene 222
King, Larry 214
King Creole 125, 136
Kings Go Forth 70, **71**, 124
Kinsey, Alfred 123
Kovacs, Ernie 117
Kramer, Stanley 72–5, 76
Kubrick, Stanley 95–6, 99–100, 122

The Lady Gambles 22, 200
Lady L 114, 121
The Ladykillers 59
Lamarr, Hedy 129–30
Lambert, Gavin 70, 124, 127
Lancaster, Burt 19, 24, 35, 51, **55**, **61**, 99, 121, 134, 144, 190, 193, 198, 200, 211, 216, 217, 223; as costar 52–66; friendship with Curtis 53–4; practical jokes played on Curtis 53–4; praised by Curtis 55; similarities to Curtis 53; suffers stroke 184; and *Sweet Smell of Success* 58–66; and *Tough Guys* 173; and *Trapeze* 52–7
Lang, Fritz 83
Langdon, Ann **103**
Lange, Hope 195
Langella, Frank 99
Lansbury, Angela 49
Lanza, Mario 192
Las Vegas, opinion on 214–5
The Last Tycoon 158–60, 161, 172
The Late Late Show 201
Laughton, Charles 95–8
Laurie, Piper 30–6, **34**, 39, 41, 108, 148; meets Curtis for first time 18; promotional tour with Curtis 32; refusal of Curtis to see her 171; relationship with Curtis 30–6; rows with Curtis 33–4; studio pressure to marry Curtis 33
Lawford, Peter 72, 116, 175, 194
Lazar, Irving "Swifty" 126–7, 133, 161, 170, 197, 210
Lederer, Charles 47
Legion of Decency 89, 95
Lehman, Ernest 58–9
Leigh, Janet 17, 24, 30–3, 35, **38**, 39–51, 56–7, 67–9, 72–3, 84, 90, 93, 104, 106–7, 109–11, 112, 117–8, 142, 153, 166, 171, 185, 195, 209–10, 213, 217; birth of Jamie Lee 88; birth of Kelly 50–1; Bob Fosse involvement 49–50; car accident 72; child custody arrangements 151; clumsiness 77; and Curtleigh 56; dates Curtis 26–7; death of Ernie Kovacs 117; in denial about affair between Curtis and Christine Kaufmann 109; on divorce 109, 112; drinking problems 102; engagement to Curtis 31; first film with Curtis 42; first impressions of Curtis 26; first marriage 26; fussiness 37; "Golden Couple" status 37–9; and *Houdini* 42–5; "improves" Curtis 39; inspiration for Curtis in *Some Like It Hot* 80; and *The Manchurian Candidate* 117–8; marital tension with Curtis 50, 102, 107; on marriage in general 48, 102; marriage perceived as career move 113; marries Curtis 33; miscarries child 46; money worries 40; as novelist 217; pregnant with Jamie Lee 67, 72; pregnant with Kelly 50; and *Psycho* 101–2; reconciliation with Curtis 182; and *Safari* 52; second marriage 26; separation anxiety 45–6, 52, 56–7, 139–40; submission under Curtis 37, 39, 42, 52, 67, 102; suicide attempt alleged by Curtis 109; suicide of father 106; and *The Vikings* 67–9; worries about safety of Curtis 42, 53
Leigh, Vivien 73, 96
Leigh, Wendy 47
Lemmon, Jack 84, 99, 129, 132, 185, 194, 196, 217; and *The Great Race* 127; Oscar nomination 89; as transvestite for *Some Like It Hot* 78–82
Leone, Sergio 133
Lepke (film) 154–5, 156, 188
Lepke, Louis 154–5
Let's Make Love 90
Levee, John 56
Lewis, Jerry 40; annoys Curtis in *Boeing Boeing* 129; card-playing with Curtis 42; disapproves of Curtis marrying Janet Leigh 32–3; makes home movies with Curtis 50
Lewis, Richard 72
Life magazine 48, 123
Lincoln, Abraham 83
Lisi, Virna 83
The List of Adrian Messenger 121
Little Miss Marker 119, 169–70
Lloyd's (insurance firm) 41, 92
Lobster Man from Mars 184
Loew, Arthur 26
Lollobrigida, Gina **55**, 64; costars with Curtis in *Trapeze* 52–4; friction with Burt Lancaster 53; tension with George Cukor 114
London, George 42
London base 146, 151
The Long Day's Dying 143
Loren, Sophia 114
Los Angeles Times 166
Louis and Frank 211
love, opinion on 206
Love Is a Survivor 219
Lovell, Curt 221
Lynley, Carol 173
Lynn, Vivienne 182

Ma and Pa Kettle 18
MacArthur, Gen Douglas 13
Mackendrick, Alexander 59–66, 133–4, 223
MacLaine, Shirley 71, 214
Mae, Elaine Tyler 123
Mafia Princess 179
The Mail 220
The Mail on Sunday 209
male chauvinism 39, 42, 126, 129, 151, 206, 208, 210, 211, 214
The Manchurian Candidate 117–8
The Manitou 163
Mankiewicz, Joseph 88
Mann, Anthony 95
Mann, Roderick 65, 172
Manoff, Dinah 170–2
Manson, Charles 135
March, Frederic 45
marriage, opinion on 31, 39, 113–4, 205
Marshall, Brenda 119
Martin, Dean 36, 50, 71, 93, 200
Martin, Deana 36

Martin, Ricky 139
Marty 51
Marvin, Lee 67
Marx, Karl 135
Marx Brothers 40
M*A*S*H 134
Maslon, Laurence 78
Maté, Rudolph 30, 46, 47
Matisse, Henri 130, 131
Matthau, Walter 14, 121, 144, 170
Maugham, Somerset 161
Maxim magazine 215
Mayer, Louis B. 104
McBain, Ed 162
McCarthy, Joseph 100, 177, 178
McCartney, Paul 135
McClelland, Doug 22
McCoy 156–7
McHale's Navy 92
McNab, Geoffrey 60, 212, 223
Me, Marilyn and the Movie 84
Meet Danny Wilson 35
The Men 28
Merrill, Dina **91**
Metalious, Grace 123
method acting, opinion on 28–9, 91–2
Meyer, Emile 63
midlife crisis 184
Midnight 183–4
The Midnight Story 56
Milland, Ray 158
Miller, Arthur 78, 83, 89–90, 114
The Million Dollar Face 174
Millstein, Gilbert 155
The Mirror Crack'd 197
The Misfits 218
mobbing 32
money 27, 37, 40, 69–70, 92, 102, 106–7, 114–5, 126, 139, 151
Monroe, Marilyn 39, 79–87, **89**, 135, 149, 152, 156, 164, 165, 168, 177, 179, 186, 192, 196–7, 202, 208, 216, 218, 223, 224; as artistic object 130–1; conspiracy theories about her death 193–4; depression of 79, 89; as diva 81; early relationship with Curtis 19; hysteria 83–4, 89–90; inability to remember lines 81–3; intuition 82; and Jill VandenBerg 217, 218; and *Lady L* 121; maligned by Curtis 82, 86, 156; method aspirations 81, 195; miscarries child 89; murder alleged after death 116; posthumous worship of 116, 196; problems with Arthur Miller 79, 83, 89–90; scattiness 81–2; sexual frustration 19; and *Some Like It Hot* 79–87, 89–90, 194; suicide alleged 194; suicide attempt 90; tantrums 79, 81–3; tensions with Curtis 78–87; unpunctuality 79, 81
Montand, Yves 83
Monte Carlo or Bust 141
Moonlighting 149
Moore, Roger 145–50, **147**, 186, 219
Moorehead, Agnes 121
Moreau, Jeanne 158

Morrison, Fred 106–7
Morrison, Helen 106–7
Motion Picture 32
Moviola: The Scarlett O'Hara War 170
Mrs. Doubtfire 194
Muhl, Ed 52
Muir, Kate 89
Mulligan, Robert 93, 102
Munn, Michael 34, 35, 93, 186
murder attempt suggested 120
Murder in Three Acts 179
Muni, Paul 29
Murphy, Audie 24–5
Murphy, Mary 57
Murray, Don 195
music 214
Music Corporation of America (MCA) 23, 46, 88, 145
Musto, Michael 101
My Sister Eileen 49, 217
Myra Breckinridge 164

Nader, George 48
Naked in New York 198
Naremore, James 84
The Nation 94
National Velvet 172
Navy 12–13
nervous breakdown 173
Neumann, Kurt 34
New York Herald Tribune 120
New York Observer 65
New York Times 45, 49, 51, 65, 108, 120, 124, 172
New Yorker 123
Newman, Paul 29, 115, 144, 199
Nicholas Nickleby 172
Nichols, Barbara 60, 63
Nicholson, Jack 149, 158, 160
Nicol, Alex 35
Niven, David 75
Nixon, Richard 104
No Room for the Groom 41
Norman, Barry 150
nostalgia 125
Not with My Wife You Don't 132
Novak, Kim 73, 172
novelist 161–3

O'Brien, Daniel 115
The Observer 64
O'Connor, Donald 23
Odets, Clifford 59–60, 62, 64, 66, 134, 162
O'Hara, Maureen 30
Oliver! 166
Olivier, Laurence 25, 73, 95–100, 131, 196
On My Way to the Crusades I Met a Girl Who... 134
On the Waterfront 51, 197
Once Upon a Time in the West 144
One, Two, Three 87
Operation Petticoat 90–2, **91**
Ophuls, Max 62
Orry-Kelly 81, 86, 89
Oscars 75, 89, 102, 106, 120, 140, 186, 194; nomination for *The Defiant Ones* 75

Ostler, Catherine 209
Oswald, Lee Harvey 193
Otash, Fred 48
Othello—The Black Commando 174
The Outsider 104–6, **105**

Pacino, Al 193
painting 9, 56, 116, 130, 139, 156, 183, 187–8, 189, 219–20
paranoia 18, 25, 139, 200
parenting problems 113, 126, 158, 211, 219, 222
Paris, Barry 35, 187
Paris When It Sizzles 119–20
Parish, James Robert 127
Parker, John 158–9
Parkinson, Michael 223
Parsons, Louella 16, 48, 111, 153, 195
Parsons, Tony 65, 149, 222
Parton, Dolly 221
Patterson, John 220
Peale, Norman Vincent 123
Pearl, Ralph 143
Pearl Harbor, invasion of 12
Peck, Gregory 120, 190
Pepitone, Nina 90
Peppard, George 104
The Perfect Furlough 77
Perkins, Anthony 101
Perlberg, William 116
Persoff, Nehemiah 78
personality 25, 70, 106, 142, 157, 164, 211
The Persuaders 145–50, **147**, 186, 210, 216, 219
Pevney, Joseph 41, 56
Peyton Place 123
Phillips, Julia 162, 168
Photoplay 37, 42, 218
Piaf, Edith 198
Picasso, Pablo 116, 120, 130, 219, 220, 224
Pickford, Mary 37, 67
Picturegoer 70
Pinter, Harold 158–9
Piscator, Erwin 14, 29
Pitt, Brad 37
Pizza with Bullets 219
Plato 184
Playboy 115, 123, 166–7
playboy image 132
Pleasance, Donald 158
Pleshette, Suzanne 119, 142
Plowright, Joan 96
Poitier, Sidney 74–5, **76**, 99
Polanski, Roman 134, 135
possessiveness 26, 139
Power, Tyrone 12–13
Presley, Elvis 23, 66, 93, 163, 195, 201; considered for *The Defiant Ones* 73–4; Curtis' influence on 25, 25; hairstyle of Curtis copied by 25, 34; meets Curtis 125; similarities to Curtis 125–6
Prime Target 186
The Prince and the Showgirl 196
Prince Valiant 35, 46
The Prince Who Was a Thief 17, 28, 30, **31**, 32–3

The Producers 184
Prom Night 166
USS *Proteus* 13
Psycho 101–2, 117, 166, 220
publicity, opinion on 126
The Purple Mask 49, 172

Quine, Richard 47, 119–20

Raft, George 78, 194
Ragtime 45
Raines, Bob 49
Rand, Jess 66
Randolph, Donald **31**
"The Rat Pack" 70–2, 102–3, 214; *see also* Sinatra, Frank
The Rat Race 93–4, **94**
rationalizations 139
Rattigan, Terence 138
The Rawhide Years 49
Reading, Mario 223
Reames, Stan 26
Redford, Robert 144
Redgrave, Lynn 183–4
Reed, Sir Carol 52–4
Reed, Oliver 54, 166
Reed, Rex 49, 157
Reflections of Evil 214
rehabilitation 173, 180, 183, 189, 202
religion 10, 198, 222
Remington Steele 149
resentment 129
retirement announcement 153
Reynolds, Burt 142
Reynolds, Debbie 121–2; anti-semitism suspicions of Curtis 110; costars with Curtis in *The Rat Race* 93; socializes with Curtis 39; witnesses Curtis meeting Janet Leigh 26
Reynolds, William **34**
Rich and Powerful 174
Rififi 94
Ritt, Martin 95
Robin and the Seven Hoods 117
Robinson, Edward G. 29, 78
Rocco, Alex 138
Roeg, Nicholas 177–9
Rogers, Will 23
Rosemary's Baby 135
Ross, Herbert 170–1
Ross, Morten 155, 156
Roth, Philip 223
Runyon, Damon 169
Russell, Jane 30
Russell, Rosalind 144
Russell, Therese 159, 177
Russo, Vito 89, 98

Sabrina 119
Safari 52, 57
The Saint 145, 148
salary negotiations 69–70, 114–5, 133, 216
Salinger, J.D. 162
Salisbury, Lesley 4, 183
Savio, Andria 174, 181, 223
Scaramouche 33
Scharbach, Petra 182

Schatz, Thomas 23
Schenck, Joe 196
Schiaffino, Rosanna 132
Schiff, Stephen 62
Schulz, Charles 221
Schumach, Murray 96
Schwartz, Bernie 25, 27, 109, 125, 131, 132, 191, 202
Schwartz, David R. 124
Schwartz, Emanuel "Manny": affection of Curtis for 88; career frustration 5, 6, 193; as couturier 27; dancing aspirations 7; death of 88; fatalism 5; heart attack suffered by 32; and lung cancer 146–7, 150; as publicity agent for Curtis 27; smoking 5, 13, 146–7; timidity of 5, 5, 14
Schwartz, Helen 193, 203; attitude to Janet Leigh 31–2; death of 155; leaves money to Bobby in will 155–6; moves to Hollywood 27; pressures Curtis about Bobby 27, 40, 47, 134–5, 199; schizophrenia 5, 6; upbringing 6; violence 5, 6, 208
Schwartz, Julius "Julie" 5, 162–3, 199, 211; accident with truck 10; artistic representation of by Curtis 188; death of 10–11; guilt of Curtis over death 14, 92; "novelization" by Curtis 162–3
Schwartz, Paul 12
Schwartz, Robert "Bobby" 5, 40, 163, 186, 198, 211; birth 12; death 186; in Hollywood 27; inherits money 155–6; institutionalized 134–5; photographed by studio 47–8; schizophrenia 14; signs self out of institution 186; in therapy 67
Schwarzenegger, Arnold 186, 193, 205, 221
Scorsese, Martin 144, 198
Scott, George C. 121, 132, 161
Seaton, Patricia 175
selfishness 221
Selznick, David O. 15, 170
Selznick, Joyce 15
sense of humor 21–3, 25, 82, 95, 112, 131, 135, 148–9, 150, 154, 159, 163, 207, 213, 216
sensitivity 22, 89, 106, 111, 131, 140, 149, 201
Separate Tables 75
Sgt. Pepper's Lonely Hearts Club Band 135
The Seven Year Itch 79
sex 19, 48, 102, 115, 129, 139, 161, 181, 202, 208, 215; with Marilyn Monroe 83, 85–7, 217
Sex and the City 124
Sex and the Single Girl (book) 123
Sex and the Single Girl (film) 123–4, 140
sex comedies 119
Sextette 164–5, 192, 197
Shane, Maxwell 22
Shatner, William 215
Shendel, Dean 214

She's in the Army Now 174
Shiloh Horse Rescue Foundation 218; *see also* VandenBerg, Jill
Shipman, David 22, 63, 132
Shurlock, Geoffrey 96
shyness 14–15, 42, 49
Siegel, "Bugsy" 141
Sierra 24
Simmons, Jean 99, 100
Simon, Neil 170–2
Simon, Paul 213
Sinatra, Barbara 21, 117
Sinatra, Frank 35, **71**, 116–8, 119, 121, 154, 155, 168, 190, 197, 214, 222, 224; considered for *Some Like It Hot* 78; costars with Curtis in *Kings Go Forth* 70; death of 211; as father figure to Curtis 72; friendship with Curtis 71–2, 102–3; gives flute to Curtis 93–4; lobbies for JFK 102–4; "Rat Pack" invitation to Curtis 70–1; reaction to death of JFK 117; visited by Curtis in old age 211
Sinatra, Tina 211
Sinyard, Neil 178
Siodmak, Robert 20, 24
Sirk, Douglas 41
Six Bridges to Cross 47
Skolsky, Sidney 27, 129
Sloane, Everett 30
Smith, Anna Nicole 207
smoking 145–7, 150
So This Is Paris 47
Socrates 104
Some Like It Hot (film) 3, 12, **86**, 101, 117, 122, 124, 129, 136, 165, 192, 194, 196, 198, 202, 220, 221, 223; costume problems with 98–9; helps casting in *Insignificance* 178; influence on Curtis' life 211–2; jacket sold at auction 224; shooting of 78–87; *see also* Lemmon, Jack; Monroe, Marilyn; Wilder, Billy
Some Like It Hot (stage musical) 216
Son of Ali Baba 33–5
Spartacus 94–100, **97**, 136, 222
Spiegel, Sam 158–9
Spielberg, Steven 46
The Square Jungle 49
Staedler, Lance 45
stage debut 15
Stanwyck, Barbara 22, 200
Star Trek: The Sequel 215
Stargames 211
Starstruck 164, 166, 168–9, 174, 182, 210
Steiger, Rod 69
Stein, David 56
stereotyping 36, 49–50, 55–6, 63, 73–4
Sterling, Jan 40
Stevens, George 35
Stewart, James 23, 48
Stone, George E. 78
Storch, Larry 13
Strasberg, Lee 28–9, 79, 156
Strasberg, Paula 79, 81, 122, 195, 196

Strasberg, Susan 164
Stratten, Dorothy 166–7
A Streetcar Named Desire 28
Stritch, Elaine 77
studio marketing 18, 20, 39–40, 51, 63, 115, 141
stunt skills 42–5, 53–4
Suddenly Last Summer 88
suicide of father-in-law 106
Summers, Anthony 103
Summers, Eve 188
The Sun 181
Sunday Independent 189
Sunday Times 205
Sunset Boulevard 184, 220
Suppose They Gave a War and Nobody Came 141–2
survival qualities 187
suspicious nature 49–50, 139, 187, 200
Susskind, David 150
Swanson, Gloria 206
Sweet Smell of Success 3, **61**, 77, 136, 198, 200, 223; chemistry with Burt Lancaster 99; debt to Alexander Mackendrick 133; importance of to career 65, 223; shooting of 58–66
The Swimmer 144

Taras Bulba 107–8, 115, 136, 198
Tarzan 221
Tate, Sharon 134, 135
Taylor, Elizabeth 41–2, 69, 110–1, 172, 197
Teicholz, Tom 211
The Telegraph 186
television 145–57, 165, 170, 174, 179
Tell Me About It Tomorrow 57
tendon problems 96
Terror Train 166
Thalberg, Irving 158, 160
therapy 49, 67, 92–3
Thomas, Jeremy 179, 223
Thompson, J. Lee 107
Thomson, David 65, 101–2, 175
Those Daring Young Men in Their Jaunty Jalopies 141
Those Magnificent Men in Their Flying Machines 129, 141
threatened by handgun 179–80
Thunder Rock 15
Time magazine 66, 89
The Times 185
Title Shot 167
Todd, Mike 110–1
"A Tony Curtis" 26
Tootsie 194
Touch of Evil 77
Tough Guys 173
Tracy, Spencer 48
transience of fame, opinion on 144, 191, 209
transvestite 12, 48, 79–80, 89
Trapeze 51–7, **55**, 198
Trow, M.J. 97, 98
True Lies 205
Trumbo, Dalton 94–6, 99
Turtlenecks 152, 154

United Artists 52
Universal Studios (U-I) 20, 49, 53, 55, 56, 100, 126, 168; bought out by MCA 88; Curtis' first paycheck 18; in debt 77; as "factory" 63; loans Curtis out for *Trapeze* 52; markets Curtis as "beefcake" 48; pressures Curtis to marry Piper Laurie 33; seeking new talent 17–28; unwilling to risk Curtis in leading role 21
upward mobility 169
The Users 165
Ustinov, Peter 95–9, 179

Valenti, Jack 46
Valentino, Rudolph 89
Van Gogh, Vincent 131
VandenBerg, Jill 208, 209, 211, 213–5, 217–20, 222, 223; age difference to Curtis 207; dates Curtis 207; family of Curtis disapproves of 205; fascination with Marilyn Monroe 207, 218; and horses 217; and inheritance from Curtis 223–4; marries Curtis 213; meets Curtis 206
vanity 207, 220, 223
Vanity Fair 216, 219, 221
Variety 93
vasectomy 154, 185
Vega$ 165
Vernon, John 166
Viagra 211, 212, 213
Vidal, Gore 99, 103–4
The Vikings 67–9, 95, 111, 210
violence 41, 184
Vitti, Monica 134
voice problems 6, 8, 18, 34–6, 49, 99, 107, 110
Von Nussink, Gerda 183
Von Sydow, Max 35

Wagner, Robert 35, 48, 70, 99, 110, 119
Waldman, Diane 130
Walker, Alexander 119, 124
Wallis, Shani 166
Walter & Carlo I Amerika 184
War and Peace 210
Warhol, Andy 224
Warner, Jack 16, 127–8, 221
Warner, John 172
Warner Brothers 123–4
Wasserman, Lew 52, 77, 116; adulation of Curtis for 51; agenting style 24; death of 216, deterioration of relationship with Curtis 210; encourages Curtis to go to Europe 133; ends agenting of Curtis 126; generosity 46; and Granarte 92; and *Lady L* 114–5; negotiating skills 23–4, 216; sells Universal 209–10; steers Curtis away from Frank Sinatra 71–2; steers Curtis away from leading man roles 56; takes over at Universal 88; and television 46; as workaholic 46

Wayne, George 216–7
Wayne, John 35
weight 175–6
Weiss, Ehrich 42
Welles, Orson 77, 175–6
West, Mae 164–5, 192
Where Is Parsifal? 175
Whitehead, J. Gordon 45
Whiting, Barbara 22
Whittel, Giles 213
Who Was That Lady? 93
Widener, Don 78
Widmark, Richard 154
Wild and Wonderful 121
Wild in the Country 66
The Wild One 22
Wilder, Audrey 56
Wilder, Billy 122, 129, 165, 179, 196–7, 205; argues with Arthur Miller over Marilyn Monroe 89–90; directs Curtis in *Some Like It Hot* 79–87, 89; encourages Curtis to collect art 56; jokes about *The Defiant Ones* 73; and Marilyn Monroe 81–7; on Monroe's death 116
Wilder, Vicki 51
will 223–4
Williams, Dick 116
Williams, Esther 30
Williams, Robin 194
Wills, Chill 23
Willson, Henry 23, 48
Winchell, Walter 57, 59–60, 66
Winchester 73 23
Winfrey, Oprah 218
Winters, Shelley 23, 28, 34, 39, 81, 179, 195, 220; befriends Curtis after arrival in Hollywood 17; denounced by Curtis 35
Wolfe, Donald 83, 87
womanizing 19, 24–5, 47, 202
Wood, Ed 208
Wood, Lana 127, 172
Wood, Natalie 110, 123–4, **128**, 130–1, 185; costars with Curtis in *Kings Go Forth* 70; makes love with Curtis 127; refuses role in *The Mirror Crack'd* 172; suicide attempt alleged by sister 127
Wood, Ronnie 90, 156
worries about aging 131, 157
A Writer's Notebook 161
writing, opinion on 161–2
Wyatt, Petronella 220
Wyler, William 99
Wynn, Keenan 77
Wynter, Dana 121

Yost, Norma **105**
You Can't Win 'Em All 142–3
You'll Never Eat Lunch in This Town Again 168

Zanuck, Darryl F. 24, 138
Zec, Donald 150–1
Zinseer, William 65
Zolotov, Maurice 83